SACRIFICE, VIOLENCE, AND
IDEOLOGY AMONG THE MOCHE

THE WILLIAM & BETTYE NOWLIN SERIES
in Art, History, and Culture of the Western Hemisphere

STEVE BOURGET

SACRIFICE, VIOLENCE, AND IDEOLOGY AMONG THE MOCHE

THE RISE OF SOCIAL COMPLEXITY IN ANCIENT PERU

University of Texas Press   *Austin*

Requests for permission to reproduce material from
this work should be sent to:
    Permissions
    University of Texas Press
    P.O. Box 7819
    Austin, TX 78713-7819
    http://utpress.utexas.edu/index.php/rp-form

♾ The paper used in this book meets the minimum
requirements of ANSI/NISO Z39.48-1992 (R1997)
(Permanence of Paper).

LIBRARY OF CONGRESS CATALOGING-IN-
PUBLICATION DATA

Bourget, Steve, 1956–, author.
Sacrifice, violence, and ideology among the Moche : the
rise of social complexity in ancient Peru / Steve Bourget.
— First edition.
        pages   cm — (The William and Bettye Nowlin
series in art, history, and culture of the Western
Hemisphere)
    Includes bibliographical references and index.
    ISBN 978-1-4773-0873-8 (cloth : alk. paper)
    ISBN 978-1-4773-0872-1 (library e-book)
    ISBN 978-1-4773-1049-6 (nonlibrary e-book)
1. Mochica Indians—Antiquities.   2. Mochica Indians—
Religion.   3. Mochica Indians—Social life and customs.
4. Mochica Indians—Rites and ceremonies.   5. Moche
(Peru)—Antiquities.   6. Human sacrifice—Peru.   I. Title.
II. Series: William & Bettye Nowlin series in art, history,
and culture of the Western Hemisphere.
    F3430.1.M6B69   2016
    985'.01—dc23
                                        2015029023

doi:10.7560/308738

*Dedicated to Christopher B. Donnan
and Marshall D. Sahlins*

*Research is always easier when
standing on the shoulders of giants*

Il s'accouda à la balustrade et fuma sa première cigarette en regardant les oiseaux tombés sur le sable: il y en avait qui palpitaient encore. Personne n'avait jamais pu lui expliquer pourquoi ils quittaient les îles du large pour venir expirer sur cette plage, à dix kilomètres au nord de Lima: Ils n'allaient jamais ni plus au nord ni plus au sud, mais sur cette étroite bande de sable longue de trois kilomètres exactement. Peut-être était-ce pour eux un lieu sacré comme Bénarès aux Indes, où les fidèles vont rendre l'âme: Ils venaient jeter leur carcasse ici avant de s'envoler vraiment. Ou peut-être volaient-ils simplement en ligne droite des îles de guano qui étaient des rochers nus et froids alors que le sable était chaud et doux lorsque leur sang commençait à se glacer et qu'il leur restait juste assez de force pour tenter la traversée. Il faut s'y résigner: il y a toujours à tout une explication scientifique.

[He leaned over the railing smoking his first cigarette while looking at the birds lying on the sand: some of them were still alive. No one had ever been able to tell him why they would leave their islands at sea to die on this beach, ten kilometers north of Lima. They never went further north or south, only on this narrow stretch of sand exactly three kilometers in length. Maybe it was for them a sacred place like Benares in India, where the faithful go to surrender their soul: they came to discard their carcasses before really taking flight. Or maybe they just flew straight from the guano islands, which were cold rocky outcrops, while the sand was warm and soft when their blood began to freeze, and they still had just enough strength to attempt the crossing. We must resign ourselves: there is always a scientific explanation for everything.]

—ROMAIN GARY, *LES OISEAUX VONT MOURIR AU PÉROU*

CONTENTS

PREFACE AND ACKNOWLEDGMENTS

This study is the result of an odyssey that began on the slopes of the Cerro Blanco and at the Huacas de Moche site, on the north coast of Peru, more than twenty years ago. As a starting point for this journey, the first part focuses on a sacrificial site and four tombs that were excavated within the Huaca de la Luna ceremonial center between 1994 and 1998. At the time, Moche sacrificial practices were mostly known from isolated contexts and through modeled and painted ceramics. Therefore the discovery of the sacrificial site, which contained the remains of at least seventy-five male individuals, often put to death during El Niño–related ecological conditions, represented a major milestone in Moche studies. It has been especially significant in demonstrating the centrality of these practices in Moche ideology and, more broadly, in understanding the role(s) of violence in the development of social complexity. In this first section, my aim is to provide a fully documented account of the archaeological contexts and to demonstrate how closely interrelated these contexts are to the rest of the material culture, including the iconography, the regalia of the elite, and the monumental architecture.

The second part of this study, which explains the contexts uncovered at the Huacas de Moche site, took much longer to complete than initially expected. Additional information that continually came to light led to new avenues of research. In the process, this truly became a multidisciplinary undertaking, drawing information from diverse disciplines such as the social, life, earth, and natural sciences. This section, which is admittedly more speculative, clearly shows how central the ritual of human sacrifice was to Moche ideology. The research also suggests that at least three other notions—divinity, ancientness, and foreignness—

are intricately connected to the concept of ritual violence.

No investigator is an island. That is especially true of this project, as numerous colleagues have been involved in various parts of the research. Several talented archaeologists and field technicians participated in the archaeological work at Huaca de la Luna, including María Montoya, Rosa Marín, José Armas Asmad, Jorge Sachun, Estuardo La Torre, Julie Beausoleil, and Jean-François Millaire. An equally important aspect was the careful study of the human remains from the sacrificial site and buried nearby on a dedicated platform. The bioarchaeology, which produced a wealth of information (and controversies about the nature of Moche warfare), could not have been so brilliantly accomplished without the expertise of John Verano (Tulane University) and some of his students, especially Laurel Anderson Hamilton and Florencia Bracamonte.

Many of the ideas expressed in the analysis of the visual culture and its relationships with the archaeological contexts grew from spirited discussions with diverse colleagues, most notably Christopher B. Donnan. Professor Donnan has pioneered some of the most important concepts of Moche iconography, including ceremonial combat, capture, and ritual sacrifice.

I would also like to take this opportunity to thank Kimberly L. Jones and Claude Chapdelaine, who read earlier versions of this text. Last but not least, I would like to express my gratitude to Santiago Uceda Castillo and Ricardo Morales, who welcomed me into the Huaca del Sol and Huaca de la Luna Archaeological Project.

INTRODUCTION

Qu'est-ce qui constitue le culte dans une religion quelconque? C'est le sacrifice. Une religion qui n'a pas de sacrifice n'a pas de culte proprement dit. Cette vérité est incontestable, puisque, chez les divers peuples de la terre, les cérémonies religieuses sont nées du sacrifice, et que ce n'est pas le sacrifice qui est sorti des cérémonies religieuses.

[What is the ritual aspect of any religion? It is the sacrifice. A religion that has no sacrifice does not have a cultic aspect as such. This truth is undeniable, since, among the various populations of the world, religious ceremonies were born from sacrifice, and it is not sacrifice that came from religious ceremonies.]

—CHATEAUBRIAND 1834: 210

Chateaubriand is categorical. Without sacrifice, a religion is without rituals. In short it is not a religion. Since his statement of this position more than two hundred years ago (1802), the practice of sacrifice in its multitudinous forms and functions has been registered in various parts of the world, including Africa (De Heusch 1985), Asia (Bujard 2000; Thachil 1985), Europe (Burkert 1983; Yerkes 1952), Polynesia (Valeri 1985), and throughout the Americas (Matos Moctezuma 1984; Sugiyama 2005; Viau 1997). The principal aim of this book is to explore the complex roles of human sacrifice in Moche culture and ideology. This ritual practice, central to their ideology, also dominated the visual discourse embedded on the walls of their temples and depicted on their portable art. I argue that this iconography—in conjunction with the practice of human sacrifice at all their main ceremonial centers—was the main device used in the establishment and development of the Moche state.

The term "ideology" is used in this book in lieu of the term "religion," as the exact role of the iconography in this domain is not clear. Although various scholars have perceived the evidence of gods and deities in the depictions of beings with supernatural attributes and zoo-anthropomorphic subjects (Giersz, Makowski, and Przadka 2005; Golte 1994), the archaeology has demonstrated that many of these representations can consistently be associated with real individuals. Beginning as early as 1946, high-status funerary chambers have revealed individuals who once donned the ritual accouterments and carried the paraphernalia seen with those anthropomorphic forms in the iconography (Alva and Donnan 1993; Bourget 2006, 2008; Strong 1947; Strong and Evans 1952). While the increasing evidence of such correspondences between the iconographic representations and archaeological contexts does not negate the existence of religious expressions in Moche visual culture, it demonstrates that social and political aspects were at the center of this system of representation and that the iconography was probably instrumental in reinforcing them. I return to this important aspect later. But from the onset I consider the iconography, in all its forms, primarily as an efficient means for disseminating complex concepts and values directly tied to Moche rulership. That said, it is likely that some of the elements and animal subjects discussed in chapter 5 on the ritual ecology of El Niño conditions delved into broader aspects of Moche religion and cosmology. High-status individuals are often depicted with animal parts amalgamated with their anatomy, their clothing, and their regalia. I suggest that by consciously and conspicuously displaying subjects and attributes pertaining to this ritual ecology—such as spiders, crabs, octopi, and seahorses—the ruling elite sought to establish a quasi-symbiotic connection with the natural world and in the process to affirm the legitimacy of their rulership.

Human sacrifice permeates the material record of Moche society. It has been found prominently depicted in all media of Moche visual culture: the ceramic vessels deposited in burials, the painted walls of mud brick huacas, and the regalia of rulers. Physical evidence of human sacrificial rituals has been found in the funerary chambers of the highest-ranking individuals and in the temple plazas. The ubiquity of sacrifice would suggest that it formed the very structure of Moche ritual apparatus and visual discourse. The practice of human sacrifice and its representations certainly provided the most powerful tropes. Given this evidence, the main questions that I posit and address in this volume are:

- Why was human sacrifice so central to Moche ideology and religion?
  and
- Why is sacrifice so intimately related to the notions of warfare and capture?

The material and conceptual foundations of this study are provided by a number of sacrificial and funerary contexts that I and others have excavated at Huaca de la Luna since 1994. This architectural complex at the Huacas de Moche site in the Moche Valley (perhaps the most important cere-

monial center of this culture between the fourth and eighth centuries AD) has produced a wealth of information on these subjects (see fig. 2.1). Since the first exploration at Huacas de Moche by Max Uhle in 1899 (Kroeber 1925; Uhle 1913), detailed excavations have been carried out in many parts of the site. Among other things, these undertakings have revealed the long history of the monumental buildings with their numerous transformations and the existence of a sprawling urban sector located between the Huaca del Sol and the Huaca de la Luna. In order to discuss the importance and the practice of human sacrifice, as well as its political and symbolic significance, I begin by examining the information collected by myself and by my colleagues at the site. I believe that the evidence of human sacrifice recovered at Huaca de la Luna forms an integral part of the development of Moche political structure and the dissemination of its concomitant ideologies. In conjunction with the iconography, the archaeological record thus serves as the basis for discussing the transformation of sacrificial practices and the evolution of rulership during the Early Intermediate Period on the Andean north coast.

This book is organized into four thematic sections consisting of eight chapters. I argue that the Moche paid great attention not only to the physical relationships between ceremonial sites and their environment but also to broader aspects of north coast ecology in order to create symbolic and ideological systems. Because of the purported importance that the Moche devoted to these aspects, the first chapter provides a brief review of the research in the ancient Andes on the general concept of sacred geography. This foundation is essential in order to frame the current undertaking in this field of study. The second part of chapter 1 discusses in general terms the ecological conditions of the north coast and the disruptions brought by environmental conditions associated with strong episodes of the El Niño Southern Oscillation (ENSO).

Chapter 2, in the second section, offers an overview of the knowledge accumulated so far on the Moche and particularly on the Huacas de Moche site. It also relates the context of discovery of the sacrificial site in Plaza 3A of Huaca de la Luna and an additional potential site for sacrifice on the flanks of the Cerro Blanco. The detection of these sacrificial precincts was achieved by conceiving a broader notion of a ritualized landscape through a detailed analysis of the archaeology and iconography. This approach generated a number of hypotheses that were eventually tested in the field and led to the detailed excavation of the Plaza 3A sacrificial site.

The third section of this book focuses specifically on the excavations of Plaza 3A and Platform II at Huaca de la Luna. Study revealed that they formed part of a single architectural project. Chapter 3 is dedicated to the detailed description of the sacrificial site proper within Plaza 3A, including the main results of forensic studies conducted on the human remains. Chapter 4 presents the excavation of the platform and examines its relationship with both the plaza and the sacrificial victims.

The fourth and final section consists of four chapters, which assess and interpret the relationships among the three distinct sets of data collected from the site of Huaca de la Luna and from the visual culture—sacrificial, funerary, and iconographic. These chapters seek to assess the broader role of human sacrifice in Moche society, state development, and ideology. Chapter 5 addresses the prominence of El Niño–related ecological species in the iconography and their part in the fashioning of Moche ideology. Chapter 6 elucidates the presence of three children buried beneath the sacrificial site and demonstrates the cohesiveness of Moche ritual systems. The remaining two chapters address some of the broader issues resulting from this inquiry, such as the function of sacrifice in the development of Moche rulership (chapter 7) and the complex role of ritual violence in the rise of social complexity (chapter 8).

SACRIFICE, VIOLENCE, AND
IDEOLOGY AMONG THE MOCHE

CHAPTER 1

A CULTURAL LANDSCAPE

Over the past forty years or so, an increasing number of studies have been focusing on the complex relationships between pre-Columbian archaeological sites in Peru and diverse aspects of their physical settings. Most of these endeavors, however, have been concentrated in the south coast region and in the central Andes. Perhaps because of the concerns of ancient Andean groups in those regions, or those of modern investigators, the main focus was on the surrounding geography and ecology.

Scholars of the Nasca culture have proposed that the largest Nasca center of Cahuachi on the south coast of Peru served primarily as a place of yearly pilgrimage. They have linked the monumental center with some of the pampas' geoglyphs and the presence of water features in the landscape (Silverman 2002). In a similar vein, the better-known geoglyphs situated nearby in the valley plain have been studied in connection with the surrounding landscape, subsurface water, local ecology, and astronomy (Aveni 1981, 1986, 1990, 2000; Reinhard 1988; Silverman and Proulx 2002). Despite such intensive research in the region, however, the Nasca themselves—who created the well-known figures of the pampas—have largely been left out of the interpretations/investigations. Early investigations by Eugenio Yacovleff (1932) and Yacovleff and F. L. Herrera (1934, 1935, 1938) noted the vast amount of identifiable floral and faunal representations in Nasca iconography—comparable even to Moche iconography. But to date no detailed research on the vast material culture remains, including numerous decorated textiles and ceramics, has been done to define their ritual ecology and their cosmovision.

In the Andean region, Inca sites and cities like Cuzco, Machu Picchu, and the Island of the Sun on Lake Titicaca have been documented in terms of their relationships with the surrounding landscape, water features, and astronomy (Bauer 1998; Bauer and Dearborn 1995; Niles 1987, 1999; Stanish and Bauer 2004; Zuidema 1964). Similar efforts have also been undertaken in the northern Peruvian highlands at Chavín de Huántar and Tiahuanaco (Benitez 2009; Burger 1992; Kolata 1993, 1997; Lumbreras, González, and Lietaer 1976; Reinhard 1987). The investigations at these two major sites have explored diverse aspects, including the ritual landscape, water and fertility, social organizations and land tenure, cosmology, astronomy, shamanism, and ancestor worship.

As diverse as they may be in terms of their objectives and methodologies, these investigations have definitely shown a growing interest in the Andean region for the study of the intrinsic consubstantiality between the natural and cultural realms. A common thread running across these contributions is the suggestion that complex attitudes toward fertility as a whole, cosmology, and religion inhabited the mindscape of ancient Andean peoples from at least the Late Preceramic Period. These concerns constituted the basic tenets of the majority of these sacred geographies. The environment in archaeology is thus not perceived as a passive matrix for human intervention or just in terms of its ecological, economical, and strategic potential but as a dynamic agent in the shaping of cosmologies, religions, ideologies, and rituals (Ashmore and Knapp 1999). Although much research remains to be done, this important avenue of investigation is increasingly providing a much more complex and comprehensive picture of the web of relations that may have existed between ancient social formations and their milieu.

In contrast to the southern highlands and coast, the Peruvian north coast has received minimal attention in terms of detailed studies of ceremonial complexes with their natural surroundings and the local environment (Bawden 1996; Conklin 1990; Donnan 1986b; Sakai 1998). The few notable examples include passing remarks on the association between Moche monumental centers and the environment and on the alignment between certain architectural features at Pacatnamú and the surrounding landscape (Donnan 1986a; Moseley, Donnan, and Keefer 2008). There have also been brief discussions on the geographical and astronomical orientations at the Early Horizon site of Chankillo and at the Chimú capital of Chan Chan (Ghezzi and Ruggles 2006; Sakai 1998). No regional or site-specific research, however, has sought to define the relationship of the local geography, the ecology, and Moche cosmovision and ideology.

In this study I argue that multilayered relationships, which are often embedded with complex metaphors but also with a rather pragmatic view of the universe, existed among Moche ideology, the natural features of the environment, and the ecology of the north coast. Such conceptual connections would have been established through ritual practice not only between certain Moche centers and their geographical and physical settings—such as cardinal orientations, valleys, mountains, lomas, rivers, the Pacific Ocean, and guano islands—but also in relation to a geoclimatic phenomenon called the El Niño Southern Oscillation (ENSO). This recurring event affects the northern coastline every seven to ten years and can bring torrential rains to an otherwise almost precipitation-free desert coast. These infrequent downpours can drastically disrupt the life of the inhabitants.

Natural indicators of ENSO events include the appearance of new marine animal species coinciding with the arrival of the warm El Niño sea current as well as subtle to drastic changes in the local marine and terrestrial ecology. I posit that these visible indicators would have served as dominant tropes in the elaboration of the Moche ritual apparatus, by substantially bolstering the symbolic system that supported it. Furthermore, I argue that Moche rulers capitalized on a symbolic and ideological linkage with this impressive and transformative natural phenomenon. It would have provided them with a powerful "stage" upon which to build the legitimacy of their rulership through myth and ritual practice.

THE NATURAL ENVIRONMENT OF THE NORTH COAST

The north coast of Peru is one of the world's driest regions. During a regular year, the region receives less than 10 mm of precipitation. This situation is due to the juxtaposition of a cold coastal current (the Humboldt Current), land warmed by an equatorial sun, and the towering mountain range of the Andes. The southwesterly tropical air masses above the Pacific Ocean condense as they travel across the colder Humboldt Current and then expand upon reaching the warmer coastal plains. The higher temperature of the landmass augments the capacity of these clouds to retain moisture, thus preventing them from releasing their rain onto the coast. The strong winds moving from west to east, from the Pacific Ocean toward the coast, then push these lighter and larger clouds up in the mountainous regions of the Andes. The humidity carried by these clouds is distributed at a higher altitude against the flanks of the mountains, creating patches of fog vegetation called lomas. The coast is thus extremely dry. Under regular conditions, apart from the occasional drizzle in the morning during the rainy season, it almost never rains on the north coast. Fresh water comes to the valleys in the form of rivers running perpendicularly across the coastal plains, from the slopes and the foothills of the Andes to the Pacific Ocean. Therefore the Moche and the people long before them devised a sophisticated hydraulic technology in order to capture the periodical water coming down from the mountains and channel it to the dry but mineral-rich land flanking the floodplains of the valleys.

The year on the north coast is divided into two broad seasons. The first is a sunnier period lasting from December to May, when it rains in the Andes. During this season, the vegetation in the lomas proliferates and numerous populations of animal species thrive, including insects, land snails, reptiles, birds, deer, foxes, and ocelots. The second period is a colder and foggier season from June to November.

In order to optimize food production, the meteorological and micro-environmental conditions would also have been closely monitored by the Moche. As in other agricultural communities around the world, a number of ecological markers could have been used to plant seasonal crops, coordinate nonagricultural social projects, and so forth. These markers may have included the growth of certain plants, the behavior of insects and arachnids, the periodic reappearance of animals from periods of dormancy (like land snails,

snakes, and toads), and the reproductive success of foxes, rodents, and other creatures.

In my initial research, I posited that the detailed observations of certain plants, animal species, and environmental conditions provided the basis for a ritual ecology expressed in the visual culture (Bourget 1990a, 1990b, 1994a, 1994b). My original interpretation of this visual ecology was that plants such as *Tillandsia* and cacti and animals such as boas, foxes, deer, owls, and others depicted in the iconography were mostly associated with the normal conditions prevailing on the coast. More recently, however, the archaeological fieldwork has provided additional evidence that another important aspect of nature played a role in Moche symbolism. Excavations carried out at three major Moche ceremonial centers have made it increasingly apparent that specific rituals were performed during the torrential rainstorms of El Niño events. At Huaca de la Luna and Huaca Cao Viejo, for example, large tombs were apparently reopened during rainstorms. Their contents were scattered or replaced by peculiar offerings and carefully resealed into the architecture of the temples (Franco, Gálvez, and Vásquez 1994, 1998). At Huaca Dos Cabezas two funerary chambers were created by carving into the craters left behind by water pouring down on the architecture (Donnan 2007).

The social and ritual activities carried out at Huaca de la Luna throughout its history took place not only during the normal conditions prevailing on the north coast of Peru but also during these ecological disturbances. The iconography is populated by animals and beings with supernatural attributes, all of which display clear associations with these conditions. In order to explore the significance of these elements and ecological circumstances in the construction of the ideological framework of power and rulership, I offer a brief description here of the ecology of the north coast and of the El Niño phenomenon.

THE EL NIÑO PHENOMENON

The normal geoclimatic equilibrium achieved by the Pacific Ocean, the Humboldt Current, trade winds, and the Andes results in an almost complete absence of rain on the north coast; this equilibrium, however, is periodically offset by a recurring large-scale ocean-atmosphere fluctuation. The El Niño/Southern Oscillation (ENSO) is a periodic climate event characterized by a rise in surface temperature in the Pacific Ocean. Often designated simply as "El Niño," this climatic event can bring torrential rains and severe floods on the desert north coast, destroying irrigation systems and crops and melting down adobe houses and temples. Mega El Niño events can last up to nine months and are often followed by long periods of intense drought and sandy winds, the corresponding climate event called "La Niña." Such El Niño events, which trigger significant ecological changes, occur irregularly (perhaps once every five to ten years; mega events can occur once every twenty to thirty years).

The appearance of El Niño is connected with changes in the Southern Oscillation, which constitutes the cycling of the Pacific Ocean circulation pattern. Stronger trade winds move large water masses from the eastern to the western part of the Pacific Ocean. This massive amount of water, warming on its way, raises the sea level in the western Pacific. When the trade winds weaken, a number of Kelvin waves are released. Their leading edge crosses the Pacific on the equator from west to east. The velocity of these Kelvin waves is about 240 km per day, so six to eight weeks are needed to cross the Pacific from Indonesia to South America. When these Kelvin waves approach the South American west coast, they deviate to the north and to a stronger degree to the south, where they run south toward the pole along the American continent. For example, during the 1982–1983 El Niño event, the sea level on the north coast rose more than forty cm in certain places. At Puerto Chicama the temperature of the water was 8° C above normal. This constitutes an enormous volume of water that can create tidal waves, flooding coastal settlements.

Contrary to earlier assessments, upwelling continues and even gets stronger as the temperature difference between the warm ocean and the even warmer coast creates a powerful onshore eastward wind, which is eventually pushed upward by the Andes. Nevertheless, the thermocline rich in nutrients is pushed farther down by the action of Kelvin waves and the flow of these warm waters. In the process only hot water, relatively poor in nutrients, is brought back to the surface (Arntz

and Fahrbach 1996: 69). The end result is a drastic diminution of phytoplankton concentrations, which severely affects the reproductive success of schools of small fishes and causes the collapse of the ecological food chain provided by the Humboldt Current. Largely deprived of their food source, the schools of anchovies and sardines disappear, leading to the demise of countless seabirds and sea mammals. This warm current is accompanied by a number of animal species that literally replace the local fauna along the Peruvian coast. The ecological conditions prevailing during these events and the repercussions for the local animal species are described more fully in chapter 5.

Perhaps the most dramatic picture of the effect of a mega El Niño event is the amount of water pouring down from the mountains and invading the coastal plains. During the most severe rain conditions, the slopes of the Andes act like a gigantic rain collector and channel the waters back toward the coast, using the rivers and the quebradas. For example, during March 1983 the Chicama River discharged 900 cubic meters of water per second (table 1.1). This massive quantity of water compared with a thirty-year mean of only 101.7 cubic meters per second for the same month, which highlights the hydraulic forces put in motion during an event of such magnitude. Numerous lives were lost, villages were flooded, bridges were destroyed, and large swaths of agricultural lands were devastated by silt. It is likely that such conditions must have disrupted the lives of prehispanic coastal inhabitants as well, as archaeological research is revealing.

An assumption that is still widely accepted is that intensive floods brought by a mega El Niño and followed by long periods of drought and windblown sand (La Niña) destroyed and buried the urban sectors at certain Moche ceremonial centers at the end of the Early Intermediate Period. Such cataclysmic events, for example, are argued to have caused the abandonment of the site of Dos Cabezas and Huacas de Moche around AD 600 (Moseley, Donnan, and Keefer 2008; Moseley and Richardson 1992; Shimada 1990). Such a doomsday hypothesis for the Huacas de Moche has been challenged by excavations carried out in its urban sector (Chapdelaine 1998). The ritual activities associated with (or performed during) El Niño events and the dates of the occu-

Table 1.1. Maximum Daily Runoff (MDR) in Cubic Meters of Water per Second of Rivers in Northern Peru (December 1982 to May 1983) and Thirty-Year Means

River	Runoff	December	January	February	March	April	May
Leche	MDR	18.9	77.2	46.2	122.5	120.9	108.1
	30-Year Mean	3.1	5.3	9.8	17.5	14.5	7.5
Chancay/Reque	MDR	135.3	138.5	60.1	720.0	477.5	73.7
	30-Year Mean	18.0	25.1	44.4	67.8	70.5	39.0
Zaña	MDR	11.7	146.2	23.0	177.5	160.0	84.3
	30-Year Mean	3.7	5.4	10.2	15.6	17.2	11.2
Jequetepeque	MDR	92.4	155.9	80.4	624.2	266.2	220.6
	30-Year Mean	13.3	19.9	50.6	72.5	58.9	28.8
Chicama	MDR	66.2	112.3	81.8	900.0	600.0	400.2
	30-Year Mean	8.9	33.4	66.6	101.7	78.2	29.7
Moche	MDR	90.0	120.0	24.0	240.0	280.3	28.8
	30-Year Mean	3.9	9.8	17.0	34.2	29.9	10.2
Virú	MDR	14.4	80.0	9.0	70.3	120.0	10.0
	30-Year Mean	1.3	4.3	10.1	14.8	10.0	4.0

Adapted from Caviedes (1984: 279, table II)

pation at the site, on the contrary, suggest that the Moche were certainly impacted by these ecological disruptions but were not forced to abandon the location. Such data show that the site was still being used as late as AD 700.

My hypothesis is that the Moche transformed this powerful and potentially cataclysmic event into an object of thought, a canvas upon which to elaborate an important part of their ideology and symbolic system, regardless of its outcome in terms of their livelihood and built environment.

The research for this book has involved both the shelves of museums and investigations on the slopes of the Cerro Blanco, at the Huacas de Moche, and at a number of other archaeological sites. Before examining the crux of the subject of human sacrifice, I present a brief summary of these research avenues and frame them in the current state of research concerning the Moche. A revolution taking place in Moche archaeology has shaken a number of assumptions and paradigms taken for granted just a few years ago.

CHAPTER 2

THE MOCHE

The Moche culture is a social formation that inhabited the north coast of Peru from the first through eighth century AD. Much research remains to be done in order to understand the nature of this cultural formation and its exact chronological sequence, but it is generally accepted that during the nearly seven hundred years of their history, the Moche occupied the region from Piura in the north to Huarmey in the south, a distance of a little more than five hundred kilometers (fig. 2.1). In each of the valleys under their dominion, the Moche constructed villages and concentrations of urban dwellings surrounding complex monumental edifices. They created and maintained elaborate systems of irrigation to reclaim vast swaths of desert coastal lands (Eling 1986). The products of a diversified agriculture were supplemented by a rich protein diet obtained from the bountiful Pacific Ocean and to a lesser degree from the valley floor and Andean foothills. For example, the diet found in the refuse of dwellings of the urban sector at the Huacas de Moche consisted of forty-three species of mollusks, six species of crustaceans, thirty-six species of fishes, fourteen species of birds, and eight species of mammals such as guinea pigs, llamas, deer, and sea lions (Vásquez et al. 2003). Although they did not possess a writing system or a clearly defined market economy, the social and political complexity of this society was the result of millennia of cultural development in the region.

The rise of the first archaic state on the north coast of Peru is usually attributed to the Moche (Carneiro 1970; Lanning 1967; Lumbreras 1974; Moseley 1982, 1983; Topic Lange 1982; Willey 1971; Wilson 1988). While the factors used to define an early state were and are still a matter of lively debate (Flannery 1999), the physical remains left behind by the Moche (such as ceremonial centers,

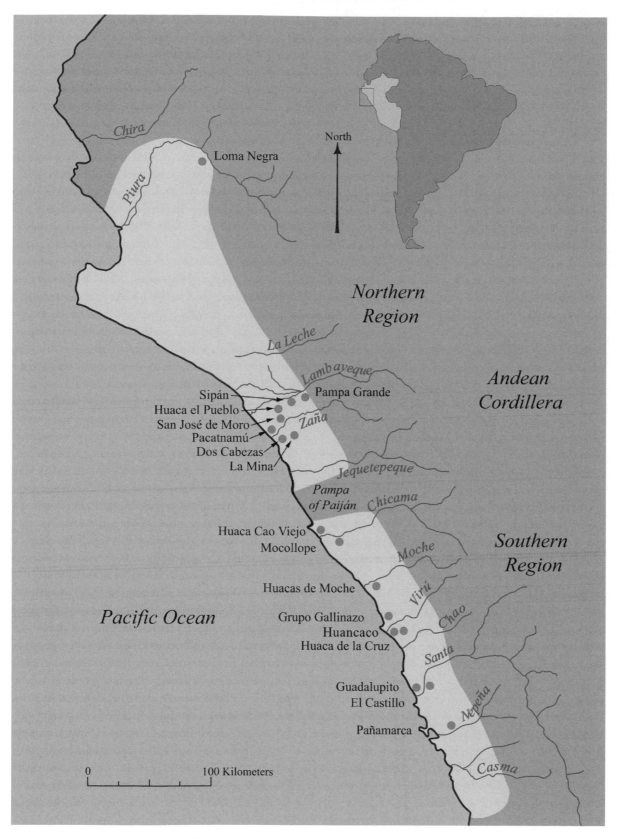

FIGURE 2.1. Map of the north coast of Peru showing the extent of Moche occupation.

complex urban sites, craft specialization, irrigation systems, elaborate funerary contexts, sacrificial rituals, solstitial calendars, and a dynamic iconographic system) continue to provide increasing evidence of their high level of social complexity (Bourget 2014). Important features summarized by Kent Flannery (1972), such as kingship, bureaucracy, state religion, and military organization, have been demonstrated at Moche burial contexts and sacrificial sites and recognized in their visual culture (Alva and Donnan 1993; Benson 1972; Bourget 2008; Verano 2001b).

Until recently, the presence of artifacts, architectural features, and archaeological contexts stylistically recognizable as Moche led scholars to draw a picture of this cultural entity as homogeneous and centralized, sharing a simple five-phase morpho-stylistic ceramic sequence (Larco Hoyle 1948). During the last few years, however, this model of a centralized state based at the Huacas de Moche has been disputed. At least two different societal systems with distinct artifactual traditions are now believed to have existed (Moseley 1992). It has been proposed that the Pampa de Paiján functioned as a natural barrier and that the territories to the north of the desert formed a series of autonomous polities distributed in the valleys of Jequetepeque, Zaña, Lambayeque, and La Leche, while the southern territories would have been under the direct control of the Huacas de Moche site (Castillo Butters and Donnan 1994; Moseley 1992). Thus the Huacas de Moche would have maintained its hegemonic position in the southern region. In the northern region, however, the Moche sites possessing monumental architecture would have been more or less independent from one another and would not have displayed formal connections with the southern region. If such a degree of semiautonomy or decentralization existed, we would expect to see much greater differences in the northern territories, based in part on their relative degree of independence in comparison with the southern "core" and its more centralized political system. We may likewise assume that the northern Moche urban centers would also have displayed greater differences from one another congruent with their degree of internal autonomy (Moseley 1992).

Since its inception, the model of a north/south division has been based on differences in material culture—especially in the style of fineware vessels—and to a lesser extent on the types of settlement patterns and monumental architecture. Apart from the use of boot-shaped burial chambers in the north and the burial of individuals in benches at Galindo in the south, Moche funerary practice is remarkably similar in the two regions (Bawden 1996; Donnan 1995; Millaire 2002). The fineware ceramics retrieved from these burials apparently show the greatest stylistic variation, not the funerary traditions. Admittedly, these broad assessments have not been subjected to detailed analyses. What might be perceived as largely similar might have been considered significative for the Moche of each region.

The five-phase seriation established by Rafael Larco Hoyle in 1948 in the southern region is still considered to be valid (Chauchat et al. 2008; Donnan 2004). The main taxonomic attributes of this seriation are the changes in the type of decorations and in the form of stirrup spout bottles; the form of the upper spout is usually sufficient to indicate the phase of the bottle (fig. 2.2). Because the morphological and stylistic differences between Phase I and Phase II have not yet been clearly established, they are presently considered together as Phase I–II (Donnan and McClelland 1999). Evidence of an early occupation has been detected at the site, but these phases have not yet been properly documented or dated (Donnan and Mackey 1978; Kroeber 1925). For the following Phase III and Phase IV, the research carried out at the Huacas de Moche site has clearly established stratigraphic and chronological correlations (Chapdelaine 2001, 2003; Chapdelaine, Pimentel, and Bernier 2001). Phase III existed from approximately AD 250 to 450, and Phase IV from approximately AD 400 until AD 700. The last phase—Phase V—has been recognized elsewhere in the Moche Valley at Galindo (Bawden 1982, 2005; Lockard 2005).

At the apogee of Moche cultural production during Phases III and IV, between the fifth and the seventh century, it appears that the main location of Moche political power in the southern region was concentrated in two contiguous valleys: the Moche and the Chicama. A number of important sites attest to the presence of the Moche in these two valleys, especially the El Brujo complex and Mocollope in the Chicama Valley and the Hua-

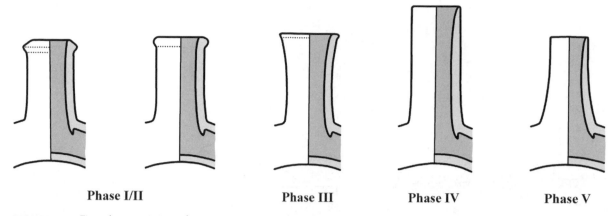

Phase I/II   **Phase III**   **Phase IV**   **Phase V**

FIGURE 2.2. Five-phase seriation of stirrup spout handles. Adapted from Donnan and McClelland 1999.

cas de Moche in the Moche Valley. Compositional and thematic similarities noted on the recent murals found at Huaca Cao Viejo (El Brujo complex) and at Huaca de la Luna (Huacas de Moche) indicate that these two sites must have maintained very close relationships at least during this period (figs. 2.3, 2.4). The architectural layout of the main plaza and the decorative programs on the walls of the buildings are broadly similar.

It is likely that in this period the whole southern region from the Chicama Valley in the north to the Huarmey Valley in the south was being influenced by the urban and ceremonial center of the Huacas de Moche. The exact nature of this influence is still a matter of debate. Nevertheless, clear indices of Moche material culture probably originating from this center have been found at numerous sites, such as Huaca de la Cruz in the Virú Valley, El Castillo in the Santa Valley, and Pañamarca in the Nepeña Valley (fig. 2.1) (Chapdelaine 2010; Donnan 1973; Proulx 1968; Strong and Evans 1952).

To the north of the Pampa de Paiján, a distinct fineware tradition has recently been recognized. This led to the establishment of a distinct and simplified typology of only three main phases—Early, Middle, and Late—for the core of the Moche period. A number of characteristics distinguish this tradition from the one established to the south. The overall form of the stirrup spout bottle is different. There is also a greater emphasis on modeled subjects rather than fineline paintings (until the Late Moche phase, that is). Certain types of ceramics common in the southern region such as the flaring bowl apparently do not exist in

the north. Luis Jaime Castillo Butters (2001: 312) has suggested that based on stylistic evidence the Middle Moche phase present at the site of San José de Moro would have been contemporary with Phase III and Phase IV found at the site of Huacas de Moche. Although the results obtained from our recent excavations at Huaca el Pueblo are still preliminary, the research at the site suggests that this first correlation between two traditions can be considerably refined. Our investigations indicate that northern Early Moche style would have been contemporaneous with the southern Phase III, whereas the Middle Moche would have been in synchrony with Phase IV (table 2.1). This statement, however, will require additional work. A clear stratigraphic sequence and an independent absolute chronology for the northern tradition remain to be developed.

Even though problems still exist within the established chronologies of the northern and southern regions, they remain largely accepted. Nevertheless, the degree of independence between the major sites of the northern region as well as between those of the northern and southern regions remains largely unknown.

The following two examples should suffice at this stage of the investigation to highlight that the Moche were unified under a singular symbolic project, regardless of the degree of stylistic differences between the southern and the northern regions. The first bottle is a Phase III sculpture depicting an amputee with its face ravaged by leishmaniasis (fig. 2.5). The figure is seated cross-legged and in his hands holds his left leg, which terminates in a prosthesis. His face is decorated

FIGURE 2.3. Huaca Cao Viejo, El Brujo complex, Chicama Valley.

FIGURE 2.4. Huaca de la Luna, Huacas de Moche site, Moche Valley.

with incised motifs representing felines and lunar foxes among other things. The exact origin of this piece is unknown, but the style is southern and very consistent with similar examples excavated at the Huacas de Moche site. The second stirrup spout bottle was found in a largely looted funerary chamber at the site of Huaca el Pueblo in the Zaña Valley (fig. 2.6). This Early Moche bottle depicts the same subject in the same position holding his right leg, which also terminates in a prosthesis.

Table 2.1. Moche Stylistic Phases in the Southern and Northern Regions

Southern Region	Northern Region
Chimú	Lambayeque/Chimú
Early Chimú	Transitional Period
Phase V	Late Moche
Phase IV (AD 400–700)	Middle Moche
Phase III (AD 250–450)	Early Moche
Phase I/II	(unknown)

FIGURE 2.5. Stirrup spout bottle depicting a left foot amputee with facial leishmaniasis. Staatliche Museen zu Berlin, Preußischer Kulturbesitz—Ethnologisches Museum. Inv. no. VA 62148.

FIGURE 2.6. Stirrup spout bottle depicting a right foot amputee with facial leishmaniasis. Huaca el Pueblo. Ministerio de Cultura Peru. Inv. no. HP-3948. Photograph by Johnathan Watts, MEG.

His face is decorated with a number of incised motifs, including insects and lizards. Although the styles are different because they originate from the southern and northern regions respectively, the two ceramic bottles boast nearly identical form and composition, rigorously showing the same subject. In the iconography this individual is associated with funerary and sacrificial contexts (Arsenault 1993; Bourget 2006: 199).

The apparent stylistic differences between the north and the south thus may be due largely to differences in local ceramic traditions; even such identified distinctions may be skewed, however, by the very nature of the archaeological research carried out so far. Most of the major projects conducted in the northern region have been concentrated on late Moche or transitional sites or on the excavation of sumptuary funerary contexts (Castillo and Donnan 1994; Alva and Donnan 1993; Donnan 2007; Shimada 1994). To the south, although the pursuit of funerary contexts has not escaped the interests of archaeologists, the recent research has largely been dedicated to the study of monumental architecture and urbanism (Chapdelaine 2001; Mujica et al. 2007; Uceda Castillo 2008). Despite these slightly different approaches, it nevertheless appears that the northern and southern regions possessed slightly distinct architectural styles and material culture. Such regional differences, however, contrast sharply with the degree of conceptual fit in the iconographic record with a more encompassing Moche ideological system. The leishmaniasis subjects mentioned earlier constitute excellent evidence that regardless of stylistic differences Moche ceremonial centers situated on either side of the Pampa de Paiján divide fully participated in a unified symbolic and ritual system employing the same type of ritual specialists. As highlighted in the following section, it is this interregional unity that allows for the identification of subjects from the northern region while using the iconography of the southern region.

WHEN ICONOGRAPHY MEETS ARCHAEOLOGY

The archaeological discoveries made at Sipán in the Lambayeque Valley have also brought into question the degree of separation between the southern and northern regions. At the site, Walter Alva and his colleagues unearthed the tombs

FIGURE 2.7. Fineline painting of the Presentation Theme (Sacrifice Ceremony), Staatliches Museum für Völkerkunde, Munich. Drawing by Donna McClelland. The Christopher B. Donnan and Donna McClelland Moche Archive, Image Collections and Fieldwork Archives, Dumbarton Oaks, Trustees for Harvard University, Washington, DC.

of high-ranking individuals buried with a retinue of people and numerous ceremonial artifacts (Alva 1994, 2001; Alva and Donnan 1993). On the basis of these associated objects, the three principal male individuals placed in Tombs 1, 2, and 3 respectively were eventually identified as the main protagonists, A, B, and D, of the Sacrifice Ceremony (fig. 2.7) (Alva and Donnan 1993; Bourget 2008).

The Sacrifice Ceremony is arguably the most complex and elaborate theme represented in Moche visual culture (Donnan 1975, 1978). In addition to Sipán, the burials of elite individuals associated with this ritual have been uncovered at Huaca el Pueblo in the Zaña Valley, at Pacatnamú in the Jequetepeque Valley, and at Huaca de la Cruz in the Virú Valley (Arsenault 1994; Bourget 2014; Donnan and Castillo Butters 1994; Ubbelohde-Doering 1983). In the northern Moche region, in addition to these locales, elements associated with this theme have also been found at Huaca Facho and Pampa Grande in the Lambayeque area and apparently at Loma Negra in Piura, the northernmost valley with a Moche presence (Donnan 2010). In the southern region depictions of this ceremony or closely related themes have been found on murals at Pañamarca in the Nepeña Valley and at El Castillo in the Santa Valley and on ceramics from most Moche sites with monumental architecture (Bonavia 1985; Wilson 1988). The mural fragment at Pañamarca shows the priestess (Individual C) holding a goblet and a gourd plate (fig. 2.8) (Bonavia 1985). The plate, which is barely

visible on the eroded mural, is held upside down and may have served to cover the contents of the goblet. This fragment indicates that the destroyed remainder of the mural may have consisted of a complete depiction of the ceremony also involving Individuals A and B (Donnan 1978: 166). The murals, the iconography, and especially the burials of individuals identified with such represented actors appear once more to challenge the supposed cultural distinction between the southern and northern parts of the Moche region. In fact, while the most elaborate Moche burials found so far have been located in the northern region, the fineline paintings of the Sacrifice Ceremony remain restricted to the southern region.

The broad distribution (from the Loma Negra in the north to Huaca Pañamarca in the south) of artifacts, buried elite individuals, and iconographic subjects that may be associated with the Sacrifice Ceremony prompted Donnan (2010) to propose the existence of a Moche state religion. He suggests that a vast ritual and symbolic system was adopted by all major Moche sites of the north coast from the Piura Valley to the Nepeña Valley and that this system spanned this whole area regardless of the purported north/south division within Moche society:

That the Sacrifice Ceremony was so widespread in both space and time strongly implies that it was part of a state religion. The ritual sacrifice of nude captives and the presentation of their blood in tall goblets appear to have been the most important religious rites, but ceremonial combat and the bleeding, parading, and ultimate dismemberment of prisoners also would have been important rituals. All available iconographic and archaeological evidence indicates that the Moche state religion, like Christianity, was a well-organized, highly structured institution that almost certainly exercised not only religious power, but economic and political power as well. And like Christianity, it would have served as an overarching religious institution that was independent of regional political boundaries. As such, it would have been a significant force in unifying the Moche state, even though local political boundaries and allegiances continued to change. (Donnan 2010: 68–69)

Such a position would apparently support the argument of Kent Flannery (1972: 407) that "[t]he critical contribution of state religion and state art styles is to legitimize that hierarchy, to confirm the divine affiliation of those at the top by inducing religious experience." Donnan perhaps uses the term "Moche state religion" here in order to circumnavigate the rather complex issue of Moche political structures and social organizations. Apart from generalized views, our understanding of these institutions is still rather rudimentary. If individuals such as A, B, C, and D of the Sacrifice Ceremony were priests who exercised some

form of political authority, would this not make the Moche ruling apparatus a sort of theocracy? Or are we confronted by a form of divine rulership with its own priestly apparatus? One fact remains: the striking homogeneity in the personae of the highest-ranking Moche individuals found both in burials and in Moche iconography suggests that the rulership of this society was organized and unified under a vast symbolic apparatus and political system, which was not segregated by the boundary of the Pampa de Paiján.

Additional individuals related to another complex ceremony were found at Huaca de la Luna, where two individuals associated with the Coca Ceremony were unearthed during the clearing of a mural in the main platform. They too were subsequently related to their iconographical counterparts (Bourget 1994b; Uceda Castillo 2008). These important identifications (discussed more fully in chapter 7) demonstrate that the individuals portrayed on ceramics were not merely mythological figures:

The art, we now realize, accurately documented real events enacted by real people. We also now realize that Moche religion involved ceremonial rituals with priests and priestesses dressed in rigidly prescribed paraphernalia.

FIGURE 2.8. Pañamarca mural depicting the Sacrifice Ceremony, Nepeña Valley. Drawing by Donna McClelland. The Christopher B. Donnan and Donna McClelland Moche Archive, Image Collections and Fieldwork Archives, Dumbarton Oaks, Trustees for Harvard University, Washington, DC.

The rituals appear to have been performed for centuries throughout the Moche kingdom without changes in the activities, the priestly roles, or the ritual attire. (Alva and Donnan 1993: 226)

One of their most well-known artistic productions is indeed this symbolic system of representation, which until very recently has been the most studied aspect of Moche culture (Benson 1972, 2008, 2012; Donnan 1978; Hocquenghem 1987). Among other themes, Moche potters artistically depicted complex rituals and activities apparently related to the elite subjects and to themes of warfare and sacrifice—such as warriors in combat, the capture of prisoners, the arrival of captives in a ceremonial precinct, the eventual sacrifice of these human victims, and the consumption of their blood by high-ranking individuals. The recognition that people, events, and places represented in the iconography really existed has critical importance in the elaboration of archaeologically testable hypotheses. This approach serves as the foundation of my present analysis, by presuming that such illustrated and enacted activities constituted an ever-refined Moche ideological program and that these activities were ultimately elaborated and disseminated from the site of Huacas de Moche. This would signify that the ceramic sculptures of leishmaniasis amputees discussed earlier indicate that such individuals actually existed at these sites and that they performed the activities depicted in the art. An amputee was found in Tomb 48 in Uhle's platform located on the west side of Huaca de la Luna Platform I (Chauchat et al. 2008). Wood fragments at the extremity of the left leg

indicate that he was wearing the sort of prosthesis shown in the iconography.

HUACAS DE MOCHE

It is widely considered that the Huacas de Moche site was the most important ceremonial and urban center of the Moche. The site is situated in the Moche Valley some six kilometers from the Pacific Ocean (fig. 2.1). The architectural complex is dominated by two pyramidal and platform mounds, the Huaca de la Luna and the Huaca del Sol (figs. 2.4, 2.9) (Bawden 1977; Larco Hoyle 1948; Topic Lange 1977). The Huaca del Sol was constructed along the eastern banks of the Moche River, while the Huaca de la Luna rests 500 m farther to the east, on the foothills of the Cerro Blanco. Although tombs and funerary platforms can be found in many parts of the site, one of the main cemeteries is spread between the Huaca de la Luna and the Cerro Blanco and sprawls all around the hill to a distance of about one kilometer. This densely packed cemetery unites the huaca with the cerro and highlights the ritual importance of the hill itself.

An intensive program of investigation including various archaeological projects has been under way since 1991. The main group, directed by Santiago Uceda Castillo and Ricardo Morales, is dedicated to the study and the protection of the Huaca de la Luna main platform. This investigation has led to numerous discoveries such as polychrome murals, elaborate tombs, complex architecture, and artisanal workshops (Uceda Castillo and Mujica 1994, 1997, 1998). Some of the main results achieved by the group are presented in this study.

The second project, under the supervision of Claude Chapdelaine, literally unearthed a city between the two main Huacas. This study has demonstrated a degree of urban planning previously unsuspected, involving streets, habitation complexes, and sectors for the production of goods such as beads, ceramics, textiles, metallic objects, and corn beer (*chicha*) (Chapdelaine 1997, 1998, 2001). Although Chapdelaine ended the urban sector excavations in 1999, the field research has been pursued by Uceda Castillo's collaborators and Claude Chauchat. Chauchat studied principally a long platform located on the western side

FIGURE 2.9. Huaca del Sol, Huacas de Moche site, Moche Valley.

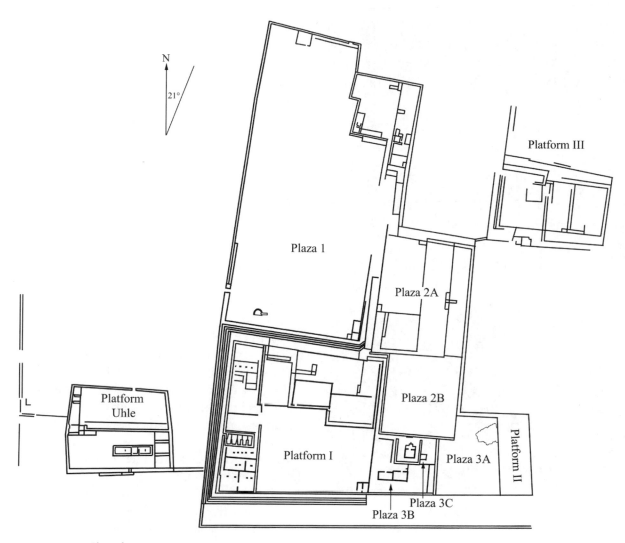

FIGURE 2.10. Plan of Huaca de la Luna, Moche Valley.

of the Huaca de la Luna main platform (1999–2009) (Chauchat et al. 2008). This structure (Platform Uhle) is the very same sector where Max Uhle extracted more than thirty tombs at the end of 1899 (Kroeber 1925).

The fourth project, under my supervision, complemented the three aforementioned projects. The principal objective of my research, begun in 1994, was to gain a greater understanding of the relationships between the Huacas de Moche site and its surroundings—in short, to discover the tenets of a sacred geography. The first part of the research entailed fieldwork on the slopes of the Cerro Blanco. The results of this first endeavor were followed by a second project, including detailed excavations in Plaza 3A and Platform II within the monumental architecture at Huaca de la Luna (fig. 2.10).

HUACA DE LA LUNA

The Huaca de la Luna, created directly on the rocky foothills of the Cerro Blanco, is a ceremonial complex measuring 290 m along its north-south axis and 210 m along its east-west axis, to a height of at least 20 m. It is composed of three main platforms connected by a series of corridors, ramps, smaller structures, and plazas (fig. 2.10). These three platforms were constructed at different times throughout the history of the site. Platform I was the first one constructed and by far the most complex. Plaza I is adjacent to the north side of Platform I (fig. 2.11). Platform II was created sometime during Phase IV. Finally, Platform III was probably elaborated toward the end of Phase IV. It is located slightly apart from the rest of the complex, on higher ground and closer to

FIGURE 2.11. North façade of Huaca de la Luna, Moche Valley.

Canziani 1993; Uceda Castillo and Mujica 1997). The earlier constructions would have been carefully buried to give a base to the new building. To date no consensus regarding the construction sequence of Platform I has been reached, and distinct propositions have been made over the years (Tufinio 2004b). Nonetheless, on average, each new building raised the floors by about 3.5 m and extended its sides by 5 m (Uceda Castillo 2007: 273). They have been alphabetically organized from F1 for the earliest structure registered so far to A for the last building. The previously established building phases B and C have been joined together, as it is now recognized that B would have constituted a remodeling affecting only the upper section and some sectors of the platform.

Building D is associated with the preparation of Plazas 3B and 3C and has yielded Phase III sherds. At this time an elaborate painted relief was created on the walls of a great patio (figs. 2.10, 2.13). Buildings E and F1 are thus deeply buried within Platform I and have been detected solely through test pits and tunnels left behind by looters. The stylistic phases for these earlier structures are unknown.

The first great patio was carefully buried, caches with offerings were left in the fill, and a new, slightly bigger patio was built on top of the previous one (fig. 2.14). Building B/C would have been contemporaneous with the use of Plazas 3B and 3C and was related at its beginning to Phase III or perhaps to transitional material Phase III/ IV (more on this later). The newly created patio was adorned with a mural similar to the previous one. It again depicts octopus beings surrounded by stylized catfish. The use of this patio continued well into Phase IV, until the abandonment of Platform I. It includes the last remodeling of Platform I (Building A) and the construction of Platform II and Plaza 3A (fig. 2.10). During this period, Plaza 3B remained functional and Plaza 3C was filled in for the creation of a small platform.

Uceda Castillo (2007) states that all the platforms and plazas are abandoned during the remaining period and a new, much smaller structure—consisting of Platform III and Plaza 4— was built (fig. 2.10). He argues that the process of abandonment of the older site platforms and plazas is evinced by the frequency of marked

the Cerro Blanco. Apart from extensive looting, Platform III has received little attention from previous researchers at the site (Kroeber 1930; Seler 1912). In 2007, however, Santiago Uceda Castillo and Ricardo Morales initiated the study and the preservation of this important part of the huaca. Of these three platforms, Platforms I and II provide the most critical information. My research in particular has concentrated on the second platform, Platform II, and its associated plaza, Plaza 3A (fig. 2.12).

PLATFORM I

The extensive work carried out on Platform I has revealed that the edifice did not constitute a single construction project but a series of at least five successive architectural structures established on top of the previous one (Uceda Castillo and

FIGURE 2.12. Plaza 3A and Cerro Blanco, Huaca de la Luna.

FIGURE 2.13. Octopus mural in the main patio of Building D, Huaca de la Luna. Photograph by Johnathan Watts, MEG.

adobes between the different phases of construction. Uceda Castillo mentions that the frequency of marked adobes in the later structures (Platform III and Plaza 4) is 95 percent, whereas in the rest of the huaca it does not even reach 10 percent. This late structure would have functioned during the final transformation of Huaca del Sol, which is also largely built with marked adobes. This hypothesis, though, is challenged by two contexts.

During the excavation of Platform II, a remodeling was noted on the summit of the struc-ture along its eastern and southern walls. These walls were constructed completely with marked adobes (Bourget and Millaire 2000: 54). Therefore Platform II would have known two construction phases, the last of which would have coincided with the creation of Platform III. In addition, even though the bases of certain walls and frag-ments of floors were all that was left of Build-ing A, the frequency of marked adobes recovered during the excavation was 24 percent (Montoya 1997: 29). It may not be too surprising to note that

FIGURE 2.14. View of the superimposed octopus murals in the main patios of Buildings B/C and D, Huaca de la Luna.

the base of Building A was not constituted solely of marked adobes, as parts of earlier structures on Platform I were dismantled and sound adobes were reused, especially at the beginning of a new project. I have noted the same process at the sites of Huaca el Pueblo and Dos Cabezas (fig. 2.1). Thus, contrary to Uceda Castillo's assumption, during its last phase of construction the Huaca de la Luna kept expanding and getting more complex with the addition of Platform III and Plaza 4. The previous two platforms—Platform I and Platform II—were also transformed with the addition of new structures, which have been largely destroyed by time and looting activities.

The relative chronologies of the edifices and their correlation with the stylistic phases have been established by the discovery of a number of burials and diagnostic material in the construction fill of these distinctive building episodes. On the basis of such corresponding material remains, Buildings D and B/C have been associated with Phase III and Phases III/IV respectively and Building A and Platform III with Phase IV (table 2.2).

At this stage, it is important to note that the last three remodeling stages of the Huaca de la Luna main platform (which formed Buildings A, B/C, and D) are associated with events of intense rainfalls. These rainfalls could only have been the result of major El Niño events.

These successive remodelings have the effect of substantially enlarging the platform over the years. It has been proposed that the successive burials of the previous structures were ritual in nature and could have been likened to a form of life cycle of each building. These layers would have coincided with the replacement of the religious elite (Uceda Castillo and Mujica 1998: 10). This process, defined as the "regeneration of the temple," by Santiago Uceda Castillo and José Canziani, would have consisted at least in the last three phases (A–B/C–D) of re-creating the architecture and the murals of the preceding phase but on a bigger scale.

The regeneration of the architecture and of the ritual
(of which the architecture is the embodiment) represents
an explanatory proposition of this process that acquires

even greater significance if one considers that, in the Central Andes, the Moche probably represented the most complex and highly developed of the state formations of a theocratic type. Their extraordinary architectural achievements were the apotheosis of old traditions that began a long time before with the development of early monumental architecture. (Uceda Castillo and Canziani 1998: 157)[1]

Admittedly, it is very difficult to assess the extent of the transformation of the huaca, as many of the murals and architectural details of an edifice would have been buried or destroyed by the successive phase. Perhaps the most important aspect at this point is that the main architectural changes that took place coincide with a transition from Phase III to Phase IV. Such synchronized changes of stylistic phases and architecture have also been noted at Huaca Cao Viejo (Franco, Gálvez, and Vásquez 2003).

PLATFORM II AND PLAZA 3A

As stated previously, Platform II and Plaza 3A constitute a prolongation of the Huaca de la Luna main platform toward Cerro Blanco during one of its latest phases of reorganization (fig. 2.10). On the basis of a number of elements—such as the construction sequence of the main platform, the ceramic seriation, the radiocarbon dates, and the contexts found in Plazas 3B and 3C—it appears that this part of the temple was constructed at about the time of the elaboration of Edifice B/C. The association between this part of the site and Platform I is important in order to present a hypothetical reconstruction of the sacrificial rituals performed in Plaza 3A and their relation with the rest of the ritual precinct.

This late extension represents a single architectural project constructed between the sixth and seventh centuries, perhaps at the beginning of Phase IV. It consists of an open plaza and a rectangular structure bisecting a rocky outcrop (fig. 2.15). The summit of Platform II and the interior of Plaza 3A cover an area of nearly 2,000 m²: 850 m² for the platform and 1,140 m² for the plaza. Study of the outer walls of the structure indicates that the north, east, and south walls were constructed first, delimiting the space that would become Platform II and Plaza 3A. This clearly demonstrates that these platform and plaza structures formed part of a single project and that they were meant to function together. In addition, inner walls were added to the north, south, and part of the west walls. The north and south walls are the highest standing walls of the Huaca de la Luna and are still between 6 and 7 m high. The bases of the inner walls of the plaza were constructed directly on yellowish sand.

The presence of a rocky outcrop within this part of the site led us to excavate in the plaza (fig. 2.12). Indeed, similar mounds surrounded by walls have also been noted at the Moche sites of Mocollope (Chicama Valley) and Pañamarca (Nepeña Valley). At Huaca de la Luna and Pañamarca, these rocks are situated deep inside the ceremonial centers and are surrounded by the highest freestanding adobe walls of these sites. At Mocollope, the selected rock seems to have been part of the

Table 2.2. Construction Sequence of Huaca de la Luna

Phases	Platform I	Plazas			Platform II	Platform III	Plaza 4
Phase IV	[Building A, Bourget] [Abandonment of Platform I, Uceda Castillo]				Platform II	Platform III	Plaza 4
Phase IV	Building A	Fill/Adobe	Plaza 3B	Plaza 3A	Platform II		
Phase III/IV	Building B/C	Plaza 3C	Plaza 3B				
Phase III	Building D	Fill Plazas 3B and 3C					
unknown	Building E						
unknown	Building F						

FIGURE 2.15. Plan of Plaza 3A and Platform II, Huaca de la Luna.

cerro itself. A vastly eroded wall now surrounds this peak. It would thus appear that the enshrinement of a rocky outcrop for ritual purposes, sacrificial or otherwise, is part of a north coast tradition at certain sites during the Early Intermediate Period. The outcrop in Plaza 3A was initially a much smaller rock formation, made more impressive by the addition of a number of loose boulders. Since then many of these rocks have fallen on top of the postoccupational sediments. Initially, however, they must have been resting on the outcrop, making it perhaps more conical in shape and

somewhat reminiscent of the form of the Cerro Blanco just behind it (fig. 2.12).

As a research hypothesis, I proposed that this mound was considered sacred by the Huaca de la Luna priestly class and that human sacrifices may have been performed in front of some of these "natural altars." In the case of Huaca de la Luna, this theoretical approach proved quite fruitful. In the northwest corner of Plaza 3A, just in front of the rocky outcrop, evidence of a number of sacrificial rituals was discovered in 1995 (Bourget 1997). Chapter 3 presents a detailed description of the plaza and the sacrificial rituals performed in that arena.

Construction of Platform II

Platform II, which formed the eastern part of Plaza 3A, is not impressive in its present state of conservation. The structure is largely eroded and has suffered greatly from the repeated assaults of tomb robbers. Nonetheless, the work carried out on it has confirmed that, like Platform I, the structure was built with vertical towers made of adobes, also called RATs (*rellenos de adobes tramados*), set one against the other and originally measuring at least 7 m in height. On average, the approximately 280 RAT units measured 2 m × 1.5 m and were formed by about 3,300 adobes each (fig. 2.16). The different side angles of these construction blocks seem to indicate that they were not set in sequence in an orderly fashion, one after the other, row after row. On the contrary, it appears that many of them were built standing alone, here

FIGURE 2.16. View of vertical tower of adobes (RAT), Platform II.

and there, and then joined together with adjacent construction blocks. It is not possible to erect a seven-meter-tall tower of adobes in just one continuous undertaking. The builders would have to wait for a while after a certain number of layers for the clay mortar to settle and dry; otherwise the sheer weight of the structure would squeeze out the mortar altogether, greatly reducing its stability. Given this RAT construction technique, a number of projects could have been started at more or less the same time. Teams of builders could have worked on each of these on a more or less rotational basis.

Three test pits excavated down to the base of the platform indicated that the structure was built on a fairly thin layer (less than 50 cm) of grayish gravely sand resting on the bedrock of the Cerro Blanco itself. Furthermore, the trench excavations carried out along the external walls of the platform, to the north and the southeast, suggest that surface material at least 1 m thick was removed in order to reach this firm base. Thus at least 1 m of sand and rocks was removed in preparing the construction site, and the remaining material was leveled.

To define the base of Platform II, three trenches were made in the southeast and northeast corners (fig. 2.15F, G, H). In each trench the base of the platform is supported by large rectangular stones set against a layer of rocks held together by a mud mortar (figs. 2.17, 2.18). Apparently to prevent the east wall of the platform from collapsing, the base of the wall was completely covered with these rocks and boulders. Being so close to the Huaca de la Luna main platform and the Cerro Blanco, this project was undertaken on a fairly coveted piece of real estate. Evidence found alongside the northern wall of Platform II indicates that a Phase III cemetery was already located there all around the rocky outcrop and probably right against the eastern limit of Plaza 3B and 3C. Propped against the north wall, the remains of these tombs were found underneath two occupation floors probably dating from the Middle Horizon (fig. 2.19). These floors, complete with postholes and the base of walls, clearly indicate that the Phase III tomb remains found underneath these contexts were not disturbed by looting activities but by the Moche themselves when the new project was

FIGURE 2.17. Southeast corner of Platform II (Trench F), Huaca de la Luna.

FIGURE 2.18. Northeast corner of Platform II (Trench G), Huaca de la Luna.

built. Among the most diagnostic artifacts recovered from this context is a sherd depicting a warrior and a dipper (figs. 2.20, 2.21).

Consequently, the Moche had to displace part of this cemetery to build this ritual complex right behind Platform I. Remains of some of the tombs, such as complete vases and dispersed human remains, were found along the north wall of the platform. The remainder of the cemetery is still in place between this same platform and Cerro Blanco (Millaire 1997). The density of the burial site alongside the eastern side of Platform II, toward the Cerro Blanco, suggests that dozens of burials must have been removed from the construction site. Where were they relocated? Given the proximity of these burials in relation to the temple, it is likely that this was the resting place of fairly high-ranking people of the community. Did the Moche thus outright discard these important funerary contexts or re-inter the bodies in another location? I suggest that the answer to these questions was located nearby.

Plaza 2B

In 2000 a platform was studied in Plaza 2B, located immediately to the west of Plaza 3A (fig. 2.10). This adobe structure had to have been created during the building of the complex Plaza 3A/Platform II because they share the same wall. In addition, this structure measuring at least 6.2 m in height was built during the burial process of Plaza 3C and the use of Building A (Tufinio 2006). Although this part also had been looted in the past, Moisés Tufinio was nonetheless able to locate twenty-five tombs, most of them severely damaged by the looters. All the diagnostic material recuperated during the clean-up of the looting or left in the tombs pertains to Phase III.

Unfortunately, the destruction was such that only two contexts—Tomb 19 and Tomb 20—could be found in situ. In both cases Tufinio proposed that the Moche reentered the tombs, as the offerings were in place but the human remains had been disturbed. As an alternative explana-

FIGURE 2.19. Middle Horizon floor at the base of the north side of Platform II (Trench H).

tion I suggest that this disturbance is the product of the re-interment of burials that were initially located in the space occupied by Plaza 3A and Platform II. Indeed the long bones, pelvis, and some of the vertebra and ribs were still in their anatomical position. This would be consistent with the moving of corpses that remained in a sandy soil for an archaeologically short period. The Phase III individuals would have remained buried for only two or three generations at most (± eighty years) before being relocated in the Phase IV platform. Consequently, parts of the shrouds would have survived and much of the desiccated soft tissue would have remained firmly attached to the major bones and articulations.

Adobes

The adobes used to build Plaza 3A and Platform II are on average 21.5 cm wide by 30.2 cm long and 9.9 cm thick. The vast majority had been made with wooden molds made with planks. In some cases canes were used to make part of the mold. Cane mold impressions have been noted for at least one side on 11 percent of the adobes. The vast majority of these adobes do not present any mark of fabrication.

The adobes used in the second phase of remodeling of the platform measure on average 21.8 cm wide by 31.6 cm long and 10.5 cm thick. They are thus slightly bigger than the earlier ones. A little more than half of them (52 percent) have cane mold impressions, probably because the same mold was used to produce many of them. All of these adobes have fabrication markings: crosses, finger marks, and diagonal lines. I suggest that this last phase of remodeling of the platform (at least the one that we could still register) was contemporaneous with the last building on Platform I (Building A) and Platform III.

The overall shape of the construction blocks (RATs) suggests that many groups were involved in the construction of the building and could have been working at the same time but in different parts of the site. Thus the platform could have been constructed fairly rapidly with fewer than 150 workers, in a matter of a few months. For example, about 980,000 adobes would have been needed to construct Platform II at its present size. If ten groups of builders working at the same time could have laid down 500 adobes per day each, it would have taken only 196 days to create the existing structure. Of course, we will never know the number of people involved or the exact time needed to build it. The point is that the construction of this platform and its plaza was not necessarily the product of a long and organized project but rather the outcome of a sudden decision made under very specific circumstances.

Building the Plaza 3A/Platform II complex may have been the product of certain historical contingencies such as the transformation of the political structure. This renewed form of leadership would also have been the driving force behind the construction of Building B/C. Important symbolic aspects would nevertheless have been maintained and perhaps reinforced, such as the relationship between the Huaca de la Luna ceremonial complex and the Cerro Blanco. To paraphrase Alphonse Karr, in the elaboration of a renewed political structure it was crucial for the Moche

FIGURE 2.20. Phase III fragment of warrior, north side of Platform II. Museo Huacas de Moche, Trujillo.

FIGURE 2.21. Phase III dipper, north side of Platform II. Museo Huacas de Moche, Trujillo.

to demonstrate that the "more it changed, the more it remained the same." The Plaza 3A sacrificial site represents a new sacrificial system introduced within a seemingly unbroken continuing tradition.

SACRED MOUNTAINS AND MOCHE TEMPLES: A SYMBIOSIS

Archaeological and iconographical data suggest that the localization of Huaca de la Luna directly at the base of the Cerro Blanco was the outcome of a long and complex decision process involving ritual and practical considerations (fig. 2.4). The association between a monumental adobe structure and a mountain is not unique to Huaca de la Luna. At least two additional Early Intermediate Period ceremonial structures have been located at the base of a cerro in the southern region. Huaca Mocollope in the Chicama Valley is situated at the base of the Cerro Mocollope, and Castillo de Huancaco in the Virú Valley rests along the foothills of the Cerro Compositán (fig. 2.22). This sort of symbiosis between a ceremonial building, such as a temple like Huaca de la Luna or a palace like Huancaco, and a mountain suggests a form of sacred geography where some of the features of the natural environment are fully integrated within the architectural layout of these buildings.

In the case of Huancaco this morphing process is even more extreme, as the bases of the hill have literally been covered with large adobe walls to give the illusion of a much larger and more imposing building (fig. 2.22). Rocky outcrops are embedded within these adobe walls in some of the larger front rooms, and the floors rest very close to the bedrock. Although the palace and the occupation cannot be ascribed to the Moche, the people living at the site around the seventh century AD were probably trying to emulate the architecture existing at the Huacas de Moche site at the time (Bourget 2000, 2010).

Archaeological indices suggest that the practice of including a mountain within an architectural project may have had greater antiquity than the Moche occupations in these valleys. Evidence of Gallinazo period occupations have been found, for example, in Plaza 3A at Huaca de la Luna and within the adobe structures at Mocollope.[2] Also,

FIGURE 2.22. Castillo de Huancaco and Cerro Compositán, Virú Valley.

Gallinazo sites in the Virú Valley such as Castillo de Tomaval and Huaca Santa Clara have been constructed using the natural features of hills like at Castillo de Huancaco. Nevertheless, Moche visual culture and features at Huaca de la Luna suggest that this association between a ceremonial structure and a prominent hill was more complex and perhaps more ideologically motivated. Moche iconography regularly portrays bottles modeled in the form of single-peaked to multipeaked mountains, on the slopes of which different activities are taking place (Donnan 1978: 144; Zighelboim 1995). The range of activities includes individuals holding manioc or corn plants, snail collecting, deer and fox hunts, and ceremonial combat. The most prominent and perhaps the most abundant scenes involve sacrificial activities. As an example of such representation, a Phase III bottle depicts Wrinkle Face and Iguana standing on each side of a conical hill (fig. 2.23). A sacrificial victim is draped over the mountain summit, and a second one lies dismembered in front of a building with a stepped roof decoration. The symbiosis between mountain and building that this scene indexes is not simply theoretical or based solely on iconographic interpretation. It rests on the almost interchangeable nature of the temple and mountain and some of the ritual activities carried out at these locales.

On a second modeled bottle Wrinkle Face and Iguana are no longer flanking a single peak mountain but frame a stepped pyramid decorated with a sort of scroll or wave on the summit (fig. 2.24). On the crest of the wave a sacrificial victim falls head first in exactly the same position as in all the

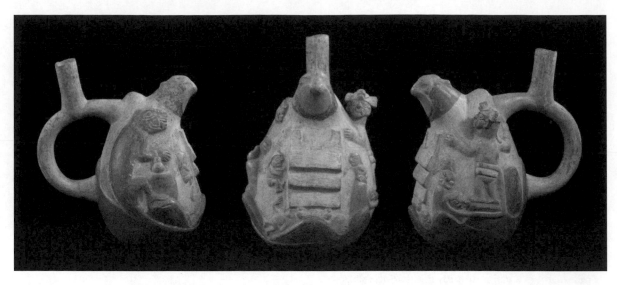

FIGURE 2.23. Bottle in the form of a mountain. Staatliche Museen zu Berlin, Preußischer Kulturbesitz—Ethnologisches Museum. Inv. no. VA 48090.

FIGURE 2.24. Bottle in the form of a stepped pyramid. Staatliche Museen zu Berlin, Preußischer Kulturbesitz—Ethnologisches Museum. Inv. no. VA 48094.

mountain scenes. A second victim rests on the lowermost step of the pyramid. The emphasis on the long mane of hair of the sacrificial victims on the summit is an important feature that may relate to the Warrior Narrative (Donnan 2010). This aspect is discussed in greater detail in chapter 7.

In the early 1990s these modeled vessels in the form of mountain peaks and temples, coupled with new discoveries at Sipán showing that real people would have personified the individuals depicted in the iconography (Alva and Donnan 1993), led me to imagine that the Moche could

physically have performed human sacrifice in a mountain setting. I also hypothesized that the best place to undertake such research was at Huaca de la Luna and the Cerro Blanco, because of the cultural prominence of the Huacas de Moche site. Therefore the search for a Moche sacrificial site that began in museum collections was pursued in 1994 on the slopes of the Cerro Blanco just behind the Huaca de la Luna. Based on the numerous modeled ceramics depicting human sacrifices taking place in a mountainous setting, it appears that the ritual consisted of having male individuals falling down from the central peak of the mountain. The bodies of these victims are often depicted lying down at the base of the hill after the fall (fig. 2.25). Thus I concentrated my initial field research on the slopes of the Cerro Blanco.

While I was the first to generate a field project around the search for a sacrificial site based on the parameters of such iconographic scenes, earlier scholars had provided the foundation for such research impetus. Elizabeth Benson (1972: 36) was probably the first scholar to recognize the symbolic importance of such Mountain Sacrifice scenes: "The sea was where the mythic battle was done; the mountains were where ceremony was carried out." Donnan (1978: 148) also noted the prevalence of mountain representations: "The number and variety of mountain scenes in Moche art suggest that the mountain played an important role in the ideology of the Moche people." Eighty years earlier, Max Uhle (October 18, 1899) had already recognized this implicit relation between the Huaca de la Luna and the Cerro Blanco and the importance of paying attention to these features: "One of the two temples built of adobes is constructed at the foot of the hill on its slope itself. My suggestion was very natural, that the hill itself must have had some relation with the ceremonies of the ancient people."

The research path thus had been laid by the iconography of Mountain Sacrifice and the setting of some Moche monumental architecture. The first problem to address, however, was how to find such a sacrificial setting on an area the size of a small mountain. Were the sacrificial rituals performed at random, here and there? Or were they carried out in a specific location? I had to admit that the former possibility would have been impossible to investigate. Making use of Georges Gusdorf's (1948) term "Theater of the Sacrifice" (which refers to the necessity of a ritual site to possess certain outstanding features), I suggested (1) that it had to be situated in a strategic place in relation to the shape of the mountain and to the Huaca de la Luna down below, (2) that it had to be sufficiently wide to accommodate an assembly of ritualists and attendants, and (3) that it had to be steep enough for the sacrifice to be properly performed. After a few days spent climbing up and down the hill, I located a promising place at about 300 m of altitude and situated right above

FIGURE 2.25. Bottle in the form of a mountain. Museo Nacional de Arqueología, Antropología e Historia del Perú. Inv. no. C-03300.

the Huaca de la Luna. The sector is marked by an arrow in figure 2.4. This location offers a commanding view of the Huacas de Moche site, the Huaca del Sol, and the Moche River farther to the west (fig. 2.26, black arrow). It is composed of a natural plateau with four niches, which seems to have been manually enlarged for the attendants to sit in (fig. 2.27). As mentioned, the hill is made of granodiorite with an extremely eroded and flaking surface, while the area of the niches seems to have been cleaned down to the underlying bedrock. The central niche is about 1.7 m wide by 2.7 m high. Just above it a natural promontory could have served as a proper place to make the sacrifice (fig. 2.28). A person pushed from this point could easily fall 100 m and would have been killed instantly upon impact. Although the purported "drop zone" area was searched, no human remains

FIGURE 2.26. Aerial view of the Huaca de Moche site, Moche Valley (adapted from Google Earth).

FIGURE 2.27. View of the rocky formation, Cerro Blanco.

FIGURE 2.28. Close-up view of the niches in the rocky formation, Cerro Blanco.

could be found. The sector consists of almost bare rock everywhere, with an accumulation of debris rarely exceeding 50 cm. Admittedly, without context we cannot know what the Moche would have done with the corpses. They might have left the bodies on the ground to be devoured by vultures, as suggested by the iconography, or they could have disposed of them in a different place. The mountain spot thus would have served as the ideal location for a ritual equivalent to the one illustrated in the Mountain Sacrifice scenes (fig. 2.25), but the lack of evidence prevents us from ever proving this function conclusively.

Another aspect that the Moche could have emphasized in their iconography is the presence of two long bands of black andesite running across the upper section of the Cerro Blanco (figs. 2.4, 2.26). This dark igneous volcanic rock is

FIGURE 2.29. Fineline painting of the Coca Ceremony, Linden-Museum, Stuttgart. Drawing by Donna McClelland. The Christopher B. Donnan and Donna McClelland Moche Archive, Image Collections and Fieldwork Archives, Dumbarton Oaks, Trustees for Harvard University, Washington, DC.

embedded within the grayish mass of granodiorite that constitutes the bulk of the cerro itself. In some cases these bands may have been represented as a bicephalous arch terminating with fox heads, a feature often illustrated in the Sacrifice and Coca Ceremonies (figs. 2.7, 2.29). One vessel (fig. 2.30) shows an individual seated cross-legged inside a temple abutted against a four-peaked mountain. A bicephalous arch is embedded in the mountain just above the human and the temple. This does not mean that the two bands of volcanic rock in the Cerro Blanco constitute the only possible meaning of these bicephalous arches populating the iconography. They most certainly refer to a wider range of significata, as hinted by a number of scholars. Anne-Marie Hocquenghem (1987: 114) sees the bicephalous arch surrounded by dark spots such as the one in the Coca Ceremony as the Milky Way in a starry sky (fig. 2.29). The dark spots are also stars for Danièle Lavallée (1970: 108–111), but she suggests that the arch symbolizes rain, water, and by extension the larger concept of fertility.

I suggest that the Moche intentionally included the andesite bands of the Cerro Blanco within the existing symbolism of the bicephalous arch (fig. 2.26). It is likely that they entertained complex beliefs about the bicephalous arch and that the discovery of the andesite bands across the Cerro Blanco led them to locate the Huaca de la Luna directly under it. Indeed the Moche began the construction of the Huaca de la Luna before the Huaca del Sol (Donnan and Mackey 1978: 59), sug-

FIGURE 2.30. Bottle in the form of a mountain with a ceremonial building at its base. Museo Nacional de Arqueología, Antropología e Historia del Perú. Inv. no. C-03312.

gesting that the planning of the ceremonial complex was initiated from the Cerro Blanco (fig. 2.4). An additional index of this ritual alignment is that domestic occupations located along the Moche River were displaced during Phase III in order to build the Huaca del Sol right in front of the Huaca de la Luna (Topic Lange 1977: 63). Therefore, in addition to including both ceremonial structures, the ritual alignment would have encompassed the Cerro Blanco and the Moche river as well (fig. 2.26).

THE SACRIFICIAL SITE OF THE HUACA

It appears that the complex Huaca de la Luna/ Cerro Blanco encompassed both constructed and conceptualized landscapes in meaningful and integrated ways. It is not easy to disentangle all the layers of meaning of such a complex and all-encompassing entity as the Huaca and Cerro. It is conceivable that Huaca de la Luna was physically built at the foot of the Cerro Blanco in a form of symbiotic dualism that was repeated in the neighboring valley at Mocollope in the Chicama Valley and at Castillo de Huancaco in the Virú Valley.

Apart from these physical locations and suggestive depictions of mountains with architecture in the iconography, specific rituals clearly connecting the two entities were missing. Archaeological evidence of human sacrifices remained to be found. Thus a new study of the iconography and of the Moche huacas was undertaken in order to find other suitable sectors of sacrifices in the perimeters of these temples. As the research progressed, it rapidly became apparent that sacrifices were also executed in the huacas. The iconography frequently shows victims led to the temples (A), instructed or prepared by women (B), and ultimately put to death during a Sacrifice Ceremony (C) in this Phase IV case (fig. 2.31).

Sacrificed victims have been found in many Moche sites. They usually accompany high-ranking individuals in their ultimate resting places (Huaca de la Cruz, San José de Moro, Sipán), are deposited or killed within plazas (Huaca de la Luna), or are the product of certain ritual practices (Huaca Cao) (Alva and Donnan 1993; Donnan and Castillo Butters 1992; Strong 1947; Strong and Evans 1952; Franco 1998).

The research was thus redirected toward the ceremonial architecture in order to locate a promising site for sacrifices. As discussed earlier, it became apparent that a number of Moche and Early Intermediate ceremonial buildings included plazas encasing rocky outcrops. Plaza 3A at Huaca de la Luna is undoubtedly one of the best examples of this type of feature (fig. 2.12).

FIGURE 2.31. Fineline painting of a Sacrifice Ceremony. Courtesy of the Division of Anthropology, American Museum of Natural History, New York. Drawing by Donna McClelland. The Christopher B. Donnan and Donna McClelland Moche Archive, Image Collections and Fieldwork Archives, Dumbarton Oaks, Trustees for Harvard University, Washington, DC.

On the basis of these similarities two research hypotheses were developed:

1. If there exist structural relationships between Cerro Blanco and Huaca de la Luna, and between the small rocky outcrop in the middle of the plaza and the temple surrounding it, then some of the sacrificial activities in the Huaca de la Luna might have been done in front of this small cerro.
2. Most of the combat scenes in the iconography depict the capture of prisoners and their eventual sacrifice, so it is plausible that the sacrificial victims were men, probably soldiers seized during combat.

In order to verify these hypotheses the first excavations at the site were conducted during the summer of 1995. The results of these excavations have certainly surpassed my wildest expectations and are described in chapter 3.

SUMMARY

The relationships that may have existed between the successive construction phases of Huaca de la Luna and the stylistic phases defined by Larco Hoyle and others cannot be explored further before describing the archaeological contexts encountered in diverse parts of the site. The discussion then returns to the hypothesis that social and political changes would have impacted other aspects of society such as ritual activities, monumental architecture, and visual culture, including the iconography found on the walls of the temples, on portable objects, and on the regalia of high-ranking individuals. Much more could be said about the Huacas de Moche site, where extensive excavations continue to be carried out in various parts. Though some other aspects of these investigations are discussed in the following chapters, my focus is on the sacrificial activities performed in Plaza 3A and Plaza 3C and the funerary contexts found on Platforms I and II.

CHAPTER 3

THE PLAZA 3A SACRIFICIAL SITE

THE FIELDWORK IN PLAZA 3A

The fieldwork in Plaza 3A began in May 1995. At the onset the plaza presented only a bare space filled with hard-packed sediments, pockmarked by looters' pits filled with windblown sand (fig. 2.12). Therefore this part of the site was mapped, and one of these looters' pits was cleaned to confirm the stratigraphy. The first human remains were found at the bottom of this test pit. Looters in search of artifacts had disturbed these bones, but they confirmed that archaeological remains rested at a depth of about one meter below the surface.

The excavation of a sacrificial site such as Plaza 3A is a long and meticulous process. Seven months over three field seasons were required to excavate an area of less than 60 m² to an average depth of about 2 m. In the process, the skeletal remains of at least seventy-five male individuals, who appear to have been ritually sacrificed and mutilated, were found in the northwest section of the plaza (fig. 2.15, Sector A). In addition to these sacrificed adults, three children were also buried in the same sector in a layer just beneath the sacrificial activities. To prevent disturbing the contextual evidence, archaeologists and field technicians worked on a scaffolding of planks, hovering about 30 cm above the surface. The human remains, some ten thousand bones, were first drawn in situ at a scale of 1:10 with the help of a drawing grid. In order to redraw each bone more precisely, these sketches were later corrected in the laboratory with the help of hundreds of photos taken perpendicularly above the human remains. After being brought to a similar scale, the photos and sketches were matched and overlapped. A final set of drawings was made on drafting film. The scale and the angles of the bones in the figures presented throughout this study are thus anatomically correct and as precise as possible. The stature of a given individual can even be roughly estimated on the basis of these drawings. The following description of the excavation process of the sacrificial site is based in great part on these drawings. Photographs of specific contexts complement the drawings.

All of the adult skeletal remains and associated artifacts were found just beneath Sediment 1, a compact and largely sterile deposit of clay, silt, and hardened sand (fig. 3.1). This extremely hard layer, some 80 to 100 cm thick, limited the efforts of the looters and probably saved the site from being completely destroyed. Nevertheless, about 25 percent of the site was damaged. The human remains were lying in a series of four distinct and alternating layers of sand and solidified clay underneath Sediment 1. The differences in thicknesses, type of material, and texture indicate clear temporal separation between the layers. They also suggest that varying environmental conditions prevailed during these periods. The mud was probably deposited during periods of intense rainfalls, whereas the sand accumulated in the open-air plaza under drier conditions. The type of fine sand and its form of deposition are consistent with material brought under windblown conditions.

As the excavation progressed, these distinct layers were successively labeled from the surface to the bedrock: Sediment 1, Sand 1, Sediment 2, Sand 2, Sediment 3, Sand 3, Sediment 4, and finally Sand 4. In order to facilitate the recording of the human remains, Sediment 2 was separated into two arbitrary levels: Sediment 2.1 and Sediment 2.2. Sand 2 represented a particularly complex layer. In order to disentangle the numerous cultural contexts lying directly on top of each other, eleven levels were created: Sand 2.1, Sand 2.2, and Sand 2.3.1 to 2.3.9. In all eighteen stratigraphically distinct levels were defined (table 3.1). For ease of description, the human remains have been assigned a code corresponding to the layer and a sequential number. For example, Individual Sa-2.1 would correspond to Individual 1 from layer Sand 2.

The drawings of some human remains were repeated from one layer to the next in a number of cases as the excavation progressed. This situa-

FIGURE 3.1. View of Sediment 1, Plaza 3A.

tion highlights the difficulty of excavating a site as complex as this one, where the human remains often have been piled up one on top of each other. For example, it is likely that a number of isolated heads originally assigned to Sand 1 (fig. 3.66) belonged to some of the headless individuals stuck in the layer of clay of Sediment 2 (fig. 3.51). Following the description and analysis of each layer and level, the archaeological evidence presented here demonstrates that it was neither a mass burial of isolated victims killed elsewhere and dumped in a jumbled mess into the plaza nor the site of discrete sacrifices accumulating over a number of years. Numerous similarities noted between rituals associated with distinct layers (say Sediment 2 and Sand 1) indicate that each sacrifice was precisely organized and probably carried out by highly skilled practitioners obeying a very precise set of rules. The proximity of the groups of human remains further indicates that fairly short periods elapsed between the rituals. Furthermore, marked differences among some of the activities demonstrate that the sacrificial rituals were complex and dynamic processes. A sacrifice is both a highly controlled procedure and a work in progress. It would respond to both agency and contingency.

The excavations in Plaza 3A have been divided into five sectors (A–E) (fig. 2.15). The first sector (A) corresponds to the sacrificial site proper. The excavations in the other four sectors were carried out in order to determine the extent of the sacrificial site proper, the limit of the west wall at its southern extremity (E), and the function, if any, of the remaining parts of the plaza (B, C, and D).

SECTOR A

STRATIGRAPHY AND RITUAL SEQUENCE

This section describes each of the natural layers and arbitrary levels of sediment and sand. In a reverse progression than in the excavation process, the sequence is presented in chronological and stratigraphical order from the most ancient to the most recent. For each layer containing human remains or artifacts, the matrix is described first, followed by a detailing of the cultural elements encountered. The altitude readings, shown at the beginning of the description, correspond to measurements taken on the surface at two different points: at the eastern extremity of the layer toward Platform II and closer to the base of the west wall. These readings were calculated from a referential benchmark situated on the summit of Platform I and arbitrarily fixed at 100.00 m by members of the Huaca de la Luna Project.

SAND 4

Sand 4 (97.42 m–96.90 m) was almost exclusively composed of fine yellowish sand (fig. 3.2). This natural deposit rested directly on the bedrock of the Cerro Blanco. Its thickness varied from 75 cm to the east to more than 150 cm to the west, near the base of the west wall. Following the same

Table 3.1. Sequence of Layers and Contexts

Layers	Contexts
Sediment 1	Postoccupational
Sand 1	Human remains: Adult males (Sa-1.1)
Sediment 2	Human remains: Adult males (Se-2.1)
Sand 2.1	Human remains: Adult males (Sa-2.1)
Sand 2.2	Human remains: Adult males (Sa-2.2)
Sand 2.3.1 to 2.3.9	Human remains: Adult males
Sediment 3	Human remains: Adult males (Se-3.1)
Sand 3	Human remains: Adult males (Sa-3.1)
Sediment 4	No human remains
Sand 4	Human remains: Children
Bedrock	Foothills of the Cerro Blanco

declination, the underlying bedrock presented a strong gradient of about 32 percent and a drop from 96.41 m to 95.30 m within a distance of less than 3.5 m. The surface of the sand was more horizontal, with a declivity of only 8 percent, dropping from 97.16 m to only 96.88 m within the same distance. It is thus likely that this layer of natural sand was leveled before the construction of the walls of the plaza began. The base of the north wall rested directly on this sand, whereas the internal section of the west wall was built on construction refuse originating from the building of the north wall. This indicates that the internal section of the north wall was built against the earlier architecture and then a second wall was erected against the original west wall.

Later excavations carried out in Plaza 2B have revealed that the external section of the west wall once formed part of a room that was eventually filled with adobes and used as a Phase III funerary platform (Tufinio 2002). This reinforces the proposition presented in chapter 2 that the Phase III burials removed for the new project were relocated in this platform.

FIGURE 3.2. View of Sand 4 in the northwest corner of Plaza 3A.

After the construction of the west wall, a small structure composed of two parallel rows of adobes was built at the base of the same wall (figs. 3.3, 3.4). It has not been possible to ascertain why this feature was constructed. It could have served as a short staircase of only three or four steps for accessing this part of the plaza, however, around the time when the children were buried. The structure seems to have been partly dismantled at one point. Some foot bones found underneath the structure may represent human remains left behind during the removal of the Phase III cemetery.

Burials of Children in Sand 4

Following the completion of the Platform II and Plaza 3A complex, one of the first rituals performed in the plaza was the burial of three children in the natural layer of fine sand (fig. 3.3). The body of one child was complete, whereas the

other two had their heads removed before burial. It would appear that these burial activities took place soon after the construction of Plaza 3A. At first sight, the presence of children resting directly beneath a sacrificial site composed exclusively of adult males appeared to be puzzling and perhaps to bear no direct correlation with it. A detailed iconographic analysis of Moche representations of children, however, hints otherwise. As chapter 6 suggests, child rituals formed part of the same symbolic system and could clearly be related to scenes of warfare and human sacrifice.

The first child (Child Sa-4.1) was found some 60 cm below the surface of Sand 4 at 96.38 m (figs. 3.3, 3.5). This complete individual was lying on its back, fully extended, with its head pointing south. Faint evidence of textiles was noted on each side of the body, indicating that the corpse was probably wrapped in some kind of shroud. This child was between two and a half and three and a half years of age. Although signs of periostitis, porosity, and swelling of the bones were noted, it has not been possible to determine if these pathologies were sufficiently severe to contribute to this child's death.[1]

The second child (Sa-4.2) also lay on its back in fully extended position (figs. 3.3, 3.6). It was placed only 10 cm below the surface of Sand 4, at 96.81 m. The feet were oriented toward the north and rested very close to the base of the north wall (fig. 3.3). This child was also about three years of age and had no head. The bones were covered with textile remains, perhaps some sort of shroud. A number of coca seeds (*Erythroxylon* sp.) and a fragment of peanut shell (*Arachis hypogaea*) were also found close to the skeleton, especially in the region of the shoulders. The child was holding two small ceramic whistles, one in each hand. The left hand had detached from the wrist and probably fell inside the funerary bundle sometime before the burial. The first whistle was thus found just below the pelvis in line with this hand. The right hand, however, was still in place and firmly holding the second whistle. The two whistles were almost identical and produced the same high-pitched note (fig. 3.7).[2] The dislocation of the left hand from the wrist indicates that some soft tissue decomposition had already taken place prior to the burial and that the child was probably not immediately buried after its death but kept else-

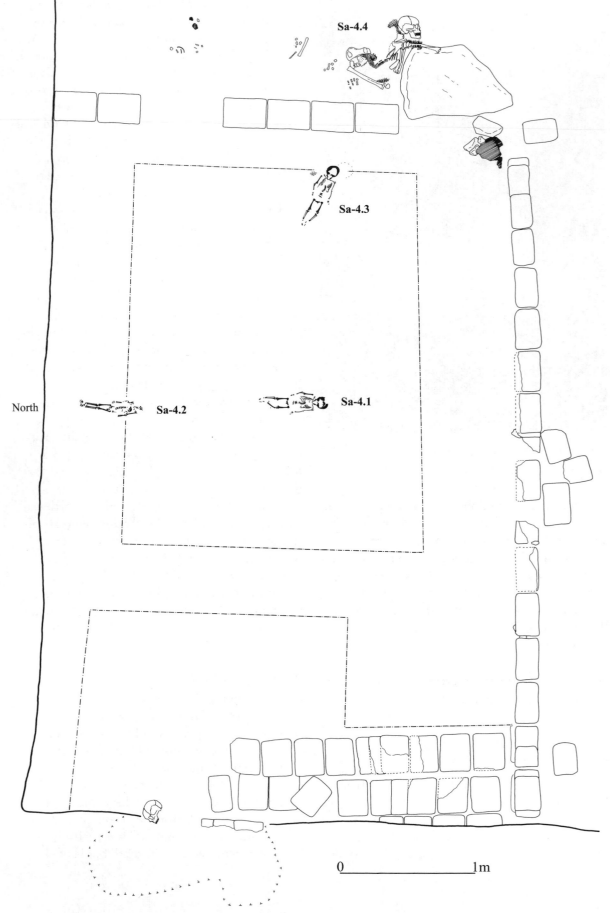

North

Sa-4.4

Sa-4.3

Sa-4.2

Sa-4.1

0   1m

FIGURE 3.4. Structure of adobes running along the west wall of Plaza 3A.

where for a while. No clear pathologies could be discerned on the bones, so the cause of death could not be determined.

The third child (Child Sa-4.3) was also headless. Its body was found about 15 cm below the surface of Sand 4 at 97.38 m (fig. 3.3). Like the two others, it was lying on its back, with its shoulders oriented toward the east. The body, in poor condition, was resting close to the line of adobes connecting the boulder to the north wall of the plaza. This single line of adobes with the southern wall created a small rectangular space. This project, which is described in the following section, included placing a large boulder (probably taken from the rocky outcrop) as the southeast cornerstone of a precinct.

A whitish mass of large seashell remains was found close to the left arm of the child, but they were too badly decomposed to be identified. Traces of decayed organic material on each side

of the body indicate that the child, perhaps like the others, was wrapped in a textile or small mat. The osteological analysis revealed that the child was about twelve months old and presented severe skeletal malformations. It appears that this very young individual, like Child Sa-4.1, might have suffered from a congenital case of periostitis or osteomyelitis. In this case, however, the illness could have been severe enough to cause death.

The close proximity of the Child Sa-4.2 to the surface of Sand 4 and to the base of the north wall indicates that it was buried after the construction of the plaza. Otherwise the shallow burial would have been disturbed by the building activities. Child Sa-4.3 was buried very close to the line of adobes marking the eastern limit of the precinct (fig. 3.3). This child could thus have been put there sometime after the others and after the completion of this simple structure. The southern wall of the precinct was more elaborate, constructed on a layer of clay brought by an episode of intense rainfall (Sediment 4), loose gravel, and sand (Sand 3) (figs. 3.3, 3.8, 3.9). The southern wall construction above clay fill indicates that Child Sa-4.1

FIGURE 3.3. (*Opposite*) Plan of the precinct in the northwest corner of Plaza 3A. Drawing by Jorge Sachun.

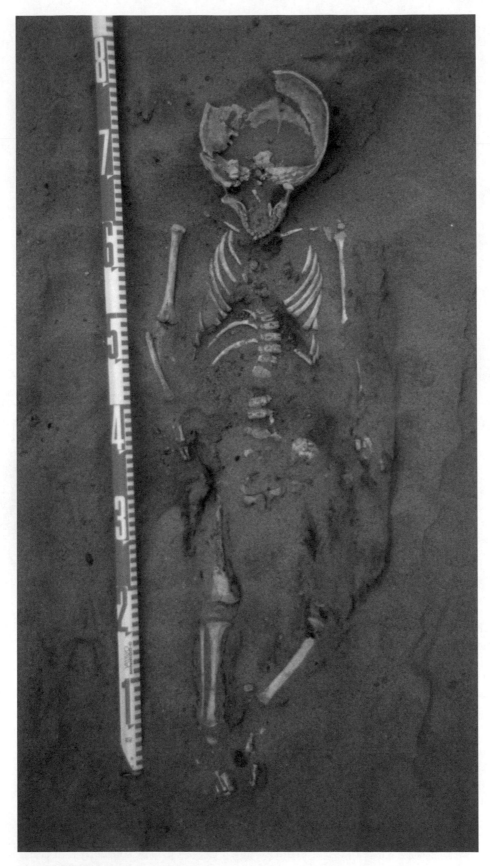

FIGURE 3.5. Child burial Sa-4.1.

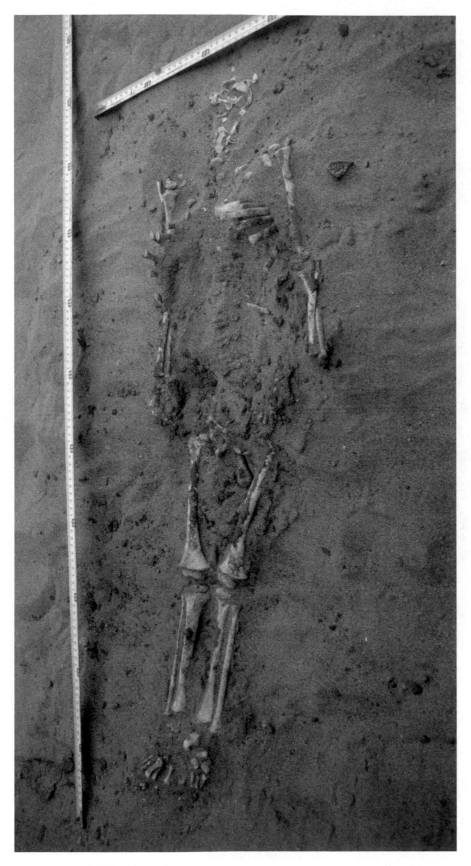

FIGURE 3.6. Child burial Sa-4.2.

FIGURE 3.7. Whistles found with Child Sa-4.2. Museo Huacas de Moche, Trujillo.

FIGURE 3.8. Base of west wall in Plaza 3A.

and Child Sa-4.2 were buried sometime before, as Sediment 4 clearly covered Sand 4 in that area. The mud did not reach over Child Sa-4.3, probably because of the slope. Hence it cannot be demonstrated that this child was also buried before the deposition of Sediment 4, but similarities noted among them indicate that the burial of these three children could have taken place during the same period of activities.

Although the heads of two of the children were missing, no evidence of decapitation could be detected on the cervical vertebrae. The absence of cut marks suggests that the heads were carefully separated from the bodies sometime after decomposition of the soft tissue took place. Furthermore, the dislocation of the second child's left hand reinforces the possibility that these three children were kept elsewhere for a time before being buried in the plaza.

The removal of the children's heads may be

part of a wider symbolic pattern. As the description of the sacrificial site shows, the Moche placed great emphasis on human heads. For example, in a room located on the western side of the Huaca de la Luna main platform, two crania were found that were transformed into some kind of vessels (Verano 2001a: 172). Severed heads are also prominently depicted in the art. It is thus likely that another ritual involving the removal of the heads of the children was also conducted, probably in some other place while the complex was being constructed. The corpses were then carefully wrapped in textiles and deposited in these shallow graves.

Why were these children buried within this part of the plaza? Why were the heads of two of the buried children removed before their burial? For the moment these questions remain difficult to answer, but it appears that the children formed part of a well-conceived plan that includes the sacrificial site of slain male warriors. The burial of these children could have been part of the whole process of preparing the sacrificial site. They may have been buried as a form of dedication to the

completion of the building, before the deposition of Sediment 4 and the construction of the precinct. This working hypothesis is substantiated by a detailed comparative iconographic analysis in chapter 6.

SEDIMENT 4

Sediment 4 (97.01 m–97.39 m) corresponds to the first layer of mud deposited in the plaza. This layer of sediment resulted from spells of torrential rains that washed down the walls (fig. 3.8). Following the natural declivity of Sand 4, the mud became concentrated in the northwest portion of the plaza to an expanse of about 12 m². Its thickness in the northwest corner was about 14 cm. This episode of rainfall could have been intense but of relatively short duration, as the deposit of clay did not cover a wide area. No ritual activity or artifact was noted in this layer. Again, this layer of sediment covered the area of Sand 4 containing the burials of Child Sa-4.1 and Child Sa-4.2, indicating that they were buried before this event took place. The south wall of the precinct rests directly on this layer and

FIGURE 3.9. Southern adobe wall connecting the boulder to the west wall.

marks the limit of Sediment 4, which does not extend to the south of the plaza past this wall.

THE PRECINCT

Shortly after the deposition of silt and clay (Sediment 4) in the northwest corner of the plaza and on top of the small structure at the base of the west wall, the southern wall of the precinct was erected perpendicular to the west wall. The southern wall was constructed with a single row two to four adobes high (figs. 3.3, 3.9). In conjunction with an eastern line of adobes and the north and west walls of the plaza, it delimited a rectangular precinct with a boulder forming its southeastern corner (figs. 2.15, 3.3). This precinct measured 3.6 m by 5.6 m, for a total area of 20.2 m².

On the basis of stratigraphic evidence, it is clear that the first event of rain (Sediment 4) preceded the construction of the south wall of the precinct and may have triggered its creation (fig. 3.9). Although we can only speculate at this stage, it would seem that the construction of the precinct came almost as an afterthought, following the deposition of the first layer of clay, as the extent of Sediment 4 closely matched the limit of the south wall. The rather limited area covered by the first layer of mud may have inspired Moche ritualists drastically to reduce the wide-open space of the plaza by creating this rectangular structure. This would imply that their intent of performing the first sacrificial ritual of adult males in a layer of mud was already set. In this regard the boulder placed in the southeastern corner could have been not only physically but also symbolically associated with the rocky outcrop less than 3 m away. Therefore this small sector could have functioned as a reduced model of the plaza itself, a microcosm of Plaza 3A with its own "sacred" rock in one corner.

Sand 3

Sand 3 (97.50 m) was a layer composed of sand, gravel, clay, and ceramic sherds, indicating that this was not clean windblown sand (fig. 3.8). The material would have been brought into the northwest corner of the plaza in order partially to level the ground within the precinct. From east to west its thickness varied between 12 and 38 cm. The area covered by this material was small and concentrated along the west and the north walls, indicating that this material was needed to readjust the rather severe declination of the ground.

Male Burial

After the burial of the children, the rains, and the construction of the precinct, Adult Male Sa-4.4 was placed in a crouched position against the east side of the boulder. The body was wrapped in a mat and at least two textiles (figs. 3.3, 3.10). Three beads and a few hematite fragments were found above the pelvis in a mass of decayed textiles that could have been a bag, together with two small quartz crystals. Some child bones were also lying nearby, midway between this body and the west wall of the plaza, suggesting relative contemporaneity in the placement of this individual against the rock and the ritual involving the children. Looting activities, noted on the surface of Sediment 1 in that area, may have disturbed the burial of this child. The adult male, who was propped against the rock, was left exposed to the elements and was not provided with any funerary offerings apart from the peculiar items just mentioned. He was thus denied a proper Moche burial. The presence of quartz crystals and hematite fragments is unusual. They suggest some form of ritual practice that may have been meant to consecrate the plaza (as in the case of the children) or to underline more specifically the special nature of the boulder. As suggested earlier, this boulder was in all likelihood taken from the rocky outcrop in order to create a smaller and more restricted ritual space. If I am correct in assuming that the rocky outcrop was considered sacred by the Moche priesthood, then the boulder may have carried a similar symbolic weight. As discussed below, the male burial was not the only ritual activity to take place against this rock, an additional indication of its importance. The placement of the man against the rock and the burial of the children were the first ritual activities involving human beings carried out in this part of the plaza. If these activities were meant to consecrate the sacrificial arena, they could have been performed within a very short period.

FIGURE 3.10. (*Opposite*) Male burial Sa-4.4 against the east side of the boulder.

FIGURE 3.11. Sediment 3 and Individual Sa-2.1.

In sum, the burial of the children, the natural deposition of the first layer of clay after the first episode of intensive rains to be detected in the plaza (Sediment 4), the intentional laying of coarse sand and gravel (Sand 3), the construction of the south wall of the precinct, and finally the placing of the adult male against the rock could have occurred quite rapidly. All these ritual actions and natural events could well have happened in a matter of a few weeks or even days. It is thus imperative to investigate whether these rituals could have been performed on purpose to serve as a foundation, so to speak, for the subsequent sacrificial rituals.

If these rituals were unrelated to one another, the complex Plaza 3A/Platform II could have been constructed initially for an altogether different reason and reused afterward as a sacrificial arena.

SEDIMENT 3

Sometime after the construction of the precinct and the positioning of the adult male against the boulder, torrential rains once again fell on Huaca de la Luna, creating Sediment 3 (97.42 m–97.65 m). The virtual absence of windblown sand deposition between Sand 3 and this new layer of mud and silt indicates that this second event took place very shortly after the coarse sand was laid down. The presence of partly melted adobes trapped in the mud in the southwest corner of the precinct clearly demonstrates that this sediment layer, like Sediment 4, resulted from the erosion of the adobe walls during pouring rains. Some of the adobes trapped in the sun-dried mud were visible just above an individual (Sa-2.1) lying on his chest (fig. 3.11). This individual (discussed later) was resting directly on the sun-dried clay. The layer of Sediment 3 covered a surface of about 22 m². Most of the clay deposit was located well within the precinct, abutting against its south and east walls. It is thus plausible that the principal aim of this rectangular space was to contain the pool of mud and in the process to act as a convenient stage for the first sacrificial ritual.

The first sacrificed individuals were found embedded in this layer of clay, which measured some 5 to 10 cm thick. Because of the proximity of the other sacrificial activities on top of this layer, it was not possible to evaluate with any degree of exactitude the number of people sacrificed in the mud. Nevertheless, the evidence indicates that at least four individuals were sacrificed (fig. 3.12). The body of Individual Se-3.1, of which only

FIGURE 3.12. (*Opposite*) Plan of Sediment 3. Drawing by Jorge Sachun.

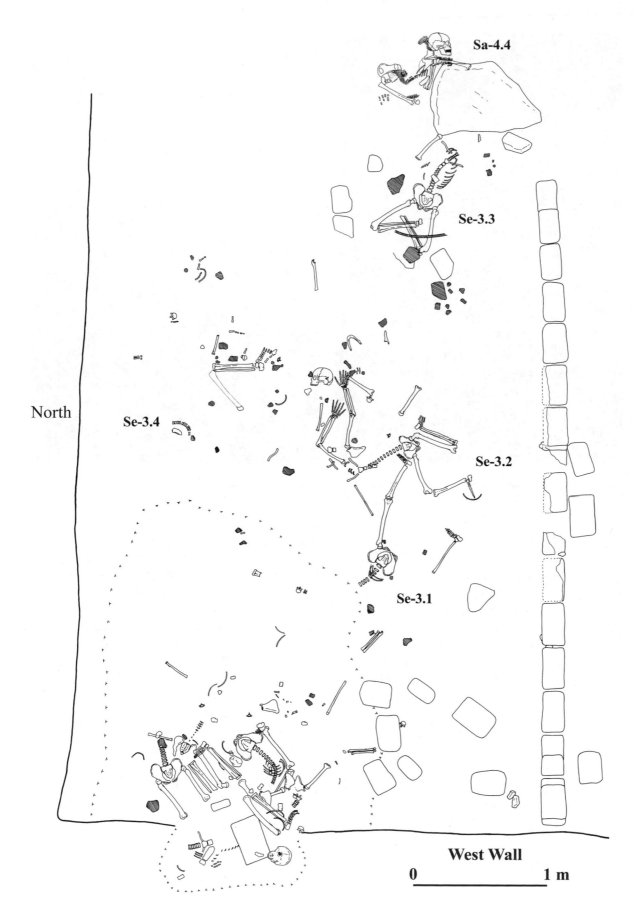

Sa-4.4

Se-3.3

North

Se-3.4

Se-3.2

Se-3.1

West Wall

0   1 m

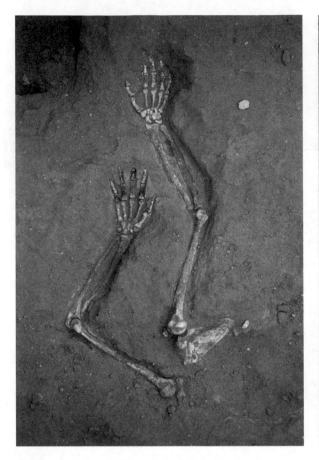

FIGURE 3.13. Bones of the arms of Individual Se-3.2.

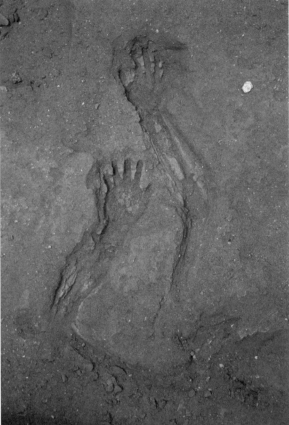

FIGURE 3.14. Imprints of the arms of Individual Se-3.2.

part of the trunk and the left leg remained, was deposited first. Individual Se-3.2 was placed there second, as evidenced by the fact that the left foot of the first man lay just underneath the pelvis of the second. Most of the body of Individual Se-3.1 had been disturbed by an activity that later took place just in front of the west wall. Both individuals were lying on their backs, and Individual Se-3.2 might have been laid to the ground with both arms stretched to one side. His right leg was slightly flexed, while the left one was folded over onto itself. As noted below, the crossing of one leg onto itself or over the body is not a rare occurrence and could have been part of some specific repositioning of the limbs by the sacrificers.

The imprints of the flesh of an isolated leg and of the arms of Individual Se-3.2 indicate that the flesh was still firmly attached to the bones when these victims were deposited in the soft mud. For example, after the excavators removed the bones of the arms of Individual Se-3.2 and gently brushed off the loose sand, the form of the fin-

gers, the hands, and the arms became clear in the impressed mud (figs. 3.13, 3.14). This shows clearly that the deposition of the mud in the plaza and the laying down of these corpses (still in a good state of conservation) were contemporaneous.

Individual Se-3.3 was placed at the base of the boulder in the southeast corner of the precinct, with his head, arms, and parts of the feet missing (fig. 3.12). The legs were crossed on top of each other. Sizable fragments of a big jar had been set around them, with the largest one resting in a standing position on top of the left leg (fig. 3.15). An additional sherd from a smaller domestic vase was placed on his chest. The position of these sherds indicates that they were intentionally placed, with the biggest one still firmly resting in equilibrium on the left leg. The careful positioning of this large ceramic fragment indicates the

FIGURE 3.15. (*Opposite*) Individual Se-3.3 lying on the west side of the boulder.

FIGURE 3.16. Cavity in the west wall.

FIGURE 3.17. Human remains in the cavity in the west wall.

degree of attention given to all the details of the ritual process.

The body of Individual Se-3.4 was apparently badly disturbed by additional sacrifices in the same area. Nevertheless, its spinal column was still trapped in the mud (fig. 3.12). Fragments of domestic ceramics were also lying scattered among the human remains. When Individual Se-3.3 was propped against the rock, Individual Sa-4.4 was still clearly visible lying on his eastern side. Therefore the positioning of the corpses on each side of the boulder seems to have reiterated the symbolic nature and the importance of this rock in the ritual sequence after Sand 3. This rock also provides a focus for attention in Sand 1.

SAND 2.3.9 TO 2.3.1

Shortly after this first sacrificial ritual in the mud, a pit was dug in the northwest part of the precinct, and a cavity was created in the west wall (fig. 3.16). The opening dug into Sediment 3 covered an area of about 5 m² (fig. 3.12). The creation of this pit certainly disturbed the first sacrificial ritual. It is possible that the bones of these earlier victims were carefully deposited back into this cavity, however, because this depression some 105 cm below the surface of Sediment 3 was crammed with skeletal remains and artifacts (fig. 3.17). The small structure that had been constructed at the base of the west wall was disturbed by this activity, further suggesting that the pit was intentional and was not the result of a natural process of erosion (figs. 3.8, 3.16).

Because of the sheer number of bones and body parts lying on top of each other in such a restricted space, the layer was divided into nine arbitrary sublayers: Sand 2.3.1 to Sand 2.3.9 (96.32 m–97.37 m) (figs. 3.18–3.26). In this location we encountered two complete corpses, five heads, seven pelvises, part of a trunk, four lower jaws, numerous legs, arms, and other body parts. Some of the remains throughout the layers were groups of bones in articulated position, indicating that soft tissue was still holding the bones together when these remains were inserted into the wall cavity. They thus seem to be the product of some dismembering activities that took place, probably in the plaza itself.

At the bottom of the pit at the junction with

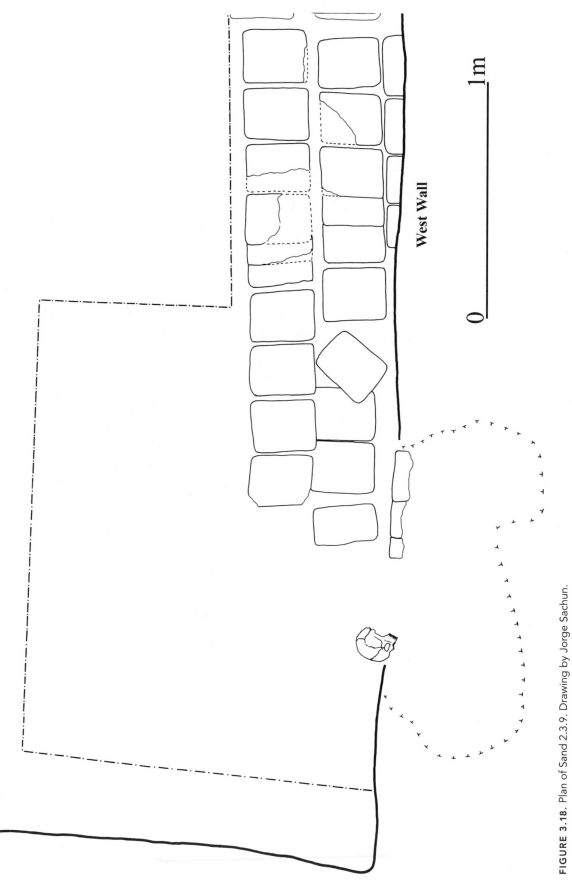

West Wall

0   1m

FIGURE 3.18. Plan of Sand 2.3.9. Drawing by Jorge Sachun.

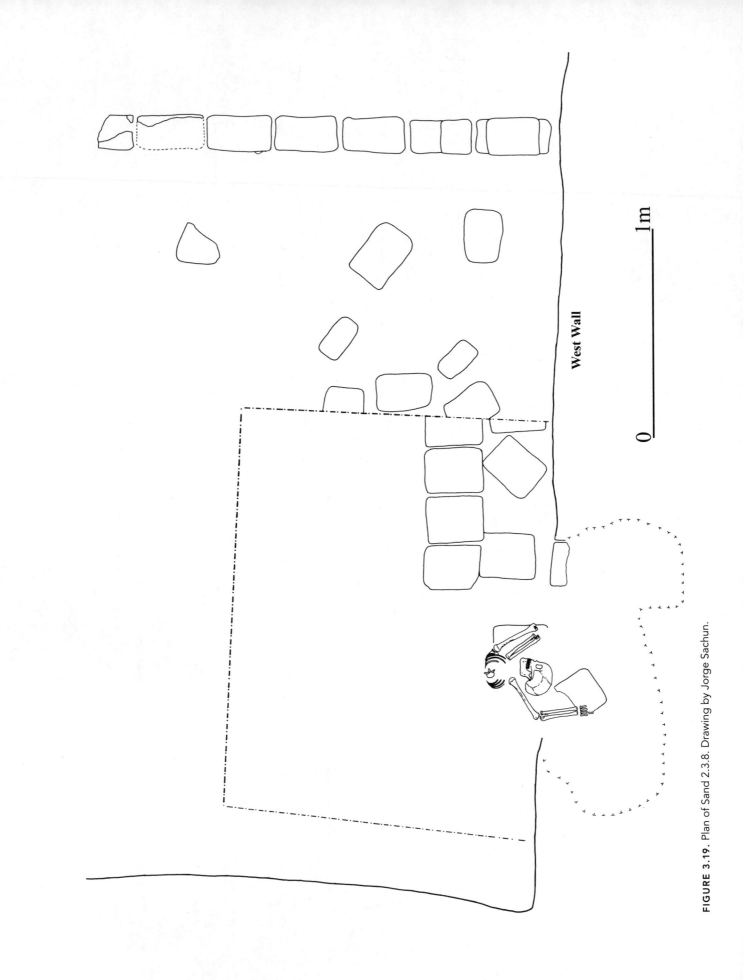

West Wall

0 1m

FIGURE 3.19. Plan of Sand 2.3.8. Drawing by Jorge Sachun.

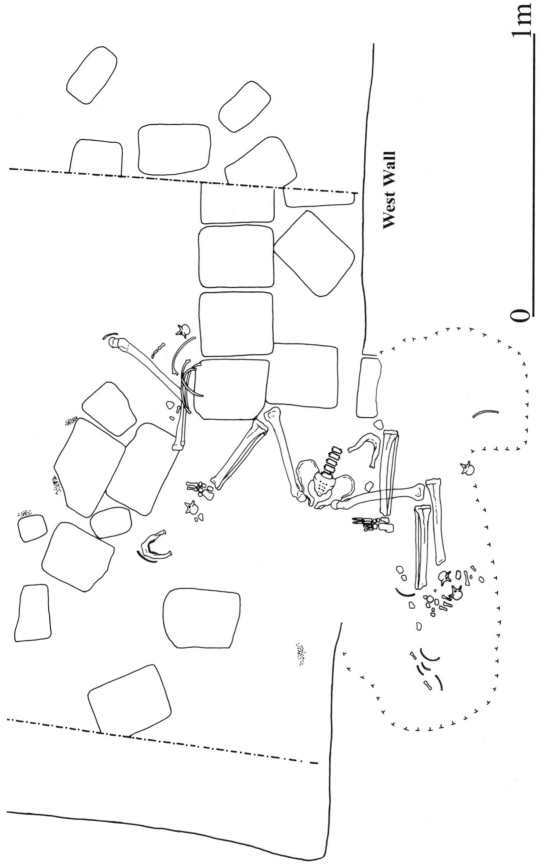

West Wall

0   1m

FIGURE 3.20. Plan of Sand 2.3.7. Drawing by Jorge Sachun.

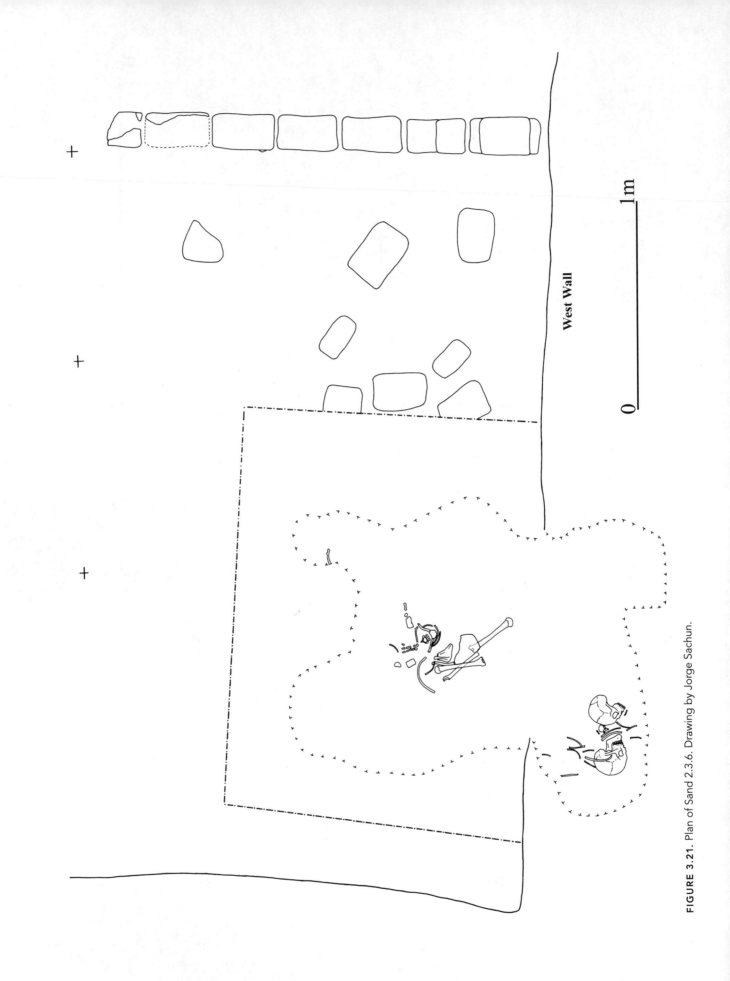

West Wall

1m

0

FIGURE 3.21. Plan of Sand 2.3.6. Drawing by Jorge Sachun.

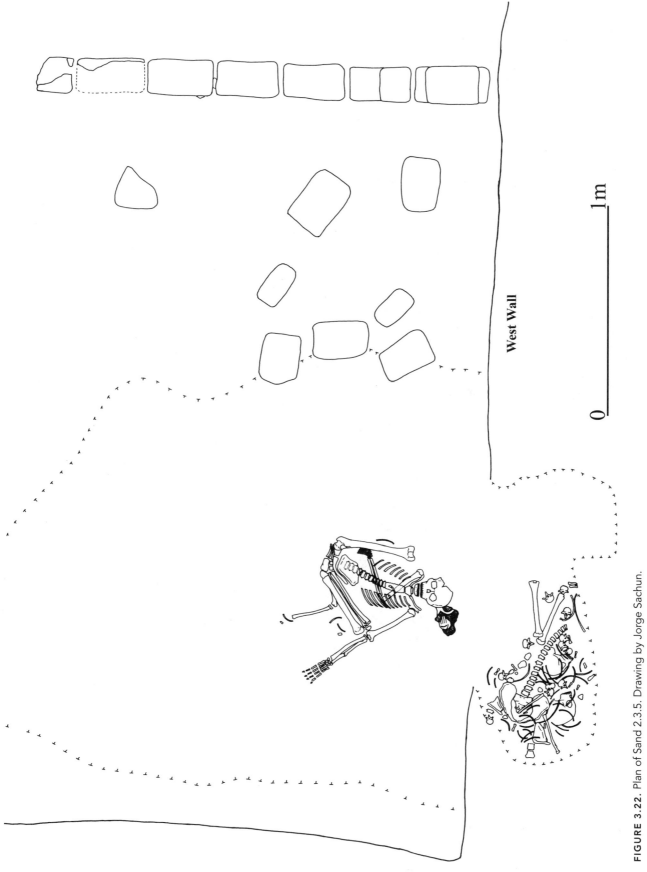

West Wall

1m

0

FIGURE 3.22. Plan of Sand 2.3.5. Drawing by Jorge Sachun.

West Wall

0   1m

FIGURE 3.23. Plan of Sand 2.3.4. Drawing by Jorge Sachun.

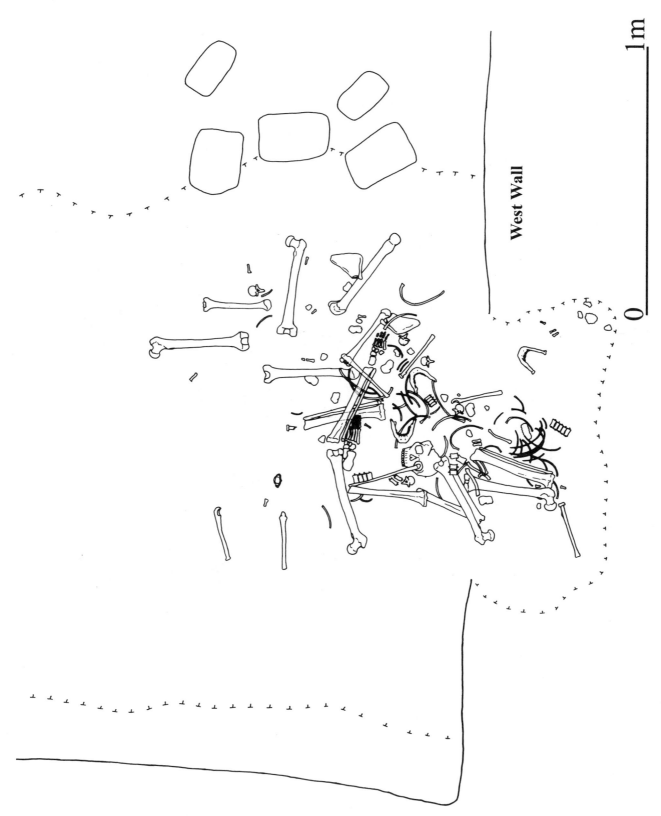

West Wall

1m

0

FIGURE 3.24. Plan of Sand 2.3.3. Drawing by Jorge Sachun.

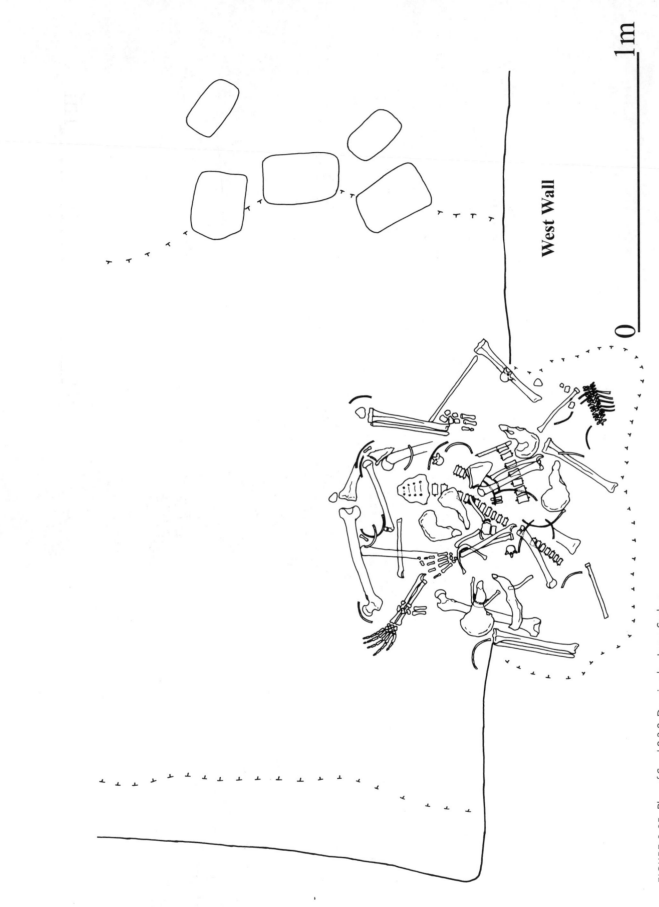

West Wall

0   1m

FIGURE 3.25. Plan of Sand 2.3.2. Drawing by Jorge Sachun.

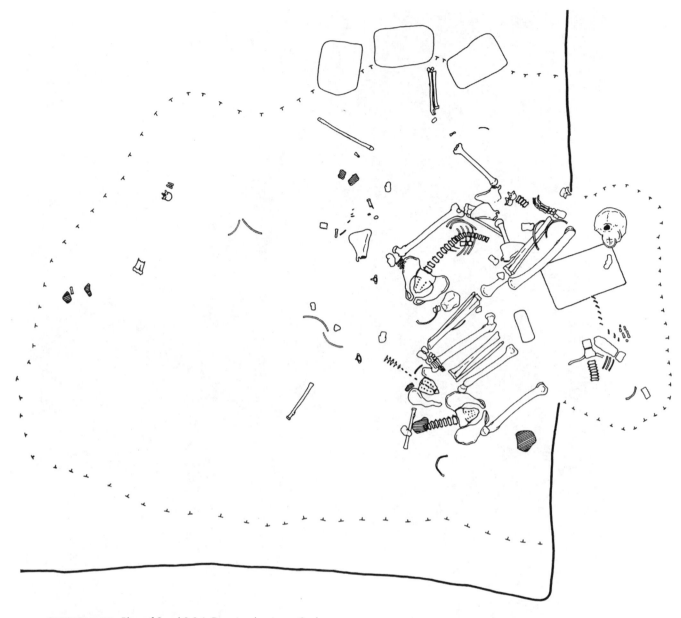

FIGURE 3.26. Plan of Sand 2.3.1. Drawing by Jorge Sachun.

the west wall and the plaza, a head was placed as a first offering (figs. 3.16, 3.18). Subsequently the trunk, arms, and head of another individual were placed just on top of it, along with some of the displaced adobes from the structure (fig. 3.19). Right after the deposition of this corpse, an incomplete corpse was placed at the entrance of the hole in the wall (fig. 3.20). This partial trunk—a pelvis with its spinal column and lower limbs still articulated but in splayed position—is fairly typical of a number of similar remains found throughout the different layers. In most cases, although the legs were still in anatomical position,

the femurs were disjointed from the hip joints and the legs were flexed at an unnatural angle. As mentioned earlier, a number of heads (such as these two placed together) were found in the west wall and in the pit (figs. 3.21, 3.27).

At some point during this process, Individual Sa-2.13 was placed on his back lying just in front of the west wall (figs. 3.22, 3.28). He had both femurs dislocated from the hip joints and was missing the superior part of his cranium. He also presented a partially healed fracture of the left ulna (fig. 3.29). A rock had tightly been inserted in his pelvis, the canine of a sea lion pup (*Otaria*

FIGURE 3.28. Individual Sa-2.13 in Sand 2.3.5.

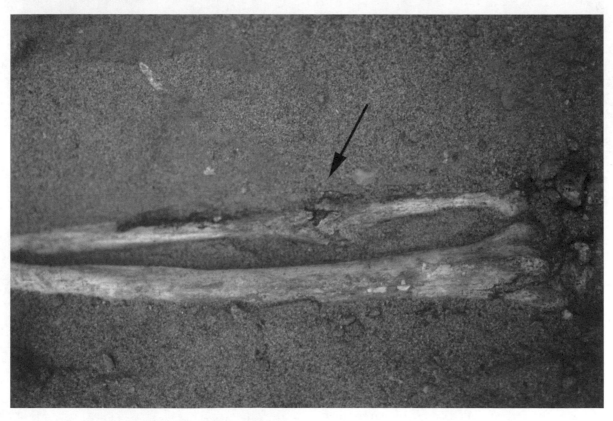

FIGURE 3.29. Left arm of Individual Sa-2.13.

FIGURE 3.27. (*Opposite*) Human remains in Sand 2.3.6.

FIGURE 3.30. Individual Sa-2.13 in Sand 2.3.5.

FIGURE 3.31. Cranium of Individual Sa-2.13.

FIGURE 3.32. Fragment of a Phase III vessel placed on the cranium of Individual Sa-2.13.

byronia) was placed on his chest, and the fragment of a Phase III ceramic vessel was found just above the left side of his head (figs. 3.30, 3.31).[3] It is possible that this ceramic fragment—which represented a bearded individual from the Coca Ceremony—was originally located directly on his face (fig. 3.32). It may have slipped to the side when other bones were placed above this individual. Additional human remains and artifacts were subsequently deposited into the pit until it was completely filled (figs. 3.24, 3.25, 3.26). The number of bones and artifacts piled on top of one another, without any sand between them, suggests that this exceptionally intense ritual took place during a very short time period.

Numerous fragments of clay statuettes and adobe bricks were mixed in with the human remains (fig. 3.33). The skeletons of four guinea pigs (*Cavia porcellus*) were also found in layer Sand 2.3.7 (fig. 3.34). An opening (sometimes even with a sort of small door) was created in the back of the statuettes in some instances (fig. 3.35), which suggests that offerings, such as the guinea pigs that were found, were inserted into these sculptures. Given the degree of fragmentation of the statuettes in this sector, it is possible that some of these effigies were thrown into the pit from the summit of the west wall.

SAND 2.3, 2.2, AND 2.1

Sand 2 is a layer of windblown sand marking an interval between two layers of clay and silt: Sediment 3 and Sediment 2. Such an accumulation of aeolian sand, which attained nearly 38 cm in thickness against the west wall, indicates that a period of time elapsed between these two episodes of rainfall. Figure 3.36 clearly shows this layer of sand wedged between the layers of clay. The sand and the subsequent layer of sediment (Sediment 2) conserved the evidence of intense rainfall that eroded the west wall and led to the earlier formation of Sediment 3. The erosion unequivocally indicates that adobe walls affected by the rain provided the layers of clay in the plaza.

The rituals performed in Sand 2 were very similar to those carried out in the cavity at the base of the west wall and likely date to the same period. Fragments of adobes, rocks, and clay statuettes were also found among the human remains in Sand 2 and clearly demonstrate the temporal continuity with the activities carried out in the depression (fig. 3.37). The main difference between Sand 2 and the cavity is the seemingly higher degree of ritual organization. The sacrifices of Sand 2 were probably realized directly on the surface of the plaza with the corpses left in place. In order to separate the skeletal remains lying directly on top of one another, I had to delineate three sublevels: Sand 2.3, 2.2, and 2.1 (97.69 m–97.60 m) (figs. 3.37, 3.38, 3.39).

At first sight it would appear that the individuals resting on the hardened clay surface of Sediment 3 were sacrificed or deposited without any apparent order, but a careful study of the distribution of the human remains suggests otherwise. Solely on the basis of the way in which the corpses

FIGURE 3.33. Clay statuettes fragments in Sand 2.

FIGURE 3.34. Skeleton of a guinea pig (*Cavia porcellus*) in Sand 2.3.7.

FIGURE 3.35. Rectangular opening in the back of a clay sculpture.

FIGURE 3.36. Stratigraphic layers (Sediment 3/Sand 2/ Sediment 2) against the west wall.

(Sa–2.1) with the positioning of Individuals Sa–2.2, Sa–2.3, and Sa–2.4 and then moving to his left side with the positioning of Individuals Sa–2.5, Sa–2.6, Sa–2.7, and Sa–2.8. It is thus likely that the placement of these individuals represents the work of a single group of practitioners.

A second sequence not physically connected to the first one was identified a few meters to the east (fig. 3.42). The first individual of this group (Sa–2.9) was laid on his back in a north-south orientation, with his shoulders toward the north wall. The second individual (Sa–2.10) was resting in an opposite direction with his right hand covering the left foot of Sa–2.9 (fig. 3.43). Like the first individual of the previous sequence (fig. 3.40, Sa–2.1), this individual had his cranium split open with a blow to the back of the head.

The elaborate sequence of deposition of the human remains makes Sand 2 one of the most complex levels of the whole sacrificial site. In addition to the deposition sequence of human remains indicating a highly organized sacrificial process, an overall view of the layer reveals an even higher degree of ritual organization.

To the east, Sa–2.9 and Sa–2.10 were placed head to head with their legs oriented in opposite directions (figs. 3.42, 3.43). Sa–2.9, the first of them to be laid to the ground, may have been decapitated. A rib was inserted into his pelvis and a lower jaw was carefully placed in his thoracic cage, just underneath the sternum (fig. 3.44). The sternum, still in its anatomical position, indicates that the jaw must have been forcibly inserted in the trunk through a cavity in the abdomen. It is thus likely that the internal organs were removed for the insertion of the lower jaw, just as the genitalia may have been removed for the placement of the rib. Sa–2.10, the second individual of the east pair, had the cranium opened with a powerful blow to the head. The cranial bone fragment was then placed against the forehead (fig. 3.42).

Individuals Sa–2.5 and Sa–2.6 (placed immediately to the west of the first pair) were also oriented in opposite directions relative to one another; however, in this case they were lying on their chests (fig. 3.42). Sa–2.6 again had an additional bone placed into the thoracic cage: a finger bone appears between the second and the third rib of his left side (fig. 3.45).

were superimposed above one another, the following order can be suggested for two groups of corpses. The first individual (Sa–2.1) to be sacrificed in this sequence was seemingly killed with a bone-shattering blow to the back of the head (fig. 3.40). He was probably forcibly held on to the ground, because he rested on his chest in a splayed position. Afterward three other individuals (Sa–2.2, 2.3, and 2.4) were killed or deposited to his right side (fig. 3.41). Four other persons (Sa–2.5, 2.6, 2.7, and 2.8) were likewise positioned, one after the other to his left (fig. 3.41). Thus the superposition of the bones indicates that they were laid in a very precise sequence, initially working to the right side of the first individual

North

West Wall

0 _____ 1m

FIGURE 3.37. Plan of Sand 2.3. Drawing by Jorge Sachun.

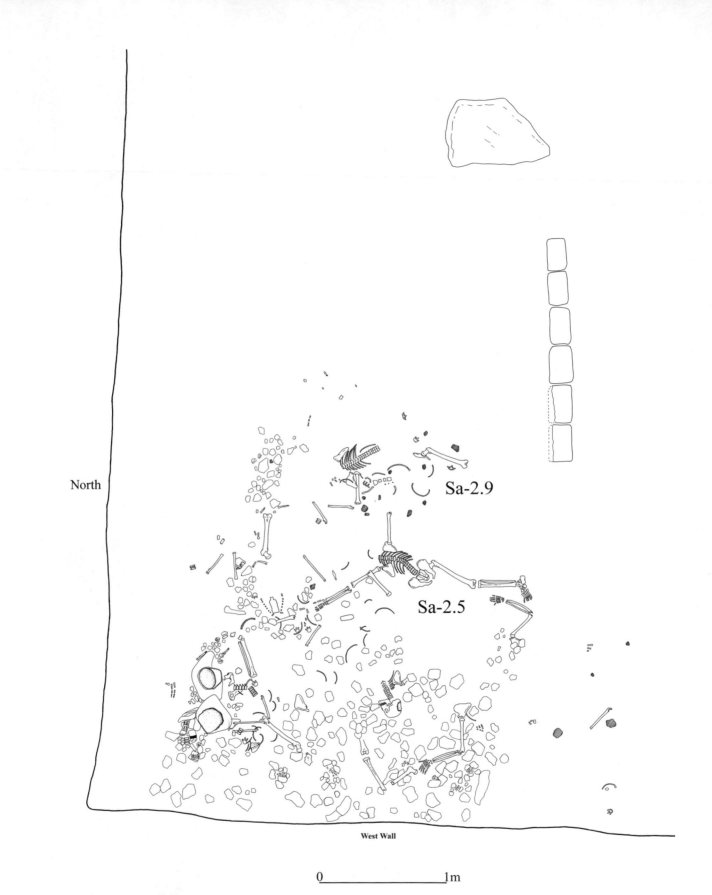

North

Sa-2.9

Sa-2.5

West Wall

0 _____ 1m

FIGURE 3.38. Plan of Sand 2.2. Drawing by Jorge Sachun.

North

Sa-2.11

Sa-2.12

West Wall

0   1m

FIGURE 3.39. Plan of Sand 2.1. Drawing by Jorge Sachun.

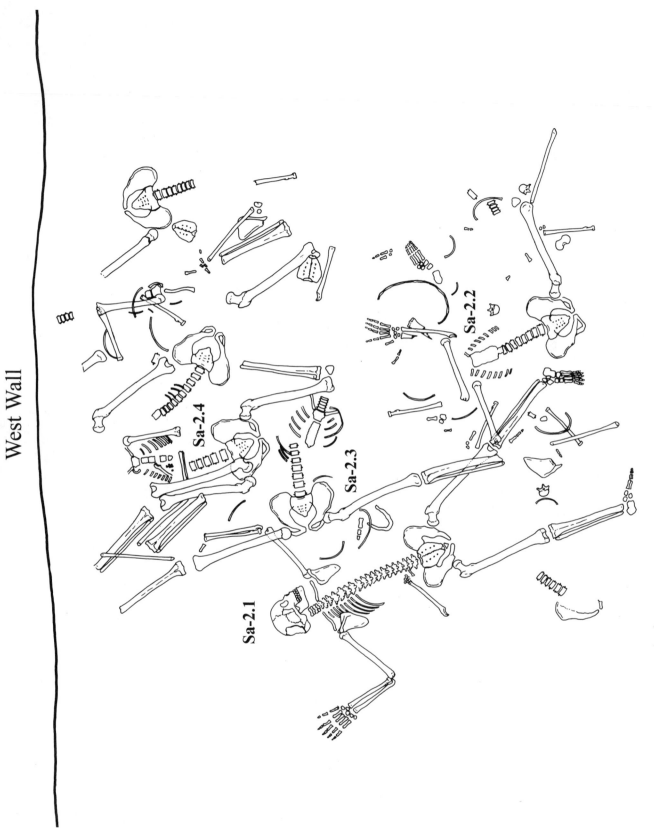

West Wall

Sa-2.2

Sa-2.4

Sa-2.3

Sa-2.1

FIGURE 3.40. Human remains in Sand 2, first group.

FIGURE 3.41. Human remains in Sand 2, second group.

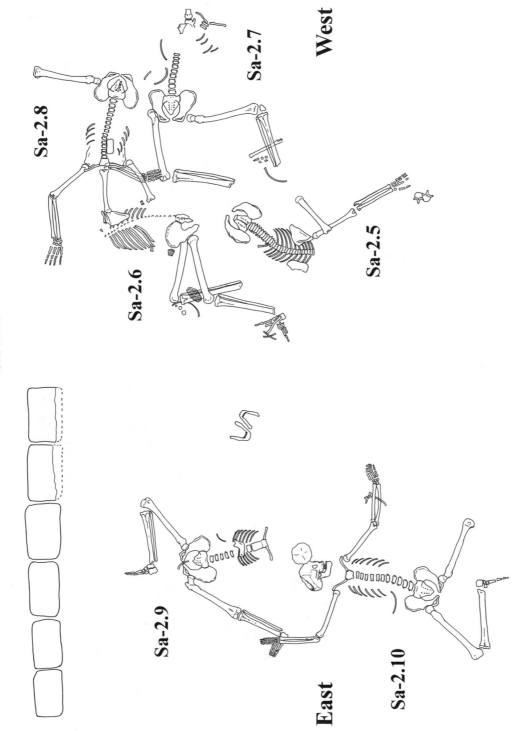

FIGURE 3.42. Human remains in Sand 2, third group.

FIGURE 3.43. Individuals Sa-2.9 and Sa-2.10.

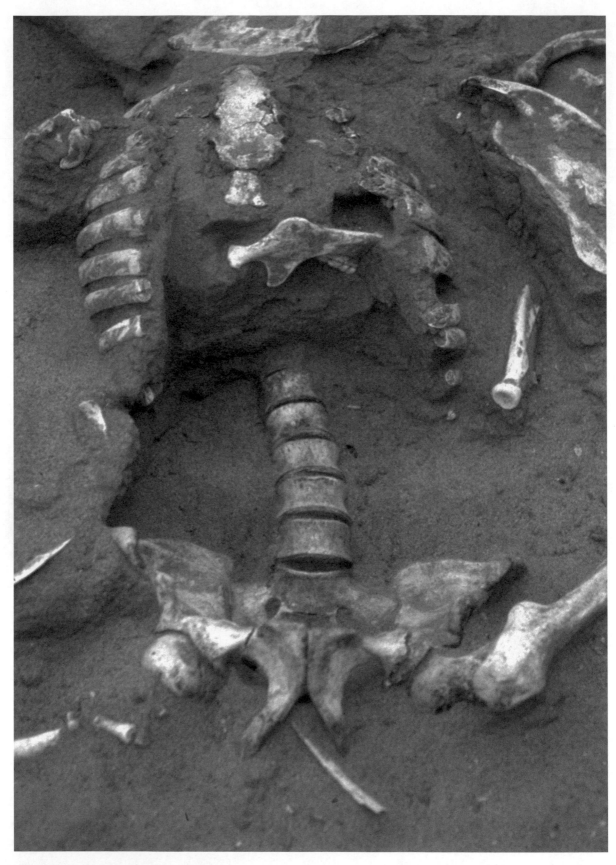

FIGURE 3.44. Details of Individual Sa-2.9.

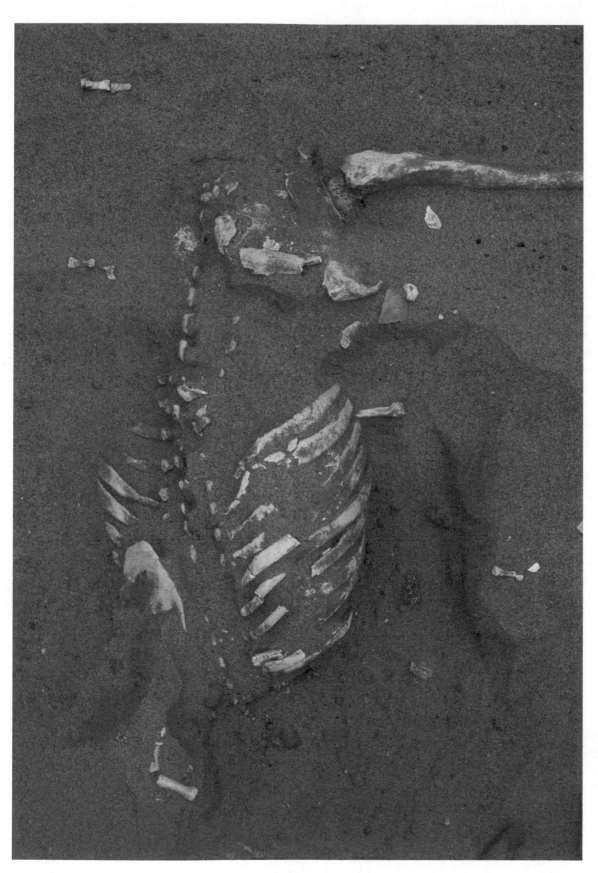

FIGURE 3.45. Individual Sa-2.6.

The third pair, Individuals Sa-2.7 and Sa-2.8 (whose heads were missing), were placed side by side in an inverted position (fig. 3.42). As with the two previous pairs, Sa-2.8, situated to the south, had a complete toe bone inserted into the middle of his pelvis (fig. 3.46). The presence of additional bones placed within the body of these individuals recalls the rock introduced into the abdomen of the man in front of the west wall (fig. 3.30).

The individuals with inserted bones were consistently lying on the southern side of the pairs. Also, the relative position of the bones in the human body from top to bottom (jaw, rib, hand bone, and foot bone) seems to have been preserved in their placement from east to west. The first individual (to the south) had a jaw and a rib, which come from the upper part of the body. The second had a finger bone. The one closest to the west wall had a toe. Furthermore, the pairing of four other bones seems to reproduce on a smaller scale the positioning of the bodies. The first pair consisted of two lower jaws placed upside down and in inverted positions, midway between the first and the second pair of individuals (figs. 3.42, 3.47). The second pairing of loose bones consisted of two inverted vertebrae resting just above the left hand of Individual Sa-2.5 (fig. 3.42).

On the basis of the evidence recovered, it appears that the intentional pairing of human remains began with Individuals Sa-2.5 and Sa-2.6 (fig. 3.42). It proceeded with the deposition of the second pair (Individuals Sa-2.7 and Sa-2.8) and culminated with the placement of the remaining two individuals of the second sequence (Sa-2.9 and Sa-2.10) to the east (figs. 3.42, 3.43). If the placement of the inserted bones reflecting their position in the human body was purposeful, it is likely that this action was undertaken after all six individuals had been placed in the plaza. The careful deposition of the bodies as well as the loose bones suggests that this complex ritual was carried out in a very specific fashion. The superposition and the placement of the corpses indicate that the sacrifices were carefully planned and could have been executed by a single group of sacrificers working on one individual at a time. A similar modus operandi was repeated in the following sacrificial layer (Sediment 2).

During the ritual reflected in Sand 2, a number of clay statuettes identical to those found in the pit were also destroyed. The deposition process indicates that the clay statuettes were placed and shattered after the human sacrifices, as none of the victims rested on any of the clay fragments. The statuettes were purposely broken with rocks and adobe bricks in at least three instances (fig. 3.48). Fragments of one statuette head were placed on the head of Individual Sa-2.11 located against the north wall (figs. 3.39, 3.49, 3.50). Additionally, two statuettes were "seated" side by side in a way that seemed to mimic the pairing of some victims (fig. 3.48). Thus a certain relation likely existed between these effigies (which represented nude males) and the sacrificial victims.

In addition, this layer presented the first individual deposited outside the precinct (Sa-2.12) (fig. 3.39). As is often the case, the hip joints of Individual Sa-2.12 were dislocated and the legs were in a flexed position. The upper part of the body was missing, but a head appeared alongside the right femur. Fragments of clay statuettes further indicate that this corpse was part of the ritual just mentioned. It is likely that additional human remains existed in between these two contexts; the looting activities have destroyed any such evidence, however, leaving behind an empty space in the central part of the sacrificial arena.

SEDIMENT 2.2 AND 2.1

The layer of clay and silt of Sediment 2.2 and 2.1 (98.44 m–97.78 m) corresponded to the deposition of sediment after what appears to have been a series of torrential rainfalls of much greater intensity than the previous ones. Spanning at least 60 m², the area covered by this clay layering was nearly three times bigger than the surface covered by Sediment 3. For the new series of sacrifices the emphasis moved south of the precinct, immediately in front of the rocky outcrop (fig. 3.51). This shift reinforces the suggestion that the boulder placed at the southeast corner of the small precinct once carried the same symbolic value as the rocky outcrop, which then possibly assumed the primary central role. Without this precinct, the sheer size of Plaza 3A, with 1,140 m², would have dwarfed the first pair of ritual areas, which covered a surface of only 20 m².

All the individuals deposited in this sector were laid down side by side, resting on their backs. From the superposition of the human remains,

FIGURE 3.46. Individuals Sa-2.7 and Sa-2.8.

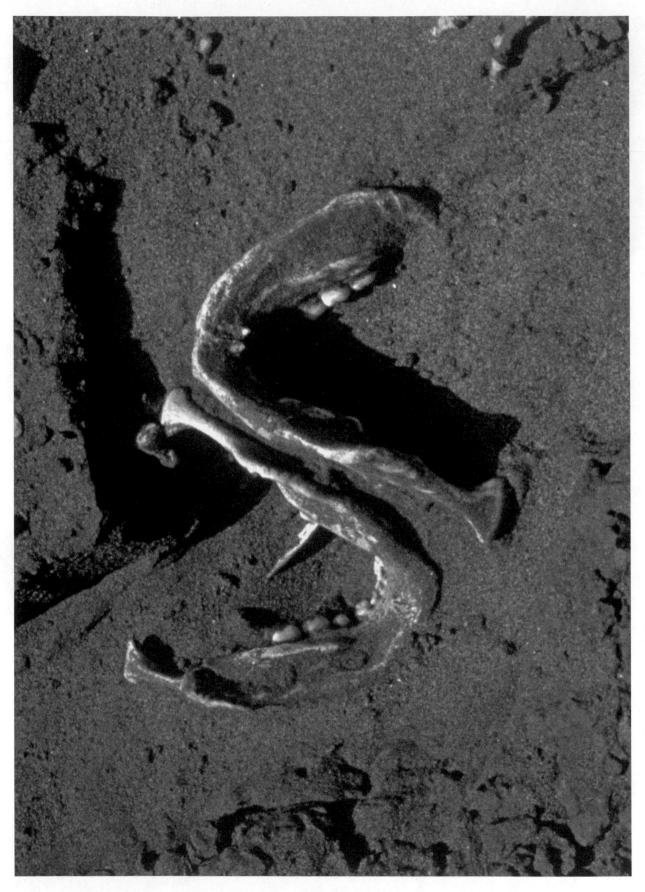

FIGURE 3.47. Pair of inverted lower jaws in Sand 2.

FIGURE 3.48. Pair of clay statuettes in Sand 2.

HUACA DE LA LUNA
ARP-2
CUADRANTE NE
CUADRICULA   13-EM,EN
ADENTRO   ARENA-2
10 07 95

FIGURE 3.49. Individual Sa-2.11 placed against the base of the north wall.

FIGURE 3.50. Fragments of a clay statuette head.

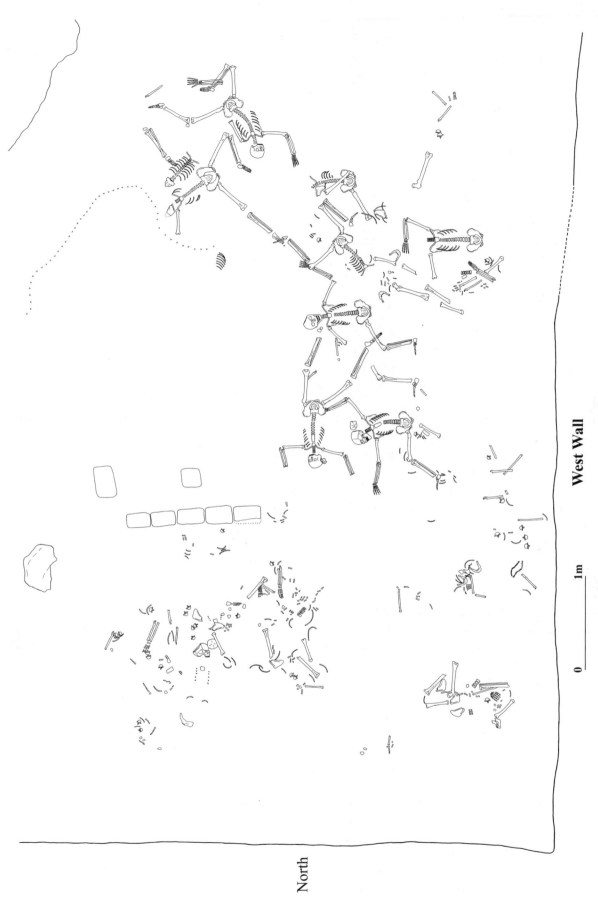

North

West Wall

0   1m

FIGURE 3.51. Plan of Sediment 2.2. Drawing by Jorge Sachun.

it is again possible to follow the sacrificial ritual almost step by step. Not surprisingly, this once more reveals a very high degree of ritual organization. The first victim (Se-2.1) had a portion of his cranial vault broken, indicating that he may have been put to death with a solid blow to the back of the head (figs. 3.52, 3.53). His left hand was resting underneath the pelvis of the second individual (Se-2.2), who had a similar skull fracture, hinting that he may also have been killed with a blow to the back of the head (fig. 3.54). Their positions relative to one another and the type of injuries indicate not only an order in the sequence but also that the practitioners were carrying out very precise sets of ritual actions (fig. 3.55). The right femur of the third individual (Se-2.3) covers the right foot of the second individual. Se-2.3 was seemingly killed with a blow to the left side of the head. His left hand was underneath the left knee of the fourth individual (Se-2.4). The head of the fourth victim was missing, and his left foot was under the right foot of the fifth person (Se-2.5) (fig. 3.52). The head of the fifth individual was also missing. The sixth individual (Se-2.6) was placed alongside the previous one, but in an inverted position (fig. 3.56). His left arm was swept across the chest of the fifth individual and even his chest slightly overlaps his predecessor's thoracic cage, indicating that he was laid to rest shortly thereafter.

Because the remaining three individuals did not overlap, it is not possible to demonstrate with complete confidence that they were sacrificed in the same sequence (fig. 3.52). Nevertheless, the left arm of Individual Se-2.7 was touching the left knee of Individual Se-2.5, which suggests that he was also laid down after the pair situated immediately to his left. His jaw and the lower part of his left arm were removed. Interestingly, a right arm was placed on his right tibia. Individuals Se-2.8 and Se-2.9 could well have been sacrificed one after the other following the sequence from left to right with Individual Se-2.1 to Individual Se-2.6 and then from right to left with Individuals Se-2.7 to Se-2.9.

This series of sacrifices, neatly arranged just in front of the rocky outcrop, recalls in many respects the sacrifices that took place previously in Sand 2, in the small precinct a few meters to the north (fig. 3.41). Indeed, it appears that the victims were executed and placed on the ground

one by one by a single group of sacrificers, as in Sand 2, emphasizing once more the ritual dimension of the practice. A number of similar wounds indicate that one of their tools of choice was a mace capable of breaking the cranium of an adult male with a single blow. The first six individuals touched each other, which does not seem to be fortuitous. I would suggest that it is more than mere coincidence. This could have been part of a well-planned and deliberately intended visual effect: the creation of a sort of *tableau macabre* where putrefying corpses and eventually skeletons were touching one another in a sort of eerie dance. It is also possible that the next three individuals (Se-2.7, 2.8, and 2.9) were initially touching each other as well. Many body parts and bones could have been disturbed by later sacrificial activities in the same area and by being left exposed to the elements. Although no clear marks of scavenging have been detected, it is further possible that carrion eaters such as vultures and foxes may have disturbed some of the remains.

The second arbitrary layer of Sediment 2 (Sediment 2.1) was slightly more difficult to evaluate than previous layers. Most of the skeletal remains lying in the plaza seem to pertain not only to this arbitrary level but also to the following one, Sand 1 (fig. 3.57). Although some of the remains were lying right on top of previous ones, they seemed to be partly trapped in the silt and yet resting on the ground as well (fig. 3.58). This only reiterates the difficulty of mapping the natural layers, the cultural processes, and the physical remains. On the southern portion of this layer, three individuals were lying face down on some of the participants in the *tableau macabre* discussed earlier. Individuals Sa-1.1, Sa-1.2, and Sa-1.3 were resting just above Individuals Se-2.9, Se-2.8, and Se-2.7 respectively (fig. 3.59). Individual Sa-1.2 was apparently held on the ground and decapitated (fig. 3.60). He presents an interesting series of healed fractures, including a left rib and the left radius and ulna, indicative of a seasoned warrior. This arm injury is consistent with a parry fracture, which could have been the result of blocking a blow (Verano 2001b). These three individuals (Sa-1.1, Sa-1.2, and Sa-1.3) are believed to form part of the following layer (Sand 1), as they were probably laid there with two other subjects during this period. In the northern section of this layer, the

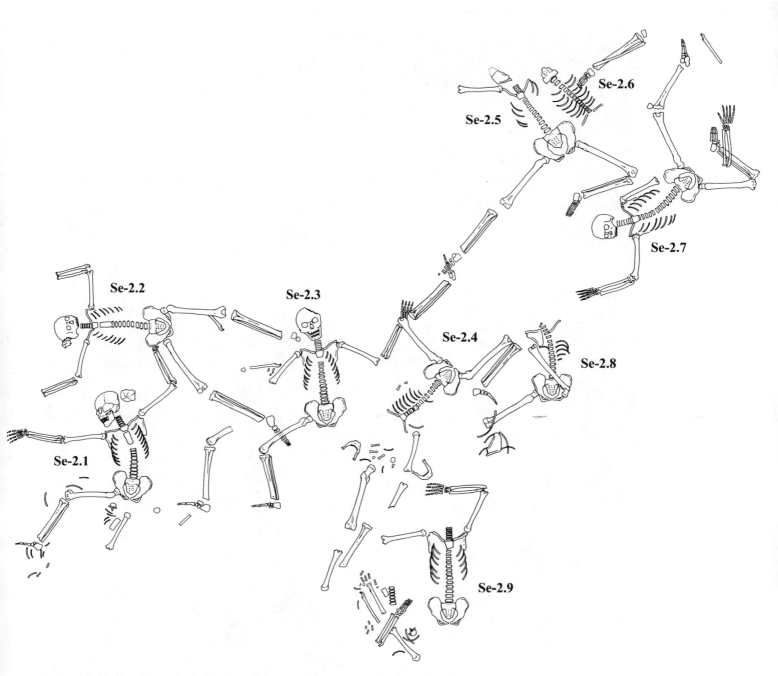

FIGURE 3.52. Human remains in Sediment 2.2.

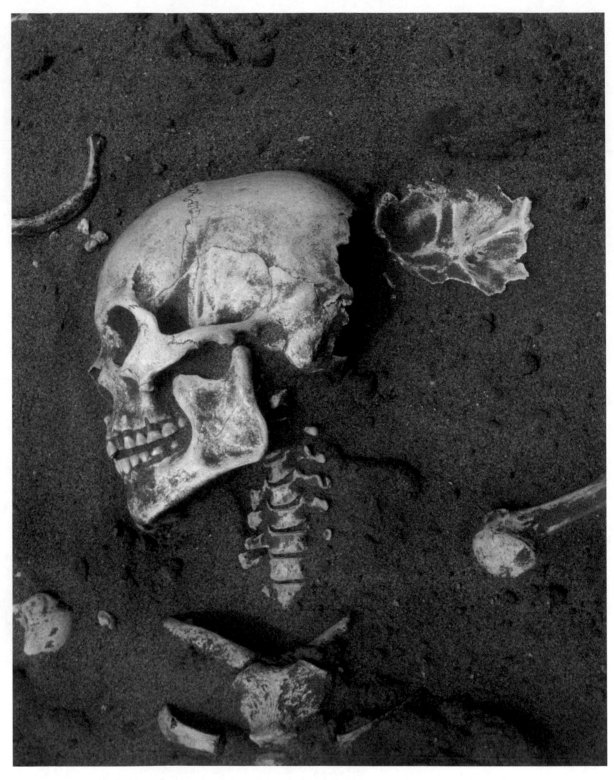

FIGURE 3.53. Individual Se-2.1.

FIGURE 3.54. Individual Se-2.2.

FIGURE 3.55. Individuals Se-2.1 and Se-2.2.

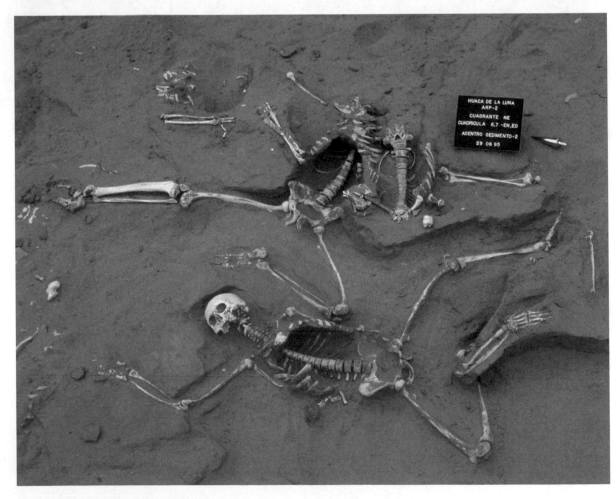

FIGURE 3.56. Individuals Se-2.5, Se-2.6, and Se-2.7.

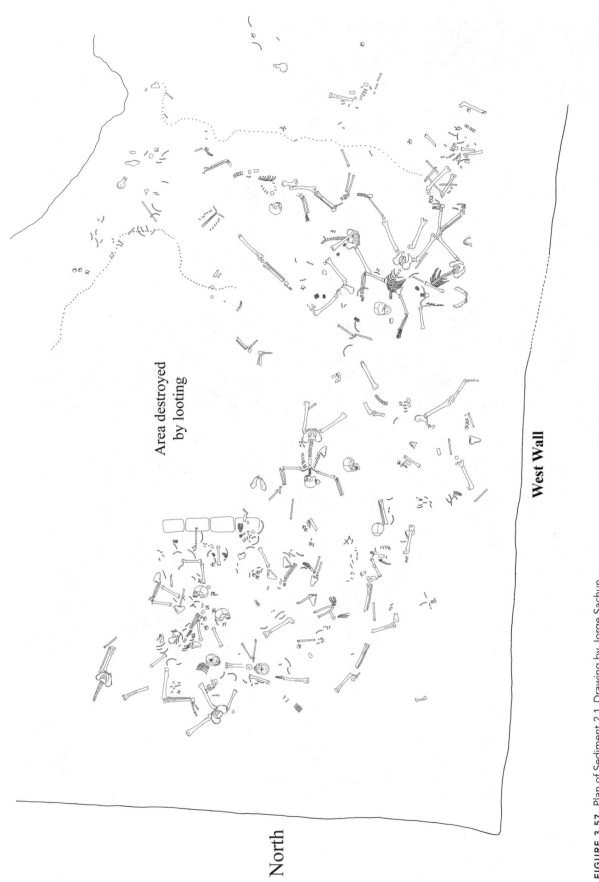

North

West Wall

Area destroyed
by looting

FIGURE 3.57. Plan of Sediment 2.1. Drawing by Jorge Sachun.

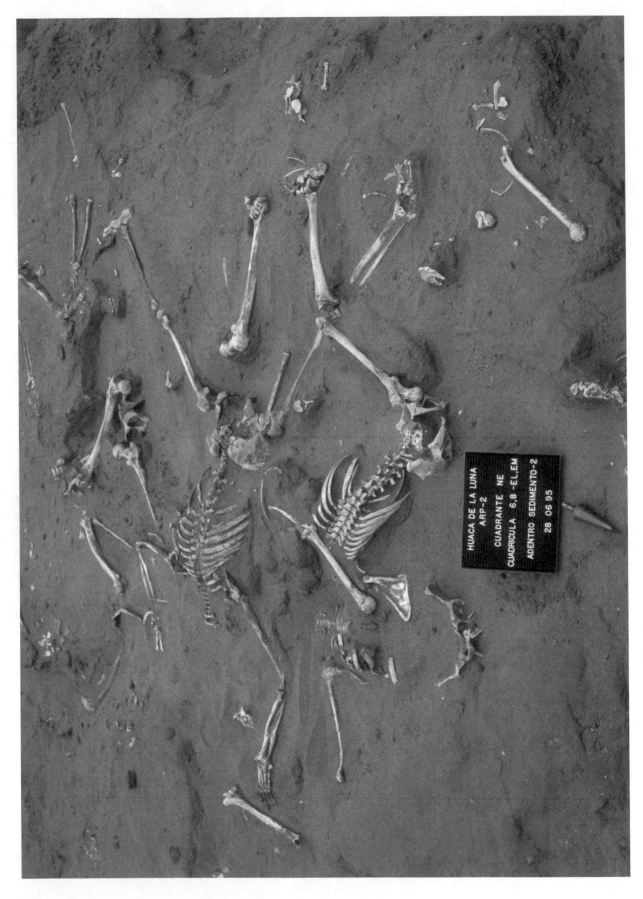

FIGURE 3.58. Individuals in Sediment 2.1 and Sand 1.

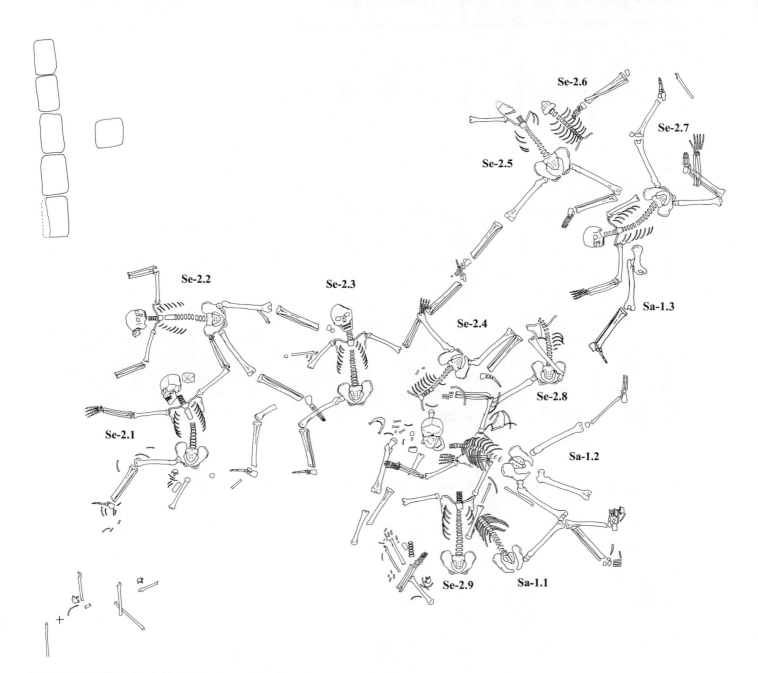

FIGURE 3.59. Plan of individuals in Sediment 2 and Sand 1.

FIGURE 3.60. Individual Sa-1.2.

FIGURE 3.61. Fragment of a Phase III sherd depicting Dance with Death figures.

human remains were much more fragmented and dispersed (fig. 3.51).

Fifty-eight domestic and six fineware sherds were recuperated from the layer of Sediment 2. Deposited alongside Individual Se-2.1 was a fragment of a ceramic vessel decorated in low relief. It represented a Dance with Death figure (Donnan 1982) (figs. 3.61, 3.62). A small whistle in the shape of a bird was found between Individuals Se-2.3 and Se-2.4 (fig. 3.63). The full significance of these two objects is discussed later. But for the moment they seem to have formed part of this ritual symbolism.

In the same mud layer but farther north along the west wall, a rope was imprinted in the clay at the extremity of an isolated ulna (fig. 3.64). This seems to indicate that some individuals may have had ropes tied around their wrists. Footprints also have been detected in the mud of Sediments 2 and 3. This constitutes further proof that people entered the sacrificial arena when the mud was still fresh. This information, in conjunction with the imprints of limbs in the mud (fig. 3.14), indicates that these sacrificial rituals were timed with El Niño conditions.

FIGURE 3.62. Low relief depicting a Danse Macabre. Drawing by Donna McClelland. The Christopher B. Donnan and Donna McClelland Moche Archive, Image Collections and Fieldwork Archives, Dumbarton Oaks, Trustees for Harvard University, Washington, DC.

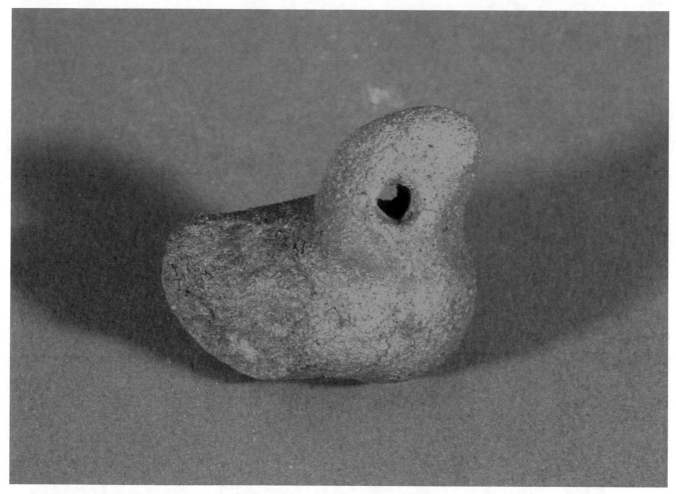

FIGURE 3.63. Small whistle in the shape of a bird.

SAND 1

The human remains encountered within this last layer (98.77 m–98.25 m) covered an area of about 48 m² and were distributed from the north wall to the front of the rocky outcrop (fig. 3.65). The remains were found in the loose windblown sand and resting directly on the hard clay surface of Sediment 2. A number of the sacrificed individuals had been placed directly on top of other victims. Twenty-two severed or isolated heads were recuperated in this layer, and evidence of decapitation was noted on a number of cervical vertebrae (Hamilton 2005). Vertebrae were still attached to the foramen magnum in some cases, indicating that flesh was present when the decapitation took place (fig. 3.66). All the individuals except one were decapitated or had their heads removed after some tissue decomposition had taken place. This important fact indicates that the sacrificial rituals consisted of a series of discrete actions that were carried out over time. It may also explain why the human remains had to be left exposed to the elements, so natural processes of decomposition could be witnessed and ritual specialists could reintervene when appropriate.

Although looters destroyed some of the evidence in the central section of the plaza, it would seem that the very last ritual activities to be performed were concentrated in the northwest corner of the plaza where the precinct used to be (fig. 3.67). Only a few human remains were found in front of the rocky outcrop, including the three individuals in the preceding layer, Sediment 2.2 (fig. 3.68).

As mentioned earlier, five individuals were found facing down directly above the others resting in Sediment 2 (fig. 3.69). Individuals Sa-1.1 and Sa-1.2 apparently were held to the ground in the same orientation and both seem to have been sacrificed by decapitation (figs. 3.59, 3.60). Individuals Sa-1.4 and Sa-1.5 were placed side by side, but in opposite directions (figs. 3.69, 3.70, 3.71). Both were apparently placed on top of the previous victims that had suffered fractured skulls (Se-2.1, Se-2.2) (fig. 3.69). Individual Sa-1.5 had clearly

been pushed on top of a previous victim: his abdomen was arched on top of Individual Se-2.2's head (fig. 3.72). Given the proximity of the human remains, it is clear that both the sacrificers and their victims had to make their way into the sacrificial arena by walking amid the previous sacrifices. Therefore it is likely that the positioning of the latest victims (Sa-1.4 and Sa-1.5) right on top of the previous ones and in inverted positions was intentional, as the previous victims were clearly visible on the ground.

In the northern section of Sand 1, among numerous dispersed human remains, at least five additional individuals were located; this time, however, they were resting on their backs (fig. 3.67). Individual Sa-1.6, close to the west wall, had his arms in a stretched position and both feet drawn together (figs. 3.67, 3.73). He was possibly decapitated. Three heads and a pelvis were placed on his lower legs and feet, while an additional pelvis was positioned on his pelvis (fig. 3.74). Individual Sa-1.7, situated closer to the north wall, was the only one in the whole sacrificial site to have been found without any missing bones (figs. 3.67, 3.75). He rested on his back in the midst of a number of heads and human remains. A deep cut to the left temporal bone by a single knife strike some 7 cm in length was the most likely cause of death (fig. 3.76). The position of his arms and legs suggests that he may have been held on to the ground while the fatal blow was delivered. The instrument was probably a crescent blade knife known as a *tumi*. This is the only type of archaeologically known tool that could have caused this type of injury. It is consistently depicted in the iconography of decapitation.

Immediately to the south of Individual Sa-1.7 was a largely dismembered individual (Sa-1.8), also placed on his back (fig. 3.67). His hands closely drawn together suggest that he was apparently laid to the ground at the moment of his death (fig. 3.77). Most of the body of this individual had been disturbed by the looter's pit. Just above Individual Sa-1.8 but on the west side of the boulder, Individual Sa-1.9 was propped against the rock in order to be sacrificed (figs. 3.67, 3.78). Both arms were drawn to the side of the rock and his legs were splayed, suggesting that three persons might have been involved in holding him on the ground as he was killed by a fourth individual.

FIGURE 3.64. (*Opposite*) Imprint of rope at the end of an isolated ulna.

FIGURE 3.65. View of layer Sand 1 and the west wall of Plaza 3A.

FIGURE 3.66. Isolated head in Sand 1.

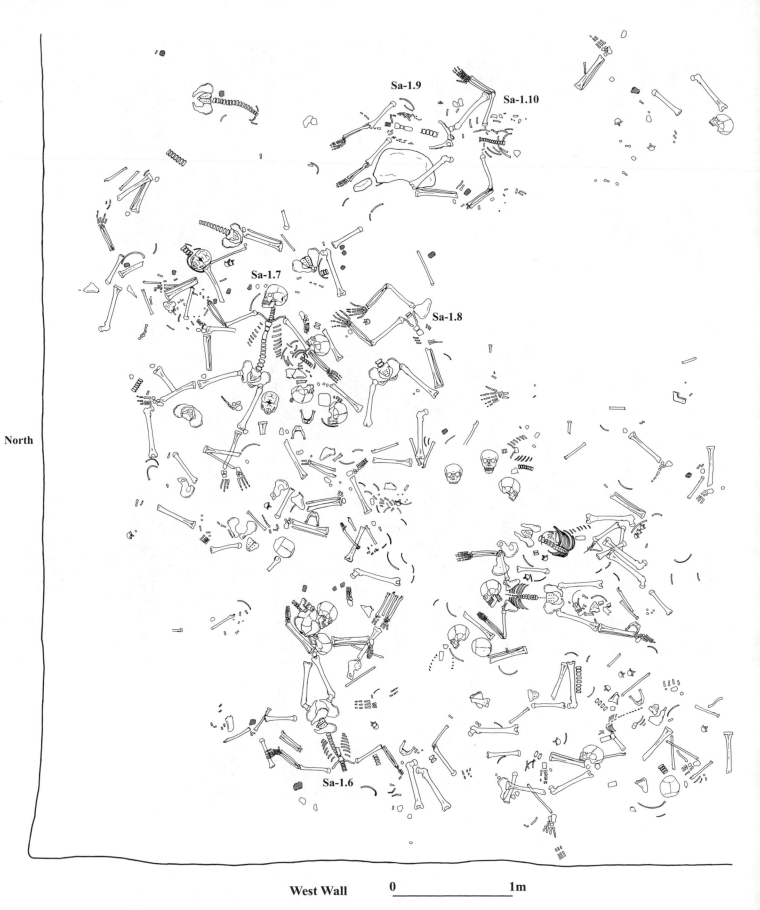

Sa-1.9

Sa-1.10

Sa-1.7

Sa-1.8

North

Sa-1.6

West Wall   0 ———————— 1m

FIGURE 3.67. Plan of the northern section of Sand 1. Drawing by Jorge Sachun.

West Wall

0 _____ 1m

FIGURE 3.68. Plan of the southern section of Sand 1. Drawing by Jorge Sachun.

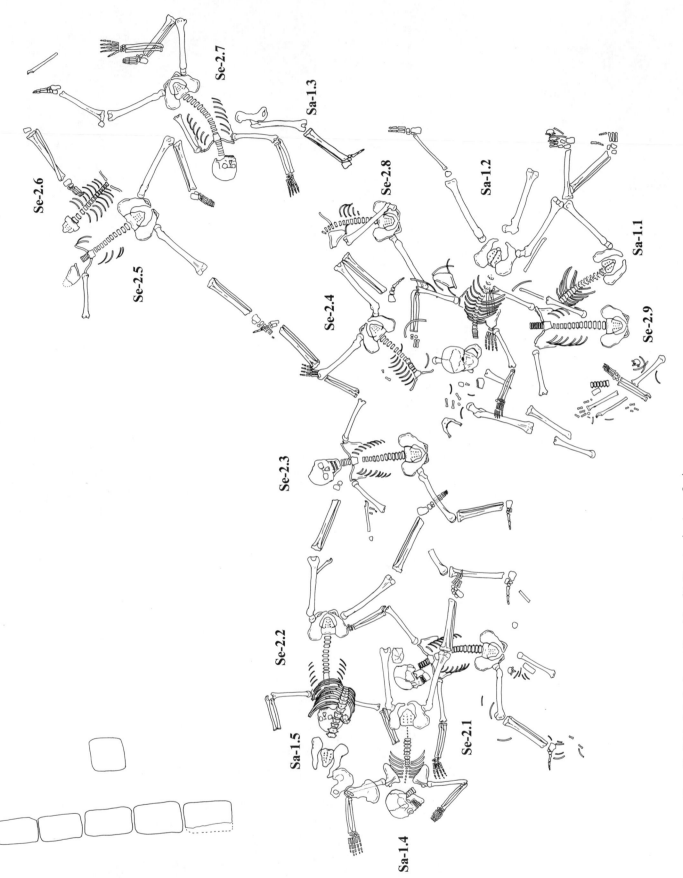

FIGURE 3.69. Plan of individuals in Sediment 2 and Sand 1. Drawing by Jorge Sachun.

FIGURE 3.70. Individuals Sa-1.4 and Sa-1.5.

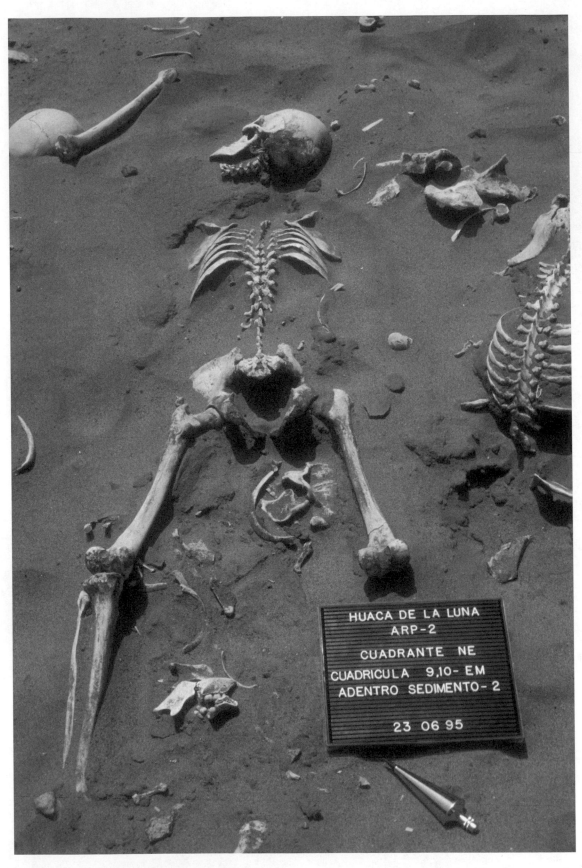

FIGURE 3.71. Individual Sa-1.4.

FIGURE 3.72. Close-up view of Individual Sa-1.5 on top of Individual Se-2.2.

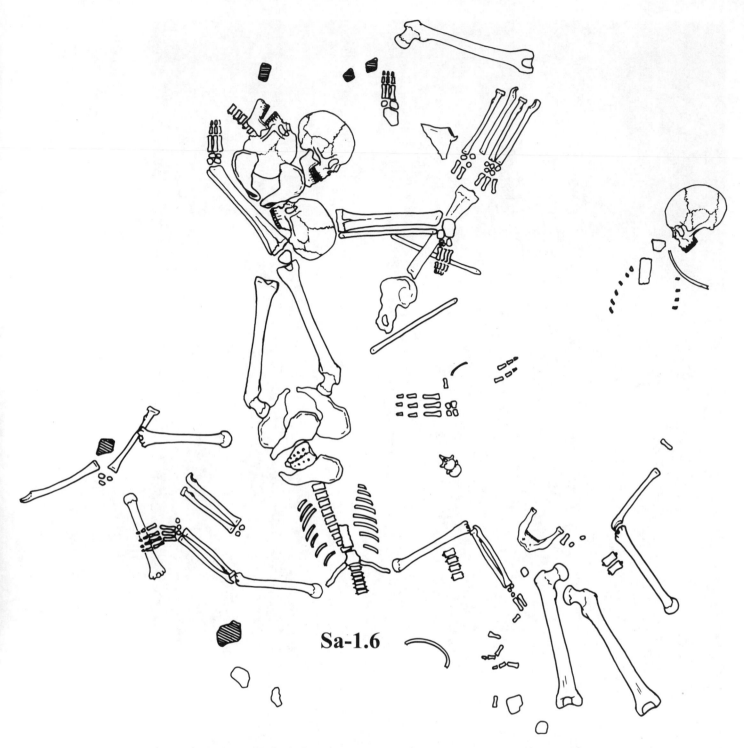

Sa-1.6

FIGURE 3.73. Position of Individual Sa-1.6.

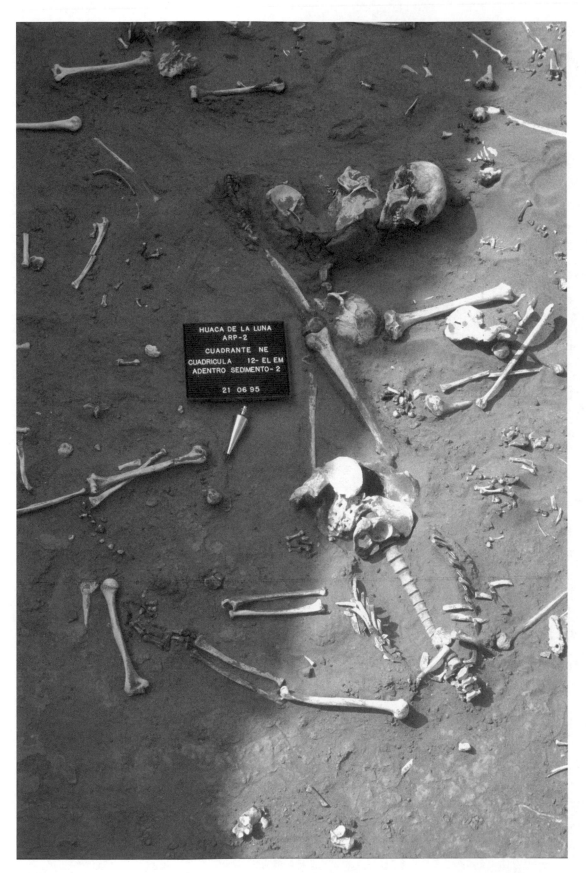

FIGURE 3.74. Individual Sa-1.6.

FIGURE 3.75. Individual Sa-1.7.

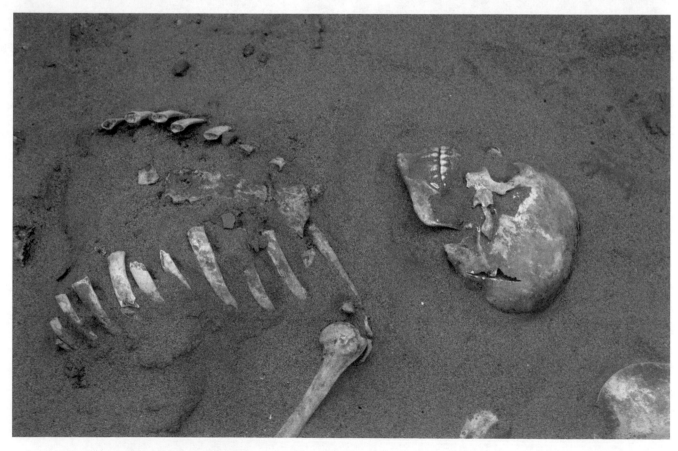

FIGURE 3.76. Close-up view of Individual Sa-1.7.

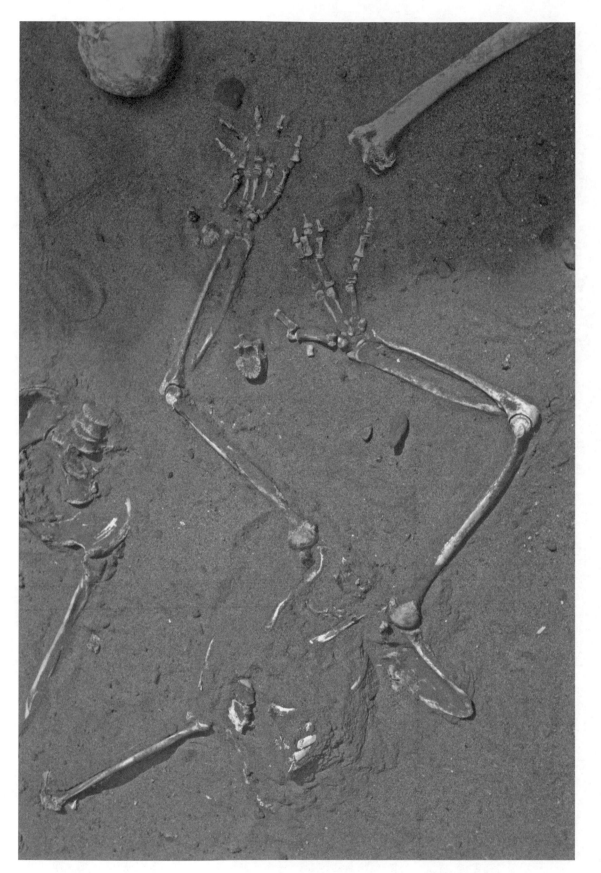

FIGURE 3.77. Arms of Individual Sa-1.8.

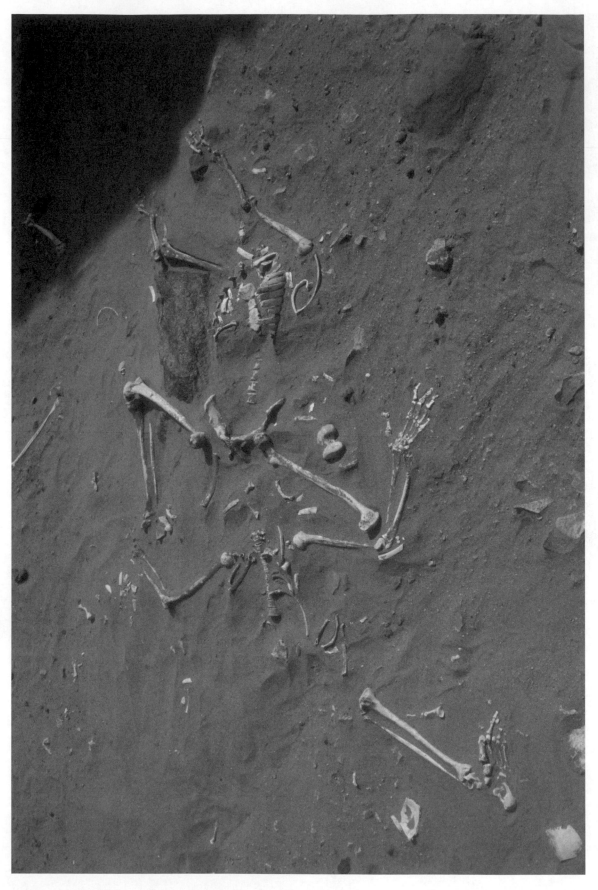

FIGURE 3.78. Individuals Sa-1.9 and Sa-1.10.

Shortly thereafter Individual Sa-1.10 was placed on the lower legs of Individual Sa-1.9, in almost the same position (figs. 3.67, 3.78). This rock is of course the same one used earlier to create the small precinct. As noted, two other individuals—Sa-4.4 and Se-3.3—were also placed against it (figs. 3.10, 3.12, 3.15). Individuals Sa-1.9 and Sa-1.10 thus demonstrate tremendous continuity between the successive rituals and underscore the symbolic importance accorded to this boulder throughout the sacrificial sequence.

It is very difficult to estimate the minimal number of individuals killed in this layer, but at least eighteen complete pelvises were identified. It is likely that some of the heads came from the individuals stuck in the layer of mud just underneath. Fifty-four ceramic sherds were recovered, including a spindle whorl resting against the pelvis of Individual Sa-1.5 (fig. 3.79). A bird motif decorates this artifact.

SEDIMENT 1

Sediment 1 (99.43 m–99.00 m), the last layer covering the sacrificial site, is postoccupational and corresponds to nearly 1,400 years of aeolian sand, erosion, and rainfall. The stratigraphy is quite complex and measures nearly a meter thick (fig. 3.1). The deposit is extremely compact and fortunately withstood the repeated efforts of looters to dig in the plaza. That is probably the sole reason this site was in great part preserved. Nevertheless, the looters managed to destroy about 5 m² of the central section of the sacrificial area (fig. 3.57).

Close attention was paid to the part of the layer lying at the base of Platform II. During the cleanup, fragments of decorative mace heads were encountered (fig. 3.80). These were ceramic objects in the form of war clubs. Such items are frequently depicted in the iconography, decorating the roofs of elaborate buildings, and many such decorative war clubs have been found in other parts of Huaca de la Luna and at other Moche sites. Therefore a roof decorated with these objects probably covered part of Platform II. Finally, two small offerings consisting of a group of marine and terrestrial shells and bones of guinea pigs were found on the ground at the base of the rocky outcrop. They probably corresponded to activities of present-day folk healing that took place sometime before 1990.

Before discussing in more detail the offerings made in the sacrificial site, such as the clay statuettes and ceramic fragments, the other sectors in Plaza 3A (Sectors B–E) are described next.

SECTOR B

The main objective of the excavation of Sector B in the southeast corner of the plaza was to determine the nature of the occupation of the southern part of the plaza during the period of the sacrifices (fig. 2.15). The sector was covered by more than 6 m of aeolian sand and clay sediments. At about 4 m deep (100.00 m), a dense concentration of animal coprolites, pieces of wood, cotton threads, and llama wool was encountered. Analysis of the coprolites revealed that they were mostly from Camelidae and to a lesser extent from dogs. Mixed in with these ecofacts were a number of Chimú domestic sherds. This concentration of refuse was resting on an accumulation of aeolian sand and a layer of clay seemingly produced by torrential rains and the trampling of the ground by human activities. The cultural material and the accumulation of sand clearly indicate that this context dated to a later period than the Moche occupation of the site (fig. 3.81). It is thus possible that the Chimú used this part of the plaza as a llama corral.

The utilization of the Huaca de la Luna by the Chimú is well attested in other parts of the site and was essentially ceremonial in nature (Tufinio 2003). It mostly consisted of burying numerous mummy bundles with sacrificed llamas and offerings on top of the abandoned Platform I. Thus some of the llamas found in Chimú burials or detected on the summit of Platform I may have been kept in this enclosure before being sacrificed during the funerary rituals. Very few animals needed to be kept at any one time for these specialized activities, which would explain the utility of such a small space, perhaps no bigger than 12 m².

Farther down, near the base of Platform II and the south wall of Plaza 3A (98.50 m), a layer of construction refuse was found (fig. 3.82). It consisted of clay fragments and complete and broken adobes, in many respects similar to the layer of debris encountered in sector A at the base of the north and west walls. Numerous fly pupae

FIGURE 3.79. Spindle whorl near Individual Sa-1.5.

FIGURE 3.80. Fragments of decorative mace heads in ceramic.

FIGURE 3.81. Chimú layer in Sector B.

FIGURE 3.82. Base of Plaza 3A in Sector B.

were found in this layer, indicating that this part of the site was exposed when the sacrificial site was in operation and that the putrefying flesh nearby attracted these sarcophagus insects. A series of trench pits also revealed that the base of Platform II was situated at 97.70 m. In the trenches, at about 97.10 m, the remains of two combustion zones contained charcoals, food remains, seeds, and domestic sherds. This occupation would have predated the construction of the plaza and the platform. A conical-shaped spindle whorl may indicate a Gallinazo Period occupation.[4] Thus the absence of Moche artifacts or structures above this earlier domestic context, the construction refuse resting on the same layer of sand as the one encountered in the northern part of the plaza, and the numerous pupa cases suggest that this part of the plaza was never really used by the Moche.

SECTOR C

The second trench dug in the center of the southern part of the plaza (Sector C) was again aimed at verifying the absence or utilization of this part of the plaza during Moche times (fig. 2.15). An 8 m² test pit was dug to a depth of about 3 m (97.64 m). The same layer of yellowish and grayish sands encountered in sectors A and B was found. Polychrome fragments of murals, Phase IV decorated sherds, and human remains were detected in the first meter of aeolian sand. The absence of structures or burials in this sector, however, suggests that this material must have come from looting activities carried out somewhere in the vicinity.

SECTOR D

The third trench in the southwest corner of the plaza (Sector D) was also excavated to verify the nature of Moche occupation (fig. 2.15). As in Sector C, painted fragments of adobe and evidence of looted Phase IV burials were unearthed. The construction sequence of this part of the plaza appears to have been slightly more complex. The remains of a floor passed underneath the south wall, which indicates that an earlier structure was dismantled during the construction of the plaza. It is likely that these transformations were conducted dur-

FIGURE 3.83. Extremity of west wall in Sector E.

ing the initial stage of construction of the plaza in order to join it to Platform I.

Evidence of rainfall was detected at different depths during the excavation of Sectors B, C, and D, which took the form of lumps of clay mixed with the windblown sand. The south wall blocking the strong winds blowing from the Pacific Ocean causes this situation by creating a vortex conducive to erratic accumulations of sand. Therefore Sectors B, C, and D did not present stratigraphically determinative layers as conclusive as those encountered in Sector A.

SECTOR E

Sector E, immediately to the south of sector A, consisted of two trenches (fig. 2.15). The first trench was made at the visible end of the west wall. It demonstrated that the wall had been partly dismantled, giving the plaza its peculiar L shape (fig. 3.83). The base of the wall was situated at

96.91 m and its summit at 98.79 m, for a height of 1.88 m. A second trench was excavated immediately to the east of the first one. The dig revealed successive layers of aeolian sand completely sterile down to the bedrock.

ACCESS TO PLAZA 3A

This series of trenches and test pits seems to indicate that the Moche never used the southern part of Plaza 3A. The fragments of polychrome murals and remnants of Phase IV burials were found in the accumulation of aeolian sand, and only construction refuse was found at the base of the walls. It thus appears that the totality of the cultural activities was conducted in the northwestern corner of the plaza, immediately in front of the rocky outcrop. The maximum area of utilization of the sector was about 60 m², which corresponds to only about 5 percent of the total area of the plaza (1,140 m²).

An inspection of the western wall was carried out in order to localize a means of access from Platform I to Plaza 3A. To our great surprise, no access whatsoever could be detected. Two Peruvian teams carried out the same research in the two small plazas, 3B and 3C, situated immediately on the other side of the west wall, and also found no access (fig. 3.84) (Gamonal 1998; Orbegoso 1998). For the moment, it would appear that the absence of an entrance between the two plazas and the nonoccupation of the southern portion of Plaza 3A corroborate the hypothesis that no direct access was ever planned. Thus the data at our disposal suggest that Plaza 3A was a closed space and that the sacrificial victims could have been pushed into this enclosure from the summit of the west wall or used a wooden ladder. As an alternate possibility, the sacrificial victims and the sacrificers may have descended the rocky outcrop as a means of accessing Plaza 3A from Platform II. Plaza 3A would thus have represented a sort of microcosm exclusively dedicated to the performance of sacrificial activities during and in between spells of torrential rains.

Interestingly, Plaza 3B seems to have functioned at least for a time very closely with the rituals carried out in Plaza 3A (fig. 3.84). In 1995 archaeologists from the Huaca de la Luna Project found under a layer of sand an earlier episode of intense rainfall together with a number of broken clay statuettes similar to those found in Sand 2. Human and guinea pig bones were found scattered among the fragments, along with sherds from both domestic and fineware vessels (Montoya 1997). These contexts constitute additional evidence that the rituals carried out in Plaza 3A could have been closely associated with other activities performed in this part of the huaca. It may have served as a sort of antechamber between Plaza 3A and Platform I.

In 1996 a number of human remains were also found in the adjoining Plaza 3C (Orbegoso 1998). On the basis of the Phase III artifacts recovered from this plaza and the radiocarbon dates obtained from some of the contexts, the rituals performed in this plaza predated the ones from Plaza 3A. With the west wall of Plaza 3A forming the east wall of these two plazas and with their west wall forming part of the mural of the Huaca de la Luna main platform, these two plazas constitute the physical connection between Plaza 3A and Platform I (fig. 3.84). Chapter 7 explores the distinctions between the ritual and sacrificial activities practiced during Phase III in Plaza 3C and those practiced during Phase IV in Plaza 3A in some detail.

THE CONSISTENT OCCURRENCES

The sacrificial site was evidently the place of a series of distinct rituals; a number of similarities throughout the sequence, however, suggest a strong homogeneity among the ritual acts. These include exposure of bodies and their manipulation. On the basis of the other trenches dug in Plaza 3A, it is clear that the preferred place for the human sacrifices and other ritual practices was situated in the vicinity of the rocky outcrop (fig. 2.15). This represents a very limited space of only 60 m², restricted by the west and north walls of the plaza. Not only would the sacrificers and their victims have had to walk amid the previously deposited human remains, but in certain cases the sacrificial acts were intentionally performed just above the preceding ones. In order to create an even more impressive altar for human sacrifice, loose boulders—probably collected from the slopes of the Cerro Blanco—were brought to the site and added to the outcrop. These observations

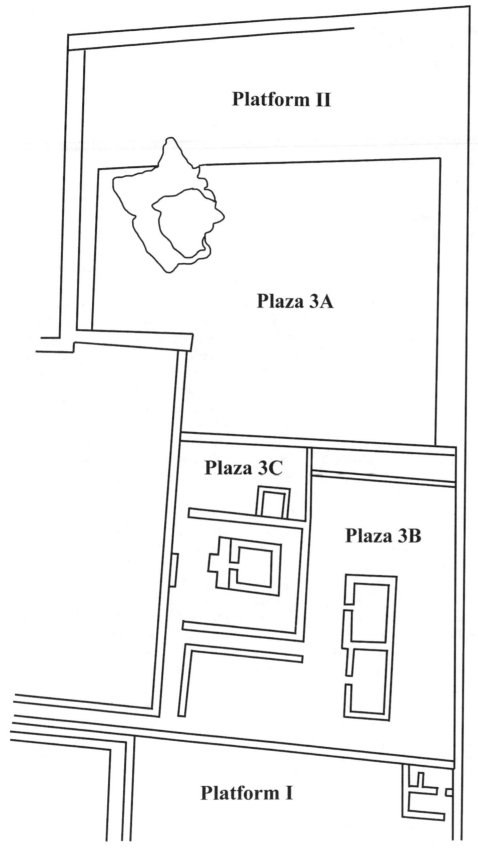

FIGURE 3.84. Plan of Plazas 3A, 3B, and 3C.

corroborate the research hypothesis that the rocky outcrop was indeed imbued with certain symbolic meanings and was intentionally included in the architecture of Huaca de la Luna.

Regarding the state of conservation of the human remains, most of the bones presented signs of surface cracking and bleaching. This indicates that the bodies were left exposed on the surface to decompose for a time. Windblown sand or a layer of clay then naturally covered the remains. These mud and silt deposits also showed signs of cracking and flaking consistent with the drying of the sun and the lashing winds of the Pacific Ocean. Numerous empty puparia of muscoid flies were also noted in all the layers containing human remains. These empty pupa cases show that the human remains were not immediately buried after the sacrifice, as scavenging insects were able to access the decomposing bodies to feed and to lay their eggs or larvae, which successfully hatched.

Both femoral heads of an individual often were out of their proper articulation with the legs, frequently splayed in an awkward position. In the two examples shown in figure 3.43, the hip joints were clearly disarticulated. One leg was splayed, while the other was partly folded. The practice was even more acute in the case of two other individuals. The legs of Individual Se-3.3 were crossed over one another, with a huge ceramic sherd firmly wedged on top of the left leg (figs. 3.12, 3.15). The lower limbs of the second individual were set in an even more extreme position, with both legs completely folded back on each side of the chest (fig. 3.22). If these articulations were not forcefully disjointed during or shortly after the sacrifices, it is possible that the Moche ritualists went back into the sacrificial arena to rearrange the bodies as the putrefaction process was taking place. Further indications that they repeatedly manipulated human remains are the sheer number of body fragments and chunks of vertebras, arms, and hands still in articulated position, found in and at the base of the west wall (Sand 2.3.1 to 2.3.9).

The large number of ceramic sherds continuously thrown into the plaza at every stage of the rituals and the numerous statuettes destroyed during the sacrificial ritual in Sand 2 clearly indicate that this theater of sacrifice was repeatedly revisited and that the rituals did not stop with the death of the victims. It is likely that the decompo-sition process and perhaps even the arrival of distinct species of necrophilous insects were keenly observed.

Further evidence implying some possible manipulation of human remains is that individuals touch one another in each of the layers. In a number of cases, the bodies were purposely rearranged in order to create a *tableau macabre*. Such examples include the two individuals head to head in Sand 2, the group of six individuals in Sediment 2, and the two incomplete skeletons against the boulder in Sand 1 (figs. 3.43, 3.52, 3.78). The corpses were not left at random. On the contrary, it would seem that the ritual practitioners enacted a precise order during each performance to achieve a certain objective. In some cases, the order recalls some form of dualist organization, where the corpses or human remains were organized in pairs and in opposite positions (fig. 3.42).

Notably, in every layer a number of body parts remain articulated. Apart from the ubiquitous severed heads (some with the cervical vertebra still attached to the foramen magnum), legs, arms, fingers, and parts of trunks have also been identified (figs. 3.85–3.88). A number of well-healed fractures and perimortem injuries, such as skull fractures or cut marks on the cervical vertebrae, were found on different individuals. The subject of such perimortem injuries is dealt with in the section on the physical anthropology of the sacrificial victims.

Significantly, rituals in the mud performed during torrential rains were always followed by others occurring on the sun-dried surface and in the windblown sand. On the basis of the depositional context of the human remains, it appears that the sacrifices from one period to the next are not disconnected but rather organized in pairs. In other words, the ritual carried out in Sediment 3 would have been related to the one conducted in Sand 2. Similarly, the one performed in Sediment 2 would have been linked with the last one in Sand 1. For example, the two victims trapped in the mud of Sediment 3 were placed on their backs, while two other victims killed afterward in Sand 2.2 (Se-3.1/Sa-2.5, Se-3.2/Sa-2.9) were situated face down directly on top of the previous ones (figs. 3.12, 3.38). This positioning was repeated in a later ritual: five individuals killed in the mud of Sediment 2 and placed on their backs were covered with an identical number of individuals

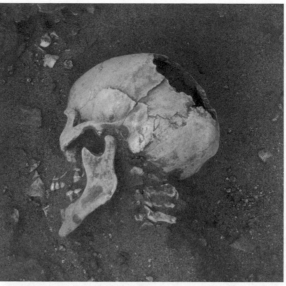

FIGURE 3.85. Severed heads.

in Sand 1 (Se-2.1/Sa-1.4, Se-2.2/Sa-1.5, Se-2.4/Sa-1.2, Se-2.7/Sa-1.3, Se-2.9/Sa-1.1) (fig. 3.69). These placements indicate a very high degree of planning and substantiate the hypothesis that the whole series of rituals was performed under similar guiding principles.

These superpositions of human remains also suggest that at least two great sacrificial rituals took place in the plaza, each composed of two episodes. This two-step ritual would have been triggered by an El Niño event and its destructive torrential rains. It is not possible to evaluate exactly how long this ritual lasted, but it had to have been performed while the mud was still in a liquid state. In some cases, the imprints of the flesh of the victims in the mud clearly indicate that the sacrifice was contemporaneous with the precipitation (figs. 3.13, 3.14). The second part of the ritual would have followed sometime after the rains stopped and the mud finally dried. The bones, which were stuck in the mud, were bleached by the sun, which also indicates that the second phase of the ritual took place sometime after the putrefaction process of these earlier remains.

As shown in figure 3.69, the organization of these corpses—the first group lying on their backs in the mud produced by the rains and second group placed upside down in relation with the first group upon the sun-baked clay, indicating that the rains had stopped—recalls a form of dualist opposition already noted in Sand 2.1 with the

FIGURE 3.86. Body parts in Sand 2.

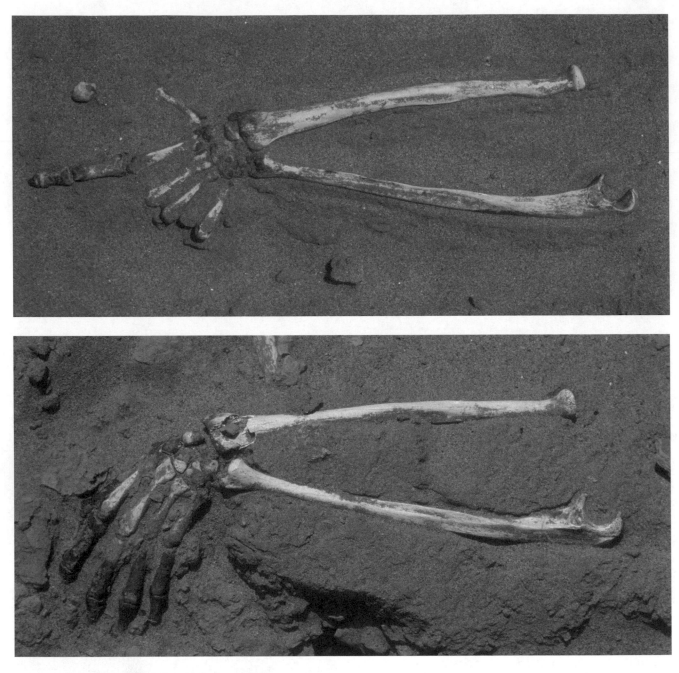

FIGURE 3.87. Isolated left arms.

pair of jaws, pair of vertebrae, and three pairs of corpses (fig. 3.42). Duality thus appears to be represented both synchronically and diachronically. Within the same ritual and period, dual organization joins the sacrificial victims together. Between two layers, skeletal remains are further positioned together, binding two chronologically distinct sets of rituals. This symbolic duality along with the production and the destruction of clay statuettes formed part of the ritual praxis of this sacrificial

system. The wide-ranging presentation of symbolic duality is considerably more complex than touched upon here and encompasses additional aspects of the Platform II/Plaza 3A ceremonial complex.

The precise sequence of sacrifice, the positioning of the corpses, and the numerous interventions in regard to the human remains indicate a complex praxis performed by highly skilled individuals. These actions acted as signifiers, reiterating the sacred and ritualized dimension of this sacrificial system. These were not random acts performed in haste but rather acts representing the expression of a complex religion and ideology based in great part on human sacrifice. Before going any further in proposing a sacrificial model, I must describe the clay statuettes found among the victims and comment on the presence of these sculptures and the numerous sherds of domestic vessels located in the midst of the sacrificial remains.

OFFERINGS IN THE SACRIFICIAL SITE

CLAY STATUETTES

We recovered a large number of unfired clay statuettes associated with the remains in Sand 2. The manufacture of these sculptures indicates that these pieces could not have been fired. In many examples, the clay lacks temper and the arms are solid, making the piece difficult, if not impossible, to fire without cracking. They were really meant to remain clay sculptures. The statuettes were found mingled among the human remains in the pit at the base of the west wall (Sand 2.3.1 to 2.3.9) and scattered around the sacrificed individuals lying atop Sediment 3 (Sand 2.1 to 2.3) (figs. 3.33, 3.38). Their broken condition and distribution among the skeletal remains indicate that the destruction of the statuettes formed an integral part of the sacrificial ritual that took place during this time.

These sculptures were purposely smashed into thousands of fragments, presenting a formidable puzzle for their reconstruction. Fashioned with clay and painted with mineral and vegetal pigments, the pieces were very fragile and had to be solidified with chemical products before any

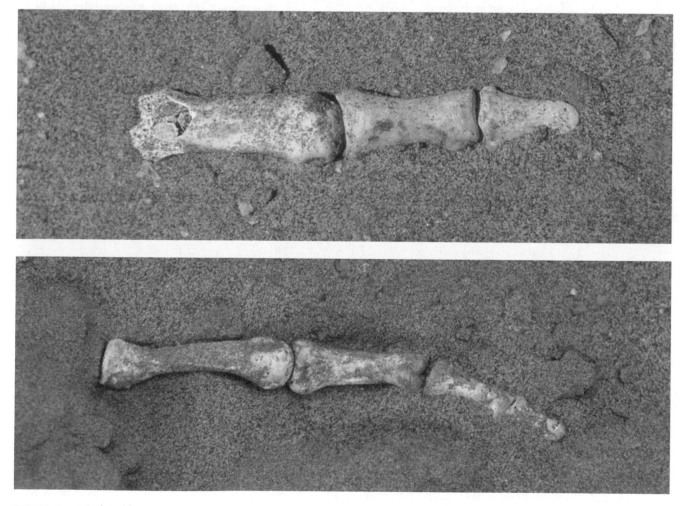

FIGURE 3.88. Isolated fingers.

reconstruction could take place. Two conservators of the Huaca de la Luna Project dedicated three months to this meticulous work. Due to the extent of destruction and degradation of many statuette fragments, it was only possible to reconstruct some of them. As I discuss below, these reconstructions, albeit incomplete, give a fairly accurate idea of the statuettes and their subjects or themes.

Most of the fragments were found at the base of the west wall, especially in the depression. Some of the statuettes were also placed among the victims and destroyed with rocks, adobe fragments, or clubs (fig. 3.48). More than a hundred stone fragments from the rocky outcrop were found among the clay fragments. One of these effigies was placed alongside the individual lying at the base of the north wall and was destroyed with rocks. As mentioned earlier, the head of one statuette was subsequently placed on the head of an individual lying at the base of the north wall in Sand 2.1 (figs. 3.39, 3.49, 3.50). Placing the sculptural head on the head of a sacrificial victim evokes possible metaphoric relationships that may have existed between them. In some cases, it appears that the same implements used to sacrifice the humans were also used to destroy the statuettes. For example, the head of a statuette was broken with a blow applied directly to the chin (fig. 3.89). This is reminiscent of the numerous skull fractures noted throughout the layers.

The statuettes are distinctive and appear to have been made by different artists. However, they generally represent nude males in a seated position, usually with their legs crossed (figs. 3.90, 3.91). A thick rope encircles their necks, with one strand resting on the chest, much like a tie (fig. 3.90). Their hands are often painted black or adorned with different motifs (fig. 3.92). Their bodies and faces are also covered with numerous representations of animals, objects, and geometric symbols (fig. 3.93). The hands are usually resting palm down on the knees (figs. 3.90, 3.91) or, more rarely, crossed over the chest or holding the rope. The estimated size of the sculptures varies between 40 and 60 cm in height.

The only parts of the statuettes to be preserved consistently in one piece were the penises. Judging by the number of penises, there were at least fifty-two statuettes (fig. 3.94). They seem to have been purposely detached from the bodies of the statuettes before their destruction. Such a gesture would recall the possible removal of the genitals of at least two victims in order to insert a rock into one and a rib in the other (figs. 3.30, 3.44). The differences in size and shape of the penises indicate that the intention of the artists was to create distinct sculptures. The foreskin was not depicted on any of these penises, suggesting that circumcision might have been practiced in Moche society. This is also consistent with the iconography, where the foreskin is never depicted. The individuality of the statuettes is made even more apparent by looking at the faces of these clay effigies. The following figures regroup twelve of these subjects (figs. 3.89, 3.95–3.105). Most of the faces are adorned with painting and in two cases marked with two or three shallow gashes on each cheek that may represent some form of scarification (figs. 3.104, 3.105).

Even if each of the statuettes is unique and may have been manufactured by a different artist, the general theme is the same: a nude male in a seated position sporting a very specific haircut (figs. 3.89, 3.95). Holes created in their slightly distended earlobes recall that the subjects depicted by these sculptures would have worn tubular earplugs such as those shown in the iconography (figs. 3.89, 3.97, 3.98). As mentioned earlier, the bodies of the statuettes were covered with fineline paintings representing diverse subjects (figs. 3.106–3.108). The style of the sculptures and painting technique clearly indicate that these statuettes belonged to the Phase IV stylistic period.

Although many of the motifs adorning these sculptures had been badly eroded, a number of subjects could be discerned. All such motifs depicted are extensively represented in the iconography. Consequently, numerous identifications have been made based on comparisons within the iconographic corpus.

The first common group to be depicted on the statuettes consists of various representations of birds. It is difficult to ascertain the exact species. One clearly represents an anthropomorphized hummingbird carrying a circular shield (fig. 3.109a), however, while another appears to depict a marine bird pertaining to the guanay family (fig. 3.109b). On the back of one statuette, the body of a bird on the right side of the trap door and the

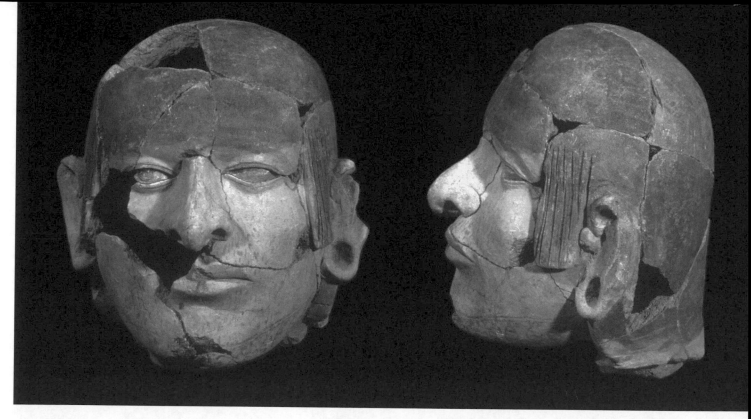

FIGURE 3.89. Head of clay statuette.

claws and tail on the other side may represent two raptorial birds facing each other (fig. 3.35).

Other types of animals were represented, such as a number of dark figures possibly referencing lizards (fig. 3.110a, b), a fox (fig. 3.110c), and a spotted feline (fig. 3.110d). One illustration shows a man facing a feline (fig. 3.111). Although the subject is poorly painted, this is a theme of great importance that was clearly represented as a mural on the walls of the small precinct of Plaza 3C (fig. 7.37). Numerous depictions of other composite animals appear, such as the snake with the head of a fox (fig. 3.112a) and the heads of foxes, sometimes with the forked tongues of reptiles appearing in their snarling mouths (fig. 3.112b, c).

Marine subjects are likewise represented in singular and composite forms. The first example depicts a sea lion with a round object just in front of its mouth. The animal is placed just behind the body of a large bird (fig. 3.113). The second example presents a composite animal with a fish body, the head of a fox, and a human arm usually holding a crescent bladed knife (fig. 3.114).

FIGURE 3.90. Body of clay statuette.

FIGURE 3.91. (*Above*) Lower section of clay statuette.

FIGURE 3.92. (*Below*) Hands of clay statuettes.

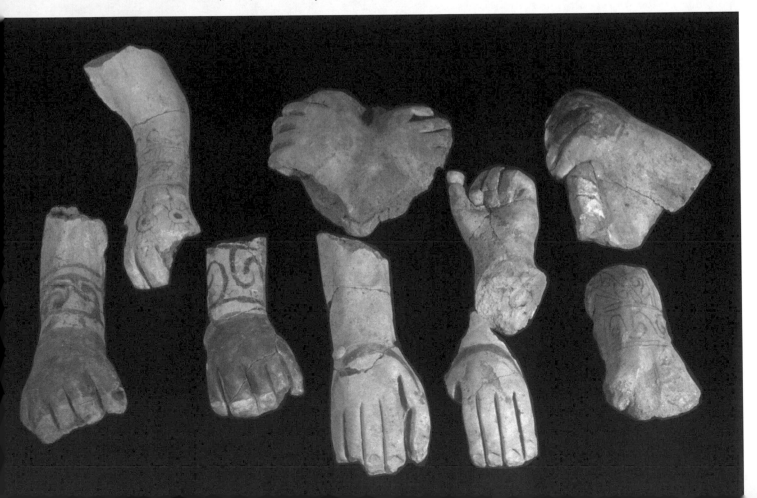

FIGURE 3.93. Torso of clay statuette.

FIGURE 3.94. Isolated penises from forty-nine clay statuettes.

FIGURE 3.95. Head of clay statuette with two gashes on the right cheek.

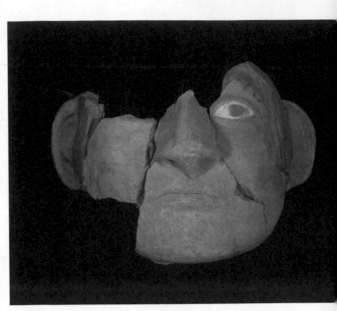

FIGURE 3.96. Head of clay statuette with the right side largely missing.

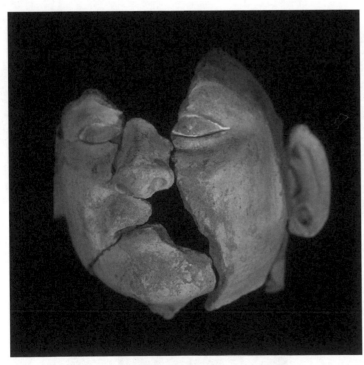

FIGURE 3.97. Head of clay statuette.

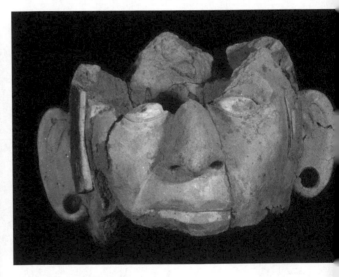

FIGURE 3.98. Head of clay statuette with round holes in the earlobes.

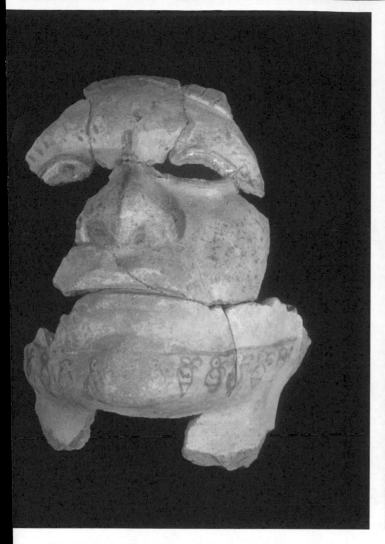

FIGURE 3.99. (*Above*) Head of clay statuette with oval elements on the lower jaw.

FIGURE 3.101. (*Below*) Head of clay statuette with step-and-fret spirals painted on each side of the nose.

FIGURE 3.100. (*Above*) Head of clay statuette with step-and-fret spirals painted on the cheeks.

FIGURE 3.102. (*Below*) Head of clay statuette with red dots symbolizing blood under the nose.

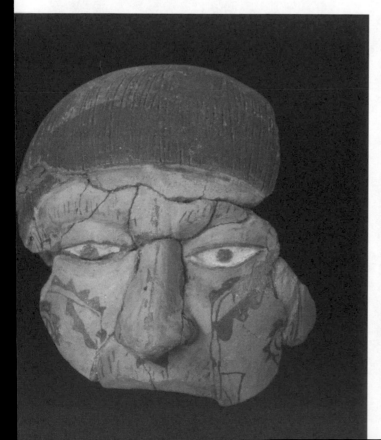

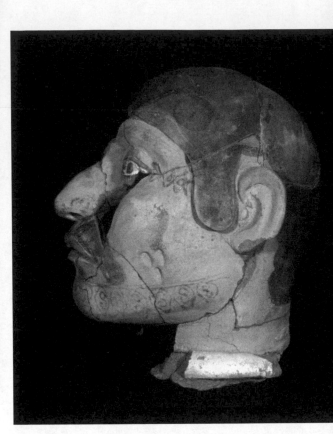

FIGURE 3.103. (*Above*) Head of clay statuette with Maltese cross.

FIGURE 3.104. (*Above*) Head of clay statuette with three gashes on the left cheek.

FIGURE 3.105. (*Below*) Close-up view of the head of clay statuette.

FIGURE 3.106. (*Below*) Body of clay statuette covered with fineline paintings.

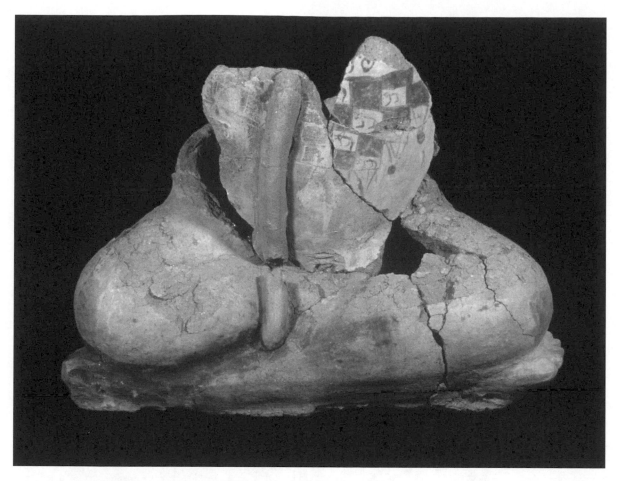

FIGURE 3.107. (*Above*) Body of clay statuette.

FIGURE 3.108. (*Below*) Torso of clay statuette.

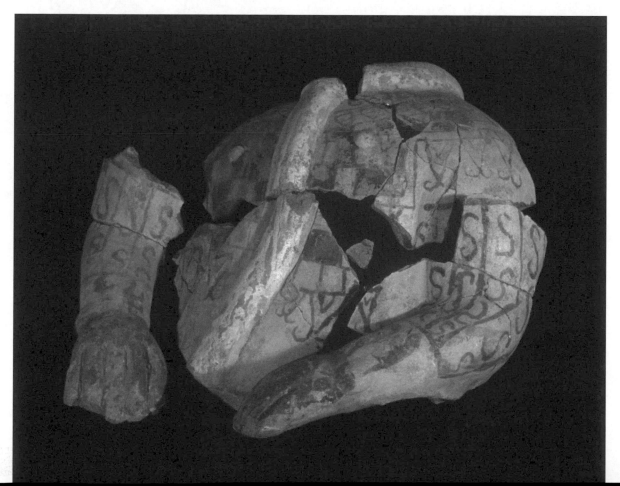

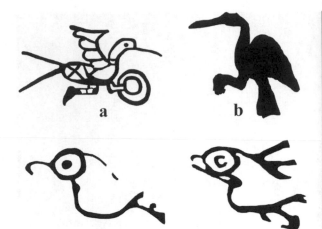

FIGURE 3.109. Paintings of birds on clay statuettes.

FIGURE 3.111. Painting on a clay statuette of a man facing a feline.

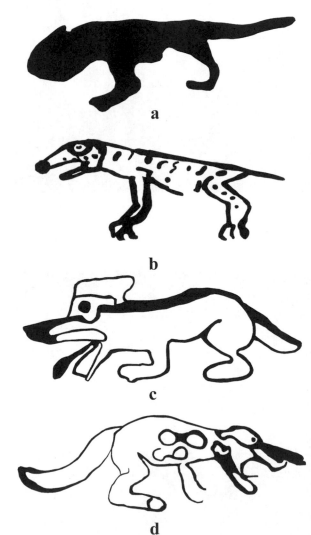

FIGURE 3.110. Paintings of mammals on clay statuettes.

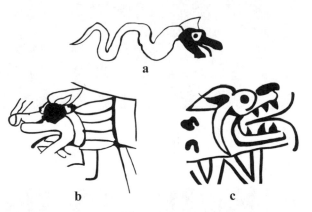

FIGURE 3.112. Paintings of a snake-fox and fox heads on clay statuettes.

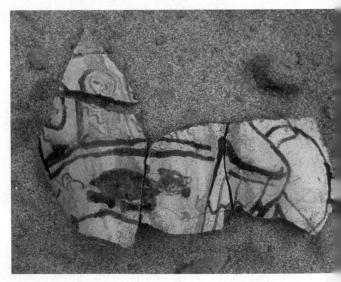

FIGURE 3.113. Painting of a sea lion on a clay statuette.

FIGURE 3.114. Paintings of borracho fish with a knife on clay statuettes.

This figure has been painted on a number of statuettes. The last marine subject is slightly more difficult to identify because the design is mostly geometric with very few recognizable features. Nevertheless, the triangular shape of the head, the two eyes, and the curved projections on each side of the head are indicative of the catfish (fig. 3.115).

Arthropods also formed part of this group, as centipedes are clearly recognizable (fig. 3.116a). The other motif is more difficult to ascertain but displays some insect-like qualities, such as an extremity similar to the centipede (fig. 3.116b). Its body seems to be contained within a cocoon.

Finally, the last living organism that could be identified is the *Tillandsia*, an epiphytic plant that covers wide stretches of the desert north coast (fig. 3.117). The plant is depicted on some of the statuettes, in an inverted position between felines and foxes (fig. 3.93). This plant and cacti are consistently depicted in scenes of warfare and Mountain Sacrifice (fig. 7.17).

The statuettes further exhibit an array of geometric symbols and a grouping of objects known as a weapon bundle. The weapon bundle is a motif extensively represented in Moche iconography. It consists of a club, a number of spears, and a shield covering these weapons (fig. 3.118). As mentioned earlier, the faces of these statuettes are often decorated with symbols. The most prominent geometric symbols are probably the step-and-fret spirals

habitually terminated by bird's heads (fig. 3.100). They are usually painted on the cheeks (figs. 3.100, 3.101, 3.119). Another motif commonly painted across the face is a Maltese cross. On the face of the only statuette covered with red pigment, such a cross decorates the cheeks, the chin, and possibly the forehead (fig. 3.103). Among the other geometric motifs commonly found on the statuettes are series of S-designs and strings of diamond-shaped incisions carved on the temples, outside of the eyes (figs. 3.120, 3.121).

Perhaps the most widespread motif represented on the statuettes is a design painted on their lower jaws, which consists of a band of oval-shaped elements extending from ear to ear (figs. 3.89, 3.99, 3.102, 3.104, 3.105). This design can also be depicted on the chest of the sculptures (figs. 3.93, 3.106). This motif takes two forms. In its simpler form it consists of a series of lozenge or oval motifs, sometimes filled in by a series of horizontal lines (fig. 3.122). In its most complex form a small circle with two lines is added to the top of the oval (fig. 3.123). I have suggested that this design might symbolize the emergence of muscoid flies from their pupal cases (Bourget 2001b).

Muscoid flies are usually the first to detect the presence of decaying flesh. The flies arrive rapidly on the bodies and lay eggs or living larvae. The eggs then hatch into larval forms and undergo successive molts before entering the inactive pupal stage (Smith 1986). The puparium

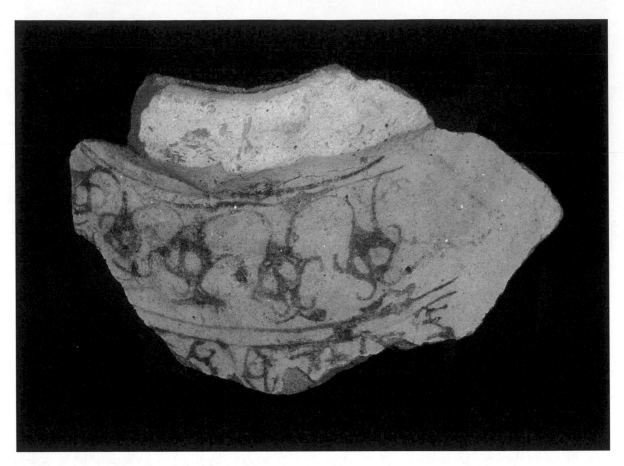

FIGURE 3.115. Painting of stylized catfish heads on a clay statuette.

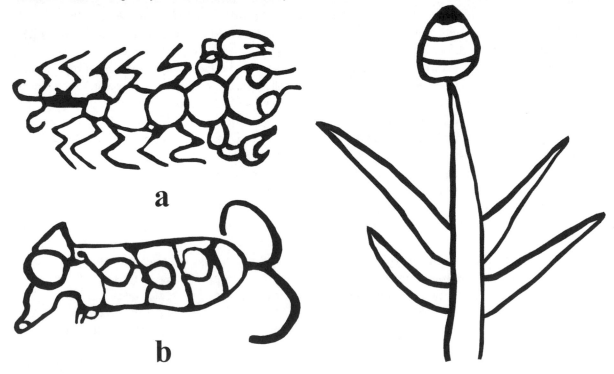

FIGURE 3.116. Paintings of a centipede and an unidentified subject on clay statuettes.

FIGURE 3.117. Painting of a *Tillandsia* on a clay statuette.

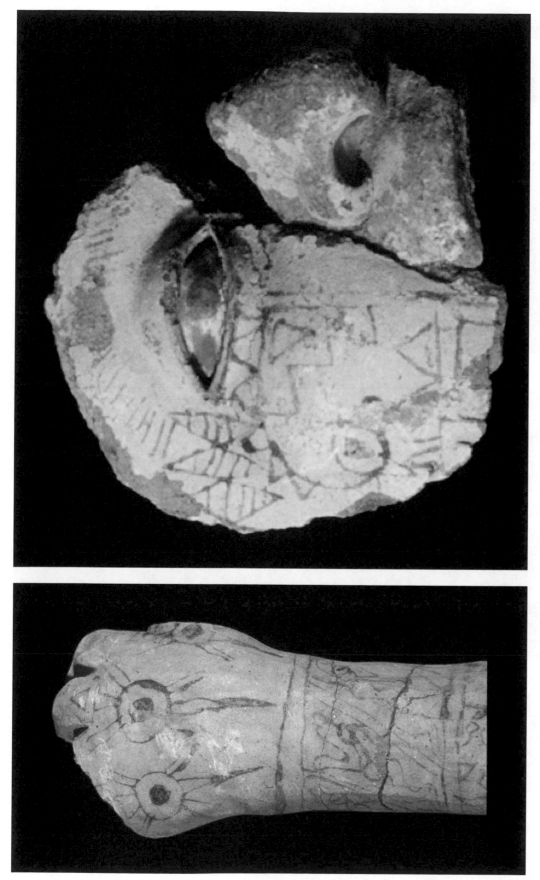

FIGURE 3.119. Painting of a step-and-fret spiral on the cheek of a clay statuette.

FIGURE 3.118. Painting of weapon bundles on a clay statuette.

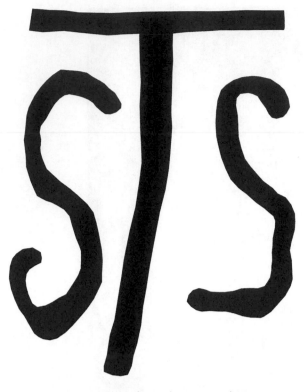

FIGURE 3.120. Painting of an S-design on a clay statuette.

is simply the hardened outer skin of the last larval stage, and the adult develops inside this protective skin. In order to emerge from the pupal case, the adult fly begins to fill with fluid a structure on the top of its head just between the eyes (fig. 3.124). When the inflated head breaks the end of the pupal case, the fly begins to extract itself with its anterior legs. Thus the design shown on the chin of statuettes precisely depicts the anterior legs and the inflated head of the fly. What appears to be an eye in the center is more likely to be the large organs used to pop open the extremity of the pupal case. On the basis of such detailed observations, it can be suggested that the first design represents unopened pupal cases. The lines drawn across the object depict the ridges of the puparium (fig. 3.122). The second design depicts the muscoid flies emerging from their pupal cases with the ubiquitous large organ and the anterior legs (fig. 3.123). This fluid-filled organ may have been mistaken for the gigantic eye depicted in the fineline paintings. Large numbers of fly puparia have been observed throughout the excavation and in all the

FIGURE 3.121. Painting of diamond-shaped designs by the eyes of a clay statuette.

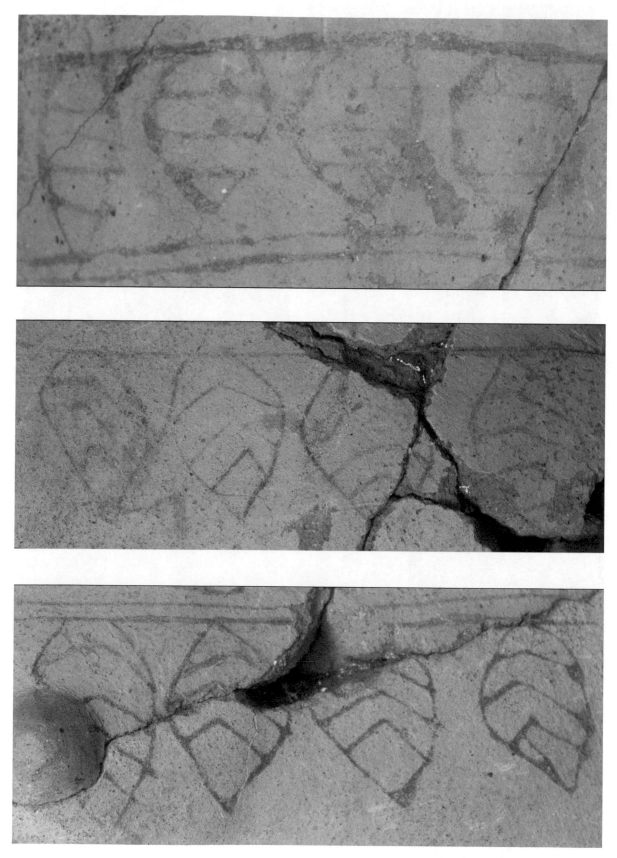

FIGURE 3.122. Paintings of unopened pupal cases on clay statuettes.

FIGURE 3.123. Paintings of flies emerging from their pupal cases on clay statuettes.

stratigraphically distinct layers. It was also noted that the anterior ends of most of the puparia were missing. This would demonstrate that the corpses were left exposed and that all the flies had successfully reached the adult stage. The emergence of flies was consistently depicted on the lower jaw, as if some connection existed between this design and that part of the anatomy.

Table 3.2 lists the motifs and subjects identified on the clay statuettes. As noted, another intriguing aspect of these statuettes is that rectangular openings were located on their backs in at least two well-preserved cases (fig. 3.35). Prior to their destruction, some of these hollowed effigies may have been filled with perishable offerings, such as the guinea pigs whose skeletons were found among the fragments of statuettes in the pit at the base of the west wall in layer Sand 2.3.7 (fig. 3.34).

FIGURE 3.124. Comparison between the design and a fly emerging from its pupal case.

connections with the larger iconographic corpus. The statuettes were not mere effigies of the sacrificial victims but represented an integral part of the ritual liturgy performed in Plaza 3A.

Although these effigies portray nude males with ropes around their necks, they do not represent prisoners as such. Contrary to numerous representations of prisoners, such as those encountered in Tomb 2 of Platform II (figs. 4.54, 4.55, 4.56), the hands of the clay statuettes are not tied behind their backs but rather rest calmly on their knees or on their chests. If these objects represent idealized portraits of the sacrificed individuals that they accompanied, then it is possible that the intention was not to depict captives of war but rather individuals offering themselves willingly.

CERAMICS

During the excavation of the sacrificial site, a total of 458 domestic and 40 fineware sherds were found (table 3.3). With regard to the domestic ware, not a single vase could be rebuilt from the

We found not only all the clay statuettes but also the most intriguing ritual practices in Sand 2 and on the dried mud. These included the organization of human remains in opposite patterns and the insertion of body parts or objects into the trunks of certain individuals, such as the lower jaw, the finger bone placed between the ribs, the complete toe, and the rock tightly squeezed into a pelvis (figs. 3.44, 3.45, 3.46, 3.30). This stone was possibly taken from the rocky outcrop itself.

Thus a reciprocal system seems to be at play in this layer. Human bones and a rock were inserted into the body of some victims by carving an opening into the abdomen and removing the internal organs. Somewhat similarly, through openings on their backs, the statuettes may have served to contain offerings such as guinea pigs. The relationship between the human and the sculptures is reiterated further by the destruction of the clay statuettes along with the sacrificed individuals and by literally covering the head of one human being with the head of a statuette (figs. 3.49, 3.104). The association between the statuettes and the sacrificial victims is made even more explicit through

Table 3.2. Motifs Identified on Statuettes

Animals:	Marine birds, raptorial birds, sea lion, fox, feline, lizard, catfish, centipede, flies' puparia
Plants:	*Tillandsia*
Subjects:	Feline with man, snake-fox, fish with knife, war bundle
Motifs:	S-design, lozenges, step and fret with spiral, Maltese cross

Table 3.3. Distribution of Ceramic Sherds per Layer

Layer	Domestic	Fineware
Sand 1	44	10
Sediment 2	58	6
Sand 2	265	24
Sediment 3	30	0
Sand 3	61	0
Total	458	40

fragments, which appear to come from a great number of vessels. These vessels were of different types (based on the rim shapes), from the smallest cup to the biggest jar, such as the sizable sherd set on the legs of the individual resting against the boulder in Sediment 3 (fig. 3.15).

Domestic Ceramics

Many domestic ceramic fragments came from vases broken long before being tossed in the plaza or from well-worn vessels with evidence of having been exposed to cooking fires. These objects could not have been brought to the site by the prevailing wind, so only two possibilities can explain their presence in this sector. They could have been accidentally brought to the site with filling material or could have been thrown into the plaza before, during, and after the rituals. As there is no domestic sector in the vicinity of the plaza, this hypothetical filling material could only have been collected from the urban sector of the Huacas de Moche site, which is situated between the Huaca del Sol and the Huaca de la Luna (fig. 2.26). The very clean sand and mud layers, however, contained only ceramic fragments and no culinary remains such as animal bones (except for the complete guinea pig skeletons) or carbonized seeds, thus largely discrediting this possibility.

The possibility that these sherds were intentionally thrown in the plaza remains the most likely scenario. This hypothesis is supported by the distribution of ceramic fragments. The sherds found in the layers associated with the preparation of the precinct (Sand 3) and with the first pair of sacrificial rituals (Sediment 3/Sand 2) were all, except for two pieces, concentrated in the northwest corner of the plaza, well within the limits of the precinct (fig. 3.125). The sherds encountered in the subsequent layers, associated with the second pair of sacrificial rituals (Sediment 2/Sand 1), were more evenly dispersed (fig. 3.126). In each case the differential distribution closely matches the location of the human remains. This clearly indicates that the ceramic fragments were not randomly brought to the site but rather directly associated with the sacrificial rituals. For example, a number of fragments were found stuck in the solidified clay of Sediment 2 and Sediment 3. Others were lying directly underneath some of the victims.

This not only indicates the close association with the victim but also their contemporaneity. Moreover, not a single sherd was found in Sand 4, the layer with the children. Therefore the deposition of these artifacts was solely associated with the sacrificial rituals of adult males.

As mentioned, most of the sherds are eroded: only 23 rims out of 458 fragments were found. The state of conservation and the great heterogeneity of this collection seem to indicate that the fragments came from numerous pots and diverse contexts such as hearths, kitchen floors, and refuse areas. Furthermore, it seems apparent that a number of people picked up these ceramic fragments in order to throw them into the sacrificial site. By far the most fragments (289, representing 51 percent of the collection) were found in Sand 2, the layer where the most complex rituals and activities were performed. This phase also witnessed the destruction of the clay effigies, the digging of the pit in front of and into the west wall, and the most complex manipulation of human remains (fig. 3.33). Thus the concentration of ceramic sherds closely matches the greater ritual investment during this period.

The sherds came from numerous vessels of different sizes and shapes and were probably thrown into the plaza during and after each ritual, which indicates not only that these artifacts must have been part of the ritual but also that the sacrificial liturgy involved various participants, possibly including some of the general population living at the site. For the moment, it is difficult to determine why eroded domestic ceramics were seen as proper offerings and who was involved in this ritual.

Fineware

The majority of the forty fineware ceramic fragments found in the plaza belong to the Phase III stylistic period. Twenty-four of these artifacts were found in Sand 2. They consist of a wide selection of fragments but, as in the case of the domestic sherds, not a single specimen could be reconstructed. The most complete example is a small jar with a face effigy modeled on the neck (fig. 3.127). Chapter 2 proposes that these ceramic sherds could have come from the cemetery displaced for the construction of the Platform II/

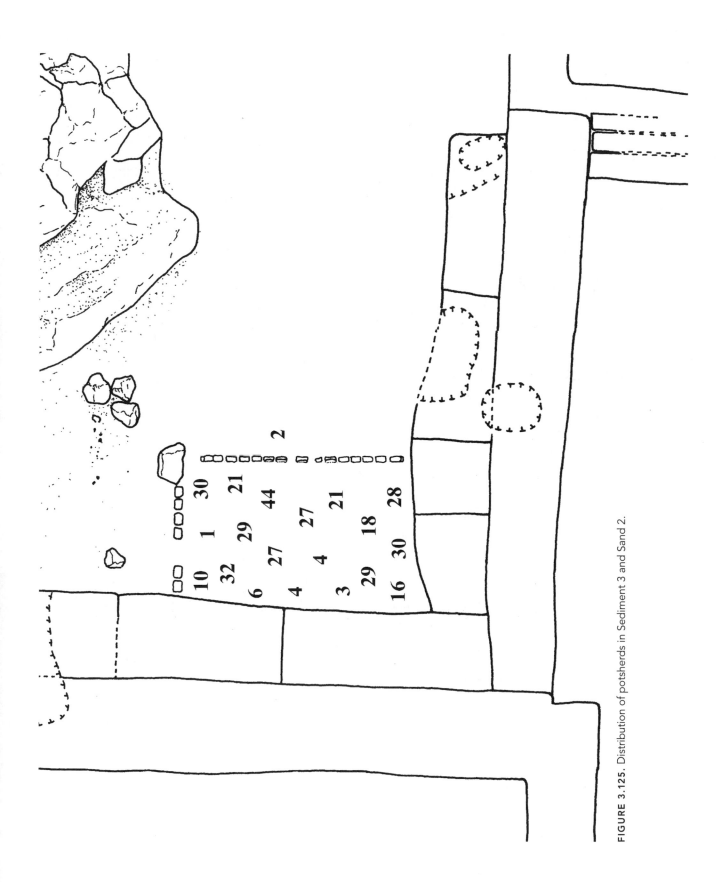

FIGURE 3.125. Distribution of potsherds in Sediment 3 and Sand 2.

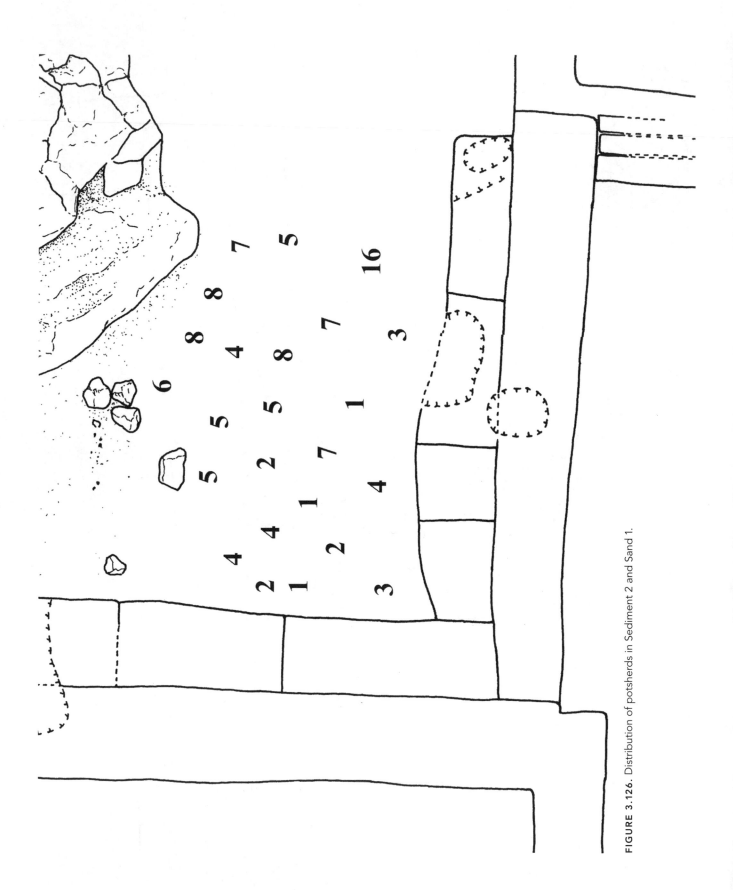

FIGURE 3.126. Distribution of potsherds in Sediment 2 and Sand 1.

Plaza 3A complex. We may recall that the fragment of a bearded figure, also representative of Phase III, was found resting against the head of the individual deposited with his legs folded on his chest (figs. 3.31, 3.32). This fragment perhaps was initially placed on the head of the sacrificed individual, just as the statuette head fragments were placed on the head of one individual in Sand 2 (fig. 3.49).

A pair of modeled ceramic ear ornaments was found among the human remains in the same layer as the bearded man (fig. 3.128). These fragments were broken from a Phase III vase, but the rest of the vessel was not recovered. It is intriguing to find a pair of ceramic ear ornaments in the midst of dozens of clay effigies of defeated male warriors, which all show earlobes with plugs removed. The iconography is more explicit on the subject and shows that such warriors themselves would have been deprived of their own ear ornaments upon being defeated (fig. 4.58). It has also been suggested that the removal of the ear ornaments would have been part of the sacrificial ritual. It is conceivable that the ear ornaments, like the bearded man fragment, were meant to reconnect this Phase IV ritual with the preceding phase. During that period, these disk ear ornaments were clearly associated with the warriors and the ritualists of the Coca Ceremony (fig. 7.26).

The final two layers presented three additional ceramic objects: a small whistle in the form of a bird (fig. 3.63), an eroded fragment depicting dancing skeletons (fig. 3.61) in Sediment 2, and a spindle whorl with a bird motif just underneath a pelvis in Sand 1 (fig. 3.129). It is unclear whether the bird motif and the whistle in the shape of a bird were meant to carry some sort of related meaning. The dancing skeletons fragment, though, may have been directly related to the group of sacrificial victims around it. After the decay of the soft tissues, the overall picture would have been a group of skeletonized individuals touching each other.

SEQUENCE

Table 3.4 represents the decisional process and the likely sequence of events that took place around the rocky outcrop at the back of the Huaca de

FIGURE 3.127. Jar with a face effigy on the neck, Sand 2.

FIGURE 3.128. Pair of modeled ceramic ear ornaments, Sand 2.3.7.

FIGURE 3.129. Spindle whorl, Sand 1.

Table 3.4. Sequence of Events and Decision Process

Before the project	1 Phase III cemetery situated to the back of Platform I and around the rocky outcrop
	2 Selection of the rocky outcrop sector as a ritual space for the project Platform II/Plaza 3A
Preparation of the project	3 Removal of the Phase III cemetery
	4 Leveling of the space for Platform II and Sand 4 for Plaza 3A
Construction	5 Construction of Platform II, north and south walls of the plaza
	6 Construction of the west wall of Plaza 3A
	7 Construction of the small structure at the base of the west wall
	8 Construction of a line of adobes from the north wall to the boulder
Consecration of the sacrificial arena	9 Burial of the children
	10 Construction of the small wall from the west wall to the boulder (Sediment 4)
	11 Burial of the man against the boulder (Sa-4.4)
Sacrificial rituals	12 Sediment 3
	13 Sand 2.3.9 to 2.3.1
	14 Sand 2.2 and 2.1
	15 Sediment 2
	16 Sand 1
Post-Moche	17 Sediment 1

la Luna main platform. The sequence has been divided into five main phases: before the project, the preparation of the sector, the construction, the consecration of the sacrificial arena, and the sacrificial rituals. The construction of Plaza 3A and Platform II coincides with a transition from Phase III to Phase IV. In chapter 7 I argue that this stylistic transition and new construction projects were triggered by equally important changes in Moche political structure.

It has been suggested that the presence of the rocky outcrop in part instigated the decision to construct the special complex of Plaza 3A/Platform II. Indeed the Moche made good use of this feature and constructed the architectural project around it, with one half of the outcrop visible in the plaza and the second half disappearing inside the solid platform (figs. 2.12, 2.15). Furthermore, all the ritual activities in the plaza took place just in front of it, and three of the four tombs of the platform were located alongside the rock (see chapter 4).

THE PHYSICAL ANTHROPOLOGY OF THE SACRIFICIAL VICTIMS

The physical anthropology of the human remains has been investigated by a number of people, including Florencia Bracamonte (1998), Laurel Anderson Hamilton (2005), and John Verano (2001a, 2001b). Their research has provided critical information regarding the population recovered in the sacrificial arena and in the tombs of Platform II. Unless otherwise indicated, this section is largely based on the results obtained by Laurel Hamilton in her 2005 PhD dissertation, which represents the most exhaustive study of this collection. Furthermore, her main concern was a detailed study of the cut marks and to a lesser degree the blows left on the sacrificial victims during their capture, their sacrifice, and in some cases after their deaths. This study gives a vivid picture of the injuries suffered by the victims and provides invaluable insight into the various aspects of a Moche sacrificial system.

COMMONALITIES

At least seventy-five male individuals were recovered in a tally of the left talus. This set includes sixty-two complete and incomplete skeletons. These robust males, largely in good physical health, range from thirteen to forty-five years in age, with a mean around twenty-five. Thus these were strong men in the prime of their lives. During the excavation of the site, I estimated that looters testing for the presence of burials destroyed about 20–25 percent of the site. Therefore it could be estimated that the site contained at least ninety to a hundred individuals prior to these disturbances.

Extensive evidence of antemortem and perimortem injuries was noted both in the field and in the laboratory. These injuries were registered on most parts of the body, including sixteen individuals with depressed skull fractures and four "parry" fractures, which occur when a

person attempts to deflect blows with a forearm. The evidence of well-healed fractures and these fresh injuries are consistent with trained warriors engaged in violent activities shortly before their deaths. Individual Sa-1.2 had an interesting set of old injuries, including parry fractures in both the radius and ulna of the left arm, broken ribs on his right side, and a broken nose (figs. 3.60, 3.69).

The majority of the cut marks were detected on the cervical vertebrae, but also on the skulls, ribs, hands, and legs. Sixty-one individuals had cut marks on cervical vertebrae, and at least forty-five of these had their throats slit. For at least seven of those individuals, this act was followed by decapitation. This clearly indicates that throat cutting was one of the preferred modes of sacrifice at the site. That is especially impressive if we consider that these numbers are based on strikes forceful enough to leave cut marks on the vertebrae of the victims. These deep cut marks at the neck suggest that these activities are consistent with the blood-collecting activities depicted in Phase IV visual culture. In addition, Hamilton mentions that at least twelve individuals showed evidence of left to right throat slitting. The iconography depicts the *tumi* held with the blade hanging down, so I would concur with part of her scenario (2005: 293):

> If capturing the victim's blood into a goblet is desired, the assailant easily could do so himself using his left hand; however, an assistant presumably would be required to restrain the victim while his throat was being cut. In the alternative (and, in my opinion, the most likely) scenario, a right-handed assailant stands behind the seated victim, uses his left hand to restrain the victim by the hair and his right to cut the victim's throat using the flexor muscles of the right arm (figure 438). If the victim's blood is collected, it would be awkward for the assailant to perform this task himself, thus an assistant holding a container in front of the victim would be necessary. (2005: 293)

My only caveat in regard to this suggestion is that it is probable that more than one individual carried out the sacrificial acts on the basis of the disposition of some of the victims in Sand 2 and Sediment 2 (figs. 3.41, 3.51). Therefore it is perhaps more likely that one sacrificer standing behind the victim was cutting the throat while assisted by two or more individuals. Decapitation was an important part of the ritual process which accompanied the act of cutting the throat.

Other injuries suggest an additional focus on the head. Hamilton (2005: 422) noted that at least nine individuals have large skull fractures resulting from "perimortem blows to the head with a blunt object or a weapon with sharp projections." In the first three cases, the impact scars around the margin of the fractured area of the skull suggest that the weapon was a mace with multiple points. In the remaining six cases, blunt objects were used to break the craniums of the victims, perhaps a rock or a club such as the one recovered from Tomb 1 on Platform II (fig. 4.14). For example, Individuals Sa-2.1, Sa-2.10, Se-2.1, Se-2.2, and Se-2.3 were dispatched in such a fashion (figs. 3.41, 3.42, 3.59). Of the nine individuals, however, eight of them had cut marks on their cervical vertebrae, indicating that their throats were slit before these additional injuries. Therefore throat slitting remains the primary mode of sacrifice.

In three cases where the shattered bones from the crania were present, the fragments were located just alongside the heads (figs. 3.42 [Sa-2.10], 3.52 [Se-2.1, Se-2.2]). In the other cases, these bones were missing altogether (figs. 3.41 [Sa-2.1], 3.52 [Se-2.3], 3.85). A blow to the head with such force would undoubtedly push the bone fragment inside the cranium, so could it be possible that this intervention was meant to remove the brain? Although this practice cannot be demonstrated archaeologically, it would be consistent with other actions, including the removal of the genital area of at least two individuals, Sa-2.13 and Sa-2.9 (figs. 3.30, 3.44).

In addition to the stab wound suffered by Individual Sa-1.7 (fig. 3.76), pointed weapons caused nonfatal injuries to a number of individuals. For example, one individual evinced a premortem stab wound to the left flank, another was stabbed in the chest (with a penetrating wound to the sternum), and a third showed cut marks on the left foot. Hamilton (2005: 422) argues that gouging wounds to some of the foot bones suggest some form of torture with "a pointed object forcibly inserted into the left foot."

Perhaps the sacrificial victim who best exemplifies the ritual process that took place before and during the sacrificial rituals is Individual Sa-2.13 (fig. 3.30). This male victim had a fractured ulna on his left arm, which was in the process of healing at the time of his death (fig. 3.29). This healing wound suggests that the warrior was captured after a hand-to-hand combat that produced this defensive parry fracture nearly a month before his death (Verano 2001b: 120). His throat was slit in the plaza, his cranium was broken with a star-shaped mace, and a rock was forced inside his pelvis after an opening was created in his abdomen. His body was rearranged during the postmortem process, with the legs bent back on the sides of the chest. Finally, a Phase III ceramic fragment was placed on his face and a sea lion canine tooth on his chest.

SUMMARY

The data recovered at the site suggest that from seventy-five to a hundred males were sacrificed during spells of torrential rains interspersed with drier conditions. The extensive evidence of old and healing injuries noted by the physical anthropologists indicates that these men in some cases had sustained combat injuries in the past and shortly before their death. The perimortem injuries further support the hypothesis that the men were taken to the Huaca de la Luna after some form of violent encounter. In some cases at least, it appears that up to four weeks elapsed after their capture before they were put to death in Plaza 3A. This would have provided ample time to carry out preliminary rituals within the huaca or to wait for the proper ecological conditions such as torrential rains. The place where these eventual victims were kept is a matter of some speculation. Nonetheless, clay statuette fragments found in Plaza 3B, which are identical to those encountered in Plaza 3A, indicate that this nearby space was contemporaneous to the sacrificial activities carried out on the other side of the dividing east wall (fig. 2.10). Furthermore, these two rooms would have been convenient places to keep these individuals.

The rituals were highly complex and entailed repeated visits to the plaza by the sacrificers and ritualists. Additional victims were brought in, bodies were displaced and rearranged, and body parts were taken or reorganized. All the human remains were kept exposed to the sun and the wind. The continuous work carried out on the remains would explain part of this exposure. It also may have been related to the decaying process and the witnessing of the diverse phases of the ritual by members of the nearby population. Their presence could be evidenced by the numerous domestic potsherds thrown into the plaza throughout the rituals (table 3.3). Chapter 7 compares the information presented here with the data recovered from Plaza 3C. This second sacrificial context dating to the Phase III stylistic period provides an important basis of comparison for reflecting upon the nature of sacrificial systems and rulership throughout Moche history.

CHAPTER 4

PLATFORM II

As discussed in chapter 2, Plaza 3A and Platform II were probably constructed as a single architectural project. A Phase III cemetery was removed from the area and largely relocated in a dedicated platform along the western wall of the plaza, a perimeter wall was erected, and the Plaza 3A/Platform II complex was purposely built bisecting a rocky outcrop (fig. 2.15). It is postulated that the plaza and the platform must have been part of a unified ritual project as well and thus also may have fulfilled related functions. The data collected in the northwest corner of the plaza (Sector A), added to the absence of artifactual remains in other sectors of the same space (Sectors B–E), clearly demonstrate that the plaza was exclusively used for a very specific series of rituals during Phase IV. These rituals included the offering of children and an adult male followed by the sacrifices of at least seventy-five men, probably warriors captured during some form of battle.

These ritual activities were solely concentrated in front of the rocky outcrop, which indicates careful planning in the utilization of space and reemphasizes the sacred nature of the rocky outcrop. Indeed the intentional use of a boulder and fragments of the same outcrop to create the cornerstone of the small precinct of Plaza 3A, to fill the stomach cavity of one of the victims (figs. 3.3, 3.30), and to throw at the victims and at the clay statuettes is further proof of the importance of the outcrop with regard to the ritual activities. Numerous rocks and boulders were probably added to the outcrop, giving it a much more substantial and impressive aspect. If this feature played such a crucial role in the plaza and became the focal point for the sacrificial rituals, it may well have had some significance during the utilization of the platform as well. The rocky outcrop would have provided the only means of reaching the platform from the plaza, as no other form of access such as a stairway or ramp could be detected during the excavation of the west wall of the platform. It is certain that the officiates making their way across the plaza filled with corpses and body parts to access the structure at the top of Platform II would have been an impressive sight indeed.

The platform has greatly suffered from erosion and looting, and only the base of walls around its perimeter and some postholes have survived. Nevertheless, these features indicate that a structure with a roof once existed on the platform. During the cleaning of its northern sector, the remains of four tombs were located (fig. 4.1) and all the looters' pits were reexcavated. The few fragments of artifacts and human remains strewn on the surface of the platform were collected and studied. They confirmed that these four tombs were the only ones in the structure. Unfortunately, all of the tombs were looted during colonial or modern times, but enough clues were left behind to suggest the social identity of two of the individuals. This section describes the fieldwork carried out on the platform and in each of these funerary contexts. I then assess the ideological and social implications of the identity of the occupants in two of these burials, especially the relationship that may have existed between these individuals and the sacrificial site.

EXCAVATION OF PLATFORM II

Somewhat like the surface of Plaza 3A, a thin layer of solidified clay mixed with aeolian sand covered most of the summit of the platform prior to its excavation. This structure has been severely looted, probably until the end of the 1980s. The first archaeological intervention consisted in cleaning the summit of the platform down to the adobe surface. A 2-m grid system was laid in place to collect all the artifacts and human remains. Of the 840 m² of the total platform surface, only 15 percent (125 m²) was left untouched by our project (fig. 4.1). The zone situated in the center of the structure was not explored because it was too eroded. No archaeological remains were detected on either side.

All the artifacts and bones collected on the surface were registered on the basis of the remaining 2 m² units. Afterward all the six looters' pits

were cleaned and precisely mapped. The materials found in each of these pits were given a different number because they could have pertained to distinct funerary contexts. In order to find other burials that escaped the attention of the looters, a series of nine test pits was excavated on the platform as well (fig. 4.1, S1–S9). The aim was to test every possible sector that presented a certain potential. Seven of these excavations were carried out in the northern part of the structure and two others in the southern part. Each of these test pits involved dismantling a whole constructive block (RAT) measuring on average 1.5 m² to a depth of about 4 m (fig. 4.2). In two cases the excavation was pursued as far as the base of the platform. Although none of these tiresome excavations yielded any funerary context, they provided a detailed study of the construction technique of the platform. This thorough survey also confirmed the extent of funerary practices in this part of Huaca de la Luna.

FUNCTION OF THE PLATFORM

Alongside the northern part of the structure three postholes were detected (fig. 4.1). At the bottom of the first one, situated immediately to the north of Tomb 1, three fragments of domestic ceramic and the vertebra of an adult sea lion (*Otaria byronia*) were found (fig. 4.3 P1, fig. 4.4). These objects were deposited inside a small recess, indicating that they were intentionally left there as offerings before the wooden post was secured. A fourth posthole was also located in the southern section of the structure. Some of these postholes may have served to support a roof of some sort that covered the platform in part or in totality. Indeed the relative altitude of the surface and the bottoms of each of these postholes seem to corroborate the hypothesis that a number of these may have supported the same superstructure: no. 1: 105.79 m–105.23 m, no. 2: 106.11 m–105.34 m, no. 3: 105.69 m–105.23 m.[1] On the basis of the size of these postholes, the posts may have measured between 22 and 25 cm in diameter. It is thus likely that the ceramics in the shape of oversized mace heads encountered in Plaza 3A along the base of the west wall of the platform served to ornament this roof (fig. 3.80).

Apart from the presence of these postholes, the

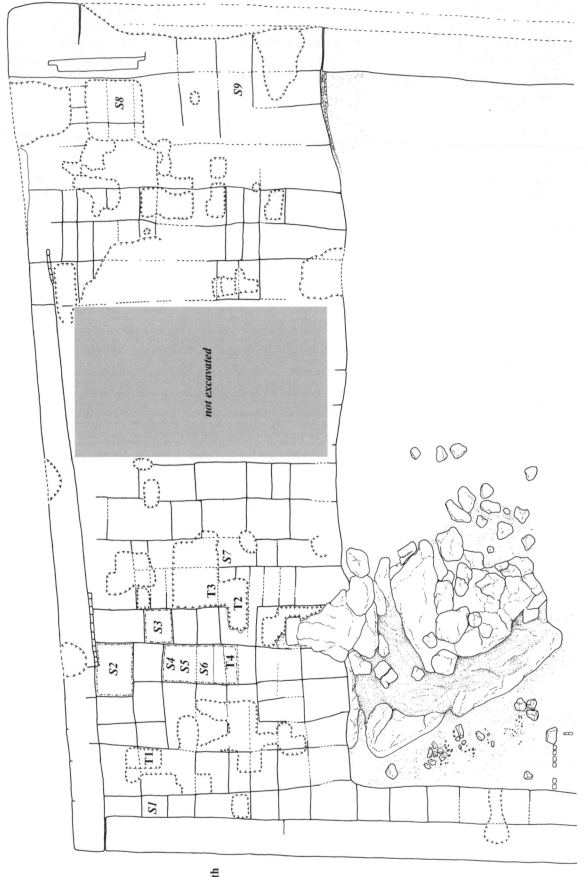

FIGURE 4.1. Plan of Platform II. Drawing by Jorge Sachun.

FIGURE 4.2. Test pit on Platform II.

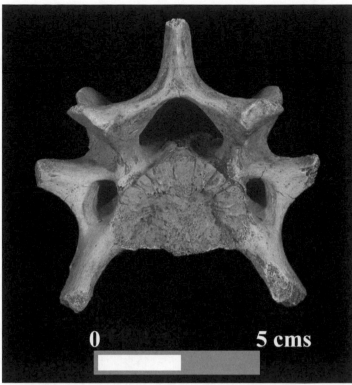

FIGURE 4.4. Sea lion vertebra (*Otaria byronia*), Posthole 1.

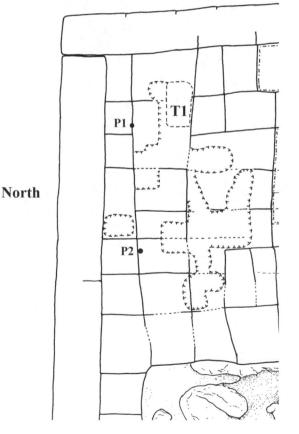

FIGURE 4.3. Plan of the northeast corner of Platform II.

only secure contexts detected are the four looted tombs. Although all of these tombs had been disturbed, they still contained important clues regarding the identity of some of their occupants and their ritual functions.

Tomb 1

This first burial encountered during the excavation was situated very close to the northeastern corner of Platform II (fig. 4.1). It consists of a simple rectangular chamber made by the deconstruction of two RATs. The chamber measures 98 cm by 205 cm and is oriented east–west (figs. 4.3, 4.5). The floor of the burial was situated at 243 cm from the summit of the construction block (104.40 m). Because of intense looting, it has not been possible to define the type of coffin or the position of the corpses. What was left of the funerary offerings and their position as a single row hiding under the rubble against the south wall make it clear that the tomb was looted during modern times (fig. 4.6). Most of the objects possessing any resale value were taken. In their haste, though, the looters overlooked this series of ceramics.

FIGURE 4.5. Tomb 1, Platform II.

Twelve vases were stacked against the south wall, eight of which were complete: two flaring bowls, four small jars, an unfired bottle, and a stirrup spout bottle in the form of a warrior wearing a conical helmet and holding a mace (fig. 4.7). This individual is in many respects similar to one found in the Warrior-Priest burial of Huaca de la Cruz, Virú Valley (fig. 4.8) (Strong and Evans 1952). Both subjects wear conical helmets, large earspools, and tunics decorated with disks. Their faces are covered with intricate designs and their hands are painted black. Incidentally, these are the same designs that were painted on the clay statuettes in Plaza 3A, indicating a symbolic continuity between the warriors and the sacrificial victims of

the iconography and between the main individual in Tomb 1 and the males in the plaza.

The two flaring bowls were placed upside down on two jars (figs. 4.6, 4.9). The designs of the associated pairs (flaring bowl and jar) were related. In one of the cases the pair may express some concept of duality with similar designs represented but in contrasting colors (fig. 4.10). In the second case, the similarity between the flaring bowl and the jar suggests that these two objects may have been

FIGURE 4.6. Ceramic offerings aligned against the south wall of the chamber, Tomb 1.

FIGURE 4.7. Bottle in the form of a warrior, Tomb 1. Museo Huacas de Moche, Trujillo. Inv. no. 000249 (H 24.1 cm).

FIGURE 4.8. Bottle in the form of a warrior, Tomb 12, Huaca de la Cruz, Museo Nacional de Arqueología, Antropología e Historia del Perú. Inv. no. C-54636.

FIGURE 4.9. Two flaring bowls on two jars, Tomb 1. Museo Huacas de Moche, Trujillo. Inv. nos. 000205, 000207, 000208, 000211.

FIGURE 4.10. Associated pair of a flaring bowl and a jar, Tomb 1. Museo Huacas de Moche, Trujillo. Inv. nos. 000205 (H 17.8 cm), 000208 (H 10.4 cm).

FIGURE 4.11. Associated pair of a flaring bowl and a jar, Tomb 1. Museo Huacas de Moche, Trujillo. Inv. nos. 000207 (H 8.9 cm), 000211 (H 18.5 cm).

produced in the same workshop (fig. 4.11). Unfortunately, this disturbed context severely limits the scope of the analysis and makes it impossible to elaborate on these subjects.

Tomb 1 contained the remains of two individuals found in the rubble and on the floor of the burial chamber. The first one was an adult male aged between fifty and sixty years, and the second one was an adolescent between fourteen and seventeen years old. Numerous pupa cases of scavenging insects indicate that the corpses were buried some time after their death. The osteological analysis shows that the adult was a very robust individual with an estimated stature of approximately 160 cm. The muscular development of this older man could indicate that in his prime he too could have been a warrior.

In addition to the human remains, the burial chamber also contained llama bones, at least one large plate made of a gourd (*Lagenaria siceraria*), and an unfired clay bottle. The vessel, in a poor state of conservation, was wedged inside the thoracic cage of the adult remains (fig. 4.12), although this may have been the outcome of the looting activities.

Outside of the burial and at the same level as the floor of the funerary chamber, a wooden club was found in an access shaft created by the looters (fig. 4.13). It had probably been extracted from the tomb and discarded because it did not possess any resale value. The club is made of hard wood and measures 70 cm in length. Showing evidence of extensive wear, it was completely encrusted with a black residue. Margaret Newman analyzed the residue by immunological analysis, and the sample showed a strong positive reaction only to human antiserum. So this artifact is literally covered with desiccated human blood (Bourget and Newman 1998). This club most certainly came from Tomb 1, which indicates that the old man was buried with a wooden tool that may have been associated with the activities carried out in the sacrificial site. This club encrusted with blood may have been used in Plaza 3A to break the bones and the crania of some of the sacrificial victims (figs. 3.53, 3.85). Although the crudeness of this object appears to have been unusual for Moche workmanship, its appearance could have been intentional and meant to emphasize its very function. In the hand of the sacrificer, a well-worn club such as this one repeat-

FIGURE 4.12. (*Above*) Thoracic cage of the adult male in Tomb 1.

edly drenched in blood from the head to the shaft could have symbolized the perennial nature of the ritual and evoked the awesome power of death (fig. 4.14).[2]

Tomb 2/Tomb 3

These two tombs were constructed side by side and share a number of similarities, indicating that they originally formed part of the same funerary context (fig. 4.1). Both tombs were most certainly looted during colonial times because dozens of vases were recovered but almost no metal was found except for a small silver disk. This disk, measuring 0.75 cm in diameter, is pierced, indicating that it may originally have been sewn onto a piece of textile with hundreds of similar disks. For example, a golden effigy found in the Huaca de la Luna main platform is covered with disks of a similar size (fig. 4.15). It has proven very difficult to separate the material belonging to each of these tombs because after looting Tomb 2 the looters gained access to the other one by tunneling into the east wall of the chamber (fig. 4.16). Consequently, most of the artifacts and human remains were extracted from Tomb 3 and dumped

FIGURE 4.13. (*Below*) Wooden club in situ, Tomb 1.

FIGURE 4.14. View of the wooden club (L 71 cm), Tomb 1.

FIGURE 4.15. Feline effigy from Platform I, Huaca de la Luna. Museo Huacas de Moche, Trujillo.

haphazardly into Tomb 2. In any case, the only secure contexts are the fragments of bones and the ceramic vessels that were left in Tomb 3. On that basis, it can be suggested that the occupant of Tomb 2 was an adolescent male approximately fourteen to seventeen years old and that Tomb 3 was the resting place of an older individual, around forty to fifty years of age.

Tomb 2

Tomb 2 was situated just alongside the rocky outcrop (fig. 4.1). The chamber is oriented north-south. Fortunately, this tomb was not as damaged as Tomb 1, so some important features were still preserved. The floor of the burial was situated at 103.05 m, some 1.7 m from the actual platform surface. Figure 4.17 shows how the ceramics and human and animal bones were piled up against the northern section of the tomb, very close to the surface. This situation clearly demonstrates the extent of the looting, and it is likely that the objects found in this first layer came from inside Tomb 3 (fig. 4.18). In fact, many ceramic fragments found in this tomb have been reunited with vases found in Tomb 3.

The funerary chamber of Tomb 2 was fashioned in more or less the same way as Tomb 1 but with some noteworthy differences. In order to build the tomb, two constructive blocks (RATs) were dismantled to an opening of 3.06 m by 1.23 m. The chamber itself then measured 2.16 m long by 90 cm wide, set inside this opened sector and incorporating small internal construction walls.

As the excavation progressed, it became clear that the disturbed material was lying on top of a central beam crossing the length of Tomb 2 (fig. 4.19). This piece of wood rested on two small walls that were constructed at the extremities of the burial. It is likely that this tree trunk served as support for the closure of the burial (fig. 4.20). Once closed with this wooden beam, the height of the chamber was 75 cm for a volume of 1.46 m³. Because of the destruction, it has not been possible to determine exactly how the tomb was actually sealed, but it is likely that other pieces of wood once were part of the original chamber roof.

Two niches were built along the eastern wall of the chamber. Only one survived the looting, as the other one was destroyed to provide access

FIGURE 4.16. Tomb 2, Platform II.

FIGURE 4.17. Tomb 2 prior to excavation.

to Tomb 3 (fig. 4.16). Niches are often found in funerary chambers at Huaca de la Luna, where they were used to stack offerings. Given the disorder within the niche in Tomb 2, it is doubtful that the objects found within it were in their original context (figs. 4.21, 4.22). These items probably were pushed inside during the systematic looting of the tombs (fig. 4.23). The artifacts found in the remaining niche and scattered throughout the chamber are presented below after the description of Tomb 3, given the blended context of these looted funerary chambers.

In all, about a hundred vases were registered pertaining to Phase IV. Although all the ceramics and human remains were drawn in situ, it became evident that the original position of the whole burial was disturbed. In their thorough and systematic search for metallic objects, the looters displaced, trampled, or pushed aside everything in the chamber. Most of the artifacts were located against the north and south walls (figs. 4.18, 4.24).

North

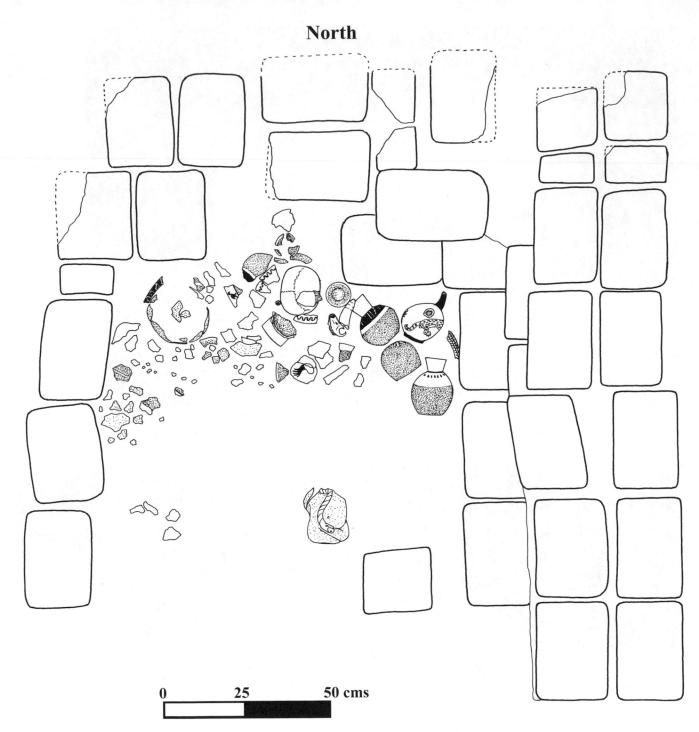

0   25   50 cms

FIGURE 4.18. Distribution of artifacts, Plan 1, Tomb 2. Drawing by Jorge Sachun.

North

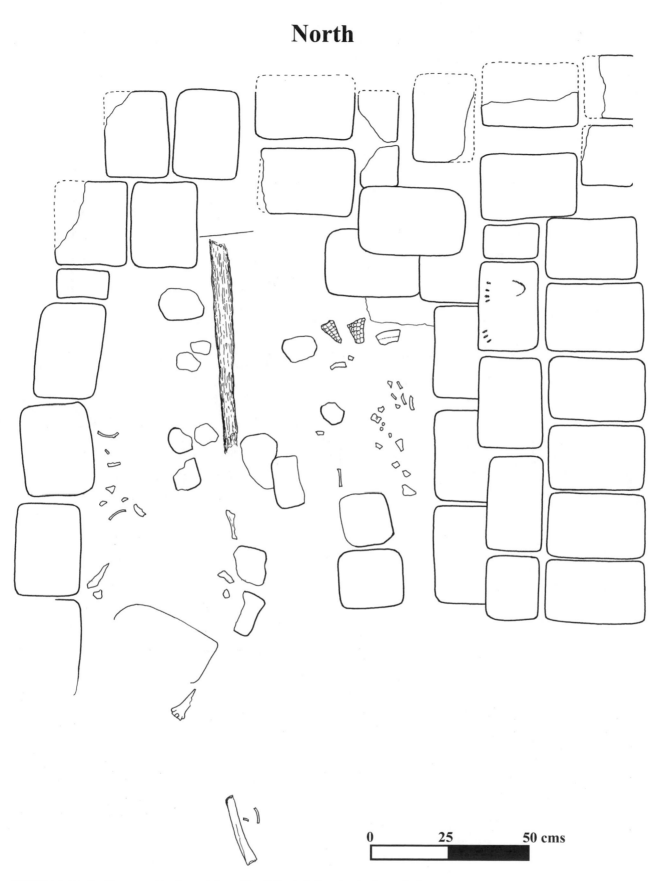

FIGURE 4.19. Roof beam and broken adobes, Plan 2, Tomb 2. Drawing by Jorge Sachun.

0   25   50 cms

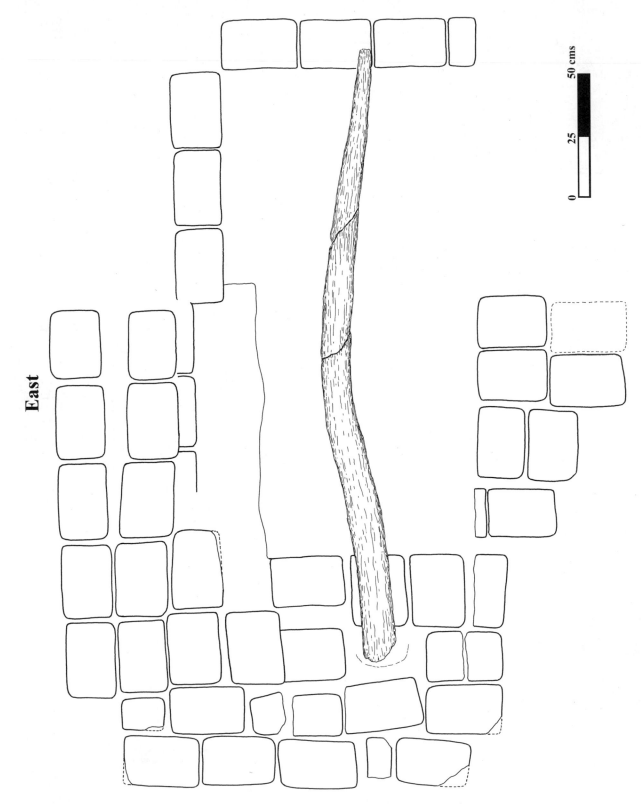

East

FIGURE 4.20. Roof beam and chamber, Plan 3, Tomb 2. Drawing by Jorge Sachun.

East

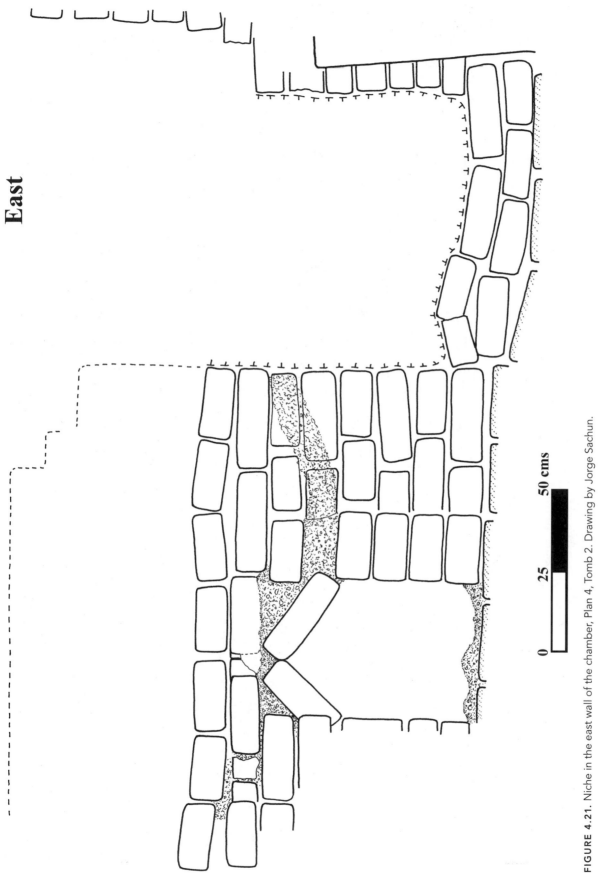

FIGURE 4.21. Niche in the east wall of the chamber, Plan 4, Tomb 2. Drawing by Jorge Sachun.

0   25   50 cms

East

FIGURE 4.22. Plan of the niche in the east wall, Plan 5, Tomb 2. Drawing by Jorge Sachun.

FIGURE 4.23. Niche in the east wall of the chamber, Tomb 2.

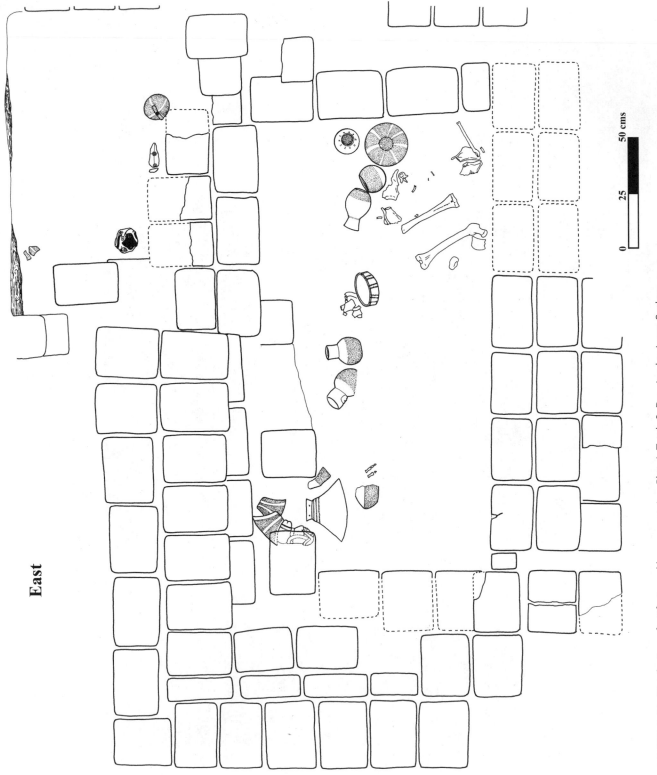

East

FIGURE 4.24. Distribution of artifacts and human remains, Plan 6, Tomb 2. Drawing by Jorge Sachun.

0   25   50 cms

Tomb 3

Tomb 3 and Tomb 2 were created side by side, probably during the same construction project. The study of the distribution of the artifacts and human remains has revealed that Tomb 2 was looted first and Tomb 3 afterward. In order to access this burial, the looters destroyed the east wall of Tomb 2, creating an opening less than 1 m² into Tomb 3 (fig. 4.25). They then systematically removed most of the artifacts and human remains from the tomb through this access tunnel. Unlike the mixed remains at the base of Tomb 2, it is thus likely that the pieces of broken ceramics or human

remains found in the bottom of Tomb 3 pertain exclusively to this tomb and not to Tomb 2.

In order to study this tomb, it was deemed necessary to excavate the original opening made by the Moche. At the beginning of this work, a bamboo tube (*caña de guayaquil*) with a large cotton thread running alongside was located at the southern extremity of the tomb (fig. 4.25 A, fig. 4.26). As in Tomb 2, the Moche had disassembled two RATs to construct this funerary chamber. After the removal of nineteen layers of adobes, it became clear that the bamboo pole, some 145 cm long, had been used to mark the position of the burial. This tomb marker descended to the

FIGURE 4.25. Tomb 2 and Tomb 3, Platform II.

FIGURE 4.26. Bamboo pole (*caña de guayaquil*) over Tomb 3.

FIGURE 4.27. Bamboo pole over Tomb 3.

beams roofing the tomb (fig. 4.27). Similar tomb markers have been reported at other Moche sites, and a bamboo pole leading to an elaborate burial chamber was also discovered at Huaca Cao Viejo (Franco, Gálvez, and Vásquez 1998; Strong and Evans 1952: 141). It is still unclear whether these markers were installed to prevent the Moche from accidentally reopening the tomb or, on the contrary, whether they were eventually used for reaccessing these burial contexts. In any case, without such a device it would have been difficult to determine the presence of a funerary chamber within an adobe platform (fig. 4.28 A). The Moche had reopened the complex funerary chamber at Huaca Cao Viejo mentioned earlier, apparently during a major El Niño event, indicating that the marker may have served to relocate the burial (Franco, Gálvez, and Vásquez 1998).

In some respects the Tomb 3 funerary chamber was constructed in much the same way as Tomb 2, and the layout was very similar. In this case, the RAT was completely dismantled down to the layer of gray sand upon which Platform II was constructed. Thus the base of the burial and the base of the platform are the same and are situated at an elevation of 101.5 m. Afterward a rectangular structure was built along the east side of the opening to house two niches (fig. 4.29). The niches were completely empty but may once have contained offerings that were removed by the looters (fig. 4.30). Following this construction, two small walls were erected at the north and south ends of

the chamber (fig. 4.31). These small walls measuring 1.10 m from the base of the tomb were used to support four wooden beams (fig. 4.32). These four beams, made with cut sections of algarrobo trees, provided the support for the roof (fig. 4.33). The funerary chamber measured 2.40 m long by 1.2 m wide and 1.10 m high, for a volume of 3.17 m³. Thus Tomb 3 was nearly 2.2 times more voluminous than Tomb 2.

After the placement of the beams, a straw mat was put on top of them (fig. 4.34). Traces of this mat found on the beams and on top of the structure containing the niches suggest that it originally covered the whole chamber. This fragment of mat was made with the split sections of totora reed (fig. 4.35). The structure of this plaited mat is 2/2 twill. Similar mats have been encountered in a Phase III burial located on the summit of the Huaca del Sol (Conklin and Versteylen 1978).

After a fine layer of clay was laid over the mat to seal the tomb, the layers of adobes were replaced. Most of the adobes of the first layer were oversized, measuring on average 30 cm wide by 40 cm long. It appears that the adobe layers

East

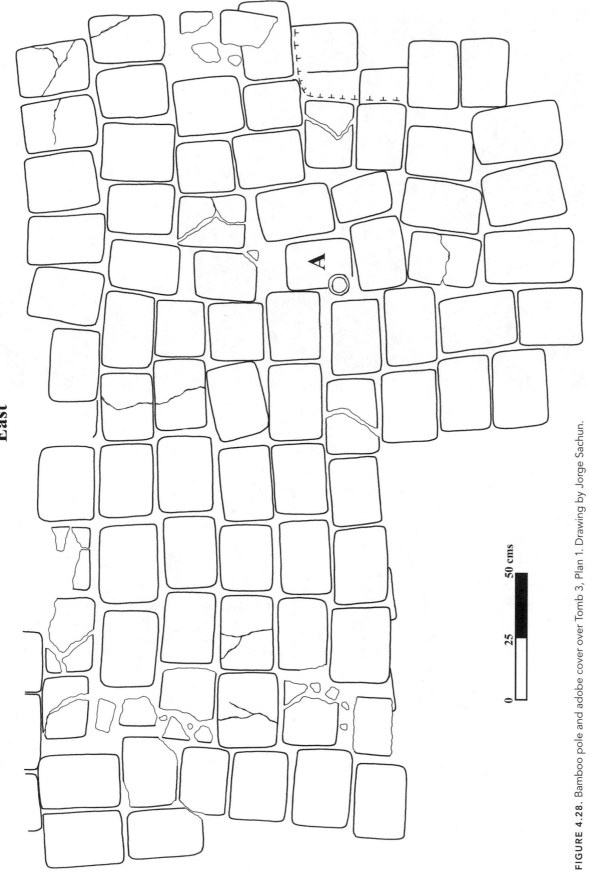

A

0   25   50 cms

FIGURE 4.28. Bamboo pole and adobe cover over Tomb 3, Plan 1. Drawing by Jorge Sachun.

FIGURE 4.29. Niches in the east wall of the chamber, Tomb 3.

East

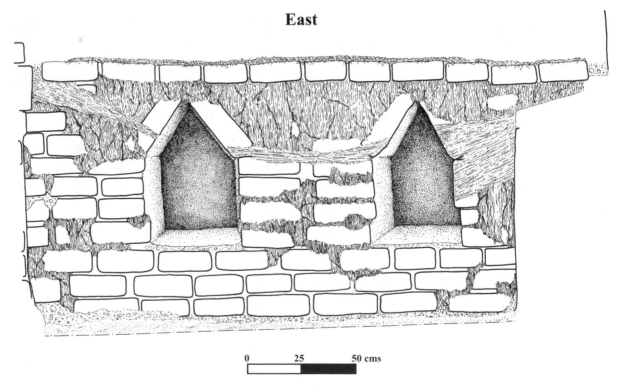

0   25   50 cms

FIGURE 4.30. Drawing of the east wall of the chamber, Tomb 3, Plan 2. Drawing by Jorge Sachun.

FIGURE 4.31. View of the funerary chamber, Tomb 3.

FIGURE 4.32. North wall of the chamber, Tomb 3.

FIGURE 4.33. Roof beams over Tomb 3.

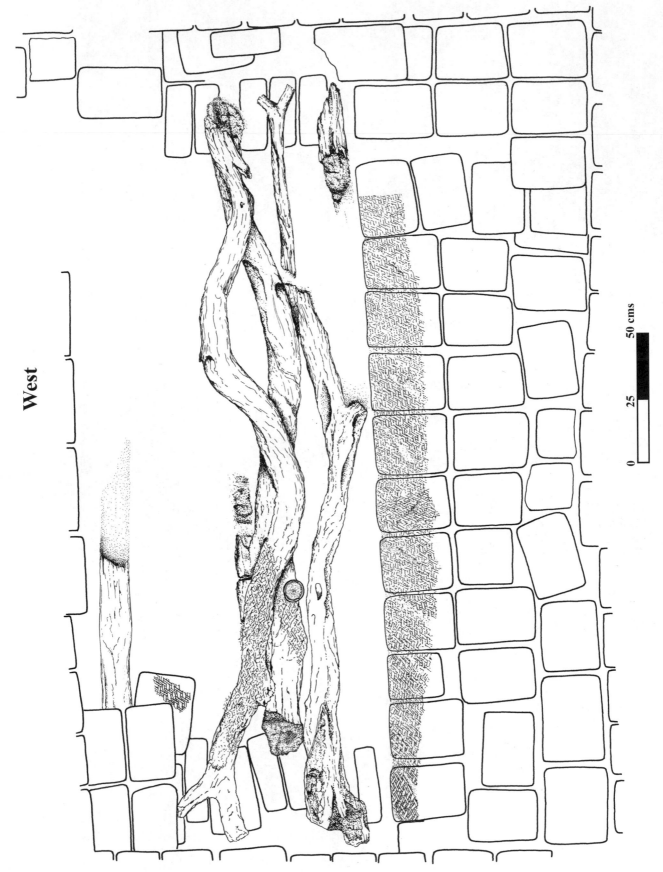

West

50 cms

25

0

FIGURE 4.34. Roof beams over Tomb 3, Plan 3. Drawing by Jorge Sachun.

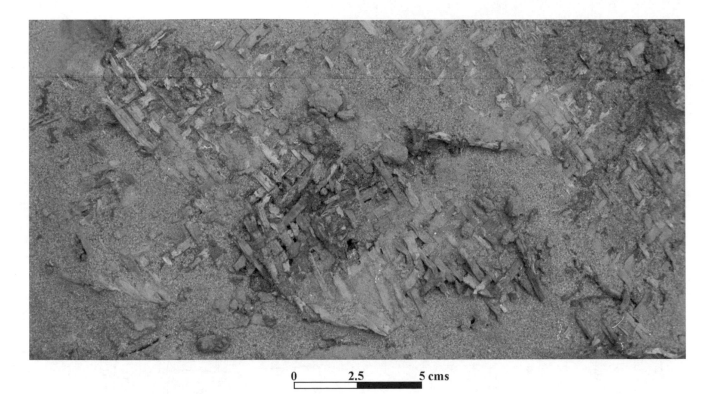

0   2.5   5 cms

FIGURE 4.35. Remnants of the reed mat over the roof beams, Tomb 3.

were laid in haste, because most of them were not joined with clay mortar. Between layers 8 and 9, it was even necessary to put a layer of sand and clay fragments some 10 cm thick in order to level the layers. The bamboo pole with its two cotton threads was wedged in between the adobe layers.

Because of the destruction of the context, it is virtually impossible to describe the spatial organization of the tomb. Nevertheless, it can be said that a fine layer of clay was deposited right on the sand matrix. The imprints of a number of wooden planks indicate that the corpse was enclosed in a plank coffin and was surrounded by numerous offerings and sacrificed llamas (fig. 4.36).

Tomb 2 and Tomb 3 each once contained the remains of a male individual whose disturbed remains were recovered within the larger looted context. The skeleton in Tomb 2 was that of an adolescent male, about thirteen to fifteen years old. Occipital flattening to the cranium indicates the application of cradle-boarding. The individual in Tomb 3 was an incomplete skeleton of an adult male estimated to be forty to fifty years old. The bones present included the right scapula, right humerus, right parietal, left radius, several ribs and thoracic vertebrae, and various hand and foot bones. The left radius showed a well-healed Colles fracture, suggesting the individual's participation in hand-to-hand combat during his lifetime. Only the bones pertaining to the older man were found in Tomb 3, suggesting that this was his resting place.

Ceramic Offerings in Tomb 2 and Tomb 3

Because of the extensive looting suffered by these two burials, the ceramic vessels cannot be reassigned to their proper context. They are thus treated as a single assemblage. This section describes the most important ceramics found in these two burials and discusses the iconographic themes or subjects to which they belong: (1) Ritual Runners, (2) the ceremonial combat, capture, and sacrifice trilogy, (3) death and duality, and (4) the world of the sea.

Ritual Runners: the first piece is a jar in the form of a seated individual (fig. 4.37). He is shown in the process of tying an elaborate headdress, consisting of a head ring incorporating the head of a feline with a large trapezoidal element on top of it. He wears tubular ear ornaments. The face painting consists of a broad vertical band of red slip applied on each side of the face. This creates a

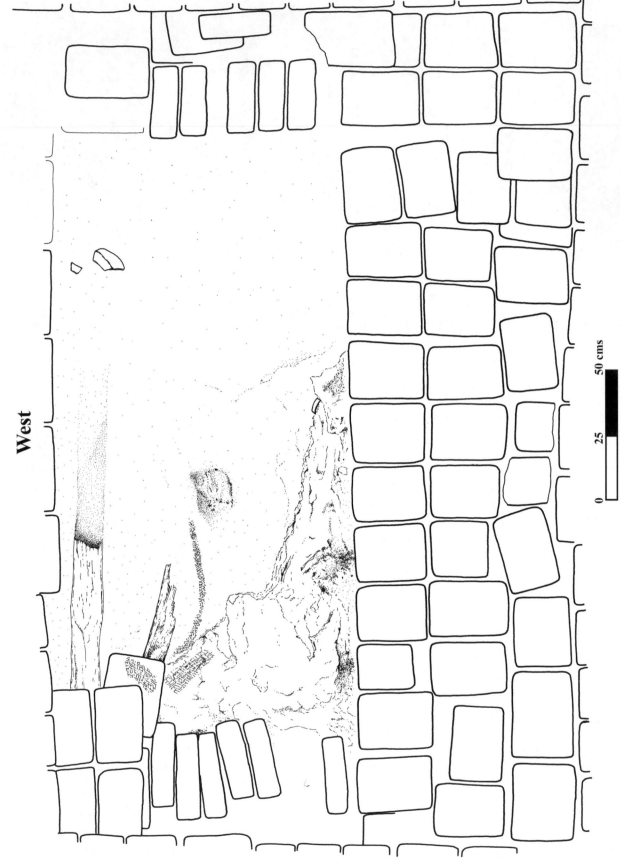

West

50 cms

25

0

FIGURE 4.36. Wood plank fragments of the coffin, Tomb 3, Plan 4. Drawing by Jorge Sachun.

FIGURE 4.37. Jar in the form of a Ritual Runner, Museo Huacas de Moche, Trujillo. Inv. no. 000245 (H 33.2 cm).

FIGURE 4.38. Fineline painting of Ritual Runners. Drawing by Donna McClelland. The Christopher B. Donnan and Donna McClelland Moche Archive, Image Collections and Fieldwork Archives, Dumbarton Oaks, Trustees for Harvard University, Washington, DC.

three-stripe effect: red-white-red. The figure has a slight bulge of the left cheek, probably indicating the presence of a coca chew in his mouth. The ribs and the sternum are clearly depicted, signaling that the individual is bare chested. The absence of a shirt and the depiction of a trapezoidal element in the headdress are clearly indicative of the Ritual Runners depicted in the iconography (fig. 4.38).

The three-stripe facial painting illustrated on

the seated individual is also frequently depicted with these Ritual Runners. The bilateral symmetry achieved by these alternating bands of color may have been inspired by the color of the fur of the desert fox (*Lycalopex sechurae*) (fig. 4.39). In figure 4.40 the same eyes have been used to join four faces together: two faces of foxes and two faces of human beings with fangs. The facial painting shown earlier is thus shared both by the human

FIGURE 4.39. Fineline painting of a fox and a scorpion.

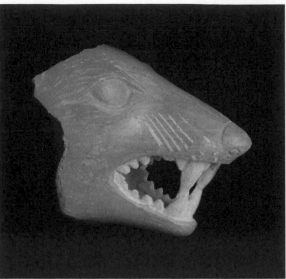

FIGURE 4.41. Ceramic fragment of a fox head, Museo Huacas de Moche, Trujillo.

FIGURE 4.40. Bottle in the form of a fanged being and heads of foxes. The Art Institute of Chicago (Gift of Nathan Cummings, 1958.688).

and the fox faces. This corresponding representation clearly indicates that this facial decoration symbolizes the fox, an animal consistently associated with Ritual Running, ceremonial combat, and human sacrifice.

The following two ceramic objects from Tomb 2/3 are also related to this animal. The first one is the well-modeled head of a fox (fig. 4.41). It probably formed part of an effigy jar. The second object is a jar with a low-relief design representing two pairs of foxes facing each other (fig. 4.42).

The ceremonial combat, capture, and sacrifice trilogy: numerous vessels contained in these burials prominently display the theme of warfare, capture, and sacrifice. Three examples depict individuals wearing a conical helmet (figs. 4.43, 4.44, 4.45). This is the same type of helmet worn by the warrior modeled on a stirrup spout bottle left behind by the looters in Tomb 1 (fig. 4.7). The conical helmet may thus represent some form of social identification and be emblematic of a specific type of warrior. Another intriguing aspect is that the three heads apparently depict the same individual but at three distinct stages of his life. On the figure to the left, the ear ornaments are almost the same size as his cheeks because of their size relative to the face (fig. 4.46 left). In the second figure, the earspools appear much smaller and the face is longer and more mature (fig. 4.46 middle). Finally, the body and face of the third

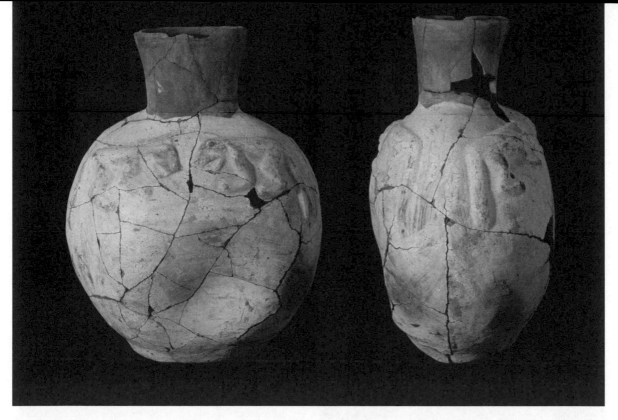

FIGURE 4.42. Jar with depiction of foxes in low relief. Museo Huacas de Moche, Trujillo. Inv. no. 0001811 (H 27.5 cm).

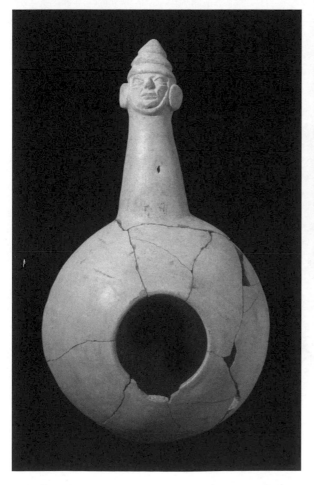

FIGURE 4.44. Dipper with the head of a warrior on the handle. Museo Huacas de Moche, Trujillo. Inv. no. 000223 (L 30.2 cm).

FIGURE 4.43. Dipper with the head of a warrior on the handle. Museo Huacas de Moche, Trujillo. Inv. no. 000222 (L 29.2 cm).

FIGURE 4.45. Jar with warrior effigy. Museo Huacas de Moche, Trujillo. Inv. no. 000221 (H 22.4 cm).

image are fatter, with the earspools resting against its bulging cheeks (figs. 4.45, 4.46 right). These faces would thus portray the same person as an adolescent, an adult in his prime, and an older man. In his extensive study of portrait vessels, Donnan (2004) also noted that a given subject may be represented at different stages of his life in some cases. One of them, dubbed Cut Lip by Donnan (2004: 156) because of diagnostic scars on his upper lip, is also shown at three distinct stages of his life: as a child, an adolescent, and an adult male seemingly in his thirties (fig. 4.47):

Since the youngest portrait of Cut Lip shows him at about age ten, his status was probably inherited rather than acquired: it is unlikely that he could have done anything by such a young age to earn a position of importance in Moche society and warrant the creation of a portrait. It is much more likely that he was ascribed high status in his youth because he was part of an elite family. Only later, as he matured into adulthood, would he have performed important activities.

In line with the same theme, Tombs 2/3 once contained a classic portrait vessel. The spout, the headdress, and the tubular ear ornaments were recovered from the looted remains, but the face itself was completely missing (fig. 4.48). Not

FIGURE 4.46. View of the warrior heads. Museo Huacas de Moche, Trujillo.

FIGURE 4.47. View of three portrait vessels showing the same individual at different ages: (a) Museo Larco, Lima, Peru. Inv. no. ML000146, (b) private collection, (c) Staatliche Museen zu Berlin, Preußischer Kulturbesitz—Ethnologisches Museum. Inv. no. VA 48030. Photograph by Christopher B. Donnan.

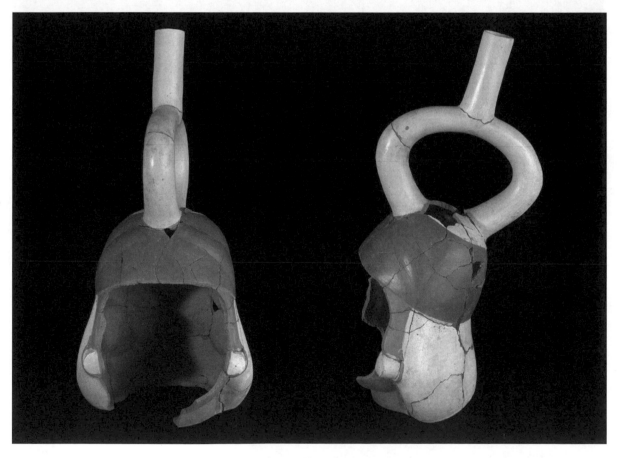

FIGURE 4.48. Portrait vessel. Museo Huacas de Moche, Trujillo. Inv. no. 000218 (H 32.4 cm).

FIGURE 4.49. Portrait vessel. Private collection. Photograph by Christopher B. Donnan.

a single sherd of it was found in the excavated collection.

With the use of a number of examples, Donnan has also made a cogent demonstration of the direct relation between the portrait vessel tradition and the practice of ceremonial combat. Nicknamed Long Nose for obvious reasons, one of these subjects is depicted on a number of vases and in diverse postures that bear many similarities to artifacts found at the site. For example, he has been depicted in the portrait vessel format wearing a bird headdress and elaborate ear ornaments decorated with war clubs (fig. 4.49) but also as a full figure in the guise of a warrior, as a prisoner with his hands tied behind his back, and as a nude male with a rope around his neck (fig. 4.50). The representations of Long Nose as a nude male with his hands free and the ear ornaments removed are almost identical to those of the clay statuettes found with the sacrificial victims of Plaza 3A (figs. 3.106, 4.51). Even the three variations of hand pos-

tures seen with the clay sculptures are depicted with Long Nose: both hands touching the rope, resting on the knees, and clasped together in front of the chest (figs. 4.50, 4.51). On the basis of this information, Donnan (2004: 138–139) suggests that the three subjects identified with these postures must have taken part in some form of combat eventually leading to sacrifice:

> Portraits of Bigote, Long Nose, and Black Stripe as captives imply that the people those images depict were defeated in combat, and the traditional scenario enacted: their clothing and armaments were made into weapon bundles, they were made to bleed from the nose, they were paraded nude by their captors, and they were taken to a ceremonial precinct where their throats were cut and their blood consumed from tall goblets by priests and priestesses. Ultimately, their bodies were dismembered.

Long Nose thus is clearly represented in all the stages associated with the practice of human sacri-

FIGURE 4.50. (*Above*) Three ceramics showing the same subject: (a) Museo Larco, Lima, Peru. Inv. no. ML000724, (b) Museo Nacional de Arqueología, Antropología e Historia del Perú, (c) Museo Arqueológico Cassinelli. Photograph by Christopher B. Donnan.

FIGURE 4.51. (*Below*) Two ceramics showing the same subject: Cassinelli Collection (left), private collection (right). Photographs by Christopher B. Donnan.

fice as documented in Plaza 3A. In contrast, for the Tomb 2/3 case it seems that the subject has maintained his status as a warrior throughout his life and was never celebrated as a sacrificial victim (fig. 4.46). That would be fitting for the adult male in the tomb, who did not terminate his career in the sacrificial site but in a high-status burial.

Warfare and the capture of prisoners are prominently depicted by a number of other pieces found in Tomb 2/3, such as a flaring bowl with weapon bundles painted inside the lip of the vessel (fig. 4.52), anthropomorphized bean warriors holding similar objects (fig. 4.53), and three jars in the form of captured individuals (figs. 4.54, 4.55, 4.56). In terms of workmanship and decorative treatment, the first two captives may have formed a pair. The third one, though, is quite different: the workmanship of the vessel and the painted designs are nearly identical to those created on some of the best clay statuettes from Plaza 3A. The overall shape of the face and the facial painting are quite similar to the subject depicted in figure 3.102, and the checkerboard design on the chest could be compared with those shown in figures 3.107 and 3.108. These elements reinforce the contemporaneity of the artifact assemblages as well as the people buried on Platform II and those sacrificed in Plaza 3A.

The subject of sacrifice also plays an important role in the offerings left in these tombs. The inside lip of a flaring bowl depicts raptorial birds holding war clubs and a series of small bowls or goblets (fig. 4.57). The birds, which are probably peregrine falcons (*Falco peregrinus*), are sometimes depicted above scenes of capture where blood is being shed (fig. 4.58). The small goblets or containers in the scene are usually associated with the recovery of human blood during certain sacrificial rituals involving profuse bleeding from the neck. The drops of blood, the bowl with a small pedestal, and the bird are occasionally presented together (fig. 4.59). The bowl also could be shown between the act of collecting the blood and the exchange of this same blood during the Sacrifice Ceremony (fig. 4.60 a). A second type of cup, a goblet, is depicted in the exchange of the collected blood in the Sacrifice Ceremony (fig. 4.60 b).

Twenty bone beads in the form of *ulluchu* fruits were found scattered on the floor of Tomb 3 (fig. 4.61). It is likely that they were once part of a necklace. Although the exact nature of these fruits has not yet been elucidated, they are prominently displayed in the scenes involving Ritual Running, the taking of human blood, and human sacrifice (figs. 4.58, 4.60 c) (McClelland 2008).

Another sculpture from this burial context is directly related to the taking of human blood and the trilogy of ceremonial combat, capture, and sacrifice. It takes the form of a seated anthropomorphized fox holding a chisel over a bowl (fig. 4.62). Chisels of this type are fairly common in collections, and that one was found in Tomb 3 at Sipán. It consists of an object with a rattle at one end and a very sharp blade at the other (fig. 4.63). A stirrup spout bottle from the Larco Museum depicts an individual holding a similar implement (fig. 4.64). The headdress, the tunic, and the posture indicate that he belongs to the same type of individual as the fox being (fig. 4.62). Long Nose is also depicted seated with a bowl on his lap and a chisel in his right hand (fig. 4.65). This confirms that this sort of representation is part of the ritual complex. It is conceivable that this type of chisel was used for cutting the jugular vein of sacrificial victims for the collection of their blood.

Death and duality: two additional broad themes that may be part of these subjects are death and duality. This theme is also clearly represented by a number of ceramic vessels in Tomb 2/3. The first example is a portrait vessel showing a mutilated face with its nose and lips excised (fig. 4.66). These types of mutilated individuals are usually involved in scenes associated with death and funerary offerings. I have suggested elsewhere (Bourget 2006) that these mutilations were performed to transform the face of a person into an authentic living dead. Chapter 5, however, explores in greater depth the association between these types of mutilations and El Niño events. Nevertheless, the play between the two states of existence—life and death—can also be understood to be represented in a human figure with the face of a monkey, as found on another ceramic from Tombs 2/3 (fig. 4.67). In such cases, a double duality may be enacted: human and animal and life and death.

An impressive number of vessels in Tombs 2/3 were intentionally and symbolically associated as dual vessels, forming a group of at least fifteen pairs. The aim of a symbolic duality is to create a link and a tension between two associated terms.

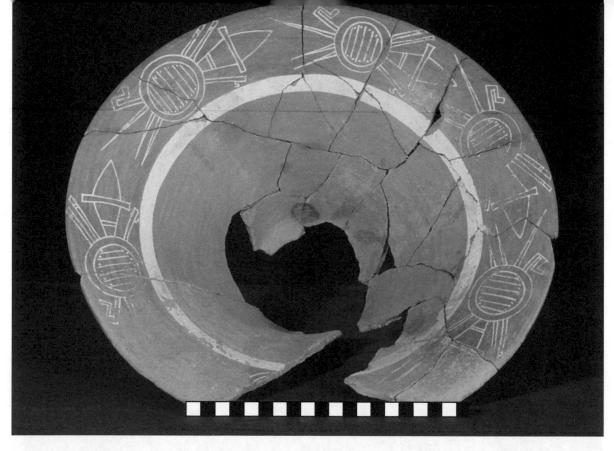

FIGURE 4.52. Flaring bowl with paintings of war bundles. Museo Huacas de Moche, Trujillo. Inv. no. 000214.

FIGURE 4.53. Flaring bowl with paintings of bean warriors. Museo Huacas de Moche, Trujillo. Inv. no. 000234 (H 21.9 cm).

FIGURE 4.54. (*Above*) Jar in the form of a captive. Museo Huacas de Moche, Trujillo. Inv. no. 000242 (H 26.5 cm).

FIGURE 4.55. (*Below*) Jar in the form of a captive. Museo Huacas de Moche, Trujillo. Inv. no. 000250 (H 26.5 cm).

FIGURE 4.56. Jar in the form of a captive. Museo Huacas de Moche, Trujillo. Inv. no. 000248 (H 30.5 cm).

FIGURE 4.57. Flaring bowl with paintings of raptorial birds and cups. Museo Huacas de Moche, Trujillo. Inv. no. 000243 (H 20 cm).

FIGURE 4.59. Fineline painting of a raptorial bird and a cup. Drawing by Donna McClelland. The Christopher B. Donnan and Donna McClelland Moche Archive, Image Collections and Fieldwork Archives, Dumbarton Oaks, Trustees for Harvard University, Washington, DC.

FIGURE 4.58. Fineline painting of a warrior holding a captive. Drawing by Donna McClelland. The Christopher B. Donnan and Donna McClelland Moche Archive, Image Collections and Fieldwork Archives, Dumbarton Oaks, Trustees for Harvard University, Washington, DC.

FIGURE 4.60. Fineline painting of an early Phase IV Sacrifice Ceremony. Drawing by Donna McClelland. The Christopher B. Donnan and Donna McClelland Moche Archive, Image Collections and Fieldwork Archives, Dumbarton Oaks, Trustees for Harvard University, Washington, DC.

FIGURE 4.61. (*Above*) Bone beads in the form of *ulluchus*. Museo Huacas de Moche, Trujillo.

FIGURE 4.62. (*Below*) Bottle in the form of a fox sacrificer. Museo Huacas de Moche, Trujillo. Inv. no. 000252 (H 24.3 cm).

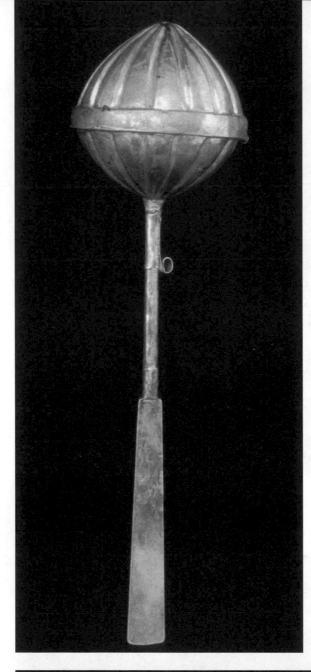

FIGURE 4.63. (*Left*) Rattle-chisel from Tomb 3, Sipán. Photograph by Christopher B. Donnan and Donald McClelland.

FIGURE 4.64. (*Above*) Individual holding a sacrificial chisel. Museo Larco, Lima, Peru. Inv. no. ML002551.

FIGURE 4.65. (*Below*) Bottle in the form of an individual holding a sacrificial chisel. Museo Nacional de Arqueología, Antropología e Historia del Perú. Inv. no. C-54557.

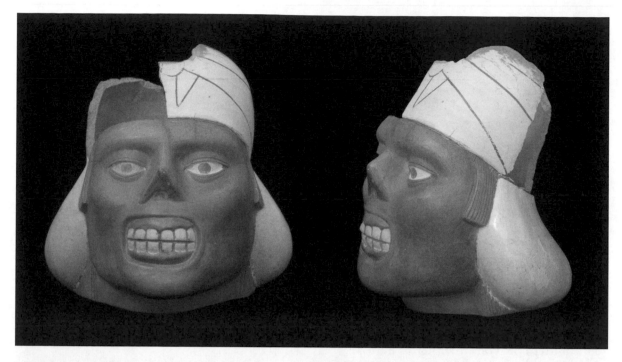

FIGURE 4.66. Portrait vessel of a mutilated man. Museo Huacas de Moche, Trujillo. Inv. no. 000246 (H 13.6 cm).

FIGURE 4.67. Bottle in the form of an anthropomorphized monkey. Museo Huacas de Moche, Trujillo. Inv. no. 000144 (H 22.8 cm).

These terms are never identical or mere opposites. They constitute a form of symbolic duality which could be expressed by the grouping of two jars. For example, one pair consists of a skeletonized face press-molded into the neck of a ceramic vessel (fig. 4.68). In this pairing, the duality is achieved by leaving the jar to the right of the mold-pressed figure unfired. In another example, the paired objects are two nearly identical jars modeled in the form of oversized corncobs (fig. 4.69). Here the duality has been achieved by firing the objects with slightly different techniques. The one to the left in the figure was fired in an oxidizing atmosphere that colored the ceramic orange, whereas the vessel to the right was fired in a smudging atmosphere, creating a gray color. In three pairs of bottles, the asymmetry between the pairs has been created by using different molds for the bottles within a pair and by making minute changes to the birds painted on either side of the rope design (figs. 4.70, 4.71, 4.72). Finally, dualities are also depicted on single vases with similar images repeated on either side of the chamber, such as a fox/deer/horned serpent (fig. 4.73) and a spotted feline (fig. 4.74). Other objects that may also have formed dualist pairs in the Tombs 2/3 contexts include dippers, small jars, and spindle whorls (figs. 4.75, 4.76). It is unfortunate that the looting of these tombs was so extensive that we have no way of knowing the exact location of these artifacts and the exact relation between these pairs.

The world of the sea: the final important theme identified in the Tombs 2/3 assemblage is the sea. Many vessels depict seabirds painted on bottles or flaring bowls but also modeled as three-dimensional sculptures (figs. 4.77, 4.78). Three other vessels found exclusively dispersed on the floor of Tomb 3 are also part of this theme. The first one is a stirrup spout bottle depicting one of the finest fineline paintings of a boat scene (fig. 4.79). The paddler journeys on a reed boat on a sea filled with borracho fish and a stingray. The central figure is surrounded by twelve seabirds. The second significant ceramic vessel with a sea theme is another stirrup spout bottle adorned with a representation of a being with supernatural attributes capturing a stingray at the end of a long fishing line (fig. 4.80). The third example is a flaring bowl decorated with a series of four borracho fish holding sacrificial knives (fig. 4.81). The significance of

these scenes and of the world of the sea in general is explored in chapter 5.

Completing the collection of objects found in these tombs were three additional dippers (fig. 4.82), twelve flaring bowls (fig. 4.83), and numerous stirrup spout bottles, straight spout bottles, and jars (figs. 4.84, 4.85, 4.86). These offerings are representative of the Huaca de la Luna ceramic offerings. Nearly identical examples have been found in various funerary contexts at the site. Because of the destruction suffered by these tombs, it is impossible to know the exact number of offerings initially deposited. Numerous fragments of others ceramic objects have been found, such as the beak of a duck, an owl, and a trumpet as well as fragments of fineline paintings of Ritual Runners and a feline. Finally, in addition to the bone beads in the form of *ulluchus*, a bone needle was recovered (fig. 4.87).

Tomb 4

Tomb 4 is situated immediately to the north of the Tomb 2 and Tomb 3 (fig. 4.1). The chamber is also in the same orientation and indicates not only a certain degree of planning but that these tombs were probably constructed in the same period. This small burial was very close to the actual surface and seems to have been looted at the same time as the other tombs: vase fragments from Tomb 2 were found inside the Tomb 4 chamber (fig. 4.88). Nevertheless, the looting of Tomb 4 was never completed. Remnants of the cane coffin were still visible to the north of the chamber, and numerous fragments of metal were still lying alongside the corpse of the child (figs. 4.88, 4.89).

The chamber was relatively simple and was constructed by removing three rows of adobe from the top of a RAT. The chamber measures 75 cm wide by 135 cm long. The child was buried in a cane coffin, and the head and the long bones of a llama were placed in the chamber (fig. 4.90). The offerings include at least two small jars and a flaring bowl with a rattle base.

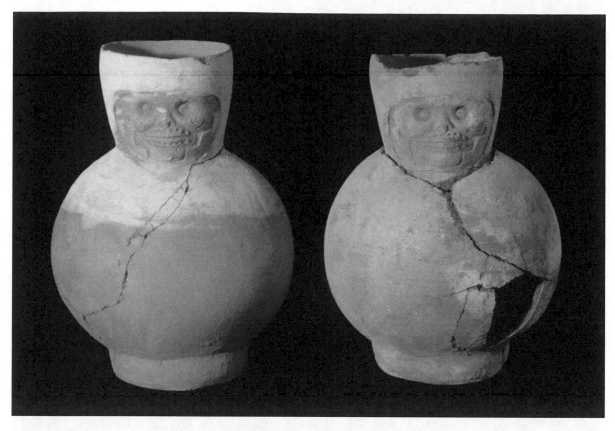

FIGURE 4.68. Pair of jars. Museo Huacas de Moche, Trujillo. Inv. nos. 000219 (H 21.4 cm), 000220 (H 21.4 cm).

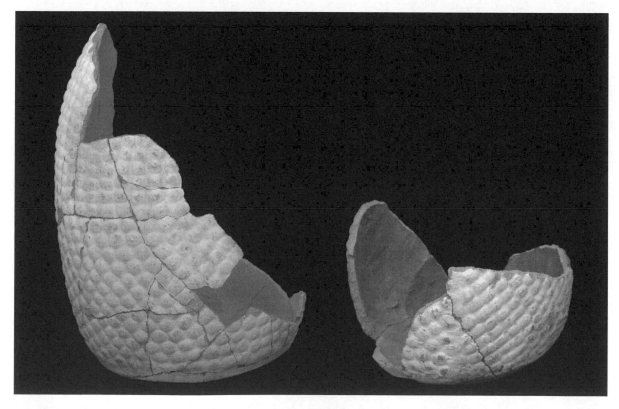

FIGURE 4.69. Pair of jars in the form of corncobs. Museo Huacas de Moche, Trujillo. Inv. no. 000198 (H 24.4 cm).

FIGURE 4.70. (*Above*) Pair of straight spout bottles. Museo Huacas de Moche, Trujillo. Inv. nos. 000183 (H 21.9 cm), 000182 (H 24.4 cm).

FIGURE 4.71. (*Below*) Pair of straight spout bottles. Museo Huacas de Moche, Trujillo. Inv. nos. 000186 (H 22.9 cm), 000187 (H 23.4 cm).

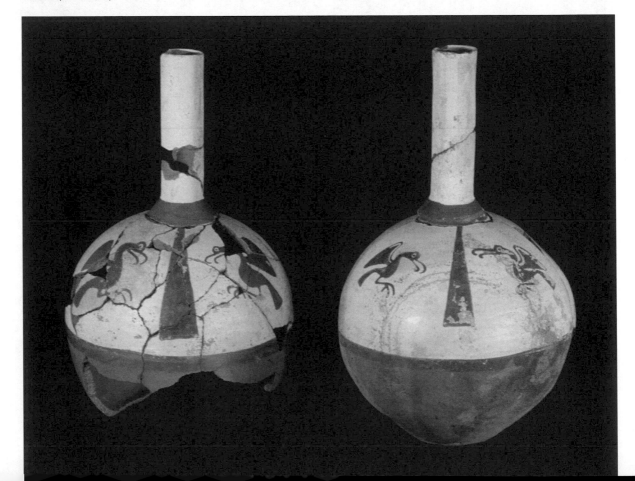

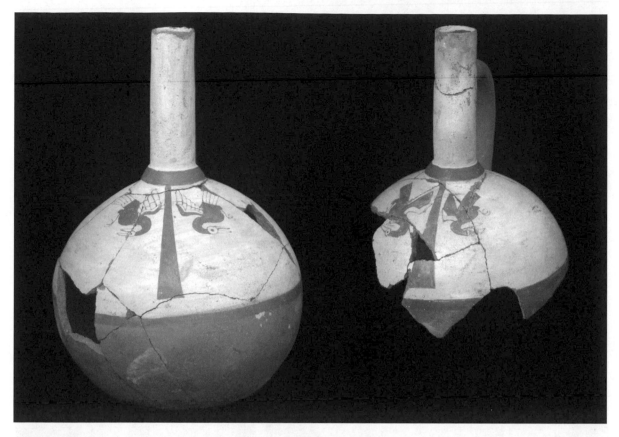

FIGURE 4.72. Pair of straight spout bottles. Museo Huacas de Moche, Trujillo. Inv. nos. 000184 (H 22.9 cm), 000185 (H 18.9 cm).

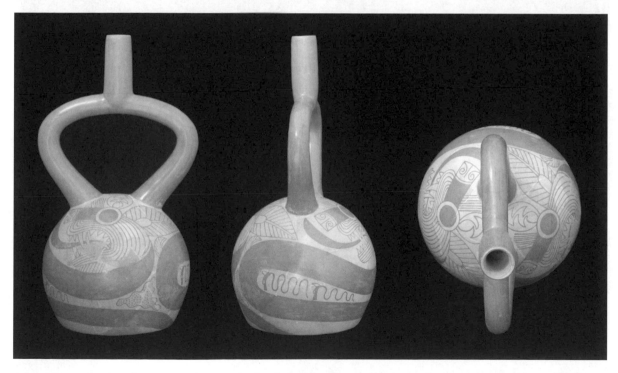

FIGURE 4.73. Bottle with paintings of two snake/fox/deer. Museo Huacas de Moche, Trujillo. Inv. no. 000251 (H 29.5 cm).

FIGURE 4.74. (*Above*) Bottle with paintings of two felines. Museo Huacas de Moche, Trujillo. Inv. no. 000247 (H 29.4 cm).

FIGURE 4.75. (*Below*) Pair of jars. Museo Huacas de Moche, Trujillo. Inv. nos. 000225 (H 18 cm), 000194 (H 17.5 cm).

FIGURE 4.76. Pair of spindle whorls. Museo Huacas de Moche, Trujillo. Inv. nos. 000236, 000235.

FIGURE 4.77. (*Above*) Flaring bowl with paintings of fishes and aquatic birds. Museo Huacas de Moche, Trujillo. Inv. no. 000167 (H 13.5 cm).

FIGURE 4.78. (*Below*) Bottle in the form of a bird. Museo Huacas de Moche, Trujillo. Inv. no. 000142 (H 13.5 cm).

FIGURE 4.79. Bottle with painting of a boat scene. Museo Huacas de Moche, Trujillo. Inv. no. 000244 (H 30 cm).

FIGURE 4.80. (*Above*) Bottle with painting of a fanged being fishing for a stingray. Museo Huacas de Moche, Trujillo. Inv. no. 000141 (H 14.4 cm).

FIGURE 4.81. (*Below*) Flaring bowl with paintings of borracho fishes and snake-fox. Museo Huacas de Moche, Trujillo. Inv. no. 000233.

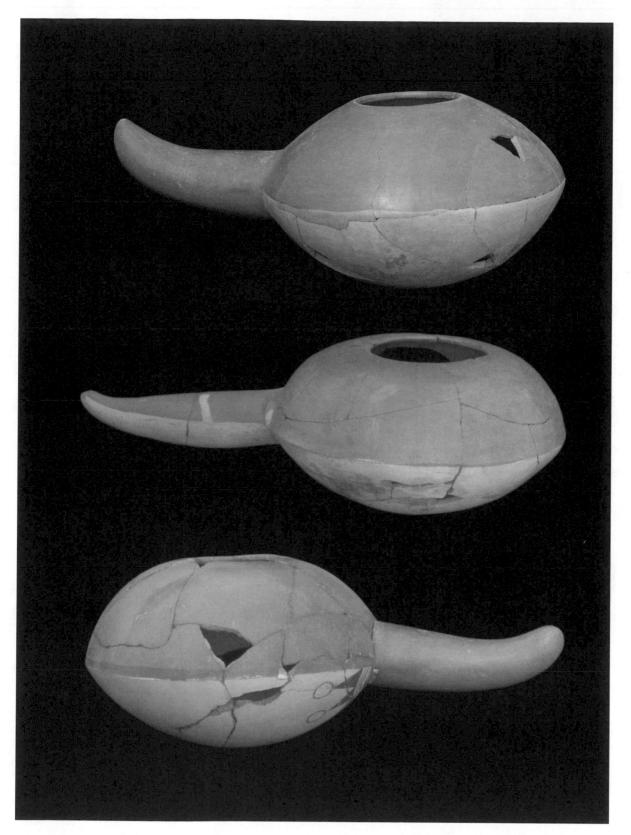

FIGURE 4.82. View of three dippers. Museo Huacas de Moche, Trujillo. Inv. nos. 000143 (L 34.2 cm), 000149 (L 27 cm), 000151 (L 23.5 cm).

FIGURE 4.83. View of twelve flaring bowls. Museo Huacas de Moche, Trujillo. Inv. nos. 000153, 155, 156, 158, 159, 160, 161, 165, 168, 170, 215.

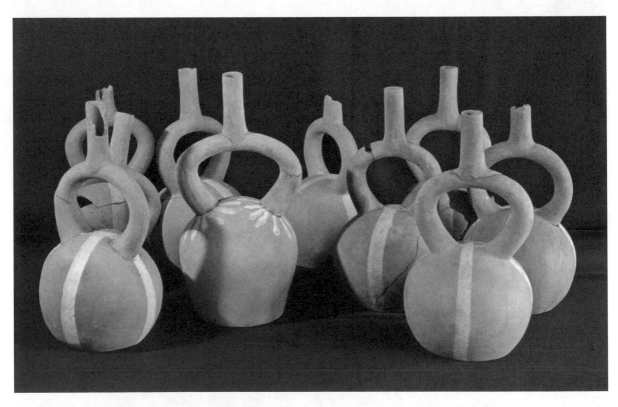

FIGURE 4.84. View of ten stirrup spout bottles. Museo Huacas de Moche, Trujillo. Inv. no. 000171-180.

FIGURE 4.85. View of two straight spout bottles. Museo Huacas de Moche, Trujillo.

FIGURE 4.86. View of sixteen jars. Museo Huacas de Moche, Trujillo. Inv. nos. 000189-193, 000189-195, 000189-196, 000224-231.

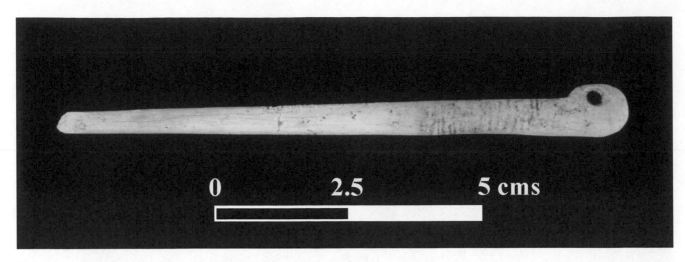

FIGURE 4.87. Bone needle. Museo Huacas de Moche, Trujillo.

FIGURE 4.88. Tomb 4, Platform II.

North

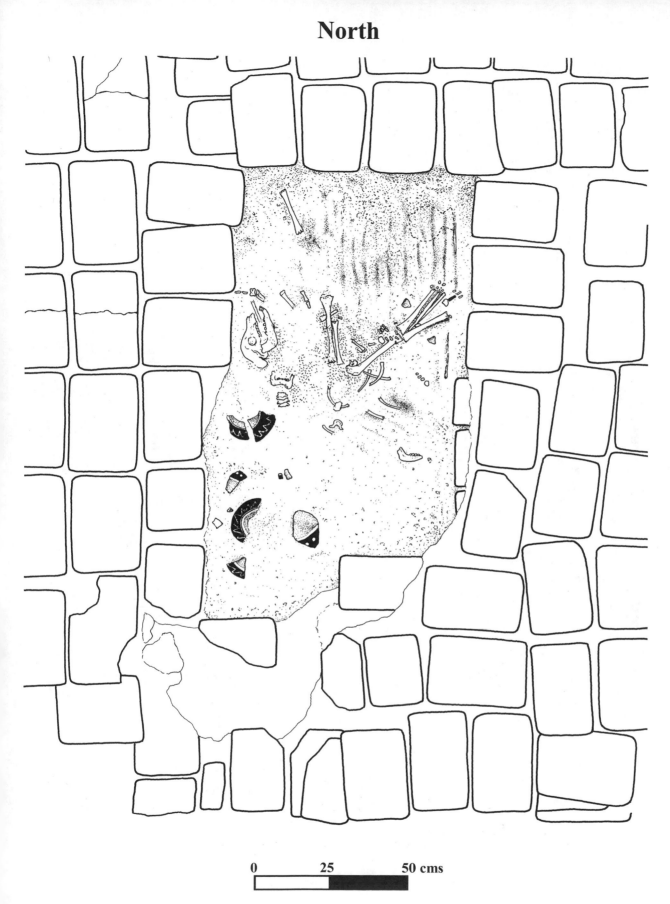

0   25   50 cms

FIGURE 4.89. Tomb 4, Plan 1. Drawing by Jorge Sachun.

North

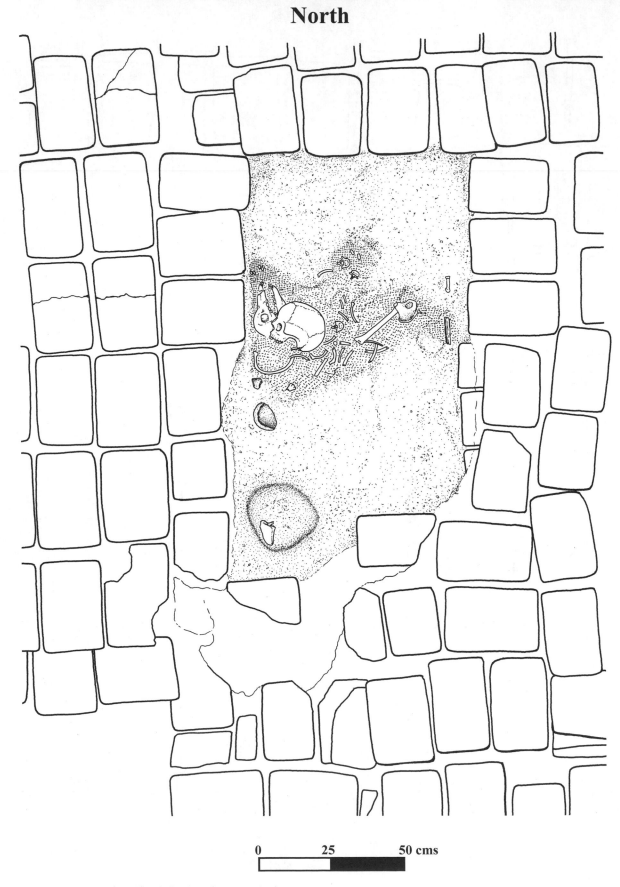

0   25   50 cms

FIGURE 4.90. Tomb 4, Plan 2. Drawing by Jorge Sachun.

ELEMENTS OF THE FUNERARY RITUAL

The proximity of Tombs 2, 3, and 4 suggests not only a high degree of planning but also that they were probably constructed at the same time. It is thus not inconceivable that the child in Tomb 4 and the adolescent in Tomb 2 were closely related and may be associated at the kinship level with the adult male in Tomb 3. The same situation might apply in Tomb 1, where an old man was associated with an adolescent.

The architecture of Tomb 2 and Tomb 3 is structurally almost identical. Both of them are dotted with small walls at each extremity that serve to support the roofing system, with two niches lining the east walls of each chamber. Before the burials proper, the bottom floors of both chambers were covered with a fine layer of clay, and they were roofed with wooden beams of hard wood (algarrobo). The main difference between the tombs is in their overall volume: Tomb 3 has a volume of about 3.17 m³ and is 2.2 times bigger than Tomb 2, which has a volume of 1.46 m³. The altitude of the bottom of the chambers was also different: Tomb 3 is situated at 101.60 m, while Tomb 2 is at 103.05 m. Thus the relative size of each funerary chamber and their position within the platform reinforce the hypothesis that Tomb 2 was the burial chamber of the adolescent and Tomb 3 the resting place of the adult male. Only bones of the adult male were found scattered on the floor of Tomb 3, which supports this hypothesis.

Tomb 3 was also more spacious than Tomb 1, which did not possess niches and in which two individuals were meant to share the same chamber. Perhaps the position of the chamber in the northeast corner of the platform is a further indication of the lesser importance of this context.

These four tombs were all situated in the northern section of Platform II, directly above the sacrificial site. Furthermore, like the sacrificial victims, three of these tombs were placed against the rocky outcrop itself. Therefore the limited number of platform burials and complete absence of other funerary contexts in the southern part of the platform reinforce the hypothesis that the Plaza 3A/Platform II ceremonial complex was used for a very short period and only in its northern part, on either side of the rocky outcrop. This select focus in the northern sector of course emphasizes the sacred nature of this rocky feature. One half of the outcrop is buried within the platform and associated with its funerary contexts. The other half of the rocky outcrop is visible in the plaza playing a critical role in an impressive display of sacrificed individuals. Based on this mediating role of the rocky outcrop itself, the platform and its content and the plaza and its content may have been elaborated to play out a wider theme of symbolic duality. To one side of the rocky outcrop was an open space located below and to the west dedicated to human sacrifices; on the other side of the same rocky feature was a solid structure placed above and to the east, containing the bodies of at least two sacrificers.

Chronology

In order to provide a chronological framework for these disturbed contexts, two radiocarbon dates were obtained from materials recovered from Tomb 2 and Tomb 3. The sample from Tomb 2 was taken from a wooden post that would have been part of the roof. The sample produced a conventional radiocarbon age of 1470 ± 80 BP (Beta-96035), with a 2 sigma calibrated result of Cal AD 412–684. The sample from Tomb 3 came from the bamboo post that served as a tomb marker. The sample produced a conventional radiocarbon age of 1370 ±50 BP (Beta-118455), with a 2 sigma calibrated result of Cal AD 580–725.

SUMMARY

The ceramic vessels located in Tomb 2 and Tomb 3 clearly establish a link between the individuals buried in these tombs and the portrait vessel tradition. Not only were portrait vessels placed with the dead, but all the aspects associated with this theme were also deposited alongside the buried individuals. Portrait vessels and their related subjects are intimately associated with the ritually charged activity of ceremonial combat, capture, and human sacrifice (Donnan 2004). All the elements encountered in the tombs are fully consistent with the theme: The different ages of the individual with the conical helmet (fig. 4.46), the presence of a portrait vessel (fig. 4.48), the pris-

Table 4.1. Symbolic and Ritual Elements in Sacrificer Tombs

Sites:	Huaca de la Cruz	Platform II	
Contexts:	Burials 12–16	Tomb 2/3	Tomb 1
Body: Old man	60+ years	40–50 years	50–60 years
Body: Boy	8–10 years	13–15 years	14–17 years
Conical helmet	*	*	*
Runner	* (m)	*	–
Ritual fishing	*	*	–
Deer	*	*	–
Cranium	*	*	–
Bean warrior	*	*	–
Shield and club	*	*	–
Portrait vessel	*	*	–
Serpent-fox	*	*	*
Tuber/facial cross	*	–	–
Wrinkle Face	*	*	–
Wooden club	*	–	*
Ritual battle	*	–	–
Bat	*	–	–
Prisoner	–	*	–

Note: m = metal, * = present, – = absent.

oners (figs. 4.54–4.56), and the numerous links with blood sacrifice (figs. 4.57, 4.62). Although Tomb 1 is slightly smaller and has been nearly destroyed by looters, several elements indicate that it may also have been the final resting place of an individual fulfilling the same social and ritual roles as the man in Tomb 3. The old man was also buried with an adolescent male, and one of the bottles left behind represented a warrior wearing a conical helmet and holding a bulbous mace in his left hand (fig. 4.7). The wooden club covered with human blood would be a further indication that this individual was probably involved in some of the sacrifices carried out in Plaza 3A (fig. 4.14).

On the basis of the artifacts, the iconography, and the context, at this stage of the analysis I suggest that the two older male individuals in Tomb 1 and Tomb 3 were sacrificers. This Sacrifice Ceremony tradition pertains fully to the Phase IV stylistic period and in all likelihood would have existed elsewhere within Huaca de la Luna and at other sites. One prominent example of another possible representation of a sacrificer is the tomb of the "Warrior-Priest" at Huaca de la Cruz in the

Virú Valley. This outstanding context (excavated by Strong and Evans in 1946) yielded almost all of the subjects and visual themes encountered in Tomb 1, Tomb 2, and Tomb 3. Indeed the tomb at Huaca de la Cruz was the resting place of an old man with an adolescent boy and contained all the key elements pertaining to the ritual trilogy of combat, capture, and sacrifice (table 4.1).

The task now is to look at the Plaza 3A/Platform II complex within the wider scheme of the Huaca de la Luna. Who were these sacrificers, and where did they stand within the social and ideological sphere of the temple? This important question is dealt with in chapter 7, which also compares the Plaza 3A sacrificial program with another sacrificial system during Phase III. Before such a discussion regarding the social and ideological sphere of the Moche state can be fully developed, a critical aspect of this symbolic program and sacrificial setting needs attention, as discussed in chapter 5. Why were the sacrifices performed during El Niño events? What was the place of these conditions within Moche symbolic and ideological systems?

FIGURE 2.6. Stirrup spout bottle depicting a right foot amputee with facial leishmaniasis. Huaca el Pueblo. Ministerio de Cultura Peru. Inv. no. HP-3948. Photograph by Johnathan Watts, MEG.

FIGURE 2.12. Plaza 3A and Cerro Blanco, Huaca de la Luna.

FIGURE 3.30. Individual Sa-2.13 in Sand 2.3.5.

FIGURE 3.43. Individuals Sa-2.9 and Sa-2.10.

FIGURE 3.53. Individual Se-2.1.

FIGURE 3.70. Individuals Sa-1.4 and Sa-1.5.

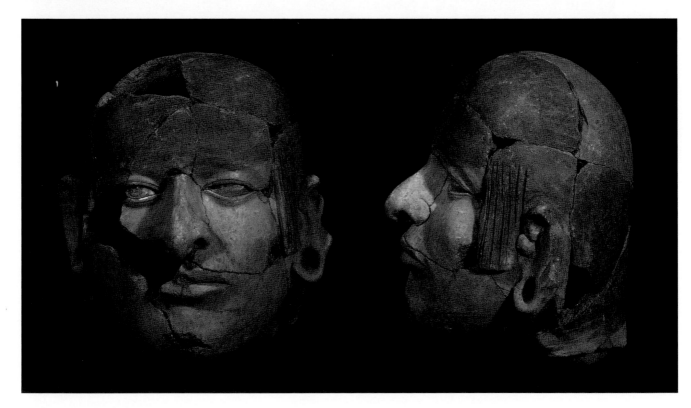

FIGURE 3.89. Head of clay statuette.

FIGURE 3.106. Body of clay statuette covered with fineline paintings.

FIGURE 4.62. Bottle in the form of a fox sacrificer. Museo Huacas de Moche, Trujillo. Inv. no. 000252 (H 24.3 cm).

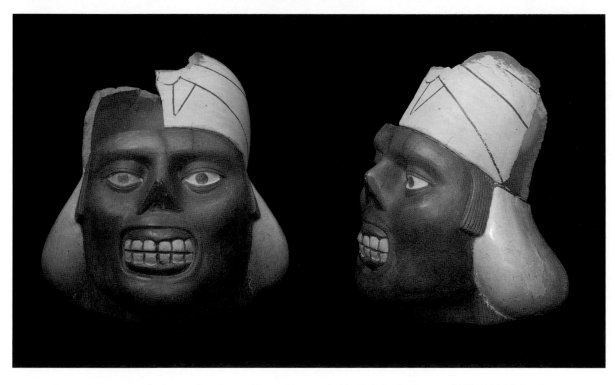

FIGURE 4.66. Portrait vessel of a mutilated man. Museo Huacas de Moche, Trujillo. Inv. no. 000246 (H 13.6 cm).

FIGURE 4.79. Bottle with painting of a boat scene. Museo Huacas de Moche, Trujillo. Inv. no. 000244 (H 30 cm).

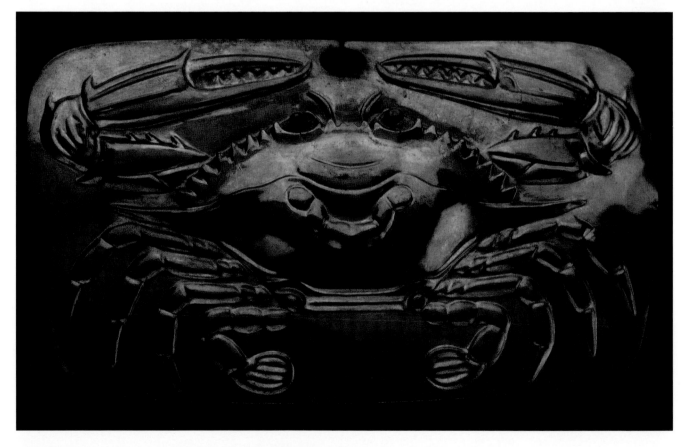

FIGURE 5.14. Nose ornament in the shape of a swimming crab (*Callinectes toxotes*). Private collection. Photograph by Christopher B. Donnan.

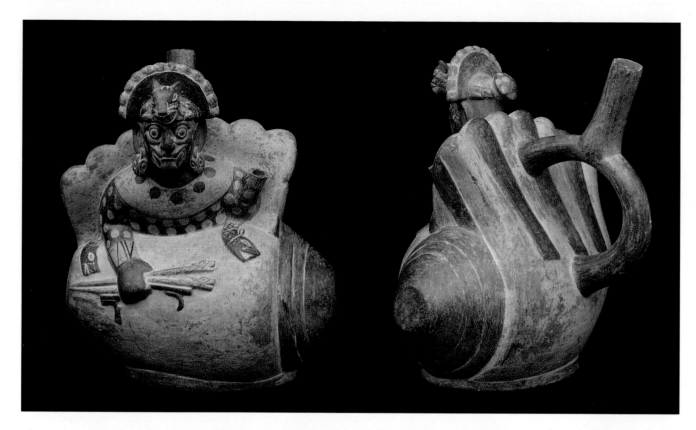

FIGURE 5.33. Being with fangs inside a *Strombus* seashell. Museo Larco, Lima, Peru. Inv. no. ML003208.

FIGURE 5.36. Musician standing on top of a Sacrifice Ceremony. Museo Nacional de Arqueología, Antropología e Historia del Perú. Inv. no. C-03315.

FIGURE 5.73. Andean condor (*Vultur gryphus*), Tomb 2, Dos Cabezas. Museo de Sitio de Chan Chan. Inv. nos. 13-01-04/IV/A–1/13,436. Photograph by Johnathan Watts, MEG.

FIGURE 5.99. Bottle in the form of a seahorse, Tomb 2, Dos Cabezas. Museo de Sitio de Chan Chan. Inv. no. 13-01-04/IV/A–1/13,453. Photograph by Johnathan Watts, MEG.

FIGURE 5.128. V-shaped diadem decorated with lizards, Lord of Ucupe burial, Huaca el Pueblo. Ministry of Culture, Peru. Inv. no. CH7-102. Photograph by Johnathan Watts, MEG.

FIGURE 5.137. West Peruvian screech owl (*Otus roboratus*), Lord of Ucupe burial, Huaca el Pueblo. Ministry of Culture, Peru. Inv. nos. CH7-141, CH7-140. Photograph by Johnathan Watts, MEG.

FIGURE 5.187. Diadem with raised arms, Lord of Ucupe burial, Huaca el Pueblo. Ministry of Culture, Peru. Inv. no. CH7-124. Photograph by Johnathan Watts, MEG.

FIGURE 6.7. Bottle in the shape of a bat warrior holding a child. Staatliche Museen zu Berlin, Preußischer Kulturbesitz—Ethnologisches Museum. Inv. no. VA 18083.

FIGURE 7.65. Individual resting on his right side. Tomb 2, Dos Cabezas. Museo de Sitio de Chan Chan. Inv. no. 13-01-04/IV/A-1/13,437. Photograph by Johnathan Watts, MEG.

FIGURE 7.81. Bottle with ceremonial combat and ritual objects, view B. Museo Larco, Lima, Peru. Inv. no. ML010849.

FIGURE 7.84. Nose ornament with low-relief scene of ceremonial combat, Lord of Ucupe burial, Huaca el Pueblo. Ministry of Culture, Peru. Inv. no. CH7-19. Photograph by Johnathan Watts, MEG.

FIGURE 8.1. Huaca Dos Cabezas, Jequetepeque Valley.

CHAPTER 5

A RITUAL ECOLOGY OF POWER

EL NIÑO IN MOCHE VISUAL CULTURE

The clay statuettes destroyed alongside the victims in Plaza 3A are a good starting point for delving into the complex and multitudinous roles of El Niño events in Moche culture and ideology. The fifty-two sculptures first established a positive link between the real warriors—in the flesh so to speak—and their depictions in the iconography (fig. 3.48). These clay sculptures, like their counterparts in ceramic and wood, depict nude males with ropes around their necks. In fineline painting, they bear strikingly similar intricate designs on their bodies and faces (fig. 5.1). In addition to representations of shields, spearthrowers, and darts, which would be befitting for warriors, their clay skins are covered with geometric motifs and insect and animal subjects such as fly puparia, birds, lizards, foxes, sea lions, and fishes (table 3.2). These sculptures were modeled and painted by numerous artists and in some cases apparently filled with offerings, including guinea pigs. At least two of them even had openings in their backs to facilitate this activity. Like the real victims, they suffered blows. In one case, the fragments of the head were distributed on the head of a man resting against the north wall of the plaza (fig. 3.49). These statuettes are thus not incidental to the ritual activities performed in Plaza 3A; they were not created after the fact but were clearly integrated in the sacrificial process. These offer important evidence that the sacrificial rituals performed in the plaza formed part of Moche core beliefs.

The elaborate iconography of ceremonial combat and the Phase IV portrait vessel tradition found in other parts of the site (such as Platform II and the urban sector) are also closely matched in all their details by the type of statuettes encountered in Plaza 3A. For example, one jar was part of

FIGURE 5.1. Comparison between a clay statuette and a painting of a captive. Drawing by Donna McClelland. The Christopher B. Donnan and Donna McClelland Moche Archive, Image Collections and Fieldwork Archives, Dumbarton Oaks, Trustees for Harvard University, Washington, DC.

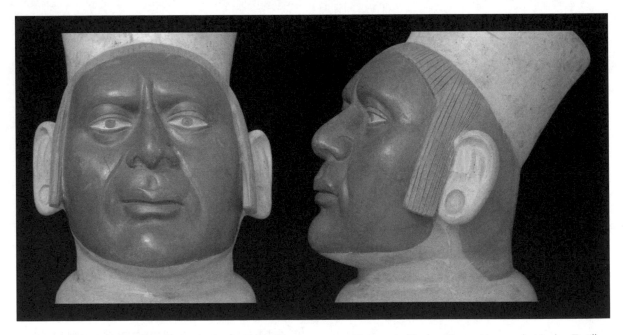

FIGURE 5.2. Portrait head on the neck of a jar. Phase IV, urban sector, Huacas de Moche. Museo Huacas de Moche, Trujillo. Inv. no. 000431.

the rich funerary assemblage of an adult woman buried beneath the floor of a ceramic workshop in the urban sector (fig. 5.2) (Uceda Castillo and Armas 1998). The head modeled on the neck of the jar is nearly identical in style and size to the heads created for the clay statuettes. It is thus likely that the same artisans produced the clay statuettes and the ceramic objects, perhaps under the guidance of ritual specialists. The portrait vessels created to commemorate the activity of ceremonial combat and human sacrifice may have been kept within the vicinity of the temple but were ultimately destined to be part of funerary assemblages, whereas the sole purpose of the clay sculptures apparently was to be destroyed with the sacrificial victims. Even the material used for each type of object—ceramic versus clay—reinforces their distinct destinations. Those that were meant to accompany an individual in the permanence of the funerary chamber were fired, while those that were meant to decay with the exposed victims were made of unprepared clay that could not be fired.

The similarity between the statuettes and Phase IV iconography shows without a doubt that the sacrifices in Plaza 3A formed an integral part of Moche ideology and ritual practices. By being incorporated with the sacrificial victims, the clay sculptures quite literally establish a direct link between the human sacrifices carried out in the plaza and the visual culture. This does not mean that the iconography served to represent this very ritual, but it clearly demonstrates that they conceptually form part of the same ritual complex. In a certain way, that erases the conceptual distance between the virtuality of the representations and the reality of the sacrificial activities. In addition, the similarities between the portrait vessel tradition and the clay statuettes indicate that the warriors implicated in these rituals might have formed part of a very select group of individuals belonging to Moche society (Donnan 2004). Indeed mitochondrial DNA (mtDNA) analyses carried out on nineteen individuals from the sacrificial site and twenty-nine others buried in the Huaca de Luna and the urban sector indicate that all of them may have formed part of the same population (Shimada et al. 2005, 2008).

Our mtDNA data also suggest that the sampled sacrificial victims pertained to the same closed population as the sacrificers and urban residents, or to a nearby population that shared the same founders or maintained regular bride exchange. The possibility that the sacrificial victims pertained to contemporaneous Cajamarca and Recuay societies centered in the adjacent upper valleys and highlands seems remote. Other lines of evidence in support of our view are presented elsewhere (Shimada et al. 2005). Here we emphasize that the Plaza 3A sacrificial victims were a very select group of warriors engaged in ritual battles . . . , and that there is a close relationship between the sacrificial site at

Huaca de la Luna, on one hand, and ritual battles and sacrifices represented in Moche iconography, on the other. (Shimada et al. 2008: 187)

These results suggest that the population living at the site or at other Moche sites participating in the same political system in all likelihood might have provided the sacrificial victims found in Plaza 3A. Basing their conclusion on biodistance method, the local origin of the victims has been challenged by Richard Sutter and John Verano (2007). This is discussed in more detail in chapter 8. Regardless of whether the victims were local or nonlocal, however, the people residing in the vicinity of the Huaca de la Luna most certainly supplied the clay statuettes and the numerous domestic sherds found intermingled with the human remains (chapter 3). We thus have archaeological, iconographical, and apparently genetic evidence supporting the hypothesis that ceremonial combat led to human sacrifice in Moche culture.

But what can we determine about the two stratigraphically distinct sacrificial rituals carried out in layers of mud? Only torrential rains triggered by El Niño events could have created the degree and thickness of mud in Sediments 2 and 3, by washing down the mud plaster and eroding the adobe walls of the plaza (fig. 3.36). What was the role of these conditions in Moche culture and cosmovision? Were the human sacrifices performed during stressful situations caused by excessive rains, as the thick mudwash appears to support? If so, were such rituals meant to petition some higher power or set of Moche gods, to put an end to these potentially catastrophic conditions? Or were they part of a well-orchestrated stratagem dedicated to the reinforcement of Moche elite political ideology? The purposely built architecture for sacrifice, rituals, and rich iconographic tradition in regard to sacrifice (discussed more fully in chapter 7) strongly suggest that the sacrifices were part of a well-conceived and thoroughly planned project. At this stage, it is not entirely clear how the El Niño conditions factored into all this, but it is apparent that they were fully integrated in the ritual activities as well.

As stated in chapter 1, the sacrifices in Plaza 3A were not the only ritual activities carried out in relation or reaction to El Niño events. It appears that these conditions would have triggered other types of rituals. Two funerary chambers at Dos Cabezas in the Jequetepeque Valley were created by enlarging the lower portions of two large erosion channels that ran along the southwest corner of the main huaca:

> After the rains stopped, Tomb 1, Tomb 2, and Tomb 3 were constructed. The location of the burial chambers of Tombs 2 and 3 seems to have been determined by the location of the two rounded concavities that were created by water erosion. These were simply enlarged and deepened to the desired size and shape of burial chambers by breaking out adobes from the recently constructed masonry bulk. (Donnan 2007: 61)

An isolated case like this would suggest only opportunistic behavior. Similar conditions, however, seem to have instigated the reopening of elite funerary chambers at Huaca de la Luna (Platform I, Tomb 5) and at Huaca Cao Viejo (Tomb 2) (Franco, Gálvez, and Vásquez 1998; Tello, Armas, and Chapdelaine 2003). In both cases, the adobe structures above the chambers were dismantled and the large chambers were reopened during severe episodes of rains. It appears that their original contents were removed and replaced by human remains and a few offerings. The chambers were then carefully resealed.

Because of the ubiquitous presence of El Niño events throughout the sacrifices and the clear link between the Huaca de la Luna sacrificial site and the representations of ceremonial combat, capture, and sacrifice, I suggest an equally strong correlation with the El Niño phenomenon in the iconography. But how can we assess the presence and the significance of such ecological disruption in Moche visual culture? The problem is complex, as the scope of ecological changes brought by an El Niño event on the north coast of Peru is widespread. It affects and transforms both the land and the sea by bringing sudden rainstorms and floods and by replacing the cold Humboldt Current with the tropical El Niño current. Any animal or subjects depicted in the iconography could theoretically have been impacted by severe El Niño conditions. Consequently, the identification of a few species that are not native to the north coast of Peru and accompanied an El Niño sea current, such as swimming crabs, would not suffice to demonstrate the importance of El Niño

conditions in Moche ideology, religion, and visual culture. It might merely indicate that the Moche were aware of these newcomers and decided to depict them. In order for these animal species to represent definitive indicators of the centrality and importance of El Niño conditions in Moche ideology, they would have had to occupy a structural position in the iconography, which placed these El Niño subjects to the fore of not only the visual culture but also the ideological system as a whole. In such a case, the depictions of these animal species would represent not solely the subjects themselves but an index of a wider and much more profound link with El Niño as a whole.

Given the actions taken during this geoclimatic disruption at different Moche sites, I suggest as a research hypothesis that the El Niño Southern Oscillation (ENSO) provided an important template for Moche ideology and that the totality of the iconographical representations relating to the sea and most of those relating to the land could be directly associated with El Niño events. I propose no less than a paradigm shift regarding this system of representation. In conjunction with the archaeological data discussed, the entire Moche worldview as understood by scholars to this point will have to be reconsidered if this hypothesis is correct. Although the presence of ENSO conditions during Moche times has been noted by investigators (Moseley, Donnan, and Keefer 2008), it has never properly been factored into most aspects of their ritual and political life, including the structure of rulership and the iconography. Therefore I propose that the Moche would have created an impressive ritual ecology based on these changing conditions to serve as the foundation for their entire symbolic system. I suggest further that the Moche would have used a number of very specific animal species as well as other elements to depict and to mark this cosmology. The research hypothesis resulting from this proposition could be synthesized as follows:

1. ENSO conditions formed an integral part of the Moche ideological system, especially the aspects most closely related to rulership.
2. In order to achieve a high degree of congruity between ENSO conditions and the ideology of power, the Moche created a complex form of ritual ecology.

3. The ritual apparatus, including sacrifice and funerary rituals, was fully integrated into ENSO conditions.

RESEARCH FRAMEWORK

The arrival of this warm sea current from the north and its consequences can be detected first by the presence of animal species not indigenous to the north coast of Peru and second by the changing behavior and the severe mortality suffered by a number of local animal species. Furthermore, other scenes that appear to depict terrestrial contexts and activities may also have been connected to the same environmental conditions.

Here I intend first to demonstrate that the animal subjects formed part of a vast system predicated by El Niño conditions and second to highlight the pervasiveness of such a system in Moche iconography, ideology, ritual practices, and rulership. The description sequence of these subjects is governed by their associations with one another. When it is logically feasible, I begin with what I perceive to be the most important subjects. Each of the main topics presented in this chapter warrants a more thorough investigation, but the arguments here clearly evince the larger visual and ideological system at play, based on the corpus of species represented.

Four distinct sections deal with the exotic as well as the local species depicted. The first one ("The Newcomers") includes the animal species that accompany the warmer oceanic sea current and do not usually inhabit the frigid waters of the Humboldt Current. The second section ("From the Northern Region") describes the subjects that may have migrated during ENSO conditions or were brought from north of the Moche region. The last two sections ("Local Species Disturbed by El Niño Events" and "Local Species Helped by El Niño Events") deal with the local species severely impacted for better or worse by the changing conditions. The section "Death and Disease" covers aspects related to the toxicity of certain plants and to a specific disease introduced during severe El Niño events. The section "Two Insignia of Power" approaches the symbolism of two types of diadems related to some of the highest-ranking individuals.

Although the diverse sections of this chapter review the most recent and relevant data regarding the ecological changes brought on by strong ENSO events, a detailed understanding of all the biological and environmental processes involved during these turbulent times on the north coast of Peru is still lacking. Different causes may explain this situation. Most of the research dedicated to El Niño's effects in Peru is geared toward economically important species such as sardines and anchovies. The other studies are mostly directed to very specific species or problems: contagious diseases affecting the local human population (Caviedes 1984), the massive death of certain species of marine mollusks (Arntz and Valdivia 1985; Glynn 1988), or the disappearance of seabirds and sea lions, for example (Tovar and Cabrera 1985; Tovar, Cabrera, and Farfán del Pino 1985). No detailed studies of the entire system have been published, apart from the more general overviews by Wolf Arntz and Eberhard Fahrbach (1996) and Cesar Caviedes (1975, 1984). This situation is understandable, as the multifaceted impacts of such conditions are often outside the specialized field of expertise of most scholars. Therefore the picture emerging from these studies is incomplete. The use of these fragments of information about such a global system nevertheless demonstrates that the Moche were not only acutely aware of these conditions but integrated the most salient characteristics into their worldview.

Another aspect limiting our understanding of the Moche symbolic system and its relationship with ENSO conditions is that the marine and coastal ecologies of the region may have changed substantially during the last 1,500 years. These changes may hamper our understanding of the local ecology and the relative importance and distribution of certain species during Moche times. Thus even under ideal circumstances it would be difficult to reconstruct the exact conditions that prevailed at the time. In addition to all these limitations, the research on the complex processes involved in these events is relatively recent. Hence the identification of species and description of their behavior must be perceived as approximate and incomplete. With this caveat in mind, the objective of this study is not to provide a natural history of the region under these geoclimatic conditions but to demonstrate that the numerous changes occurring during this period provided the template for the elaboration of a vast symbolic and ideological apparatus.

The Moche symbolic system was largely based on the imperative of embedding the ecological system created by El Niño conditions in the ideological precepts disseminated by the ruling elite, which resulted in a specialized taxonomy relating to specific needs. The Moche's choices for creating such a system may have been unique to them, but such a classificatory system based on largely symbolic and political necessities is not unique. These folk taxonomies elaborated on the basis of very distinct ecologies have been noted among many cultures around the world by diverse scholars, including Claude Lévi-Strauss (1966) (the Americas), Stanley Tambiah (1985) (Southeast Asia), and Marshall Sahlins (1985, 1995) (Polynesia):

> The folk taxonomy is a cultural ontology, comprehending nature in terms set by human relationships and activities. But systematic biology would be the language of nature itself: a nomenclature of the world, each specific name in a one-to-one relation to what there really is—the self-expression of nature in the form of human speech. . . . Accordingly, the folk classifications of plants and animals are integrated with many other aspects of human existence. The categories are factored by their relationships to persons and purposes as socially constituted—to local distinctions of groups and genders, habitats and directions, times and places, modes of production and reproduction, categories of kinship, and concepts of spirit. In brief, the creatures are embedded in a total cosmology from which it is possible to abstract them as things-in-themselves only at the cost of their social identities. (Sahlins 1995: 158–159)

The notion of social identities mentioned by Sahlins is crucial for understanding the demonstration that follows. This taxonomy of necessity may have been predicated on the need to establish a symbolic system dedicated to the formulation of an ideology of power and the legitimation of rulership. The four categories used here to demonstrate the existence of a symbolic system dominated by El Niño are somewhat arbitrary, like any external classification imposed upon an ancient system of representation. They mostly facilitate the description of the subjects. Symbolic systems are governed by rules that often unite fairly disparate subjects: nocturnal habits, voraciousness, or

seasonality. They may also include other unifiers relating to their origin, relative size, and reproductive success. As quickly becomes apparent, a considerable amount of overlap among the species and representations testifies to a certain degree of arbitrariness regarding the four categories but also to the degree of cohesion of Moche iconography. In order to mitigate the loss of "their social identities" by singling them out or putting them into one of the four categories, here I systematically highlight the links that unite them. These links, which are often made by the artists themselves by associating distinct species in the same fineline painting or modeled on the same pot, also act as methodological justifications for the categories and associations created here. In some cases, when the complexity of a scene demonstrates considerable overlap, species that belong to one category (such as "The Newcomers") are described further in another section in order to reduce the degree of arbitrariness created by such categories.

THE NEWCOMERS

As described in more detail in chapter 1, the onset of an El Niño event on the Peruvian north coast is related to changes in the Southern Oscillation (ENSO), which is the entire weather system over the Pacific. When stronger trade winds shift large water masses from the eastern to the western part of the Pacific Ocean, the traditionally cool Humboldt Current and its undercurrent then suffer a change to subtropical or even tropical conditions. The upwelling system that brings nutrients to the surface ceases to perform adequately as the thermocline can no longer be reached, provoking the rapid collapse of the entire food chain and the disappearance of numerous local species. Several animal species accompany this warm current, in many instances literally replacing the local fauna along the Peruvian coast. The information concerning the description and changes brought by an El Niño is mostly drawn from the study of the 1982–1983 episode. This was perhaps the most severe and arguably the most studied ENSO event of the twentieth century:

> Nonetheless, the first indices of radical changes in the region of the Humboldt Current appeared in 1982–83. During December of 1982, the fishers of the central coast of Peru

signaled that the majority of local fish species had disappeared from the area up to 30 m in depth exploited by the artisanal fisheries. Among them, we can mention all the lenguados (*Paralichthys adspersus* and other species), the cojinoba (*Seriolella violacea*), the corvina (*Sciaena gilberti*), and also the pejerrey (*Odonthestes regia regia*) that live close to the surface. Initially these species were replaced solely by borrachitos, small fish that are not sold in the markets. With the progressive warming of the waters occurred a diversified invasion of tropical and subtropical species that lasted in the south of Peru until April 1983 and in the north until the end of ENSO: barrilete (*Katsuwonus pelamis*) and dorado (*Coryphaena hippurus*), sierra (*Scomberomorus maculatus sierra*), and yellowfin tuna (*Thunnus albacares*). . . . Diverse species of sharks (especially hammerheads, *Sphyrna* spp. and shortfin mako sharks, *Isurus oxyrhynchus*), large eagle rays (*Myliobatis* spp.), and manta rays (*Manta hamiltoni*) destroyed fishing nets not designed for capturing such gigantic immigrants. (Arntz and Fahrbach 1996: 138)[1]

In this excerpt Arntz and Fahrbach highlight the dramatic changes taking place in Peruvian waters. These tropical waters caused the disappearance of numerous local species and brought with them a number of foreign species in the vicinity of the Peruvian north coast, including large rays, schools of sharks, sea turtles, and large swimming crabs. Certain species in this foreign fauna would have served as powerful tropes for the symbolization of El Niño conditions and, I suggest, were the animals that the Moche selected to depict.

Eagle Rays

Arntz and Fahrbach (1996) mention that some of the most prominent creatures to make their appearance on the local scene are species of rays. A particular species of eagle ray, *Myliobatis peruvianus*, becomes much more abundant during the ENSO conditions. While this species exists in Peruvian waters under normal conditions, the Peruvian eagle ray has only been recorded in the open ocean over the continental shelf and slope. This region was clearly beyond the reach of Moche fishers. The appearance of the fish in the benthic waters along the north coast would have been a clear marker of the changing climatic and oceanic conditions. Their behavior during ENSO events, and even during regular conditions, is poorly known to say the least. But perhaps in El Niño

conditions the rays are driven closer to the coast in their quest for food. During the 1982–1983 event, Peruvian eagle rays were apparently much more abundant and were clearly associated with manta rays, which are species from tropical waters.

Three species of ray are identifiable in the iconography, including the Peruvian eagle ray, Pacific cownose ray, and manta ray. The cownose ray and manta ray clearly pertain to tropical currents. The Peruvian eagle ray is by far the most widely depicted of the group, so I begin this section by addressing this particular ocean creature.

The rays in general, and above all the Peruvian eagle ray, may be the single most important subject to index marine representations and their association with ENSO conditions. Moche artists have clearly shown these species on numerous vessels. In figure 5.3, the general shape of the stingray is depicted very accurately: the pectoral fin is expanded and covers most of the small pelvic fins located on each side of the tail. Eagle rays can measure up to 1.8 m in length, including the tail. On the vessel, only the long whip-like tail has been proportionately shortened. The quadrangular shape of the mouth of the ray is also precisely depicted just above the human face (fig. 5.4). This design is slightly more complex: the mouth of the ray also creates an additional feature on the forehead of the individual. The significance of this human face and its decorations including the design on the forehead is explored in chapter 7, but for now I would only suggest that it highlights the importance of the eagle ray.

The upper body of the stingray is decorated with two aquatic birds, three octopuses (the suckers are visible on the one painted on the head of the fish), and two stingrays, one on each wing (fig. 5.3). Although the general form of the eagle ray has been respected on the paintings, the head of the animal has been transformed into a frontal mask. These paintings are of great importance because they clearly establish that the stingrays depicted in this format in other fineline paintings in fact represent an eagle ray and not some other yet unidentified species. For example, in one rather crudely made Phase III painting, a fanged being stands in a reed boat located in front of an oversized eagle ray (fig. 5.5). He holds a fishing net in his right hand and an additional eagle ray in his left. His tunic is decorated with a double spiral

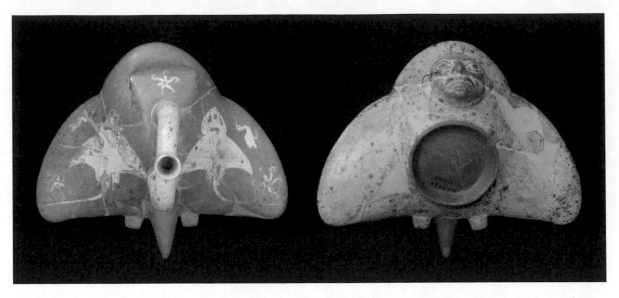

FIGURE 5.3. Stingray (*Myliobatis peruvianus*) with a human face. Phase III. Museo Nacional de Arqueología, Antropología e Historia del Perú. Inv. no. C-54484.

FIGURE 5.4. Detail of a stingray with a human face. Museo Nacional de Arqueología, Antropología e Historia del Perú. Inv. no. C-54484.

FIGURE 5.5. Painting of a fanged being in a boat and a stingray. Drawing by Donna McClelland. The Christopher B. Donnan and Donna McClelland Moche Archive, Image Collections and Fieldwork Archives, Dumbarton Oaks, Trustees for Harvard University, Washington, DC.

FIGURE 5.6. Section of a Huaca Cao Viejo mural showing stylized rays and catfishes.

of interlocking rays. Therefore the main activity depicted here is the netting of eagle rays by this being. The design on his garment may have been based on the eagle ray as well, especially since the triangular form recalls the shape of the fish. Interestingly, a similar motif has been found on an impressive mural from Huaca Cao Viejo (fig. 5.6). It highlights the importance of this motif but also shows that the same design was seen fit to cover somewhat indiscriminately the body of a fanged being or the walls of a huaca. This stingray also represents an important marker for the identification of additional marine species.

Pacific Cownose Rays

The Pacific cownose ray (*Rhinoptera steindachneri*) is a member of the Rhinopteridae family and indubitably accompanies El Niño sea currents. Once more the Moche have faithfully captured the form, especially the rectangular head with the median notch just below the forehead

(fig. 5.7). Apart from this representation, the role of this ray is unclear. Its general form is similar to that of the eagle ray, so it is possible that the rays participate in the same symbolism. In the best ceramic examples, the two species were nevertheless clearly recognized and separately considered by the Moche.

Manta Rays

The third type of ray, which also makes its appearance with the El Niño oceanic current, is represented by two closely related species, *Manta hamiltoni* and *Mobula lucasana* (Arntz and Fahrbach 1996; Valdivia and Arntz 1985). The manta rays are the largest of the rays. They can measure more than 7 m across their pectoral fins and reach a weight of nearly 3,000 kg. On the bottle presented in figure 5.8, the manta ray is located near the tail of the boat-fish just underneath the right hand of the paddler. The general form of the fish has been well reproduced, especially the broad head laterally

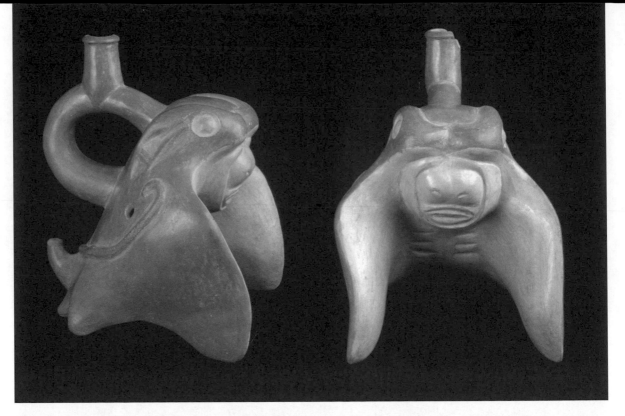

FIGURE 5.7. Modeled stirrup spout bottle in the shape of a Pacific cownose ray (*Rhinoptera steindachneri*). Private collection. Photograph by Christopher B. Donnan.

FIGURE 5.8. Man sitting in a boat in the shape of a borracho fish (*Scartichthys gigas*). Wereldmuseum, Rotterdam. Inv. no. 71625. Photograph by Edward de Bock.

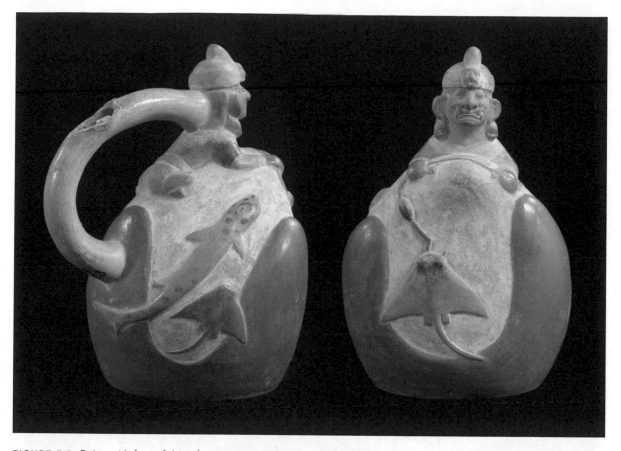

FIGURE 5.9. Being with fangs fishing for a stingray and surrounded by a second ray and a shark. Staatliche Museen zu Berlin, Preußischer Kulturbesitz—Ethnologisches Museum, VA 18023.

connected to cephalic fins. This family of ray is not as extensively represented as the eagle ray. Perhaps the main reason is that manta rays feed exclusively on plankton and consequently cannot be captured at the end of a fishing line. The manta ray nonetheless is accurately depicted and would have been included in the overall symbolism associated with these cartilaginous fishes. Like their natural counterparts, when rendered in sculpture these rays are faithfully depicted with a dark dorsal and a lighter ventral surface.

Sharks

Sharks also visit the region with the El Niño current. They are represented by a number of different species. In the iconography, sharks are often shown on the same vessel in conjunction with eagle rays or Pacific cownose rays, establishing a clear association not only between these species but also with the oceanic conditions that bring such creatures together along the north coast of

Peru. Consequently, the presence of these rays indicates that the whole context presented on the ceramic vessel pertains to El Niño conditions. The shark was used extensively as an ecological marker. Therefore it can equally be used to elucidate the identity of other animal species. This important methodology is employed throughout this survey.

On the frontal part of the bottle in figure 5.9, a being with supernatural attributes is capturing an eagle ray at the end of a fishing line. To the right of this being, a shark is located directly on top of a second eagle ray. Therefore the presence of the eagle rays indicates that the marine scene is related to the warmer seas and the near tropical conditions of an El Niño event. Thus this shark must also appear on the coast of Peru during these conditions. Although it is much more difficult to ascertain the exact species depicted, the head of the shark and the small dorsal fin located near the tail may represent the bluntnose sevengill shark (*Notorynchus maculatus*), a species locally known as the *gatita*. This large shark, which can measure

FIGURE 5.10. Osprey (*Pandion haliaetus*) capturing a shark. Museo Nacional de Arqueología, Antropología e Historia del Perú. Inv. no. C-54501.

up to 3 m in length and weigh more than 100 kg, has a broad head and a characteristically short and blunt nose. The dorsal fin is located far back on the body of the fish. This opportunistic feeder is potentially dangerous to humans.

In figure 5.10, what appears to be an osprey (*Pandion haliaetus*) is seizing another species of shark in its claws. The dark spots and the same general shape may indicate two different species: the tiger shark (*Galeocerdo cuvier*) and the whale shark (*Rhincodon typus*). Both species may appear near the Peruvian coast during El Niño conditions. Their sizes and feeding habits are markedly different. Tiger sharks are large and aggressive. They can measure nearly 9 m long and reach a weight of 800 kg. The whale shark is much bigger, reaching a length of nearly 13 m and weighing as much as 35,000 kg but poses no threat to human beings. This shark is a filter-feeding fish subsisting

exclusively on plankton and small fishes. The relative sizes of the osprey and the shark in this scene, be it a whale shark or a tiger shark, are of course disproportionate. But such a hierarchy of scale was probably established to emphasize the notion of capture by the osprey, which usually captures fish after hovering and clasps the prey in its claws in such a fashion.

The presence of sharks and stingrays depicted alongside complex iconographic contexts may indicate that the ensemble as a whole relates to the El Niño warm current and not the normal Humboldt Current. This is of critical importance, as scenes in maritime settings have usually been associated with the generic context of north coast conditions. For example, the *totora* boats that are frequently depicted have often been likened to their modern-day counterparts, suggesting that the events represented took place during the normal ecological conditions of the north coast (Benson 1972; Donnan 1978). Consequently, the presence of an eagle ray and a shark lying just behind the paddler of the example in figure 5.11 is clearly indicative of the relations between the paddler and a warm ocean. Concerning this vessel, it must be stated that the relative sizes of the subjects are not representative of their real dimensions. Given the limitation of this mode of representation, the Moche rarely adhere to these rules.

Most fineline paintings that depict boat scenes also show a ray similar to those painted on the eagle ray presented at the beginning of this section (figs. 5.3, 5.12). It is therefore likely that the intent of representing these painted examples on the perfectly modeled eagle ray was to indicate that regardless of the representational techniques both belonged to the same species and indicated the same oceanic conditions.

Swimming Crabs

Scores of swimming crabs are another important immigrant species to the north coast. During the 1982–1983 El Niño event, four different species of swimming crabs were recorded: *Euphylax robustus*, *Portunus acuminatus*, *Portunus asper*, and *Callinectes arcuatus* (Arntz and Valdivia 1985). These crustaceans can easily be identified by the fifth pair of legs that are flattened into paddles for swimming (fig. 5.13). These gigantic crabs normally live in great numbers in the warmer waters of Ecuador and Colombia. On the north coast, during severe El Niño events, most local species of crabs are severely depleted. In some cases thousands of dead crabs cover the beaches in thick layers.

Swimming crabs are faithfully reproduced in gold as ornaments, indicating the importance of this type of representation for Moche rulers. For

FIGURE 5.11. Boatman carrying a shark and a ray. Linden-Museum, Stuttgart. Inv. no. 53253.

FIGURE 5.12. Anthropomorphized duck and being with fangs capturing a ray and a borracho fish. Drawing by Donna McClelland. The Christopher B. Donnan and Donna McClelland Moche Archive, Image Collections and Fieldwork Archives, Dumbarton Oaks, Trustees for Harvard University, Washington, DC.

FIGURE 5.13. Swimming crab. Museo Larco, Lima, Peru. Inv. no. ML012859.

example, two nose ornaments from the looted tomb of La Mina in the Jequetepeque Valley were exquisitely chiseled and formed in the shape of two distinct species of swimming crabs: *Callinectes toxotes* (fig. 5.14), and *Euphylax dovii* (fig. 5.15).

Numerous other metallic artifacts found in this tomb by the looters and now in private collections were adorned with or took the form of animal species related to the present study. It is not clear why at least two nose ornaments depicting

FIGURE 5.14. Nose ornament in the shape of a swimming crab (*Callinectes toxotes*). Private collection. Photograph by Christopher B. Donnan.

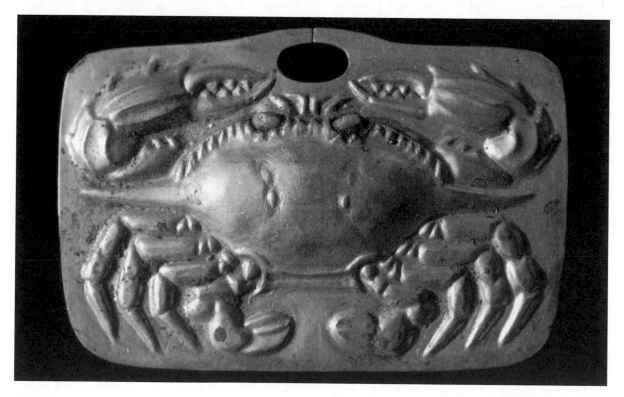

FIGURE 5.15. Nose ornament in the shape of a swimming crab (*Euphylax dovii*). Private collection. Photograph by Christopher B. Donnan.

two distinct species of swimming crabs were made for this high-ranking individual. Nevertheless, it demonstrates the importance of each species for the elite and the degree of precision that could sometimes be achieved by Moche artisans.

Figure 5.16 shows a fanged being in the form of a crab. The posterior legs of the crustacean have been transformed into human legs, and it holds an eagle ray at the end of a fishing line. Once more the stingray marks the scene as being related to El Niño conditions. In this example the general shape of the crab's shell is markedly different from that of the two species of swimming crabs presented earlier. It is not clear what species of crab the fanged being is supposed to embody. In the fineline paintings such as this one showing a battle between two fanged beings, the form of the shells is usually much more consistent with a distinct group resembling the swimming crabs (fig. 5.17).

Lobster and Shrimp

A second species of crustacean that makes it way along the Peruvian coast in the warm sea current is the green spiny lobster (*Panulirus gracilis*). The carapace of this large crustacean can measure up to 32 cm in length. It has no claws and possesses five pairs of walking limbs.

The beautifully modeled crustacean in figure 5.18 is clearly a faithful rendition of a green spiny lobster. Although no absolutely diagnostic attribute could be singled out, the features and form are meticulously rendered. The crustacean species is more ambiguous in its anthropomorphized form (fig. 5.19). In this case, the fanged being has human legs and arms but has claws instead of hands. The general form of the body resembles more closely the body of two species of shrimp that also invade the region in massive numbers during ENSO conditions: *Xiphopenaeus riveti* and *Penaeus* sp. (Arntz and Fahrbach 1996: 130–133). The position of the subject and the headdress with a V-shaped diadem are identical to those of the crab presented earlier, indicating that they probably refer to the same type of individual in different animal forms (fig. 5.16). Paired vessels depicting a crab on one and a shrimp or a lobster on the other have been found in Tomb 2 at Huaca el Pueblo and in a number of burials at Sipán,

indicating that the two species are conceptually perceived as related subjects.

Sea Turtle

The leatherback turtle (*Dermochelys coriacea*) is also a marine animal rarely seen in Peruvian waters. This is the biggest species of turtle in the world. During an El Niño event, the leatherback turtle extends its range to the south and is seen with a certain regularity on the Peruvian north coast (Arntz and Farhbach 1996: 200).

In the iconography, the turtle species can usually be recognized by the seven diagnostic ridges running in parallel lines along its shell and in some cases also by a series of white dots that closely resemble the markings on the back of the animal (fig. 5.20). The adults average 1.35 m to nearly 1.8 m in carapace length and weigh from 290 to 540 kg. The shell of the reptile is either black or bluish-black with small white and yellowish spots. The belly is cream-colored or whitish. Figure 5.20 faithfully reflects all these characteristics. The overall shape of the shell in figure 5.21 adopts the form of the shell of the leatherback turtle more closely. Although the outer surface of the shell is now completely white, it may have been painted with a fugitive paint that has now disappeared.

Puffer Fish

The last subject in this category is probably the most difficult to identify conclusively. It is nonetheless important, because it is directly associated with the depiction of sacrificial victims. On this Phase III example in figure 5.22, the fish is modeled on top of the bottle, with smaller ones interspersed among the sacrificial victims. The headless victims are warriors with metallic backflaps dangling between their legs. The quadrangular design depicted on the head of the fish may refer to a fishing net. The semicircular "apron" located just below the head of the fish is unusual and has not been found on any of the species consulted. But the round form of the body, the globular eyes, and the dots may refer to the genus *Sphoeroides*. In figure 5.23 the same type of fish is repeated in a similar context. The main difference is that the

FIGURE 5.16. (*Above*) Being with fangs in the form of a crab fishing for a stingray. Museo Nacional de Arqueología, Antropología e Historia del Perú. Inv. no. C-03257.

FIGURE 5.17. (*Below*) Battle between two fanged beings. The subject to the right has the body of a crab. Drawing by Donna McClelland. The Christopher B. Donnan and Donna McClelland Moche Archive, Image Collections and Fieldwork Archives, Dumbarton Oaks, Trustees for Harvard University, Washington, DC.

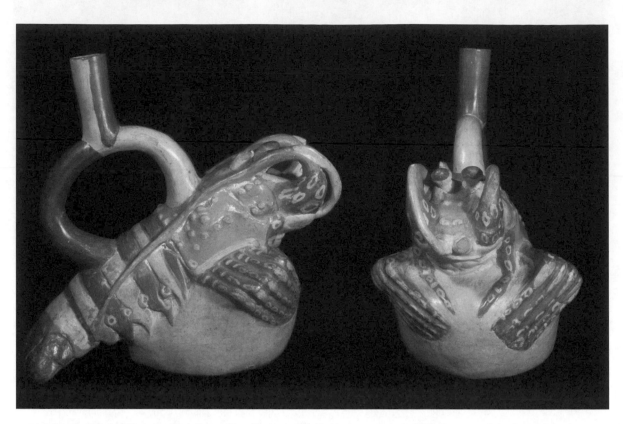

FIGURE 5.18. (*Above*) Green spiny lobster (*Panulirus gracilis*). By kind permission of the Trustees of the British Museum, London. Am1939,-.5.

FIGURE 5.19. (*Below*) Being with fangs in the form of a crustacean. Museo Nacional de Arqueología, Antropología e Historia del Perú. Inv. no. C-01330.

FIGURE 5.20. Leatherback turtle (*Dermochelys coriacea*). Museo Nacional de Arqueología, Antropología e Historia del Perú. Inv. no. C-01493.

FIGURE 5.21. Leatherback turtle. Museo Nacional de Arqueología, Antropología e Historia del Perú. Inv. no. C-01547.

FIGURE 5.22. Puffer fishes and sacrificial victims. Museo de Arqueología, Antropología e Historia, Universidad Nacional de Trujillo.

FIGURE 5.23. Puffer fishes (genus *Sphoeroides*) and captives. The Art Institute of Chicago (Gift of Nathan Cummings, 1957.402).

fish are not surrounded by headless victims but by warriors with their hair tied into a topknot.

The third example (fig. 5.24) highlights the importance of the puffer fish in relation to the El Niño conditions. Right above the animals, a fanged being is capturing the fish at the end of a long fishing line. Surrounding this activity are one dead seabird, two sea lions, an eagle ray, an octopus, three limpets, and two human beings wielding clubs (fig. 5.25). The eagle ray once more signals that the situation is related to the El Niño sea current. This bottle is in many respects similar to a bottle (fig. 5.59, discussed later) depicting an individual fishing for an eagle ray surrounded by some of the same animals. This demonstrates that an eagle ray and a puffer fish are nearly interchangeable as catch and carry the same symbolical charge.

The identification of these subjects provides a drastically revised outlook on Moche iconography (table 5.1). Two additional subjects—the snowy egret and the muscovy duck—are discussed in the section on the local species helped by El Niño conditions because of their level of interaction with the local fauna.

The species presented in this section suggest that the El Niño phenomenon provided the template for the symbolic system depicted by these representations. The totality of the maritime scenes of Moche iconography can no longer be considered to depict the natural conditions of the Peruvian north coast. The ritual significance of some of these subjects with the practice of ceremonial combat and human sacrifice suggested by the human subjects depicted in figures 5.3, 5.22, and 5.23 is explored later in the chapter.

FROM THE NORTHERN REGION

In addition to the sea animals that migrate down the coast in association with the northern tropical currents, an additional group of exotic subjects is extensively depicted. These tropical animals—iguanas, monkeys, mollusks, and parrots—probably do not accompany El Niño oceanic currents, as they apparently do not migrate as far south as the Moche region. But because they live in northern Peru or southern Ecuador, the general area from which the El Niño current originated upon reaching the coast, these animals

shared an analogous symbolism. They would have been brought from the north by humans into the Moche region.

Iguanas

The first subject with a northern provenance is the iguana, already alluded to earlier. Three species could have inspired the Moche: the marine iguana (*Amblyrhynchus cristatus*) and two species of land iguanas (*Conolophus subcristatus* and *Conolophus pallidus*). Iguanas generally are found only in the tropical or subtropical conditions to the north.

An iguana figure is extensively represented in Moche iconography and is usually associated with a fanged being wearing a snake belt. As a pair, they perform a number of ritual activities, such as offering conch shells, battles against other beings with supernatural attributes, and the Mountain Sacrifice (figs. 5.26, 5.27, 5.28). In figure 5.28, Iguana, wearing its ubiquitous condor headdress, is standing to the left side of the central peak and holding a bulbous club. The fanged being is on the other side of the same peak. Between the two subjects, a victim is about to fall down. An already dismembered individual is lying on the ground, at the base of the foothill. The Mountain Sacrifice is one of the most important sacrificial rituals of the iconography. Its significance for Moche cosmology and rulership is discussed in chapter 7, but for now it highlights the important role of a northern tropical species in the Moche sacrificial system.

The theme of warfare is also associated with the iguana, which in some cases is depicted in the process of devouring a warrior, which it firmly holds in its claws (fig. 5.29). This supports my overarching argument in this chapter that ceremonial combat and human sacrifice are key elements closely associated with the broad concept of El Niño. Iguana is also regularly depicted in a seated position with its hands clasped together (fig. 5.30). He can be represented alone but in this posture is usually witnessing an activity performed by Wrinkle Face, such as a scene of copulation (fig. 5.31). Iguana is depicted immediately to the left of the couple in the company of a mammal. Monkeys populate the tree above the couple—another subject from the northern region described later.

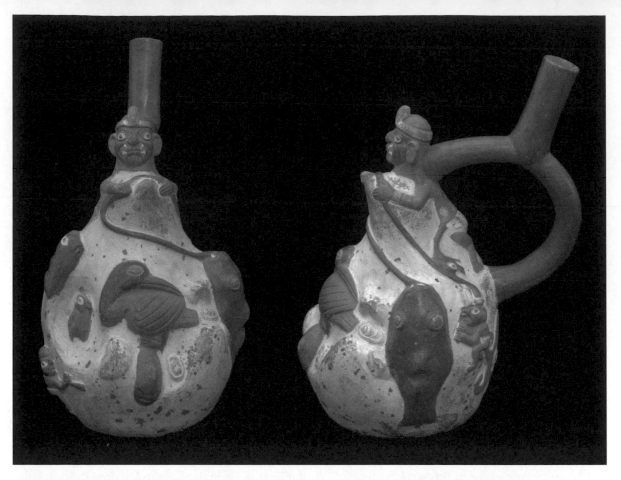

FIGURE 5.24. Fanged being fishing for a puffer fish, view A. Museo Larco, Lima, Peru. Inv. no. ML013002.

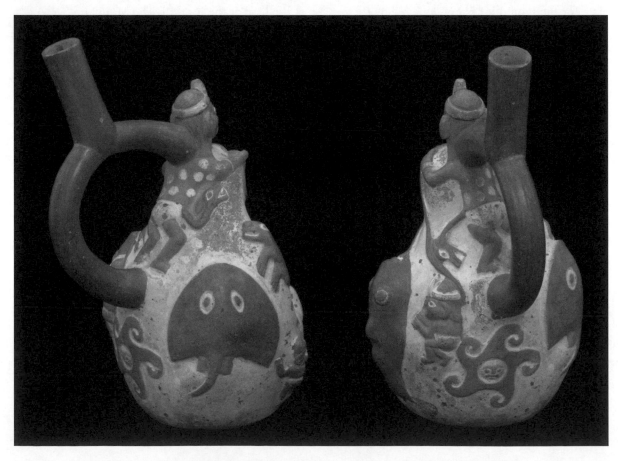

FIGURE 5.25. Fanged being fishing for a puffer fish, view B. Museo Larco, Lima, Peru. Inv. no. ML013002.

Table 5.1. Animal Species Associated with El Niño Conditions

Eagle ray	*Myliobatis peruvianus*
Manta ray	*Manta hamiltoni, Mobula lucasana*
Pacific cownose ray	*Rhinoptera steindachneri*
Sevengill shark	*Notorynchus maculatus*
Shark	*Galeocerdo cuvieri, Rhincodon typus*
Swimming crab	*Euphylax robustus, Portunus acuminatus, Portunus asper, Callinectes arcuatus*
Green spiny lobster	*Panulirus gracilis*
Shrimp	*Xiphopenaeus riveti, Penaeus* sp.
Leatherback turtle	*Dermochelys coriacea*
Puffer fish	*Sphoeroides* sp.
Snowy egret	*Egretta thula*
Muscovy duck	*Cairina moschata*

FIGURE 5.26. (*Below, top*) Being with fangs presenting a *Strombus* seashell (*Strombus galeatus*) to a high-ranking individual. Drawing by Donna McClelland. The Christopher B. Donnan and Donna McClelland Moche Archive, Image Collections and Fieldwork Archives, Dumbarton Oaks, Trustees for Harvard University, Washington, DC.

FIGURE 5.27. (*Below, bottom*) Battle between fanged beings. Drawing by Donna McClelland. The Christopher B. Donnan and Donna McClelland Moche Archive, Image Collections and Fieldwork Archives, Dumbarton Oaks, Trustees for Harvard University, Washington, DC.

FIGURE 5.28. Mountain Sacrifice. Museo Nacional de Arqueología, Antropología e Historia del Perú. Inv. no. C-54716.

FIGURE 5.29. Iguana capturing a warrior. Museo Nacional de Arqueología, Antropología e Historia del Perú. Inv. no. C-54692.

FIGURE 5.30. (*Right*) Anthropomorphized iguana. Museo Cassinelli, Trujillo. Photograph by Christopher B. Donnan.

FIGURE 5.31. (*Below*) Fineline painting of a Copulation Ceremony. Drawing by Donna McClelland. The Christopher B. Donnan and Donna McClelland Moche Archive, Image Collections and Fieldwork Archives, Dumbarton Oaks, Trustees for Harvard University, Washington, DC.

Strombus

The second subject in this section is *Strombus galeatus*. These mollusks inhabiting these shells live in the warm seas along the coast of Ecuador. Together with thorny oysters, the massive conch shells have been imported into the north coast region of Peru since at least 500 BC (Paulsen 1974). The discovery of *Strombus* shells fashioned into trumpets at Formative Period sites such as Chavín de Huántar and Kuntur Wasi and the representation of these shells in Chavín and Cupisnique art suggest that the Moche built part of their ritual ecology on a much older tradition.

In contrast to the Formative Period examples, the *Strombus* shells are fairly rare in Moche archaeological assemblages. Nevertheless, the Moche made numerous ceramic examples (fig. 5.32), which (like the real examples from Chavín and Kuntur Wasi) are in fact musical instruments: trumpets. The mouthpiece is situated at the end and the internal spires of the natural shell are accurately reproduced.

Perhaps because of the ancient usage of *Strombus* shells as trumpets on the north coast, these objects are among the most symbolically charged Moche ritual paraphernalia. In many Moche visual scenes, human beings with supernatural attributes are literally emerging from the shell trumpets as if the sound produced by these musical instruments might in some way be associated with their emergence (fig. 5.33). Shell trumpet players are also depicted in association with some of the most complex scenes of the iconography. In a fineline painting on a flaring bowl, the musicians stand in the middle of a battlefield (figs. 5.34, 5.35). The sound of the conch trumpets not only accompanies the capture of the warriors but can also be heard during the sacrifices themselves. The conch shell trumpet player is standing on top of a bottle in figure 5.36. As he is playing his instrument, an elaborate scene of human sacrifice is taking place just underneath (fig. 5.37). This early Phase IV rendition of the Sacrifice Ceremony depicts an anthropomorphized bat on the left bleeding a prisoner and collecting his blood in a cup. To the right two human beings with supernatural attributes are exchanging a goblet. The importance of the conch shell trumpet and the sound it pro-

duces cannot be overestimated: they play a central role in the most prominent rituals, especially those relating to ceremonial combat and human sacrifice.

Finally, the *Strombus* shell trumpet is consistently represented in the hands of beings with supernatural attributes (fig. 5.38). The conch shells may be offered by Wrinkle Face and Iguana to a high-ranking individual seated inside a building (figure 5.26). This scene, which dates to the Phase IV stylistic period, is part of the Burial Theme, one of the most elaborate fineline paintings in Phase V (fig. 5.39) (Donnan and McClelland 1979). The offering of shells takes place inside the building to the left of the representation. I have suggested (Bourget 2006) that the offering of conch shells was part of a reinstatement ritual in the afterworld of a recently deceased ruler. Both the *Strombus* shell and the fanged being probably originated from the Late Formative Period. By delving into more ancient traditions, their presence in these rituals would, among other things, serve to legitimate the ritual actions and those taking part in them.

Conus

Like *Strombus*, another species of univalve is sometimes represented with a being with fangs located in it (fig. 5.40). I identify this as *Conus fergusoni*. Just underneath the leg of this *Conus* being is a *Strombus* inhabited by a fox (fig. 5.41). Although *Conus* is not as prominent in the iconography as *Strombus*, whole shells have been found in large numbers in high-ranking burials and have been used extensively to inlay objects and to fashion pectorals.

Spondylus

An additional marine shell, the thorny oyster (*Spondylus* sp.), forms also part of this contingent of marine shells from the coastline north of Moche territories. This bivalve is not present in the cold Humboldt Current. Like *Strombus* and *Conus*, it is only found in the tropical waters along the Ecuadorian coast, north of the Santa Elena Peninsula. Surprisingly, *Spondylus* shells are seemingly not represented in the iconography before

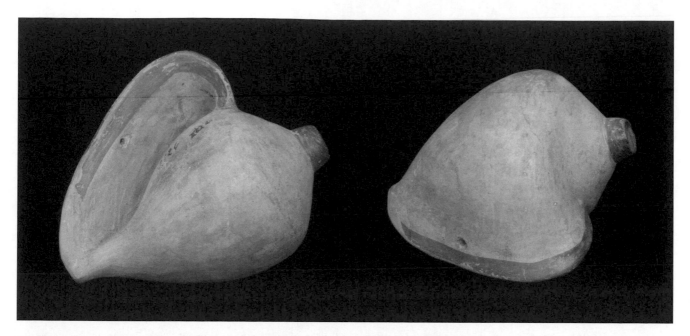

FIGURE 5.32. Trumpet in the form of a *Strombus* seashell. Museo Nacional de Arqueología, Antropología e Historia del Perú. Inv. no. MNAAH 1-2622.

FIGURE 5.33. Being with fangs inside a *Strombus* seashell. Museo Larco, Lima, Peru. Inv. no. ML003208.

FIGURE 5.34. Flaring bowl with scenes of ceremonial combat and capture. Museo Amano, Lima. Photograph by Christopher B. Donnan.

FIGURE 5.35. Ceremonial combat and capture. Drawing by Donna McClelland. The Christopher B. Donnan and Donna McClelland Moche Archive, Image Collections and Fieldwork Archives, Dumbarton Oaks, Trustees for Harvard University, Washington, DC.

FIGURE 5.36. Musician standing on top of a Sacrifice Ceremony. Museo Nacional de Arqueología, Antropología e Historia del Perú. Inv. no. C-03315.

FIGURE 5.37. Sacrifice Ceremony. Drawing by Donna McClelland. The Christopher B. Donnan and Donna McClelland Moche Archive, Image Collections and Fieldwork Archives, Dumbarton Oaks, Trustees for Harvard University, Washington, DC.

FIGURE 5.38. Fanged being holding a *Strombus* shell trumpet. Linden-Museum, Stuttgart. Inv. no. M 30.163.

FIGURE 5.39. Burial Theme. Drawing by Donna McClelland. The Christopher B. Donnan and Donna McClelland Moche Archive, Image Collections and Fieldwork Archives, Dumbarton Oaks, Trustees for Harvard University, Washington, DC.

FIGURE 5.40. Being with fangs inside a *Conus* seashell (*Conus fergusoni*). Museo Nacional de Arqueología, Antropología e Historia del Perú. Inv. no. C-04395.

FIGURE 5.41. Being with fangs inside a *Conus* seashell. Drawing by Steve Bourget. Museo Nacional de Arqueología, Antropología e Historia del Perú. Inv. no. C-04395.

the end of Phase V (fig. 5.42), but Moche artisans made extensive use of two species—*Spondylus cal-cifer* and *Spondylus princeps*—along with *Conus* to make beads for bracelets and large pectorals and for inlays in intricate objects. Whole *Spondylus* and *Conus* seashells also frequently have been found in high-status burials (Alva and Donnan 1993). The trading system that brought *Spondylus, Strombus,* and *Conus* to the north coast was already well established in the Preceramic Period (3000–1800 BCE) and became extremely important for the Chimú during the Late Intermediate Period (900–1460 CE) (Paulsen 1974; Pillsbury 1996). Although the inclusion of *Spondylus* in this chapter may not appear to be fully justified because of its absence

from most of Moche iconography, it is important to note that all the jewelry and regalia made from these red seashells for high-ranking individuals would have been immediately recognizable by the Moche as pertaining to the genus. Therefore its presence was probably ubiquitous and added a symbolic charge to the objects that it adorned.

Monkeys and Cerithium

The trade system established from an early date with the north probably led to the introduction of monkeys on the coast. The exact origin of these primates is unclear, but they may have been brought from southern Ecuador. Monkeys are rarely represented in the iconography in their natural state. The general look of the primate corresponds to spider monkeys (*Ateles*), with facial features closely resembling those of the brown-headed spider monkey (*Ateles fusciceps*) (fig. 5.43). The monkey figures are most often depicted with human attributes and clothes: resting their heads on a jar (fig. 5.44), holding fruits or *Nectandra* seeds (fig. 5.45), collecting *ulluchu* fruits in the tree above the Copulation Ceremony (fig. 5.31), or even in the guise of a coca taker (fig. 5.46). It is notable that the coca taker relates directly to activities of ceremonial combat and sacrifice initiated at least during Phase III. The correspondence of the monkey form with coca takers thus implies the association of monkeys with these activities.

Two examples of ceramic monkey representations form a pair that may have been looted from the same burial (fig. 5.47). They represent two monkeys in the shape of tubers. The subject painted in a cream color has a painted lock of hair on its forehead and disk ear ornaments. These elements are consistent with captured warriors depicted in Phase III, an additional indication that monkeys are clearly related to this ritual activity. A blackware bottle in the general shape of a tuber

also depicts monkeys (fig. 5.48). On the summit of this exceptional piece rests a tuber-monkey dominating a group consisting of (from right to left) an iguana, an additional monkey with a bag, and a coca taker. The presence of an iguana and a monkey together on the same vessel supports the suggestion that they can be listed under the same category.

The monkey and the skeleton-monkey could also be seen inhabiting the shell of a land snail (fig. 5.49) or a sea snail (*Cerithium*) (fig. 5.50). In line with *Strombus*, *Conus*, and the limpet (discussed later: see fig. 5.71), the *Cerithium* seashell can also be occupied by a fanged being (fig. 5.51). The sea snail inhabits tropical waters and during ENSO extends its range to the Peruvian north coast. Shells of this mollusk have been found at Sipán, reinforcing their archaeological relevance.

Much more could be said about monkeys, but one final example suffices to show the range of activities and situations involving monkeys. It depicts a simian in the guise of a skeleton carrying a dead deer on its back (fig. 5.52). This scene thus links monkeys to the whole range of activities associated with the trilogy of warfare, capture, and sacrifice but also with the broader concept of death.

FIGURE 5.42. *Spondylus* being. Drawing by Donna McClelland. The Christopher B. Donnan and Donna McClelland Moche Archive, Image Collections and Fieldwork Archives, Dumbarton Oaks, Trustees for Harvard University, Washington, DC.

FIGURE 5.43. Spider monkey (*Ateles fusciceps*) holding a fruit in its paw. Museo Nacional de Arqueología, Antropología e Historia del Perú. Inv. no. C-01200.

FIGURE 5.44. Anthropomorphized monkey resting its head on a jar. Museo Nacional de Arqueología, Antropología e Historia del Perú. Inv. no. 1-2567.

FIGURE 5.45. Anthropomorphized monkey holding *Nectandra* seeds. Museo Nacional de Arqueología, Antropología e Historia del Perú. Inv. no. C-63270.

FIGURE 5.46. Coca taker in the form of an anthropomorphized monkey. Museo Nacional de Arqueología, Antropología e Historia del Perú. Inv. no. C-01221.

FIGURE 5.47. Monkeys taking the form of tubers. Museo Nacional de Arqueología, Antropología e Historia del Perú. Inv. nos. C-01184, C-01186.

FIGURE 5.48. Bottle in the form of a tuber with monkeys, a coca taker, and an iguana. Museo Nacional de Arqueología, Antropología e Historia del Perú. Inv. no. C-03085.

FIGURE 5.49. Monkey inside a land snail. Museo Larco, Lima, Peru. Inv. no. ML003876.

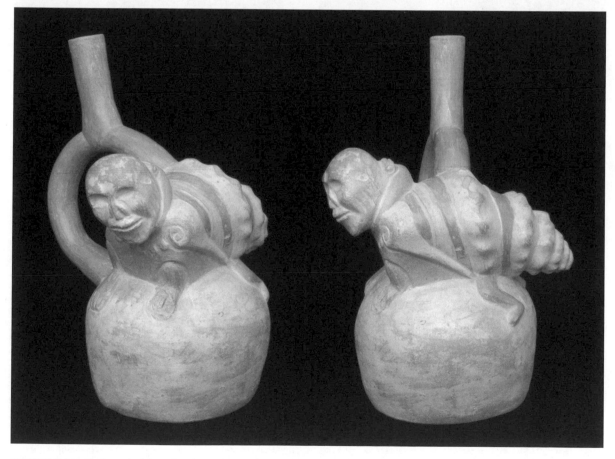

FIGURE 5.50. Skeleton inside a *Cerithium*. Museo Larco, Lima, Peru. Inv. no. ML003870.

FIGURE 5.51. Fanged being inside a *Cerithium*. Courtesy of the Division of Anthropology, American Museum of Natural History, New York. Inv. no. 41.2/7430.

FIGURE 5.52. Skeletonized monkey carrying a deer. Museo Nacional de Arqueología, Antropología e Historia del Perú. Inv. no. C-55074.

The monkey is an alter ego for humans in the iconography, at least for those involved in Moche ritualism. Monkeys do ancillary activities: they do not engage fully in the Burial Theme, take part in battle, or directly hunt deer, but they hold funerary offerings, collect the *ulluchu* for blood sacrifice, carry deer, partake in the coca ritual, and stand as sacrificial victims. Under the skin of their head lurks a human cranium.

Parrots

Species of parrots would also have been obtained from the northern regions, probably through the same trade routes. The naturalistic example of a parrot in figure 5.53 was unearthed on the western platform of the Huaca el Pueblo main monumental structure. The shape of the head, beak, and tail of this sculpture are very similar to those of the macaw (*Ara* sp.). The recess marking each side of the head around the eyes may have been created to highlight the bare facial skin of macaws. These large, long-tailed, and colorful parrots are found in the northern subtropical forests and in the Ecuadorian lowlands (Ridgely and Greenfield 2001). In the iconography, parrots are often shown using their dexterous feet to hold onto corncobs while nibbling at the kernels (fig. 5.54). The exact species represented is difficult to ascertain. But the remains of six birds were found distributed in four tombs at the site of Dos Cabezas (Donnan 2007). Four of the skeletons were probably those of military macaws (*Ara* cf. *militaris*) and the other two of the yellow-lored Amazon macaw (*Amazona* sp.) (Wake 2007). Tomb 2 contained the remains of two of these macaws as well as a double-chambered whistling bottle in the shape of a macaw's head (fig. 5.55). The general shape of the head and the semicircular striations between the eye and the beak mimic very convincingly the facial design of the real military macaw, with its white skin and lines of small black feathers.

Notwithstanding their relative scarcity in the iconography, parrots are clearly linked to ceremonial combat when they appear in complex scenes or unnaturalistic modeled forms. The summit of one stirrup spout bottle takes the form of a human cranium wearing a warrior headdress (fig. 5.56). The body painted on the bottle is that of a parrot grasping a corncob. Therefore the treatment of this subject is similar to the monkey-skeleton (fig. 5.52): the cranium of a human associated with the body of an animal. This tension between human and animal appears to be depicted in a portrait vessel (fig. 5.57). The headdress and the cranium of the warrior recall the images of figure 5.56 and also the protruding orbits of monkeys. Thus this complex portrait includes human, simian, and death features that could refer to parrot symbolism. In addition, the noses of subjects display facial lesions (leishmaniasis). This additional aspect is discussed later in the chapter.

Parrots are also shown in the midst of an encounter between two pairs of bearded individuals (fig. 5.58). The individuals depicted on this Phase III bottle pertain to the Coca Ceremony. Therefore the birds, like the monkey and other animal species presented in this chapter, relate to this ritual activity and to the trilogy of warfare, capture, and sacrifice (table 5.2).

Most of the subjects identified in the first two categories formed a central part of Moche symbolism. Their presence (most notably that of the eagle ray and to a lesser degree the shark and the puffer fish) in other scenes alongside species of local origin further documents their crucial importance for our understanding of this symbolic system.

LOCAL SPECIES DISTURBED BY EL NIÑO EVENTS

The third group is marked by the high mortality suffered by local species during an El Niño event. The local impact of a major El Niño event is somewhat more difficult to assess in the iconography, as such disruptive occurrences frequently affect the whole ecology of the north coast. Rivers that usually carry very little water burst their banks, invade settlements and agricultural fields, and leave behind destruction and deposits of silt that may take years to plow back into the ground. Dormant vegetation is activated by the rains, and vast stretches of desert landscape suddenly bloom (Caviedes 1984: 287). Lomas profit from the humidity as well, and the usually dull gray or brown Andean hillsides become a vibrant green. The environmental effects of such climate phenomena are thus widespread.

FIGURE 5.53. Bottle in the shape of a macaw, Huaca el Pueblo. Ministry of Culture, Peru. Inv. no. HP-1.

FIGURE 5.55. Whistling bottle in the shape of a macaw's head, Tomb 2, Dos Cabezas. Museo de Sitio de Chan Chan. Inv. no. 13-01-04/IV/A-1/13,430. Photograph by Johnathan Watts, MEG.

FIGURE 5.54. Parrot grasping a corncob. Museo Nacional de Arqueología, Antropología e Historia del Perú. Inv. no. C-03021.

FIGURE 5.56. (*Above*) Subject composed of the cranium of a man and the body of a parrot grasping a corncob. Museo Nacional de Arqueología, Antropología e Historia del Perú. Inv. no. C-03166.

FIGURE 5.57. (*Left*) Portrait vessel representing a blend of a human, a monkey, and a cranium. Museo Larco, Lima, Peru. Inv. no. ML004305.

FIGURE 5.58. (*Below*) Four seated individuals. Drawing by Donna McClelland. The Christopher B. Donnan and Donna McClelland Moche Archive, Image Collections and Fieldwork Archives, Dumbarton Oaks, Trustees for Harvard University, Washington, DC.

Table 5.2. Animal Species from the Northern Region

Iguana	*Conolophus subcristatus, C. pallidus, Amblyrhynchus cristatus*
Strombus	*Strombus galeatus*
Conus	*Conus fergusonii*
Spondylus	*Spondylus* sp.
Spider monkey	Family Atelidae
Sea snail	Genus *Cerithium*
Parrot	*Ara* cf. *militaris, Amazona* sp.

As the rivers flood and water penetrates the desert and the burrows of its inhabitants, mammals, reptiles, and insects (such as rodents, snakes, lizards, spiders, scorpions, and centipedes) are flushed out of the earth, move to higher ground, and invade human habitations. Thus the ecological effects are equally widespread, and most local species are disturbed in one way or another during these drastic changes. Given this situation, nearly all the animal subjects depicted in the iconography are likely to have been impacted by such changes. This makes their selection in this section fairly arbitrary, as they cannot be related to El Niño with confidence. Therefore, at the beginning of this section I present only those that can be associated directly with the ecological markers just mentioned, focusing on those animals directly associated with the invading species.

Three local species are represented on one remarkable ceramic vessel alongside two accurately depicted eagle rays: a sea lion, a seabird, and three gastropods (figs. 5.59, 5.60). As in the example illustrated earlier (fig. 5.9), the man capturing an eagle ray at the end of a fishing line constitutes an index of the El Niño oceanic current, so the figures surrounding him ought to be associated with these conditions. On either side of the man lie a sea lion and a marine bird, possibly a cormorant (figs. 5.59, 5.60). The eyes of the animals are closed, and their general posture may indicate that they are dead. Immediately behind the bird is a second anthropomorphic individual collecting limpets (*Fissurella* sp.) (fig. 5.60). On another bottle associated with the same theme discussed earlier, the fanged being fishing for a puffer fish is surrounded by similar subjects—sea lion, seabird, and eagle ray—in addition to an octopus

(figs. 5.24, 5.25). These three subjects seem to spell death in a vivid manner: the sea lion, the seabird, and the limpet.

Sea Lion

The local species perhaps worst affected by the changing conditions is the sea lion (*Otaria byronia*) (fig. 5.61). Because of the disappearance of their habitual food sources—the fish and the calamari from the ocean surface—these marine mammals have to multiply their outings to the sea. Like the seabirds, they also need to plunge deeper and deeper to locate their prey. Scores of sea lions leave the islands in largely futile attempts to find food in the shallow waters along the coast. As they are driven closer to the shores by hunger, their carcasses eventually cover the beaches of the north coast (Caviedes 1984: 276). Consequently, sea lion carcasses are sometimes portrayed being eaten by condors and represent apt metaphors of the most ritual aspects of Moche symbolism. Condors feeding on sea lions become equivalent to condors feeding on humans, as shown below (see fig. 5.75).

The sea mammals are also depicted being clubbed by humans wearing two-pronged headdresses (figs. 5.62, 5.63). I have suggested (Bourget 2001b) that this activity was analogous to ceremonial combat and that the clubbing of the animal was somewhat akin to the clubbing of an opponent for eventual capture and sacrifice (fig. 5.64). As discussed more fully in chapter 6, this suggestion is clearly similar to Donnan's position with regard to the ritual hunting of deer (Donnan 1997). Deer hunters sometimes even use the same type of clubs used with sea lions (fig. 5.65). This gesture is also an act of war, and the individual is dressed as a fully garbed warrior. This hypothesis of hunting as combat is reinforced by figure 5.66, where the three sea lion hunters wearing similar two-pronged headdresses and clubs also carry a circular shield on their right arm, undoubtedly linking them to ceremonial combat as well.

The importance of sea lions for symbolically charged activities such as ceremonial combat and sacrifice cannot be overestimated. As excavation of the sacrificial site revealed, a sea lion canine tooth had been deposited on the chest of one of the victims and a sea lion was depicted on one of the clay statuettes (figs. 3.30, 3.113).

FIGURE 5.59. Man fishing for a stingray, flanked by a dead sea lion and a dead seabird, view A. Museo Nacional de Arqueología, Antropología e Historia del Perú. Inv. no. C-54483.

FIGURE 5.60. Man fishing for a stingray, flanked by a dead sea lion and a dead seabird, view B. Museo Nacional de Arqueología, Antropología e Historia del Perú. Inv. no. C-54483.

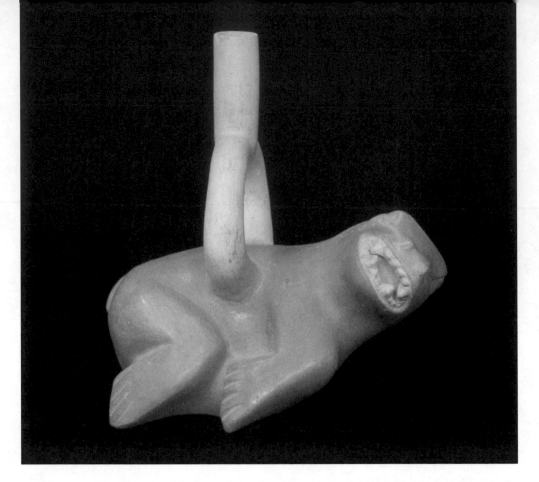

FIGURE 5.61. (*Above*) Bottle in the form of a sea lion (*Otaria byronia*). Museo Nacional de Arqueología, Antropología e Historia del Perú. Inv. no. C-03300.

FIGURE 5.62. (*Below*) Sea lion hunters. Private collection. Photograph by Christopher B. Donnan.

FIGURE 5.63. Hunt of sea lions. Drawing by Donna McClelland. The Christopher B. Donnan and Donna McClelland Moche Archive, Image Collections and Fieldwork Archives, Dumbarton Oaks, Trustees for Harvard University, Washington, DC.

FIGURE 5.64. Ceremonial combat. Drawing by Donna McClelland. The Christopher B. Donnan and Donna McClelland Moche Archive, Image Collections and Fieldwork Archives, Dumbarton Oaks, Trustees for Harvard University, Washington, DC.

FIGURE 5.65. Deer hunting. Drawing by Donna McClelland. The Christopher B. Donnan and Donna McClelland Moche Archive, Image Collections and Fieldwork Archives, Dumbarton Oaks, Trustees for Harvard University, Washington, DC.

FIGURE 5.66. Sea lion hunters. Museo Larco, Lima, Peru. Inv. no. ML013615.

FIGURE 5.67. Pair of drummers in the form of anthropomorphized sea lions. Museo Nacional de Arqueología, Antropología e Historia del Perú. Inv. nos. C-08322, C-07850.

Also, the large vertebra of an adult sea lion was deposited in a recess at the bottom of a posthole on Platform II (fig. 4.4). As suggested in chapter 6, this may have served to anchor a sacrificial rack, perhaps similar to the one depicted in figure 6.13. Therefore the link between sea lions and sacrifice was established symbolically by painting sea lions on the statuettes but also ritually by placing a sea lion canine tooth and vertebra in the plaza and the platform respectively (I return to this important subject below).

Sea lions are also shown as drummers wearing the two-pronged headdresses (fig. 5.67). Drumming is a highly charged activity in Moche iconography. In this case, by wearing the two-pronged headdress, the hunted sea lion has virtually become the hunter. The role of drumming in this scene is also quite significant in terms of this ritual inversion. This musical activity is discussed below in the sections on seabirds and leishmaniasis.

Seabirds

The next group of subjects is exemplified by the seabird lying on the right side of the fisher in figure 5.60. During the 1982–1983 El Niño event, deprived of their food resources (mainly the schools of anchovies and sardines), seabirds died by the millions. Their bodies littered the beaches of the north coast. Driven mad by hunger, the birds drastically altered their behavior. They lost their fear of humans and entered houses and restaurants trying to snatch some food morsel from tables or garbage bins. Hundreds of birds crowded fishing boats attempting to get a few fish through the meshes of the nets. Birds of different species also congregated on rocky outcrops and stopped diving for food altogether. Distinctive species of seabirds intermingling is a most unusual sight and only occurs during extreme conditions. These birds do not nest in the same sites and do not fish together or in the same way.

An extraordinary scene is painted on a bottle recovered from Tomb 3 on Platform II (figs. 4.79, 5.68). The boatman is surrounded by twelve birds, with the ubiquitous eagle ray following the reed boat, indexing El Niño conditions. The three species of seabirds flying jumbled together around the boat may be meant to suggest this loss of

FIGURE 5.68. Boatman surrounded by seabirds. Drawing by Donna McClelland. The Christopher B. Donnan and Donna McClelland Moche Archive, Image Collections and Fieldwork Archives, Dumbarton Oaks, Trustees for Harvard University, Washington, DC.

FIGURE 5.69. Drummers in the form of seabirds. Museo Nacional de Arqueología, Antropología e Historia del Perú, Moche Archive. Inv. nos. C-02920 (left), C-62601 (right).

intraspecific behavior triggered by hunger. It is fitting that what may be such a specific reference to El Niño emerged from the tomb of a likely sacrificer from Huaca de la Luna.

In their zoo-anthropomorphic forms, seabirds perform a number of ritual activities, including ritual running and drum playing, such as a pelican (*Pelecanus thagus*) and guanay cormorant (*Leucocarbo bougainvillii*) (fig. 5.69). Seabirds are also promi-

nently depicted with other subjects covered in this chapter.

Penguin

The Humboldt penguin (*Spheniscus humboldti*) is rarely depicted and does not appear in association with the eagle ray. I am therefore straying from the rules by showing this animal. But rules are

FIGURE 5.70. Humboldt penguin (*Spheniscus humboldti*). Banco Central de Reserva del Perú. Inv. no. ACE-365.

sometimes meant to be broken, and I think that this penguin is worth mentioning because it shares the same ecological settings as the other mammals living in the Humboldt sea current. This flightless seabird is usually shown as a finely modeled sculpture (fig. 5.70). These gregarious birds live on offshore islands, where they nest in small colonies. During El Niño, they suffer the same fate as the sea lions and most of the seabirds. Heavy rains and floods often destroy their breeding sites, and large numbers of these birds starve to death. In search of food, many of them suddenly appear on the littoral, a rare sight because the coast is not adequate for their survival (Caviedes 1984: 276).

Limpet

The fourth local subject is a species of gastropod, the limpet (*Fissurella* sp.) (fig. 5.60). Limpets are depicted being gathered by an individual wearing the two-pronged headdress associated with boatmen and sea lion hunters. This species is nearly eradicated by severe El Niño events (Arntz and

Valdivia 1985). It is not the only one to suffer such a fate, but it has been singled out by the Moche and is prominently depicted in many marine representations. On the bottle shown in figure 5.71, four modeled limpets are surrounded by octopi and borracho fish. Both the octopus and the borrachos multiply during El Niño conditions and are discussed in the following section. The shell of the limpet is often inhabited by an individual with fangs (fig. 5.72), replicating an association also seen with *Strombus*, *Conus*, and *Cerithium* shells (figs. 5.33, 5.40, 5.51). The emergence of this being from the shell clearly highlights the importance of this subject.

Other species probably are severely depleted by these conditions, such as crabs and various types of mollusks, which have been depicted by the Moche. But the sea lions, the seabirds, and the limpets are some of the worst affected and are most portrayed by the Moche. Table 5.3 may be incomplete, but the objective of this section is not to list all the subjects depicted and systematically link them to El Niño events. Rather the analysis is

FIGURE 5.71. (*Above*) Bottle decorated with four limpets (*Fissurella* sp.). Staatliche Museen zu Berlin, Preußischer Kulturbesitz—Ethnologisches Museum. Inv. no. VA 740.

FIGURE 5.72. (*Below*) Being with fangs inside the shell of a limpet. Museo Nacional de Arqueología, Antropología e Historia del Perú. Inv. no. C-54703.

Table 5.3. Animal Species Disturbed by El Niño Conditions

Sea lion	*Otaria byronia*
Pelican	*Pelecanus thagus*
Peruvian booby	*Sula variegata*
Guanay cormorant	*Leucocarbo bougainvillii*
Humboldt penguin	*Spheniscus humboldti*
Limpet	*Fissurella* sp.

limited (except for penguins) to those animals that could be associated with an ecological marker of these conditions.

LOCAL SPECIES HELPED BY EL NIÑO EVENTS

During the exceptional conditions brought by El Niño events on the north coast, the disappearance and massive deaths of certain species in the ocean provide other animal groups with opportunities to reproduce and thrive. The humid conditions on land further prompt tremendous growth in coastal plant life and in the lomas. Such conditions provide numerous terrestrial species with unusual opportunities to multiply and extend their range. As noted, the effects of an El Niño event are widespread. Consequently, in order to identify the local species selected to form part of the symbolic system under consideration links must be established with the ecological markers of these conditions. I concentrate here on the subjects that could be associated with some of the subjects discussed in the previous sections.

Condor

With a maximum wingspan of 3 m and a weight of up to 15 kg, the Andean condor (*Vultur gryphus*) is the largest vulture in South America. The condor normally occupies the high Andes but may also be observed roosting in some coastal mountains. When the beaches are littered with dead sea mammals and marine birds, these scavengers visit the littoral to feed on the carcasses.

In addition to their increased presence along the coast under such unique feeding conditions, a recent study has demonstrated that the reproductive success of an Andean condor popula-

tion located on the Andean foothills was linked to the 1982–1983 ENSO event. Michael Wallace and Stanley Temple (1988) observed that the birds spaced their birthing and only bore chicks under these conditions. It is difficult to demonstrate whether Andean condors would have behaved the same way during Moche times, but Wallace and Temple's findings show how finely tuned the behaviors of animal species are in relation to the environmental changes brought by these conditions. In any case, the food supply for carrion eaters such as seabirds, penguins, and sea lions would have been as great or even greater than today. It would certainly have been beneficial for Andean condors.

In one of the finest ceramic examples portraying an Andean condor, the overall shape of the bird, the color of the feathers, the carbuncle (the fleshy wattle over the beak), and the white neck ruff are clearly and beautifully delineated (fig. 5.73). As noted, sea lions are homologous with sacrificial victims. Therefore condors are illustrated feeding on the sea mammals as well as on human beings of both sexes (figs. 5.74, 5.75). In the Late Moche Phase a woman being pecked by a carrion eater, in those cases black vultures, is part of the Burial Theme (Bourget 2006).

Figure 5.76 is intriguing at many levels because it represents two distinct species of vultures involved with a sacrificial victim. On the lower register, two black vultures (*Coragyps atratus*) peck at the head and the foot of a man lying on the ground. Right above the scene, a large modeled condor is seemingly looking at the activity. The way in which the vultures handle the human is unusual, as they are usually depicted feeding on eyes or genitals (see fig. 5.127 below). The whole depiction would suggest that the two black vultures are actually presenting the victim to the condor. Given the prominence of the bird and its powerful beak, the Andean condor would feed first on carrion, tearing out at the flesh and therefore facilitating access to the entrails for the vultures afterward.

A subject with four volutes ending in condor heads is prominently depicted on the north side of Platform I at Huaca de la Luna (fig. 5.77). The frontal figure has upward-looking eyes and an angular mouth reminiscent of Cupisnique iconography. He holds a *tumi* knife in his left hand and

FIGURE 5.73. Andean condor (*Vultur gryphus*), Tomb 2, Dos Cabezas. Museo de Sitio de Chan Chan. Inv. nos. 13-01-04/ IV/A–1/13,436. Photograph by Johnathan Watts, MEG.

a human head in his right one. This mural clearly shows that the most prominent subjects of the present study are likely to be represented as fanged beings as if this is an added quality indexing their importance in this symbolic system.

Borracho Fish

The borracho fish is a species prominently displayed in most of the scenes related to the world of the sea. In the boat scene discussed earlier (fig. 5.68), ten identical fish are under the boat just in front of the eagle ray. The exact species of the fish depicted is difficult to assess, as it has been represented in various ways by diverse artists (fig. 5.78). It is nonetheless possible to recognize a number of repetitive anatomical elements indicating that it may refer to the same type of fish: the head and the body have the same proportions and the dorsal, caudal, pelvic and pectoral fins are located at

FIGURE 5.74. (*Left*) Condor feeding on a human being. Museo Nacional de Arqueología, Antropología e Historia del Perú. Inv. no. C-63131.

FIGURE 5.75. (*Below*) Condor feeding on a human being. Museo Nacional de Arqueología, Antropología e Historia del Perú. Inv. no. C-54612.

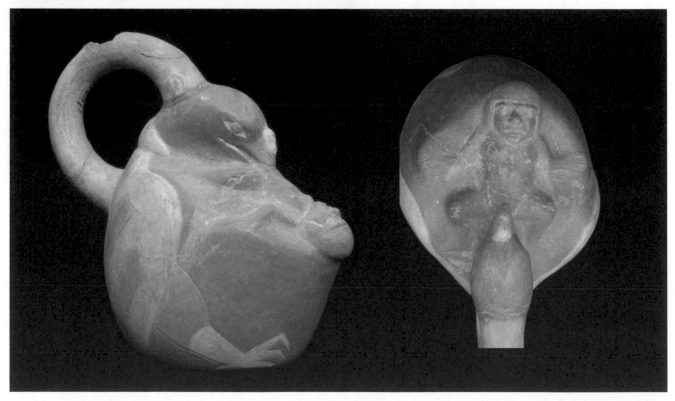

FIGURE 5.76. (*Above*) Sacrificial victim offered to a condor by two black vultures (*Coragyps atratus*). Museo Larco, Lima, Peru. Inv. no. ML001480.

FIGURE 5.77. (*Below*) Huaca de la Luna mural inspired from the Cupisnique Period and depicting a condor being, Moche Valley.

FIGURE 5.78. Borracho fish from diverse scenes. Drawings by Donna McClelland.

FIGURE 5.79. Photograph of *Scartichthys gigas* taken in the Moche Valley.

the same places. Most of these fish also possess two appendages at the inferior junction of the head and the body. A comparison between these depictions and *Scartichthys gigas*, which inhabits the shallow waters of the north coast, clearly shows a number of shared characteristics, including the two appendages located at the juncture between the head and the body (fig. 5.79).

Scartichthys gigas is locally known as *pez borracho* (drunken fish) because of the effects experienced during the consumption of their heads.[2] Numerous inhabitants of the north coast have indicated that when the heads are eaten or mixed in a soup they provoke sleepiness and induce dreaming and vivid nightmares (Schweigger 1947: 178). Because of its propensity to provoke dreaming, one species

(not specified) was even called *sueño* (dream) by fishers operating around the Chincha Islands (Murphy 1923: 605). Bruce Halstead (1978: 590) mentions that this form of intoxication is relatively common following the ingestion of species of coral fish:

> The poison is reputedly concentrated in the head of the fish which is believed to be the most dangerous part of the fish to eat. . . . The poison is not destroyed by any ordinary cooking procedure. The poison affects primarily the central nervous system. The symptoms may develop within minutes to 2 hours after ingestion, persisting up to 24 hours or more. Symptoms consist of dizziness, loss of equilibrium, lack of motor coordination, hallucinations, and mental depression. A common complaint of the victim is that "someone is sitting on my chest," or there is a sensation of a tight constriction around the chest. The conviction that they are going to die or other frightening nightmares are a characteristic part of the clinical picture. Other complaints consist of itching, burning of the throat, muscular weakness, and rare abdominal distress. No fatalities have been reported, and in comparison with other forms of Ichthyosarcotoxin, hallucinogenic fish poisoning is relatively mild.

As stated by Arntz and Fahrbach (1996), at the onset of the 1982–1983 El Niño episode, most of the usual catch from fishers operating on the Peruvian central coast was replaced by *borrachitos*. Although the authors do not mention the exact species, it is likely that they belonged to the Blennidae family. These fishes feed mostly on plants, crustaceans, and small mollusks. Therefore the high mortality suffered by local crabs and other mollusks would be beneficial for the *borrachitos* during ENSO changes and would likely lead to their reproductive success.

In the iconography, the borracho fish shows great variability from the more naturalistic to fantastic forms (fig. 5.80). For example, a human arm wielding a *tumi* knife regularly replaces the appendages at the juncture of the head and the body. In many cases, the borracho-like figure may also possess a warrior's leg. On the body of a bottle excavated by Max Uhle on the western side of the Huaca de la Luna main platform, a borracho fish is painted just underneath an impressive octopus being (fig. 5.81). An eagle ray is depicted in front of the borracho, and puffer fishes are interspersed between the arms of the cephalopod.

FIGURE 5.80. Borracho fish from diverse scenes. Drawings by Donna McClelland.

FIGURE 5.81. Octopus being with stingray and borracho fish. Courtesy of the Phoebe A. Hearst Museum of Anthropology and the Regents of the University of California. Inv. no. 4-3111.

Fanged beings (sometimes with an octopus being in the center of their body) and fishers are frequently depicted on a reed boat capturing borracho monsters at the end of their fishing line (fig. 5.82). The feat may also be performed by an individual on foot standing almost as an equal against the beast (fig. 5.83). In these instances, both the natural and fantastic subjects are usually represented side by side. In other representations, the fish become a fantastic reed boat carrying humans and beings with fangs or zoomorphic attributes to unknown destinations (figs. 5.12, 5.84). The stingrays regularly shown in these scenes (around the boats or at the end of a fishing line) are clearly eagle rays on the basis of the example discussed at the beginning of the chapter (fig. 5.3).

In sculptures, the boats have literally been transformed into a borracho fish. In the first example of this type mentioned earlier (fig. 5.8), a clear association has been made between the borracho boat and a manta ray. On another stirrup spout bottle, modeled as a fish, a fanged paddler is accompanied by two sacrificial victims (fig. 5.85). The victim attached to the tail of the fish or the prow of the boat has a rope around his neck and his hands tied behind his back. The long hair of this individual would suggest that he may be part of the Mountain Sacrifice Ceremony. As described in chapter 7, the male victims selected for this ritual always have long flowing hair covering their shoulders and upper backs (fig. 5.28).

The second victim is resting against the back of the boatman (fig. 5.86). His jugular vein protrudes from his neck and a sea lion is standing nearby and holding a vessel, probably for the collection of the victim's blood. Therefore the sacrificial theme is clearly part of this complex sculpture, with the fanged being carrying two sacrificial victims on a borracho boat and the sea lion playing an active role in the ritual. Unlike the first victim associated with the Mountain Sacrifice, this second victim seems to reflect the Blood Ceremony (Bourget 2006). Blood sacrifice becomes perhaps the most important form of sacrificial ritual in Phase IV, culminating in the Sacrifice Ceremony. As mentioned in chapter 3, most of the actual sacrificial victims in Plaza 3A presented clear cut marks on their cervical vertebrae, indicating that throat cutting was the prevalent form of sacrifice. The prow

and the stern of the boat may also be decorated with sea lion heads, highlighting once more the association with marine activities, sea lions, and the overall theme of sacrifice (fig. 5.87).

Scallops and Octopi

Two other indigenous species that do extremely well during El Niño events are the scallop and the octopus. During the 1982–1983 El Niño, the marine bivalve mollusk *Argopecten purpuratus* (the Peruvian calico scallop) became so abundant that it even extended its range along the coast. This proliferation of the scallop led in turn to a strong augmentation of octopi, which fed almost exclusively on these mollusks. The scallop is not the only mollusk to have some reproductive success during these conditions, but none of them show such an impressive abundance (Wolff 1985). Moche art clearly displays this mollusk in its accurate form, sometimes as a beautiful container (fig. 5.88). In one Phase III fineline painting, the mollusk becomes a fanged being capturing a seabird (fig. 5.89). The scallop beings are surrounded by other seabirds and borracho fish. The gesture of holding the seabird takes us back to the notion of capture and sacrifice. Dragonflies and land snails that also multiply during this time are depicted under the same guise, "sacrificing" seabirds (see figs. 5.109, 5.116 below). This constitutes further indication of the validity of creating this category.

The octopus (*Octopus* sp.) already has been mentioned as depicted on an eagle ray (fig. 5.3) and as a boatman capturing a borracho monster (fig. 5.82). This cephalopod is extensively depicted in the iconography. It was one of the single most important subjects of this system of representation. Resting on the summit of a stirrup spout bottle discussed earlier, the octopus is shown with a set of fangs, bi-globular ears, and a straight haircut (fig. 5.81).

The peculiar ears and fangs are similar to those of the subject in the Huaca de la Luna main mural in the Great Patio (see figs. 2.13, 5.102). Though this subject has been identified under different names, including a mountain deity (Uceda Castillo 2000), it is clearly an octopus with shortened tentacles. It rests in the center of a rhomboidal design surrounded by stylized catfish. The globular eyes of the being on the mural closely resemble those

FIGURE 5.82. Fanged being fishing for a borracho fish. Drawing by Donna McClelland. The Christopher B. Donnan and Donna McClelland Moche Archive, Image Collections and Fieldwork Archives, Dumbarton Oaks, Trustees for Harvard University, Washington, DC.

FIGURE 5.83. Fanged beings fishing for borracho fish. Drawing by Donna McClelland. The Christopher B. Donnan and Donna McClelland Moche Archive, Image Collections and Fieldwork Archives, Dumbarton Oaks, Trustees for Harvard University, Washington, DC.

FIGURE 5.84. Boatman on a borracho boat. Drawing by Donna McClelland. The Christopher B. Donnan and Donna McClelland Moche Archive, Image Collections and Fieldwork Archives, Dumbarton Oaks, Trustees for Harvard University, Washington, DC.

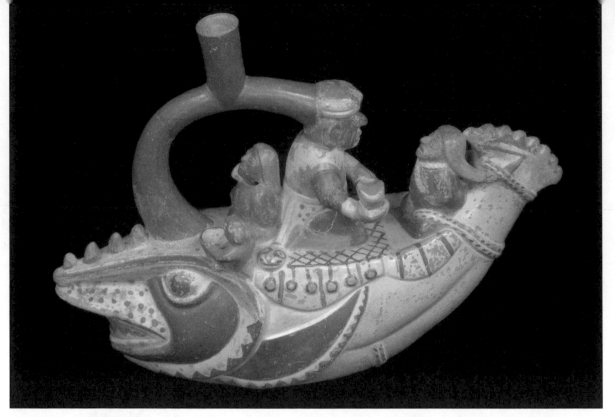

FIGURE 5.85. (*Above*) Man with two sacrificial victims on a boat in the form of a borracho fish, view A. Museo Banco Central de Reserva del Perú. Inv. no. ACE-2975.

FIGURE 5.86. (*Below*) Man with two sacrificial victims on a boat in the form of a borracho fish, view B. Banco Central de Reserva del Perú. Inv. no. ACE-2975.

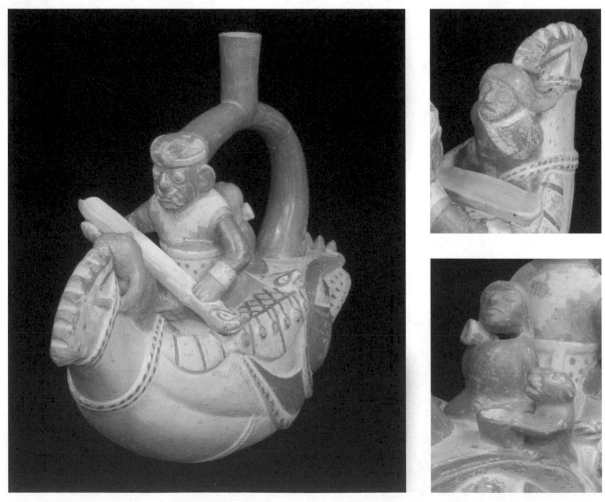

FIGURE 5.87. Boatman on a boat decorated with sea lion heads. Museo Larco, Lima, Peru. Inv. no. ML003201.

FIGURE 5.88. Peruvian calico scallop (*Argopecten purpuratus*). Museo Larco, Lima, Peru. Inv. no. ML009565.

FIGURE 5.89. Scallop being capturing a seabird. Drawing by Donna McClelland. The Christopher B. Donnan and Donna McClelland Moche Archive, Image Collections and Fieldwork Archives, Dumbarton Oaks, Trustees for Harvard University, Washington, DC.

FIGURE 5.90. Individual wearing an octopus diadem and a necklace of human heads. Banco Central de Reserva del Perú. Inv. no. ACE-459.

of an octopus, and the bi-globular ears may refer to the suction cups that are usually organized in pairs running along its arms.[3]

The importance of the octopus motif is clearly delineated by depictions of individuals wearing impressive headdresses in the shape of octopus tentacles (fig. 5.90). These headdresses usually have a series of semicurled tentacles and the claws and the head of an owl in their center (figs. 5.90, 5.91). In addition, it is worth noting that the example in figure 5.90 wears a necklace made of five human heads, whereas the one in figure 5.91 has a similar necklace of five sea lion heads. This corroborates once more the quasi-interchangeability between sacrificial victims and these sea mammals. The La Mina tomb, which contained the swimming crab nose ornaments (figs. 5.14, 5.15), also contained a large octopus headdress made of gold. The eight tentacles, disposed in two opposite sets of four, terminate with stylized heads of catfishes. This

mask, recently uncovered from a Middle Moche tomb at Huaca el Pueblo then christened the "Lord of Ucupe" by the local population, depicts a high-ranking person wearing a disk nose ornament, disk ear ornaments, and an elaborate octopus diadem (fig. 5.92). The central part of the diadem and the necklace are all decorated with owls' heads. The four pairs of arms on all octopi are bilaterally symmetric, and this is beautifully rendered on the diadems and the Huaca de la Luna mural. The symbolic link between the owl and the octopus that justifies their juxtaposition on most diadems is discussed further in the spider section, as they form part of a sort of triad.

Catfish

The catfish is an important motif, often depicted on ceramics, on textiles, and on the walls of temples (fig. 5.93). In conjunction with the octo-

FIGURE 5.91. Individual wearing an octopus diadem and a necklace of sea lion heads, Tomb 2, Dos Cabezas. Museo de Sitio de Chan Chan. Inv. no. 13-01-04/IV/A–1/13,439. Photograph by Johnathan Watts, MEG.

FIGURE 5.92. Metallic effigy depicting a high-ranking individual wearing an octopus diadem, Lord of Ucupe burial, Huaca el Pueblo. Ministry of Culture, Peru. Inv. no. CH7-89. Photograph by Johnathan Watts, MEG.

pus, this subject regularly forms part of the regalia of high-ranking individuals. For example, a male individual buried in Tomb 3 at Sipán possessed a large pectoral in the form of octopus tentacles and numerous objects, including two additional pectorals and two wristbands with catfishes on them (Alva and Donnan 1993). Although catfish can be represented in their natural form, only the head is usually shown in a stylized fashion, usually with the prominent barbels clearly delineated (figs.

5.94, 5.95, 5.96). Sixteen stylized heads of catfish on the Huaca de la Luna mural form a black and yellow lozenge around the head of the octopus being (fig. 2.13).

The exact species represented is difficult to ascertain, given the frequently stylized format of the representations. In the most explicit examples, however, the spots on the body of the fish may indicate that the artists were depicting the *life* (*Trichomycterus* sp.). This freshwater fish measures up to 20 cm and can occur in large schools. During El Niño events, *Trichomycterus* abound, as these conditions may provide these insectivore fishes with an abundant supply of aquatic insects and immature Diptera to feed on.

The catfish can also be shown as an anthropomorphic subject, highlighting its iconographical prominence. In one case, the catfish is accompanied by a borracho fish and is about to be decapitated by Wrinkle Face (fig. 5.97). The full significance of catfish, and particularly of the *life*, in Moche symbolism is not yet fully understood, but it is clearly associated with the main marine subjects. The stylized catfish head is an important motif that appears often in conjunction with the octopus, the stingray, and the seahorse.

Seahorse

Perhaps the most unusual sea creature to profit from the El Niño conditions is the Pacific seahorse (*Hippocampus ingens*) (fig. 5.98). This is the largest species of seahorse, with a maximum recorded

FIGURE 5.93. (*Right*) Fragment of a mural depicting a catfish, Huaca de la Luna.

FIGURE 5.94. (*Below*) Fragment of a mural depicting stylized catfish, Huaca Cao Viejo.

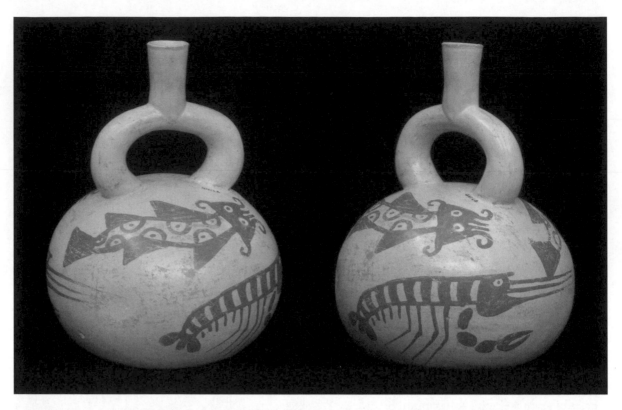

FIGURE 5.95. Painting on a bottle depicting a catfish and a shrimp. Museo Nacional de Arqueología, Antropología e Historia del Perú. Inv. no. C-04355.

FIGURE 5.96. Individual holding a shirt with a catfish design. Staatliche Museen zu Berlin, Preußischer Kulturbesitz—Ethnologisches Museum. Inv. no. VA 4639.

FIGURE 5.97. Wrinkle Face sacrificing a catfish being. Drawing by Donna McClelland. The Christopher B. Donnan and Donna McClelland Moche Archive, Image Collections and Fieldwork Archives, Dumbarton Oaks, Trustees for Harvard University, Washington, DC.

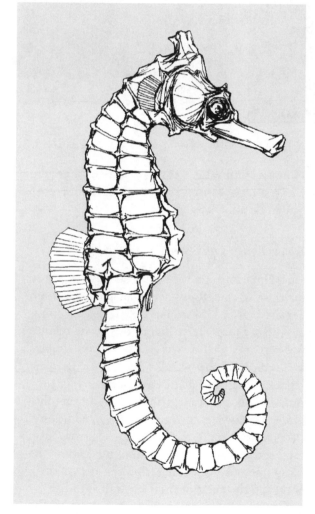

FIGURE 5.98. Drawing of a Pacific seahorse (*Hippocampus ingens*). Redrawn from Lourie et al. 2004: 58.

FIGURE 5.99. Bottle in the form of a seahorse, Tomb 2, Dos Cabezas. Museo de Sitio de Chan Chan. Inv. no. 13-01-04/IV/A–1/13,453. Photograph by Johnathan Watts, MEG.

height of 31 cm. The exact biological processes involved with seahorses during the ENSO marine changes are unknown. A fisher from the village of Jequetepeque told me that during El Niño events they are caught in large numbers in fishing nets.

Tomb 2, excavated by Donnan at Dos Cabezas in the same valley, contained two magnificent stirrup spout bottles in the shape of a fox with no hind legs and a curved tail (fig. 5.99). As noted by

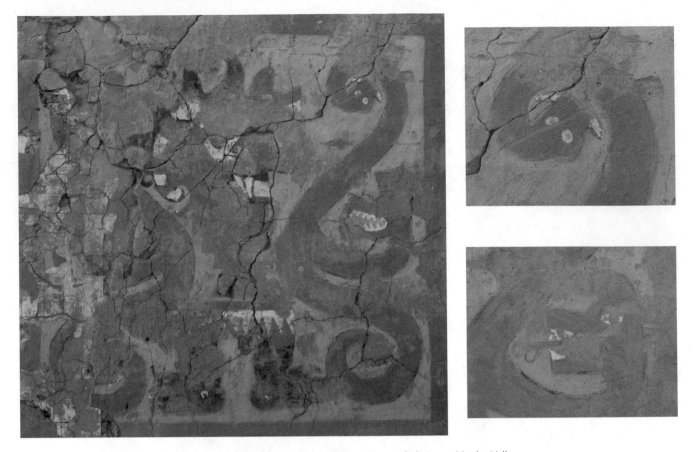

FIGURE 5.100. Painted mural depicting a seahorse being. Huaca de la Luna, Moche Valley.

Donnan (2007: 120), this curved tail and the small crest on top of the head of the animal are reminiscent of the attributes of the seahorse. There is no known naturalistic rendition of seahorses in the iconography. Perhaps the example shown here was perceived as the proper depiction of such a strange-looking animal: part fish and part fox. After all, the genus name derives from the Greek *hippos* (horse) and *campus* (sea monster).

A mural from the Huaca de la Luna main platform depicts a fanged being with the crested animal or seahorse as a sort of headdress (fig. 5.100). At the extremity of the volutes attached to the front and the back of this subject are the heads of catfish and foxes. On the basis of this depiction, I suggest that the Moche might have perceived the seahorse mythologically as having been conceived by the interaction between a fox and a catfish. This may not be too farfetched, as the dots on the Dos Cabezas seahorse's body are also reminiscent of those applied to catfish (figs. 5.95, 5.97). On diadem 10 from the Lord of Ucupe tomb, crested animals are depicted holding the severed head of

a human victim (fig. 5.101). The three volutes with serrated edges forming part of their bodies terminate in catfish heads.

Snowy Egrets, Ducks, and Dragonflies

On an interior mural at Huaca de la Luna, just to the right of an octopus being, an ancient graffito depicts a water bird seizing a borracho fish in its beak (fig. 5.102). The maker of this crude rendition was certainly well versed in Moche iconography, as this bird and the overall subject are extensively represented in an aquatic environment (fig. 5.103). A number of physical attributes suggest that this bird is a snowy egret (*Egretta thula*). In addition to the general form of the bird, Moche artists have captured perhaps its most distinctive feature, the filmy aigrettes protruding from the crown, the back, and the chest of these birds (fig. 5.104).

Caviedes (1984: 282) mentions that during the 1982–1983 El Niño vast stretches of desert landscape were flooded by the intensive rainfalls and transformed into shallow lakes, providing the

FIGURE 5.101. Semicircular diadem with seahorse subject at extremities, Lord of Ucupe burial, Huaca el Pueblo. Ministry of Culture, Peru. Inv. no. CH7-96. Photograph by Johnathan Watts, MEG.

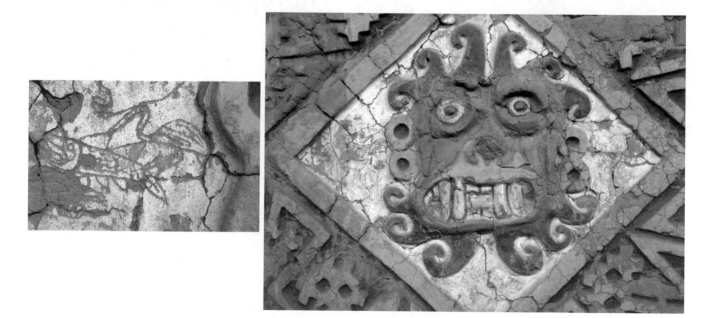

FIGURE 5.102. Graffiti of a borracho fish captured by a snowy egret (*Egretta thula*). Huaca de la Luna, Moche Valley.

FIGURE 5.103. Aquatic scene. Drawing by Donna McClelland. The Christopher B. Donnan and Donna McClelland Moche Archive, Image Collections and Fieldwork Archives, Dumbarton Oaks, Trustees for Harvard University, Washington, DC.

FIGURE 5.104. Muscovy duck (*Cairina moschata*) resting on top of an aquatic scene. By kind permission of the Trustees of the British Museum, London. Inv. no. Am1909,1218.75. Photograph by Christopher B. Donnan. Drawing by Donna McClelland. The Christopher B. Donnan and Donna McClelland Moche Archive, Image Collections and Fieldwork Archives, Dumbarton Oaks, Trustees for Harvard University, Washington, DC.

biotic support for thousands upon thousands of snowy egrets. Consequently, the arrival of these large flocks of birds coincided with the transformation of the desert landscape into a lacustrine environment. Turning large swaths of one of the driest deserts in the world into large ponds must have produced an extremely unusual sight, as lakes are virtually nonexistent on the north coast, and served as testimony to the awesome power of El Niño.

Modeled on top of the bottle in figure 5.104, a Muscovy duck (*Cairina moschata*), recognizable by the crest and the carbuncle on the bill, seems to be presiding over the whole scene taking place just underneath, including snowy egrets, borracho fish, and a catfish. It is difficult to assess the migratory displacement of wild Muscovy ducks during prehistory, as populations of these birds have been severely depleted in modern times. Nonetheless, it could be envisioned that these birds followed the egrets south to take advantage of the lacustrine environments created by El Niño conditions. Residual populations of these ducks can still be found in the gulf of Guayaquil. They are depicted

FIGURE 5.105. Muscovy duck (*Cairina moschata*). Banco Central de Reserva del Perú. Inv. no. ACE-713.

in the iconography in their natural form, as fierce warriors (figs. 5.105, 5.106), and as a fanged being capturing an eagle ray from a borracho boat (fig. 5.12). They are also shown in the arms of coca takers, a gesture relating to the notions of offering and sacrifice (fig. 5.107).

These lacustrine environments also provided a milieu favorable for the development of vast swarms of dragonflies. These insects are usually depicted in association with warriors' implements or in the form of a being with fangs sacrificing ducks and seabirds (figs. 5.108, 5.109). The dragonfly can also be depicted in the hands of a spider being, about to be devoured or decapitated; perhaps this is not too different from the fate of many dragonflies (fig. 5.110).

The lakes, the swelling rivers bursting their banks, and the augmentation of humidity on the coast lead to numerous changes in the overall landscape. Dormant desert vegetation blooms and the lomas farther up (in the 1,000–1,500 m range)

FIGURE 5.106. Muscovy duck in the form of a Moche warrior, Tomb 2, Platform I, Huaca de la Luna. Museo Huacas de Moche, Trujillo. Inv. no. PI-026.

FIGURE 5.107. Coca taker holding a Muscovy duck. Museo Nacional de Arqueología, Antropología e Historia del Perú. Inv. no. C-00743.

expand and turn a brilliant green. The wetter conditions, stagnant waters, and vegetation are beneficial to numerous animal species (including insects, land snails, rodents, and their predators, such as spiders, centipedes, boa snakes, foxes, and owls).

Land Snail

Land snails (*Scutalus* sp.) (fig. 5.111) are extensively represented in the context of the Mountain Sacrifice. They thus appear to have a particularly complex relation with the theme of human sacrifice. In one ceramic scene of the Mountain Sacrifice, the ritual is rather elaborate (fig. 5.112). It depicts the victim on the central summit surrounded by numerous modeled officiates, some of which are now missing. At least four individuals with long hair are collecting land snails on the slopes of the mountain in the midst of cacti. At the base of the mountain lies a group of nine skeletons. The land snails are not placed in these mountain scenes just to indicate the ecological conditions that may have prevailed during the sacrifices. Rather, the land snails are strongly associated with the sacrificial victim on the summit of the mountain. In some cases, the victim may even be replaced by a land snail (fig. 5.113).

This would represent a form of consubstantiality between mountain sacrificial victims and land snails. In a extraordinary ceramic vessel found in Huaca Cao Viejo, the victim is literally swallowed by a land snail (fig. 5.114). The man adopts

FIGURE 5.108. War bundles with birds and dragonflies. Museo Amano, Lima. Photograph by Christopher B. Donnan. Drawing by Donna McClelland. The Christopher B. Donnan and Donna McClelland Moche Archive, Image Collections and Fieldwork Archives, Dumbarton Oaks, Trustees for Harvard University, Washington, DC.

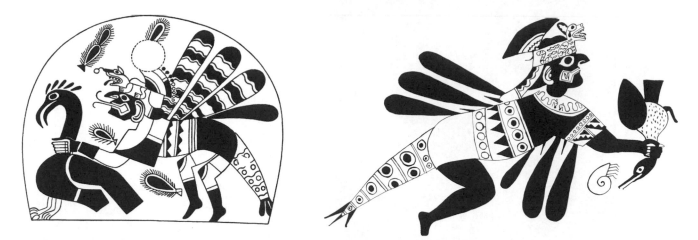

FIGURE 5.109. Fanged beings in the form of dragonflies. Drawing by Donna McClelland. The Christopher B. Donnan and Donna McClelland Moche Archive, Image Collections and Fieldwork Archives, Dumbarton Oaks, Trustees for Harvard University, Washington, DC.

FIGURE 5.110. Fanged being in the form of a spider holding a dragonfly. Museo de America. Inv. no. 01399.

FIGURE 5.111. (*Left*) Bottle in the form of a snail. Museo Nacional de Arqueología, Antropología e Historia del Perú. Inv. no. C-54504.

FIGURE 5.112. (*Below*) Mountain Sacrifice with land snails and skeletons. Drawing by Donna McClelland. The Christopher B. Donnan and Donna McClelland Moche Archive, Image Collections and Fieldwork Archives, Dumbarton Oaks, Trustees for Harvard University, Washington, DC. Private collection. Photograph by Christopher B. Donnan.

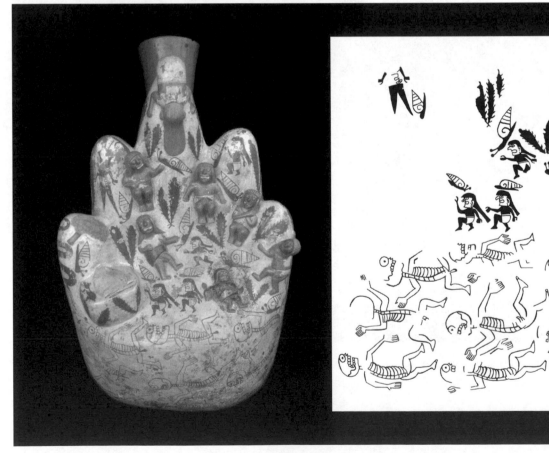

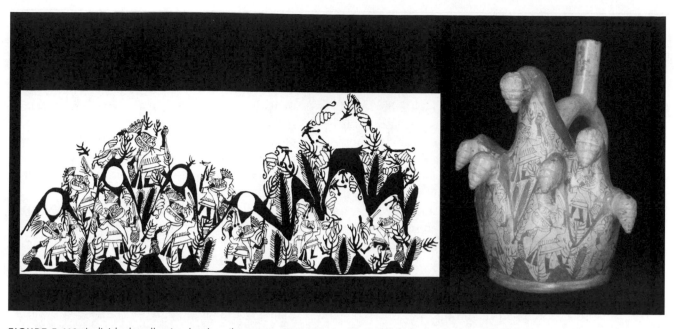

FIGURE 5.113. Individuals collecting land snails on a mountain. Museo Nacional de Arqueología, Antropología e Historia del Perú. Photograph by Christopher B. Donnan. Drawing by Donna McClelland. The Christopher B. Donnan and Donna McClelland Moche Archive, Image Collections and Fieldwork Archives, Dumbarton Oaks, Trustees for Harvard University, Washington, DC.

FIGURE 5.114. Human being crawling inside a land snail. Museo de Cao, Chicama Valley.

the standard position of the victim perched on the central peak of the mountain (fig. 5.28), but only his bent legs and his lower back are still visible as he enters the land snail.

This connection between land snail and sacrificial victim may have to do with the overall concept of capture that forms part of the ritual trilogy. Many of the individuals shown scurrying around the countryside and collecting the snails with sticks are dressed in the same attire worn by warriors and deer hunters (fig. 5.113). In other cases, the tunics and headdresses are those of the sea lion hunters and also those of the mountain sacrificial victims with long hair (fig. 5.115). These outfits clearly establish links between the individuals performing these activities. It also reinforces the proposition that snail collecting is also a form of ritual hunting and as such could be considered a metaphor of ceremonial combat and human sacrifice. The theme of sacrifice is carried further in other instances by depicting land snail beings about to sacrifice seabirds (fig. 5.116) or collecting *ulluchu* fruits (fig. 5.117).

In addition to the link between land snails and sacrificial victims, a symbiotic relationship exists between this snail and *Strombus galeatus*. The *Strombus* monster, which is often shown with warriors or in confrontation with Wrinkle Face, is in fact an amalgam of diverse species, including *Strombus*, the antennas of the land snail, the head of a fox, the tongue of a snake, and sometimes the tail of an iguana (figs. 5.118, 5.119) (Donnan 1978: 63). As Donnan mentions, the Moche apparently established a connection between the diminutive land snail and the gigantic *Strombus*. This association is not limited to the form of the shells and is also carried forward with other ritual aspects, including warfare and sacrifice. This composite being linked two distinct but symbolically associated species. The gigantic *Strombus* seashells are imported from the north, whereas the native land snails multiply during El Niño events. An additional relation that may have existed in Moche symbolism is the general similarity between the shells of the two species.

Spider

Néstor Ignacio Alva Meneses (2008) has made an important contribution to Moche iconographic studies by identifying the naturalistic spiders and spider beings with supernatural attributes as recalling *Argiope argentata*, an orb-weaving spider common to the north coast of Peru (fig. 5.120). It has a distinctive white and golden body, as is particularly well rendered on a ceramic (fig. 5.121). Although it can easily be observed under normal conditions, this spider becomes particularly abundant during El Niño events. It is of course an ideal period for arthropods in general, as insects—their main prey—multiply as well.

It has been suggested that the paired legs position of the spider creating an "X" was faithfully captured by the Moche on many objects, including numerous metallic bells at Sipán (fig. 5.122) (Alva Meneses 2008: 258; Alva and Donnan 1993: 139; Cordy-Collins 1992). This entity is known as the Spider Decapitator. I agree with the identification of the species *Argiope argentata* in Moche iconography. In this section I expand on this contribution by looking at other aspects of this spider that have been overlooked and their further ramifications in the iconography.

In addition to the general form of *Argiope*, an additional feature merits attention and has found its way into Moche symbolism. The spider constructs a structure in the center of its web, consisting of a series of trapezoidal bands of zigzag silk. The number of these bands varies from one to four, but usually four are arranged in a pattern that forms a diagonal cross (fig. 5.120). These zigzag diagonal features on a spider's web are known by entomologists as stabilimenta. The exact function of the stabilimenta is unclear. Entomologists have posited, for example, that they may serve to attract prey or conversely to ward off predators (Schoener and Spiller 1992). The striking object shown in figure 5.123, some 117 cm long, displays in its center a Spider Decapitator with the cruciform design included in its body. It holds a human head in its right hand and a sacrificial knife hangs on its back. This is clearly the same individual depicted on the metallic bell from Sipán (fig. 5.122). The wooden object terminates in a sort of paddle in a trapezoidal form, which in turn resembles the outline of the stabilimenta.

The outline of the cruciform stabilimenta recalls a number of visual motifs in Moche iconography, including the Maltese cross and undulating snake-foxes. As an example, the trapezoidal

FIGURE 5.115. Individuals collecting land snails. Drawing by Donna McClelland. The Christopher B. Donnan and Donna McClelland Moche Archive, Image Collections and Fieldwork Archives, Dumbarton Oaks, Trustees for Harvard University, Washington, DC.

FIGURE 5.116. Land snail beings holding seabirds. Drawing by Donna McClelland. The Christopher B. Donnan and Donna McClelland Moche Archive, Image Collections and Fieldwork Archives, Dumbarton Oaks, Trustees for Harvard University, Washington, DC.

FIGURE 5.117. Human being with a snail shell on his back collecting *ulluchus*. Museo Nacional de Arqueología, Antropología e Historia del Perú. Inv. no. C-04451.

FIGURE 5.118. Warriors seated in front of *Strombus* monsters. Drawing by Donna McClelland. The Christopher B. Donnan and Donna McClelland Moche Archive, Image Collections and Fieldwork Archives, Dumbarton Oaks, Trustees for Harvard University, Washington, DC.

FIGURE 5.119. Wrinkle Face fighting a *Strombus* monster. Drawing by Donna McClelland. The Christopher B. Donnan and Donna McClelland Moche Archive, Image Collections and Fieldwork Archives, Dumbarton Oaks, Trustees for Harvard University, Washington, DC.

FIGURE 5.120. Spider (*Argiope argentata*) on its web. Courtesy of WillWig at en.wikipedia.

FIGURE 5.121. Spider (*Argiope argentata*). Banco Central de Reserva del Perú. Inv. no. ACE-593.

FIGURE 5.122. Gold ornament depicting a spider being holding a human head and a sacrificial knife, Sipán. Museo Tumbas Reales de Sipán. Inv. no. MNTRS-12-INC-02. Photograph by Johnathan Watts, MEG.

FIGURE 5.123. Wooden implement depicting a spider being holding a human head. Musées Royaux d'Art et d'Histoire, Brussels. Inv. no. AAM 39.8.

form of the stabilimenta and the zigzag silk may have been depicted by gold objects (fig. 5.124). These objects were cached in the Huaca de la Luna main platform in the fill of Building D. Uceda Castillo (2008: 169) recently proposed that these were originally part of the frontal section of a coca-taker headdress (fig. 5.124 A). In this case, the snake-fox zigzagging inside the gold pieces could symbolize the silk weaving across the thread of the web. Reinforcing this hypothesis, the coca taker is seated with his back against a weapon bundle with the shield decorated with a Maltese cross (fig. 5.124 B). This subject is only a section of a more elaborate scene, discussed in more detail in chapter 7.

The relationship between the undulating snake-fox and the cross is further reinforced by the scene with the two shields presented on figure 5.108. The center of the shield to the right, with dragonflies on each side, is decorated with the Maltese cross and the zigzagging snake-fox. The other shield, which is flanked by hummingbirds, bears an octopus design. Hummingbirds are discussed later, but

along with dragonflies, octopi, and spiders they multiply during El Niño events.

In addition to the unique design created by the zigzag stabilimenta, *Argiope argentata* regularly places its four pairs of legs to coincide with the crisscross diagonal format of the four bands. The Sipán Spider Decapitator (fig. 5.122) constitutes a conflation between the paired legs of the spider and the trapezoidal stabilimenta. The alternating bands on the legs recall the alternating black and beige markings of the spider's legs: even the fingernails are clearly visible on the artifact. Therefore legs are etched within the cross motif. In some cases, the lower and upper pairs of these appendages can be separated and represented by fanged beings holding a knife and a severed head. One example depicts one of these subjects with a pair of legs within stabilimenta on each side of its body (fig. 5.125). The treatment of the legs is identical to those etched in the metal of the Sipán artifact (fig. 5.122). The fanged being wears an imposing octopus diadem with an owl's head and claws in its center. This diadem is nearly identical to

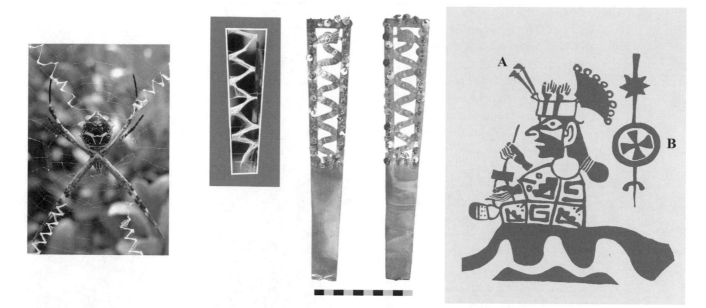

FIGURE 5.124. Correlations of a spider, the offerings, and the iconography.

FIGURE 5.125. Fanged being wearing an octopus diadem. Banco Central de Reserva del Perú. Inv. no. ACE-507.

those worn by the two subjects shown in figures 5.90 and 5.91. The arms, now missing, in all likelihood would have held a knife in one hand and a human head in the other.

The second example is a small sculpture at the extremity of a silver knife: once more a decapitator wearing an octopus diadem (fig. 5.126). The trapezoidal forms, perhaps inspired by the upper pair of stabilimenta, are now in the inverted position, in the proper V shape. The importance of the V-shaped symbol formed by the pair of arachnid legs and the overall shape of the stabilimenta cannot be overstated. This shape may take the form of a certain sacrificial structure in which a man is attached to it and sometimes delivered to the rapaciousness of vultures (figs. 5.127, 7.2, 7.3). The symbolism associated with the V-shaped design is multivocal and encompasses a number of animal species and plants, including not only the octopus and the spider but also the owl and the yucca (see the discussion below).

As noted, arthropods possess eight legs and usually use a silky web to capture and conserve their prey and to lay their eggs. The possession of eight legs, eight arms, or eight claws for capture seems to be one of the features that led the Moche regularly to associate the spider with the octopus and the owl. This similarity in numbers may have reinforced their belief in some kind of shared qualities.

During the Middle Moche/Phase IV periods V-shaped diadems are frequently associated with Individual D of the Sacrifice Ceremony (figs. 5.37, 7.50), and the real diadems have been found in a number of tombs at diverse archaeological sites. The Lord of Ucupe regalia at Huaca el Pueblo included nine such diadems. One example from this context depicts a lizard on each side and in the center of the rectangular extensions forming the V (fig. 5.128).

An additional and final aspect is the overall body shape of the silver *Argiope*. Seen from above and upside down in its web, the dorsal part of the body with its white and orange-reddish abdomen seems to recall the form of certain mountain scenes in Moche art. In one example, the base of the mountain with a white slip mimics almost exactly the form of the white part of the abdomen of the arachnid (fig. 5.129). The three mountain peaks and the interspersed heads of the casqued

FIGURE 5.126. Sacrificial knife depicting a spider being holding a human head and a sacrificial knife. Museo Larco, Lima, Peru. Inv. no. ML013582.

warriors also recall the form of the lower part of the abdomen, with its two pairs of projections along the abdominal margins making a conical shape with five lobes. The overall form of the second mountain scene is similar (fig. 5.130). It depicts the classic scene of the sacrificial victim falling from the central peak of the mountain. Clearly reinforcing this identification, the fanged being overseeing the ritual wears a V-shaped diadem

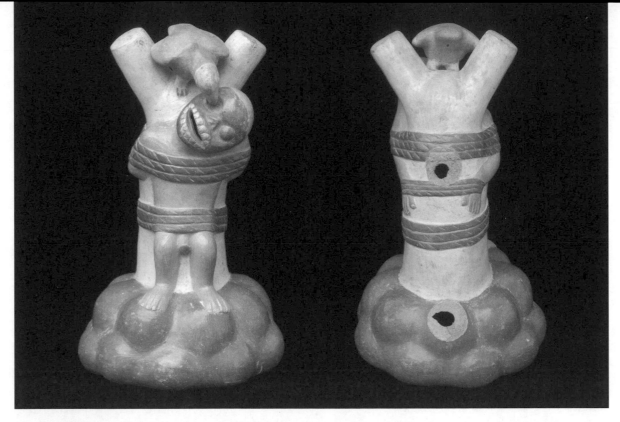

FIGURE 5.127. Sacrificial victim attached to a V-shaped structure. Museo Larco, Lima, Peru. Inv. no. ML001478.

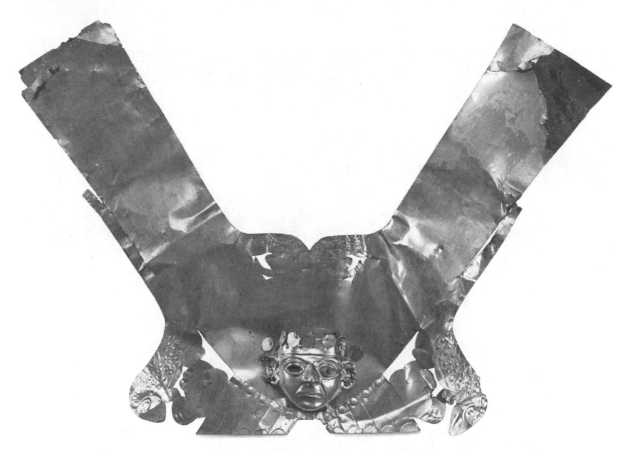

FIGURE 5.128. V-shaped diadem decorated with lizards, Lord of Ucupe burial, Huaca el Pueblo. Ministry of Culture, Peru. Inv. no. CH7-102. Photograph by Johnathan Watts, MEG.

FIGURE 5.129. (*Above*) Comparison between the spider and a bottle in the form of a mountain. Staatliche Museen zu Berlin, Preußischer Kulturbesitz—Ethnologisches Museum. Inv. no. VA 18290.

FIGURE 5.130. (*Below*) Mountain Sacrifice. Staatliche Museen zu Berlin, Preußischer Kulturbesitz—Ethnologisches Museum. Inv. no. VA 4669.

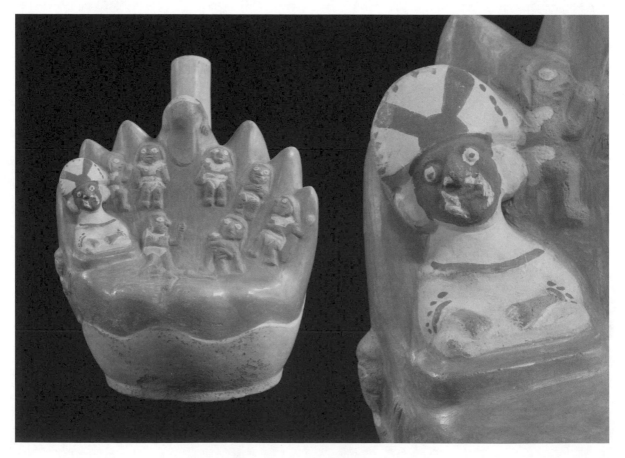

FIGURE 5.131. Rodent eating a corncob. Museo Nacional de Arqueología, Antropología e Historia del Perú. Inv. no. C-54509.

which I associate with the ensemble of arachnid legs and stabilimenta.

Rodents and Their Predators

Rodents are quite commonly illustrated in Moche ceramics performing various actions, including eating and copulating. The relationship of rodents to environmental conditions in the Moche region is unclear. No biological or environmental studies to date deal specifically with rodents of the north coast of Peru. In other regions of western South America, however, the unusually high rainfalls of El Niño events have been seen as one of the causal factors of population outbreaks of rodents (Lima, Keymer, and Jaksic 1999). Because of the unusual growth of vegetation, the rodents usually thrive during these conditions and wreak havoc in the agricultural fields. In the iconography,

they are frequently shown feasting and fattening on corncobs (fig. 5.131). The reproductive success of rodents is further highlighted by a number of ceramics depicting copulating rodents, sometimes surrounded by their numerous offspring (fig. 5.132). This copulation scene is part of a complex subject, and its wider significance has been treated in some detail elsewhere (Bourget 2006).

The main predators of rodents are boas, foxes, and owls. In the most naturalistic representations, these three animals are shown feasting on rodents or carrying them on their backs (figs. 5.133, 5.134, 5.135). Thus their predatory activities are perhaps the most important shared aspects that bring these three animal species together as creatures facilitated by El Niño conditions. In the ENSO conditions, the presence and reproductive success of owls, foxes, and snakes are notably enhanced by the proliferation of rodents. These predatory

species apparently form a sort of trilogy in the iconography. Their roles are complex, interrelated, and clearly associated with the most profound aspects of rulership, political authority, ceremonial combat, and sacrifice. A complete description of each subject is outside of the realm of the discussion here. The scope of this chapter is more limited: I intend to establish their identifications and describe only some of their main attributes.

Owls

At least four distinct species of owl have been identified so far: the burrowing owl (*Athene cunicularia*), the barn owl (*Tyto alba*) (figs. 5.134, 5.136), the west Peruvian screech owl (*Otus roboratus*) (fig.

FIGURE 5.132. (*Left*) Rodents copulating on the summit of a temple. Museo Nacional de Arqueología, Antropología e Historia del Perú. Inv. no. C-01748.

FIGURE 5.133. (*Below*) Snake eating a rodent. Museo Banco Central de Reserva del Perú. Inv. no. ACE-285.

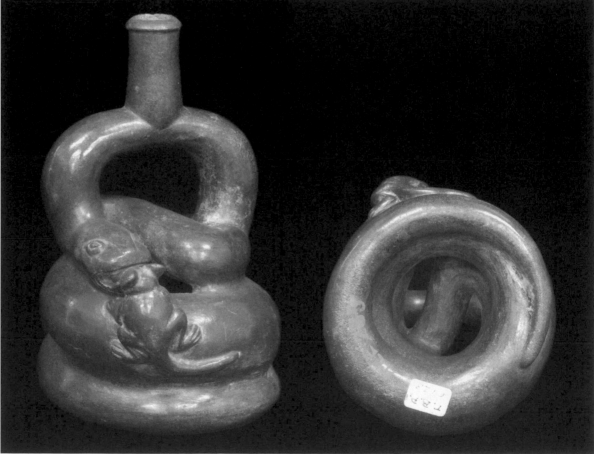

FIGURE 5.134. (*Right*) Burrowing owl (*Athene cunicularia*) with a rodent in its beak. The Art Institute of Chicago (Gift of Nathan Cummings, 1957.404).

FIGURE 5.135. (*Below, top*) Fox carrying a dead rodent. Museo Nacional de Arqueología, Antropología e Historia del Perú. Inv. no. C-54467.

FIGURE 5.136. (*Below, bottom*) Barn owl (*Tyto alba*). Museo Nacional de Arqueología, Antropología e Historia del Perú. Inv. no. C-63138.

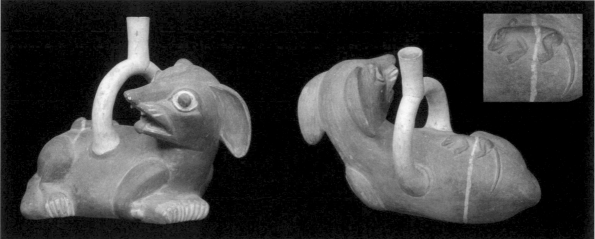

FIGURE 5.137. West Peruvian screech owl (*Otus roboratus*), Lord of Ucupe burial, Huaca el Pueblo. Ministry of Culture, Peru. Inv. nos. CH7-141, CH7-140. Photograph by Johnathan Watts, MEG.

5.137), and the great horned owl (*Bubo virginianus*). In its numerous anthropomorphized versions, the great horned owl plays the most important role. It is often depicted as a high-ranking warrior (fig. 5.138), as a sacrificer (fig. 5.139), and as Individual B of the Sacrifice Ceremony (figs. 5.140, 7.50).

Owl beings in other depictions are dealing with funerary matters, including carrying dead people on their backs (fig. 5.141) (Bourget 1996). The long hairdo of the individual tied by the neck on the owl's back suggests that he may be a sacrificial victim. This act is reminiscent of the fox carrying a dead rodent on its back in figure 5.135. The psychopomp function of the owl may nevertheless still be associated with El Niño, as the bird being has a large double wave motif painted across its body (fig. 5.141).

The double wave motif is extensively depicted both on portable art and on the murals of the temples. It consists of a white wave and a red wave intertwined, with the white wave usually riding on top of the red one. One of the most dramatic changes on the north coast of Peru during an El Niño event is the replacement of cool Humboldt Current by a warm, nearly tropical sea current. This current carries more water, raising the water level along the coast up to 40 cm in certain cases. It also flows in a different direction. Although a stronger argument cannot be made at this stage, it is tempting to see the white wave design as representing the new current moving in a west-east direction, replacing the Humboldt Current that travels roughly from south to north.

Another sculpture reinforces the connection between the owls and the El Niño event. In this case, a west Peruvian screech owl does not carry a human being on its back but is instead burdened with a trumpet in the form of a large *Strombus galeatus* (fig. 5.142). This species of owl populates the southwest portion of Ecuador as well, reinforcing the connection between the bird and the seashell. This recalls the transport of *Strombus*

by Iguana, another subject inhabiting the northern regions (fig. 5.26).

Fox

The link between rodent invasions and foxes is very strong. The iconography contains numerous depictions of foxes with rodents. Even in its anthropomorphic form, the fox can be depicted holding a rodent in its hands and another one tightly clenched in its jaws (fig. 5.143). Half of the male rodent's body has been cleverly painted on the lower jaw of the subject in this beautiful example. During rodent population outbreaks, the reproductive success of foxes is ensured. It is thus most likely that the population of foxes (*Lycalopex sechurae*) is also augmented during prolonged El Niño periods.

FIGURE 5.138. (*Left*) Anthropomorphized owl warrior. Museo Nacional de Arqueología, Antropología e Historia del Perú. Inv. no. C-00483.

FIGURE 5.139. (*Below*) Owl being sacrificing a captive. Staatliche Museen zu Berlin, Preußischer Kulturbesitz—Ethnologisches Museum. Inv. no. VA 18096.

FIGURE 5.140. Anthropomorphized owl. The Art Institute of Chicago. Inv. no. 55.2317.

(*Opposite*)

FIGURE 5.141. (*Top*) Owl being carrying a dead man on its back. Museo Nacional de Arqueología, Antropología e Historia del Perú. Inv. no. C-01044.

FIGURE 5.142. (*Middle*) Owl carrying a trumpet in the form of a *Strombus* seashell. Museo Nacional de Arqueología, Antropología e Historia del Perú. Inv. no. C-63235.

FIGURE 5.143. (*Bottom*) Anthropomorphized fox holding rodents. Museo de Arqueología, Antropología e Historia, Universidad Nacional de Trujillo.

FIGURE 5.144. Anthropomorphized fox as a warrior. Museo Nacional de Arqueología, Antropología e Historia del Perú. Inv. no. C-01215.

The fox is most notably associated with warriors, sacrificers, and Ritual Runners in the ceramic scenes (figs. 5.144, 5.145). Sometimes the relation between human sacrifice and the fox is subtler. It can be expressed simply by a human wearing the hairdo and tubular earplugs of a warrior and victim to be, holding a restful fox on his lap (fig. 5.146). The man's facial painting recalls the bicolor fur of the desert fox. The head of the animal is an important trope used to form the snake-fox, the *Strombus* monster, the borracho, the lunar fox, the bicephalous arch, the seahorse, and other forms.

Boa

Snakes depicted in their natural state are fairly rare in the iconography. In the most faithful rendition, such as in an example of a snake capturing a toad (fig. 5.147), the reptile undoubtedly belongs to the Boidae family. The artist has faithfully reproduced the general form of the head of the boa, the powerful muscles on each side of the jaw, and, with a fine incision, the dark tear drop design

behind the eye that is diagnostic of this family of snakes.

One main representative of this family on the north coast is the Orton's boa (*Boa constrictor ortonii*). Locally known as the *macanche*, it can reach about 3 m in length and mostly feeds on rodents, lizards, batrachians, and small iguanas. Abundant rains and humidity certainly provide boas with more prey. Therefore they are bound to become much more visible during these periods. The life cycle of Boidae is roughly cyclical. During the dry season, when food is scarce, the snake can fast for many months and remain underground in a state of semihibernation. As an opportunistic feeder, the boa reemerges during the rainy season and starts feeding aggressively to reconstitute its reserves.

The snake-fox motif is perhaps the most extensively depicted subject of the iconography. It adorns the walls of temples. It hangs like a belt from the sides and the backs of fanged beings and other subjects (figs. 5.26, 5.31, 5.41, 5.42). As a bicephalous arch, it is embedded in the moun-

FIGURE 5.145. (*Above*) Anthropomorphized fox warrior as a Ritual Runner. Museo Nacional de Arqueología, Antropología e Historia del Perú. Inv. no. C-01207.

FIGURE 5.146. (*Below*) Individual with a forelock holding a desert fox (*Lycalopex sechurae*). Museo Larco, Lima, Peru. Inv. no. ML001156.

FIGURE 5.147. Boa capturing a toad. Museum of Natural History, New York. Inv. no. 41.2/7848.

tain (fig. 2.30), arches across the sky in the Coca Ceremony (fig. 2.29), and separates some Sacrifice Ceremony images into two sections (fig. 2.7). This truly polysemic motif indexes most subjects possessing supernatural attributes.

Toads

The reproductive success of toads is directly tied to relative humidity (fig. 5.148). They share many of the same behavioral characteristics with the boas. During the dry season, they adopt a lethargic state and stay mostly underground to a depth of nearly 50 cm. The reproduction period is triggered by the onset of the humid season. Their sexual instinct is so strong that numerous males may attempt to fertilize the eggs of a single female. The males may even try to attach themselves to males of the same species or to objects vaguely resembling the form of a toad, such as rocks (Lutz 1971: 438–446). Of the nearly fifty species of the Bufonidae family found in South America, *Rhinella limensis* dominates in the lomas and alongside

riverbeds, whereas the coastal marshes are usually populated by *Rhinella poeppiggi*. Like the boas, the toads are often depicted with a pair of mammal ears: feline ears for the toads instead of fox ears for the snakes (fig. 5.149). Those ears may replace the parotid glands located just behind their eyes, on the back of their heads.

Perhaps most striking is the phytomorphic appearance of the toads. In this form the back of the toad takes the form of a manioc (*Manihot utilissima*) and the body is decorated with lima beans, cornstalks, and chili peppers (fig. 5.150). The presence of a tuber forming the back of the toad is part of a much more elaborate concept, part of which can be appreciated with this yucca being (fig. 5.151). The twin stalks of the yucca form the V-shaped headdress of the subject. A toad carries a younger toad in its arms in a second example (fig. 5.152). As demonstrated in chapter 6, this subject forms part of a theme involving the offering of children.

A very similar concept is the V-shaped sacrificial rack shown on figure 5.127. In this case it

FIGURE 5.148. Copulating toads. Museo Nacional de Arqueología, Antropología e Historia del Perú. Inv. no. C-01758.

FIGURE 5.149. Toad with ears of a feline. Museo Nacional de Arqueología, Antropología e Historia del Perú.
Inv. no. C-01596.

FIGURE 5.150. Toad with diverse plants depicted on its body. Museo Nacional de Arqueología, Antropología e Historia del Perú. Inv. no. C-01561.

FIGURE 5.151. Fanged being in the shape of a yucca. Linden-Museum, Stuttgart. Inv. no. L93489.

FIGURE 5.152. Toad being holding a smaller toad in its arms. Staatliche Museen zu Berlin, Preußischer Kulturbesitz—Ethnologisches Museum. Inv. no. VA 18202.

would seem that the victim stands on top of a tuber, reinforcing the relation between this type of vegetable and the subject of sacrifice and El Niño events. As suggested, the V-shaped design may also be connected to the paired legs of the spider *Argiope argentata* and its stabilimenta. The two aspects are not mutually exclusive, however; as Victor Turner (1967, 1992) notes, a dominant symbol such as the V-shaped design may encompass a wider variety of subjects and significata.

Centipede and Scorpion

The centipede and the scorpion are not extensively represented in the iconography. The centipede is largely depicted as a double-headed animal (fig. 5.153). This is of course highly reminiscent of the bicephalous arch associated with the most important rituals such as the Coca Ceremony and the Sacrifice Ceremony. The information regarding the behavior of centipedes in El Niño conditions is also scarce. These arthropods may have

been perceived as multiplying during El Niño events, as it is likely that the downpours triggered by these conditions would have had the effect of flushing them out of their habitat along with other underground dwellers, such as scorpions. They would have to seek higher ground and new shelters and therefore enter human dwellings.

The centipede found on the north coast is the Peruvian giant yellowleg centipede (*Scolopendra gigantea*). This striking and venomous arthropod is carnivorous and feeds on frogs, mice, birds, and lizards. It can reach an impressive length of nearly 30 cm. The centipede is depicted on a jar in the form of a tuber alongside a crab, a lizard, sea lions, and seabirds, confirming its association with the rest of the bestiary explored in this chapter (fig. 5.154). The centipede regularly adorns the stirrup spout of bottles of Phase IV with complex fineline scenery, including the Sacrifice Ceremony. In this elaborate representation of Individual A carried in a litter and accompanied by a plethora of zoo-anthropomorphized warriors, centipedes are

FIGURE 5.153. Bottle decorated with a bicephalous centipede. Museo Larco, Lima, Peru. Inv. no. ML009629.

depicted with snake-foxes on each fragment of the remaining stirrup spout (figs. 5.155, 5.156). At least ten distinct animal species are traveling with Individual A in the painting.

The scorpion is sometimes modeled on the summit of the chamber (fig. 5.157). It can also be found in association with other animals of the iconography such as the fox (fig. 4.39). The most widespread species on the north coast is the alacran scorpion (*Hadruroides charcasus*). This slightly venomous arthropod can reach a length of about 10 cm. In its polyiconic form, it is associated with the feline to form an unusual-looking subject (fig. 5.158).

Bats and Hummingbirds

The final two subjects of this section are bats and hummingbirds. The information regarding these

FIGURE 5.154. Jar in the shape of a tuber decorated with diverse animal species. Collection Cassinelli, Trujillo. Inv. no. 315.

animals in ENSO conditions is almost nonexistent. No study for the northern region on this subject exists, so I have extrapolated the data collected by Catherine Sahley (1996) for southwestern Peru. The research was conducted during the 1991–1992 El Niño event. During this period, her study area around Arequipa suffered a decrease in nectar-feeding bats due to drought conditions that severely limited the flower production of columnar cacti (*Weberbauerocereus weberbaueri*). Given the similarities in ecology between the two regions, it is likely that the more humid conditions prevailing in the Moche region during this period—instead of drought—would have led to increased flowering of columnar cacti. As such, the nectar-feeding animals including bats and hummingbirds would likely have expanded in numbers. As soon as the large white flowers appear on cacti, they are rapidly pollinated by long-snouted bats (*Platalina genovensium*) and giant hummingbirds (*Patagona gigas*), which move in great numbers into these regions. The nectivorous long-snouted bat does not apparently play an important role in the ico-

FIGURE 5.155. Zoo-anthropomorphized warriors accompanying Individual A in a litter. Staatliche Museen zu Berlin, Preußischer Kulturbesitz—Ethnologisches Museum. Inv. no. VA 48016. Photograph by Christopher B. Donnan.

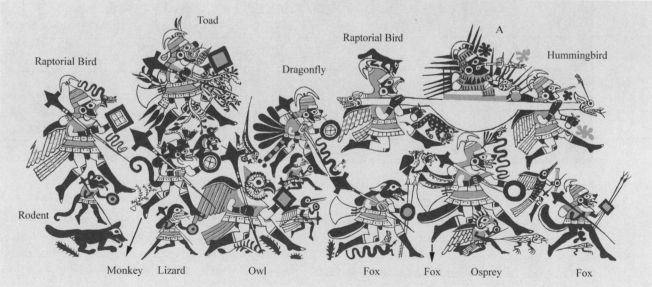

FIGURE 5.156. Painting of zoo-anthropomorphized warriors accompanying Individual A in a litter. Drawing by Donna McClelland. The Christopher B. Donnan and Donna McClelland Moche Archive, Image Collections and Fieldwork Archives, Dumbarton Oaks, Trustees for Harvard University, Washington, DC.

FIGURE 5.157. Scorpion modeled on the summit of a bottle. Museo de América, Madrid. Inv. no. 01299.

FIGURE 5.158. Feline-scorpion. Museo Nacional de Arqueología, Antropología e Historia del Perú. Inv. no. C-01218.

nography. It is usually depicted resting on a fruit form (fig. 5.159). More research is needed to elucidate this subject.

The giant hummingbird may measure as much as 23 cm in length and weigh 22 grams. Compared with local species such as the oasis hummingbird (*Rhodopis vesper*), which measures only 13 cm and reaches a weight of 4 grams, the difference is

quite striking. It is not possible to discriminate the species depicted in the iconography, but the bird is prominently depicted in activities of ritual running and warfare (figs. 5.64, 5.108, 5.156).

Table 5.4 clearly shows how extensive and varied the animal species selected by the Moche are. This diversity is clearly intended to touch all the ecological zones that they inhabited. Perhaps

FIGURE 5.159. Fruit bat placed on a fruit. Museo Nacional de Arqueología, Antropología e Historia del Perú. Inv. no. C-03086.

Table 5.4. Animal Species Helped by El Niño Conditions

Andean condor	*Vultur gryphus*
Borracho	*Scartichthys gigas*
Octopus	*Octopus mimus*
Catfish	*Trichomycterus* sp.
Calico scallop	*Argopecten purpuratus*
Land snail	*Scutalus* sp.
Centipede	*Scolopendra gigantea*
Scorpion	*Hadruroides charcasus*
Spider	*Argiope argentata*
Fox	*Lycalopex sechurae*
Snake	*Boa constrictor ortonii*
Owl	*Athene cunicularia, Tyto alba, Otus roboratus, Bubo virginianus*
Toad	*Rhinella limensis, R. poeppiggi*
Rodent	—
Dragonfly	—
Snowy egret	*Egretta thula*
Hummingbird	*Patagona gigas, Rodhopis vesper*
Nectivorous bat	*Platalina genovensium*

one of the aims was to demonstrate how wide-ranging the powers of the gods and rulers were.

DEATH AND DISEASE

This section includes lima beans, deer, and a parasitic disease. My intent is to review a number of distinct representations, regrouping important but disparate subjects of the iconography. In addition to decimating certain animal populations by depriving them of their food sources, severe El Niño events create deleterious conditions triggering the onset of infectious diseases or change the properties of certain plants, rendering them unfit for animal and human consumption. Two broad cases are considered here: the release of hydrocyanic acid in certain plants and the transmission of leishmaniasis parasites. These two aspects affect distinct populations of local species, deer and humans respectively.

Lima Beans and Deer

Lima beans (*Phaseolus lunatus*) and the white-tailed deer (*Odocoileus virginianus*) play an intriguing role in the iconography. They are often paired in scenes predominantly related to the activities of ceremonial combat and human sacrifice. Lima beans are regularly depicted as Moche warriors parading with war implements and shields or as sculptural warriors (figs. 5.160, 5.161). The deer may be depicted as a warrior but also as a sacrificial victim (figs. 5.162, 5.163). The bean warrior, however, is never depicted as destined for sacrifice. Bean warriors consistently engage deer warriors in one-to-one combat in battles (fig. 5.164). Both subjects literally stand for human warriors. But the outcome of the battles is already determined. In these violent activities, as in all the other situations depicting deer (such as ritual hunting), the animals are consistently shown with their tongues hanging out of their mouths, a sure sign of their actual or impending death (Donnan 1997: 54).

But what could the connection between lima beans and deer be to create such an unlikely pair of protagonists? Perhaps part of the answer lies in these fineline paintings depicting Moche warriors hunting deer with clubs and atlatls. Small bushes or vine-like plants in the background are shown laden with bean pods alongside cornstalks (fig.

5.165). These pod-bearing plants have variously been interpreted as algarrobos (Donnan 1978) or as the hallucinogenic plant *Anadenanthera peregrina* (Dobkin de Rios 1984). With the persistent and bellicose association between the lima bean and the deer, I suggest as an alternative hypothesis that the plants that most clearly look like vines are *Phaseolus lunatus* and that part of the answer in regard to the quasi-symbiotic relationship with deer may lie once more with El Niño events. In these humid conditions, the bean plants in their wild state grow rapidly; these young, fast-growing plants are more likely to contain high levels of prussic acid. Ruminants such as deer grazing on these plants release the hydrocyanic acid contained within the plants through chewing and ingestion. The effects of the poison are rapid and quite dramatic:

FIGURE 5.160. (*Left*) Anthropomorphized lima bean warriors. Museo Nacional de Arqueología, Antropología e Historia del Perú. Inv. no. C-04440.

FIGURE 5.161. (*Below*) Anthropomorphized lima bean warrior. Museo Nacional de Arqueología, Antropología e Historia del Perú. Inv. no. C-00559.

FIGURE 5.162. Anthropomorphized deer warrior. Museo Nacional de Arqueología, Antropología e Historia del Perú. Inv. no. C-01227.

Cyanide is a potent, rapidly acting poison. Signs of cyanide poisoning can occur within 15 to 20 minutes to a few hours after animals consume the toxic forage. Animals often are found dead. Clinical signs, when noticed, occur in rapid succession. Excitement, rapid pulse and generalized muscle tremors occur initially, followed by rapid and labored breathing, staggering and collapse. Signs also may include salivation (drooling), lacrimation (runny eyes), and voiding of urine and feces. The mucous membranes are usually bright pink, and the blood will be a characteristic bright cherry red. (Stoltenow and Lardy 2012: 1)

Therefore lima bean plants may have constituted a potential danger for deer grazing on them. Although the use of lima beans for foraging in ancient Andean Peru is unknown and a stronger connection between *Phaseolus lunatus* and El Niño conditions cannot be made at this stage, the following subject may provide further evidence that these beans are linked with the overall theme explored in this chapter. A stirrup spout bottle in the form of an anthropomorphized lima bean

FIGURE 5.163. Anthropomorphized deer as a captive and sacrificial victim. Museo Nacional Arqueología, Antropología e Historia del Perú. Inv. no. C-01280.

FIGURE 5.164. Ceremonial combat between anthropomorphized lima beans and deer. Drawing by Donna McClelland. The Christopher B. Donnan and Donna McClelland Moche Archive, Image Collections and Fieldwork Archives, Dumbarton Oaks, Trustees for Harvard University, Washington, DC.

FIGURE 5.165. Deer hunting ritual. Drawing by Donna McClelland. The Christopher B. Donnan and Donna McClelland Moche Archive, Image Collections and Fieldwork Archives, Dumbarton Oaks, Trustees for Harvard University, Washington, DC.

with some extraordinary features depicts a male warrior resting on his knees with both feet amputated (fig. 5.166). He wears tubular earplugs, and his face and his conical helmet have been modeled to resemble the overall form of the bean. In addition to the amputations, his nose and his upper lip have been destroyed by the leishmaniasis disease.

The significance of this affliction is discussed in the following section.

The Transformation of Humans

Representations of individuals showing facial and cutaneous lesions generated some of the earliest

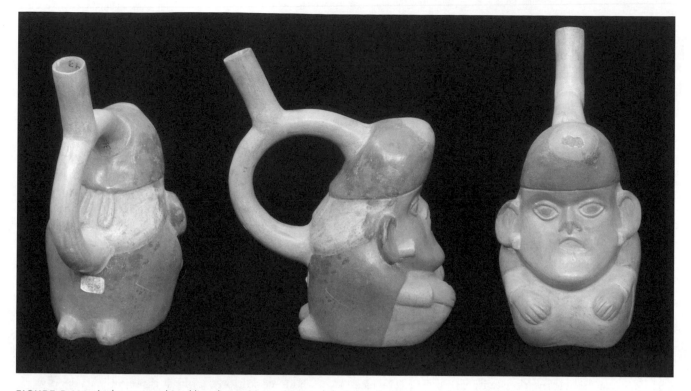

FIGURE 5.166. Anthropomorphized lima bean. Museo Nacional de Arqueología, Antropología e Historia del Perú. Inv. no. C-00290.

studies of Moche iconography. These facial lesions were associated with facial mutilations or with the ravages of leishmaniasis (Palma 1913; Vélez López 1913; Weiss 1961). Leishmaniasis (caused by *Leishmania peruviana*) is a parasitic disease transmitted to humans by the bite of infected sandflies (*Lutzomyia longipalpis*). Mammalian hosts for leishmanial parasites in ancient coastal Peru could have included rodents, dogs, monkeys, and humans. Leishmaniasis has four principal forms:

- Cutaneous leishmaniasis causes skin sores at the bite site. The sores can change in size and appearance over time. The sores often end up looking somewhat like a volcano, with a raised edge and central crater. Skin sores can develop within weeks of being infected. The disease usually heals by itself after a few months but often leaves large scars.
- Mucocutaneous leishmaniasis is perhaps the most impressive form of cutaneous leishmaniasis. As the name suggests, it affects the mucal and sinus regions of the face. It can thus destroy the nose, the palate, and the lips, producing disfigurement of the face.

- Diffuse cutaneous leishmaniasis is visually akin to leprosy. The subject develops multiple skin lesions. If left untreated, the lesions can spread all over the body.
- Finally, visceral leishmaniasis affects some of the internal organs of the body, such as the spleen, liver, and bone marrow. This is the most serious form of the disease. Without proper medication, it is almost always lethal.

Julie Kenner and Peter Weina (2005) note that the majority (90 percent) of cutaneous forms of the disease heal spontaneously after a few months, leaving scarred tissue or disfigurement. Therefore this form of leishmaniasis does not kill the stricken subjects in most cases but leaves them transformed, with vivid reminders of the ailment inscribed permanently on their faces and bodies.

Some studies have indicated that by facilitating the reproduction of sandflies the extremely humid conditions created by El Niño events would therefore facilitate the transmission of leishmaniasis in a local population (Cabaniel et al. 2005). Pools of stagnant waters or shallow lakes left in the wake of torrential rains would have constituted ideal breeding conditions for these insects on the north coast. For example, during the 1982–1983 El Niño event an epidemic of cutaneous leishmaniasis spread among the children of Canchaque, a village in the Piura Valley, causing panic among the population (Caviedes 1984: 280). This recent episode demonstrates how fast this disease can appear and become a serious nuisance even while an El Niño event is still in progress.

The various forms of cutaneous leishmaniasis are clearly shown in the iconography. In one example, the Moche artist has precisely depicted an active lesion in nasal mucosal tissue followed by the perforation of the septum and the swelling of the lips (figs. 5.167, 5.168). The Maltese cross painted on the face of the subject further reaffirms the association between the leishmaniasis subjects and the others discussed so far. In a second case, the subject is depicted with what appears to be a case of cutaneous leishmaniasis (fig. 5.169).

The Moche also included other types of facial deformations with this theme. The face of a Moche warrior on the summit of a potato-shaped bottle bears the evidence of leishmaniasis, whereas the second face depicted just underneath is afflicted by a cleft lip (fig. 5.170). Cleft lip (*cheiloschisis*) and cleft palate (*palatoschisis*) are fairly frequent congenital anomalies. The third aspect is ritual mutilation. The nose and the lips have apparently been excised on the face of a portrait vessel found in Tomb 3 (fig. 4.66).

It is quite certain that individuals born with a cleft lip, scarred by leishmaniasis, or transformed by such mutilations took part in ritual events. They are extensively depicted in the iconography carrying out various activities, sometimes with additional mutilations such as a foot or even both feet missing (figs. 2.5, 2.6). In addition, masks representing individuals with leishmaniasis may have been used during certain performances, including dances. The first mask wearer (A) appears to be wearing a leishmaniasis mask on the lower register of a fineline painting (fig. 5.171). Referring to this scene, Donnan (2008: 71) discusses the nature of masks that were used during rituals:

> Moche masks that were made to be worn by the living have two consistent features: (1) the eyes are open so the person wearing them could see, and (2) the mouths are open, suggesting that the individuals wearing them were expected to

speak or sing. This correlates well with the fineline painting portraying this type of mask being worn in a dance procession. The open eyes on the masks would have allowed the dancers to see and thus move about freely. Meanwhile, the open mouth would have allowed them to speak or sing.

Therefore Donnan contends that the ceramic mask shown in figure 5.172 could have been worn by dance and ritual participants. The two holes on the top would have facilitated fastening the mask to the head of the performer. Among other activities, leishmaniasis amputees would have played a role during the funerary rituals of high-ranking individuals (Arsenault 1993, 1994; Bourget 2006).

Individuals with leishmaniasis are also clearly linked to additional subjects already discussed in this survey. The owl is standing on top of a potato-shaped bottle (fig. 5.173). The bird looks down on a sea lion, while on each side the head of an individual with leishmaniasis is surrounded by a seabird. Thus the owl, which proliferates under El Niño conditions, looks at three subjects deeply affected by these same conditions. The sea lion is further associated with this subject. One representation of a sea lion has a V-shaped upper lip, apparently to depict a case of mucocutaneous leishmaniasis (fig. 5.174). The double spiral motif on this tunic is inspired by the double wave motif. The leishmaniasis drummer kneeling on top of a dancing procession on another bottle adopts the exact body position of two sea lion drummers discussed earlier (figs. 5.175, 5.67). The musician is also a double amputee: the missing feet are in a certain manner reminiscent of the form of the flippers of sea lions. This may not be as farfetched as it seems. Other representations depict the same human subject resting on his belly in a position also adopted by sea lions (fig. 5.176).

Polysemic Tubers

Manioc (*Manihot* sp.) and potato (*Solanum* sp.) tubers are probably the plants most often represented by the Moche. They are truly polysemic (Bourget 1990b). Many of the subjects presented in this chapter can take the form of a tuber, including monkeys (figs. 5.47, 5.48), toads (fig. 5.150), seabirds, sea lions, and humans. The tuber itself can also transform into a fanged being, highlighting its deep connection with the subjects presented in

FIGURE 5.167. Portrait vessel of an individual with leishmaniasis. Staatliche Museen zu Berlin, Preußischer Kulturbesitz— Ethnologisches Museum. Inv. no. VA 4633.

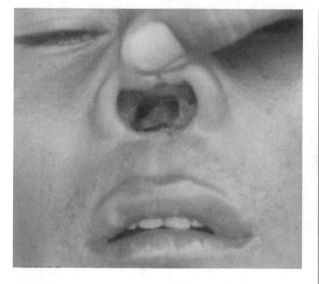

FIGURE 5.168. Mucocutaneous leishmaniasis. Courtesy of http://simple-health-secrets.com/leishmaniasis-image -leishmaniasis-pictures/.

FIGURE 5.169. Individual with leishmaniasis. Museo Larco, Lima, Peru. Inv. no. ML004297.

FIGURE 5.170. Potato-shaped bottle with three main subjects. Museo Nacional de Arqueología, Antropología e Historia del Perú. Inv. no. C-02926.

A

FIGURE 5.171. Dancers and musicians. Drawing by Donna McClelland. The Christopher B. Donnan and Donna McClelland Moche Archive, Image Collections and Fieldwork Archives, Dumbarton Oaks, Trustees for Harvard University, Washington, DC.

FIGURE 5.172. (*Above*) Mask of a leishmaniasis subject. Staatliche Museen zu Berlin, Preußischer Kulturbesitz—Ethnologisches Museum. Inv. no. VA 18056.

FIGURE 5.173. (*Below*) Owl looking at a sea lion. Museo Nacional de Arqueología, Antropología e Historia del Perú. Inv. no. C-01060.

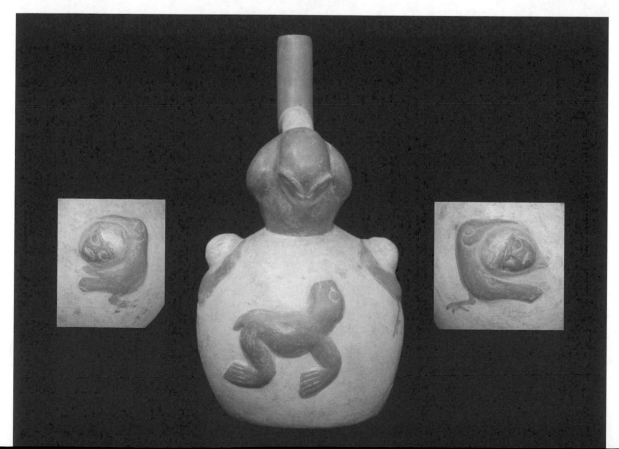

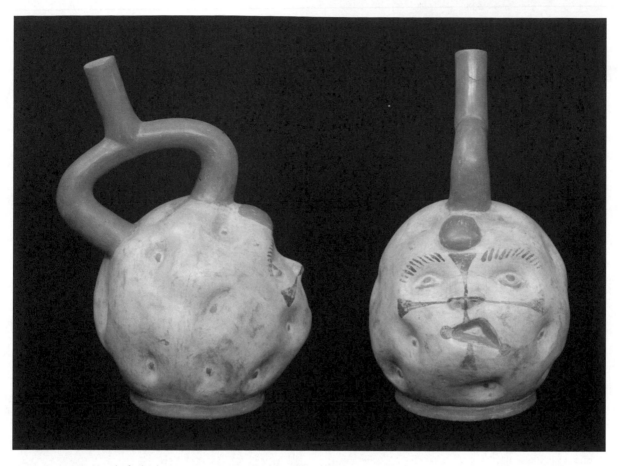

FIGURE 5.177. Head of a leishmaniasis victim in the form of a potato. Museo Nacional de Arqueología, Antropología e Historia del Perú. Inv. no. C-02926.

this chapter (fig. 5.151). Tubers also stand out in the iconography for their propensity to display large numbers of seemingly distinct subjects simultaneously on a single ceramic. A review, however, quickly reveals that in most cases the tubers are associated with subjects that are severely affected by El Niño conditions. In one dramatic example, the head of an individual with leishmaniasis may even take the form of a potato (fig. 5.177). The natural deformations of the tuber have been cleverly used to create the facial features of the individual. This type of representation may have been inspired by a rather acute case of dermal leish-

maniasis, such as the example presented in figure 5.178. This bottle excavated by Uhle on the west-side platform of Huaca de la Luna magnificently shows how interconnected all the subjects of this chapter are with human sacrifice (fig. 5.179). This potato-shaped portrait vessel depicts an individual with leishmaniasis bearing many of the facial decorations found on the clay statuettes from Plaza 3A. It includes the lozenge motifs on each side of the eyes and the string of emerging muscoid flies on the lower jaw (figs. 3.122, 3.124).

Numerous subjects can be found on a single tuber in the most intricate examples. On a large

(Opposite)

FIGURE 5.174. (Top) Sea lion with a V-shaped upper lip. Staatliche Museen zu Berlin, Preußischer Kulturbesitz—Ethnologisches Museum. Inv. no. VA 48112.

FIGURE 5.175. (Middle) Leishmaniasis drummer kneeling on top of a dancing procession. Museo Nacional de Arqueología, Antropología e Historia del Perú. Inv. no. 35-1390.

FIGURE 5.176. (Bottom) Individual with leishmaniasis and sea lion. Museo de América, Madrid. Inv. no. 01440 (left). Museo Nacional de Arqueología, Antropología e Historia del Perú. Inv. no. C-01502 (right).

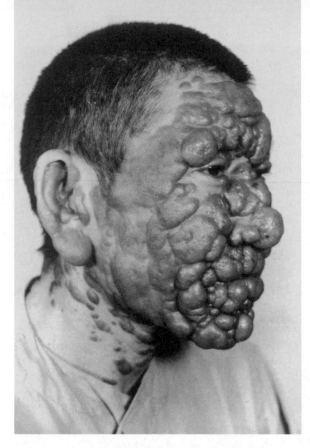

FIGURE 5.178. (*Above*) Mucocutaneous leishmaniasis. Courtesy of http://www.rainforesteducation.com/terrors /leishmaniasis/leish.htm.

FIGURE 5.179. (*Below*) Portrait vessel of an individual with leishmaniasis. Courtesy of the Phoebe A. Hearst Museum of Anthropology and the Regents of the University of California. Inv. no. 4-2814.

and exceptionally complex tuber-shaped jar, a monkey presides over an array of subjects, including a man holding the tail of a large snake-fox (fig. 5.180). Near the lower left side of the figure, the same man is seemingly sitting on the left arm of a fanged being making a fist gesture with its left hand and holding a round stone with its right (fig. 5.181). Within the drawn outline of the snake-fox are an amputee on his knees and a large feline holding a small deer in its claws (figs. 5.182, 5.183). Just behind a monkey and immediately underneath a rather large lizard is a cadaverous person with leishmaniasis blowing a *Strombus* trumpet. In front of this disfigured individual is a sea lion with a round stone in its mouth (fig. 5.184). Therefore the spider monkey—originating from the northern region—presides over numerous actors closely associated with the notion of ritual hunting and sacrifice, such as a feline capturing a deer and a sea lion coughing out a stone. The tuber shown in figure 5.48 is somewhat reminiscent of the same treatment. The monkeys, the iguana, and the coca taker modeled on its lobes clearly show how the Phase III Coca Ceremony and Mountain Sacrifice themes are embedded within the El Niño symbolic system.

Figure 5.184 suggests that at least one species of lizard is as important as the monkey. The monkey and lizard figures are both above the rest of the subjects. Unfortunately, the literature is mute on the subject of how north coast lizards are affected by El Niño events. Nevertheless, they are important subjects in the iconography: they regularly adorn the regalia of high-ranking individuals and fulfill functions like those of the other subjects (figs. 5.128, 5.156).

One ceramic bottle shows the insistence with which the Moche imbue fruits and tubers that grow underground with information relating to

(*Opposite*)

FIGURE 5.180. (*Top*) Jar in the form of a tuber with numerous subjects, view A. Staatliche Museen zu Berlin, Preußischer Kulturbesitz—Ethnologisches Museum. Inv. no. VA 65979.

FIGURE 5.181. (*Bottom*) Jar in the form of a tuber with numerous subjects, view B. Staatliche Museen zu Berlin, Preußischer Kulturbesitz—Ethnologisches Museum. Inv. no. VA 65979.

their symbolic system. The vessel recalls a manioc which has been further shaped into the form of a man whistling, with his face decorated with a Maltese cross (fig. 5.185). He tightly holds a monkey holding an *ulluchu* fruit in his left arm. He is also burdened with a net bundle. The Maltese cross on his face and the lump on his forehead recall the features on the human face depicted on the eagle ray (fig. 5.4) and the potato head effigy (fig. 5.177). The protuberance or design on the forehead also refers to the lump of hair associated with a specific group of ritual warriors and sacrificial victims that first appear in Phase III. The same is also true for the Maltese crosses. The act of whistling, the monkey carried under the arm, and the net bundle are specific themes that refer to the offering of children and deer hunting. These subjects are explored in chapter 6.

The final example of this theme shows a large potato-shaped jar with an important group of subjects already presented in this chapter: a snake-fox, the head of an osprey, and a sea lion (fig. 5.186). A person with a net design on the face is just above the sea lion. This is a relatively rare subject, but in some cases it is associated with the display of offerings. The part of the potato forming a head deserves further attention. It depicts a sea lion with two stones in a mouth with an upper lip bearing the scars of leishmaniasis. The decorated band on its chin is adorned with six pupa cases. This band on the lower jaw is nearly identical to those painted on the chins of the clay statuettes encountered in Plaza 3A. Therefore, as with a number of the statuettes, the sea lion head shown in fig. 5.186 clearly links the sea lion, leishmaniasis subjects, pupa cases, and the victims of the sacrifi-

FIGURE 5.182. (*Top*) Jar in the form of a tuber with numerous subjects, view C. Staatliche Museen zu Berlin, Preußischer Kulturbesitz—Ethnologisches Museum. Inv. no. VA 65979.

FIGURE 5.183. (*Middle*) Jar in the form of a tuber with numerous subjects, view D. Staatliche Museen zu Berlin, Preußischer Kulturbesitz—Ethnologisches Museum. Inv. no. VA 65979.

FIGURE 5.184. (*Bottom*) Jar in the form of a tuber with numerous subjects, view E. Staatliche Museen zu Berlin, Preußischer Kulturbesitz—Ethnologisches Museum. Inv. no. VA 65979.

FIGURE 5.185. Bottle in the shape of a tuber with a whistling man and a monkey. Museo Nacional de Arqueología, Antropología e Historia del Perú. Inv. no. C-03115.

FIGURE 5.186. Jar in the form of a tuber with numerous subjects. Museo Nacional de Arqueología, Antropología e Historia del Perú. Inv. no. C-2923.

cial sites. Those individuals sacrificed in the pools of mud could, metaphorically speaking, stand for sea lions being ritually hunted and clubbed. Perhaps part of the reason for tightly inserting a rock into the victim Sa-2.13's pelvis and depositing the canine of an immature sea lion on his chest was to transform him in a symbolic sea lion (fig. 3.30).

Much more could be said about these tubers, which clearly provide a backdrop for some of the most important subjects of the Moche symbolic apparatus (table 5.5). Their exact roles in the symbolic system under consideration are unclear. In

some cases, they depict subjects that are negatively affected by the adverse conditions, like sea lions and seabirds. In other cases, the symbolism is linked with animal species that apparently thrive under the same conditions, including toads, catfish, and owls. The polysemy of tubers is also made apparent by the number of human actors and beings with supernatural attributes shown on them. They clearly provide for the reunion of subjects that are usually depicted separately. In that regard they offer further testimony of how tightly connected all the elements of the iconography are.

Table 5.5. Subjects Depicted on Tubers

Human	Person with leishmaniasis
	Amputee, whistler, coca taker
	Drum player, conch shell player
	Mountain victim with long hair
	Victim with forelock
	Person with Maltese cross
Skeleton	Skeleton panpipe player
	Skeleton with erection
	Procession of skeletons
	Human cranium, dead persons
Beings with supernatural attributes	Being with fangs
	Strombus monster, snake-fox
Animals	Owl, osprey, Andean condor, seabirds (dead)
	Monkey, feline, deer, duck, rodent
	Sea lion, catfish, stingray
	Iguana, lizard, toad
Objects	Jar/bottle, net bundle

TWO INSIGNIA OF POWER: THE STRAIGHT V AND THE CURVED V SYMBOLS

V-shaped diadems come in two forms: a straight V and a curved one. The straight V diadems are particularly abundant and have been found in context at Sipán in Tombs 2, 3, and 14, and at Huaca el Pueblo in Tomb CH-7 (the Lord of Ucupe burial), which contained the only archaeologically documented curved V-shaped diadem (fig. 5.187). I have suggested in this chapter that the source of inspiration for the first form—the straight V diadem—is the trapezoidal form of the stabilimenta of *Argiope argentata* (fig. 5.120). But what about the second one? Is this only a variant of the same type or does it carry further symbolic associations? In order to tease out an additional subject that may have been added to the overall symbolism of this insignia of power, I begin with an outstanding sculpture that was found in Tomb 14 at Sipán (fig. 5.188). This solid lost wax copper figure features an owl being standing on top of a platform. He carries a club, a spearthrower, and a round shield. His diadem depicts an owl with outstretched wings, and a second owl in a similar position is tied across his back. The supplementary wings affixed to the diadem, just above the owl effigy, are striking. These wings have been simpli-

fied into curved appendages much like the curved V-shaped diadem (fig. 5.189). Therefore I suggest that the curved V symbol was created to add the owl to the spider symbolism. Two nose ornaments from Tomb 3 at Sipán offer further support for this proposition. The first one depicts a standing warrior wearing the owl diadem with outstretched wings (fig. 5.190). On top of the wings of the animal lie a pair of curve-shaped wings. The second nose ornament depicts an individual with raised arms wearing a straight V-shaped diadem (fig. 5.191). It would appear that each of these nose ornaments carries one part of the Ucupe diadem shown in figure 5.187: the raised hands are now associated with the straight V diadem, while simplified wings are clearly in the form of the curved V-shaped diadem. Perhaps the most striking example of the relationship between the curved V and the bulk of the symbolism associated with *Argiope argentata* and its stabilimenta is a pair of unprovenanced metallic plumes from the Metropolitan Museum of Art (fig. 5.192). The overall shape of these plumes, which may have been attached to a crown of some sort, is the shape of the curved V diadem, yet its body contains cutout representations of six X-shaped beings or Spider Decapitators. Thus these plumes clearly bring the two themes together.

This section ends with a rather unusual depic-

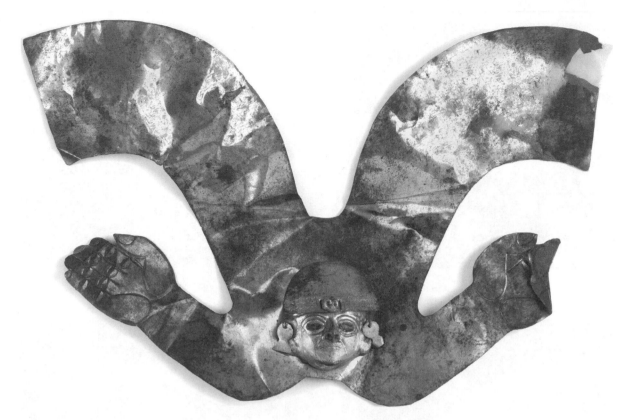

FIGURE 5.187. (*Above*) Diadem with raised arms, Lord of Ucupe burial, Huaca el Pueblo. Ministry of Culture, Peru. Inv. no. CH7-124. Photograph by Johnathan Watts, MEG.

FIGURE 5.188. (*Below*) Copper figure of an owl being, Tomb 14, Sipán. Museo de Sitio de Sipán.

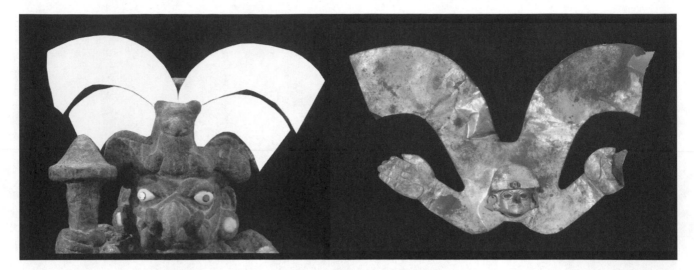

FIGURE 5.189. Comparison between the diadem of the owl being and the diadem CH7-124.

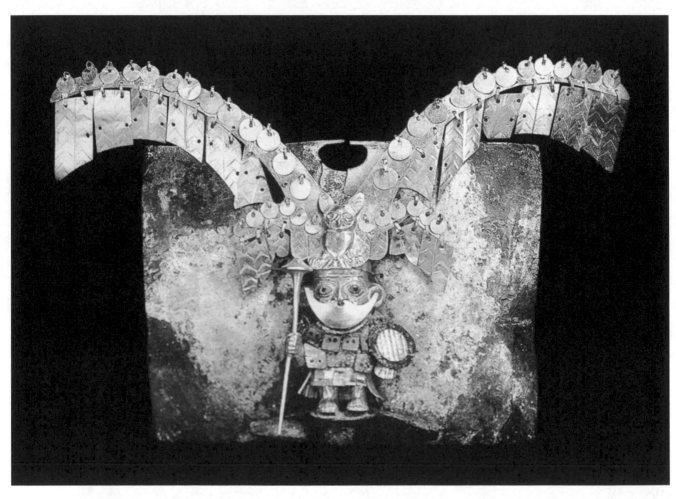

FIGURE 5.190. Nose ornament from Tomb 3, Sipán. Museo Tumbas Reales de Sipán. Photograph by Christopher B. Donnan and Donald McClelland.

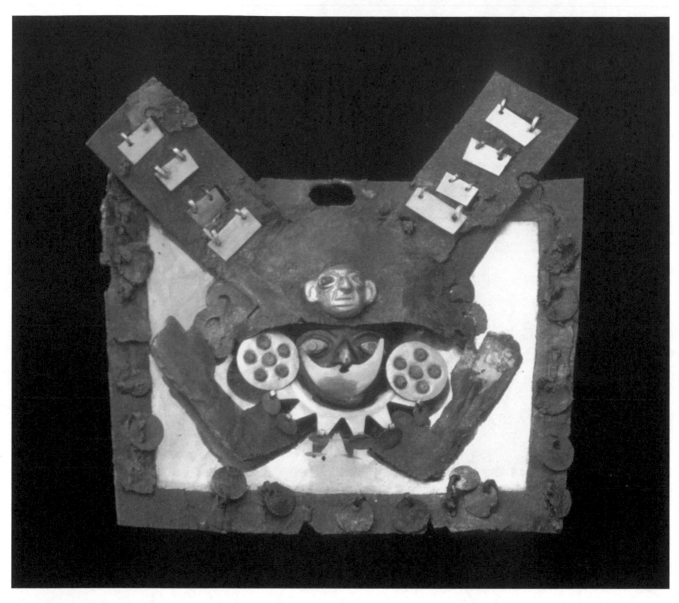

FIGURE 5.191. Nose ornament from Tomb 3, Sipán. Museo Tumbas Reales de Sipán. Photograph by Christopher B. Donnan and Donald McClelland.

FIGURE 5.192. Metallic plumes from a diadem. Metropolitan Museum of Art, New York. Inv. no. 1987.394.87–88.

FIGURE 5.193. Late Phase IV rendition of the Sacrifice Ceremony. Private collection. Photograph by Christopher B. Donnan.

tion of members of the Sacrifice Ceremony. The overall form of the bottle and the spout and the treatment of the subject matter indicate that this is a Late Phase IV (or transitional Phase IV/V) example (fig. 5.193). In the fineline painting in figure 5.194, five spider beings are wearing straight V-shaped diadems of Individual D. An individual seated inside a crescent-shaped moon above the scene is holding a cup. Stylistically, this is perhaps one of the earliest renditions of the Net Shirt woman so prominently depicted at San José de Moro. The Individual D figures are helping Individual A to climb a ladder. The sides of the ladder end in fox heads. To the lower right of the scene, an individual wearing an octopus diadem lies in a splayed position. To the far left, at the same level, a seated person wears a curved V-shaped diadem. The overall appearance of this subject and its proximity with Individual A would suggest that it refers to Individual B. Therefore this scene brings together the three main animal subjects associated with Individuals B and D: the spider, the owl, and the octopus. The truth of the matter is that Individuals B and D may pertain to the same type of subject. Physical remains of individuals impersonating this social and political entity have been found at Sipán in Tombs 2, 3, and 14 and at Huaca el Pueblo in tomb CH-7. The importance of these subjects and of the Sacrifice Ceremony is explored in chapter 7.

SUMMARY

The aim of a metaphorical system such as the one devised by the Moche was not to create an exhaustive listing of all the animal and plants species negatively or positively affected by El Niño conditions. Its main objective was to provide a rationale for the exercise of power and rulership, an ontological view of the world that makes rulership and its activities necessary and inevitable for the proper functioning of the Moche society.

FIGURE 5.194. Late Phase IV rendition of the Sacrifice Ceremony. Drawing by Donna McClelland. The Christopher B. Donnan and Donna McClelland Moche Archive, Image Collections and Fieldwork Archives, Dumbarton Oaks, Trustees for Harvard University, Washington, DC.

Table 5.6. Subjects Depicted in High-Ranking Burials

Animals	P	Lady Cao	La Mina	CH-7	Tomb 3
		Early Moche		Middle Moche	
Eagle ray	1	X	X		
Swimming crab	1		X		X
Lobster	1				
Monkey	2	X	X		
Parrot	2	X			
Snowy egret	2	X	X		
Iguana	2	X	X	X	
Dragonfly	2		X		
Sea lion	3		X		
Crab	3	X	X		
Pelican	3	X			
Fox	4	X		X	X
Feline	4	X	X	X	X
Owl	4	X	X	X	X
Boa	4	X	X	X	
Rodent	4	X			
Condor	4	X	X		X
Spider	4	X	X	X	X
Centipede	4		X		
Scorpion	4	X			
Snail	4	X	X		
Catfish	4	X	X		X
Borracho fish	4	X			X
Octopus	4		X	X	X
Seahorse	4	X	X	X	
Lizard	4		X		

Provenance (P): 1 The Newcomers, 2 From the Northern Region, 3 Local Species Disturbed by El Niño Events, 4 Local Species Helped by El Niño Events

Each of the subjects whether big or small, playing a prominent role or not, participates in this overall program. Each of them constitutes only one small part of the system, which is the reason why singling them out for analysis is not productive. Therefore the dominant enterprise in this chapter has been to give justice to the system and try to present as many subjects as possible and clarify the intricacies of their ramifications. Table 5.6 permits us to appreciate how important these animal species were for Moche rulers in the Chi-cama (Lady Cao, Huaca Cao Viejo), Jequetepeque (La Mina), Zaña (CH-7, Huaca el Puebo), and Lambayeque (Tomb 3, Sipán) Valleys. They literally decked themselves with these creatures and, by association, with their associated symbolism.

Size and number matter in the symbolic system highlighted in this chapter. The subjects accompanying the warm El Niño oceanic current are often impressively large: manta rays, whale sharks, green lobsters, leatherback turtles. A certain amount of pairing is also suggested: the lizards with the iguanas, the black vultures with the Andean condors, the land snails with *Strombus*, the local crabs with the swimming crabs, and the shrimp with the green spiny lobsters. It would appear that the Moche were intentionally pairing them together to emphasize these size differences. An added strategy for highlighting the importance of these subjects and marking their connections with the most profound aspects of Moche symbolism was to transform many of them into fanged beings. As mentioned earlier in the chapter, beings with large fangs protruding from their mouths are an ancient theme probably inherited from the Late Formative Period. Bestowing those attributes on these subjects was perhaps a way of making them ancient: validating their presence and importance with ancientness. It may also index a certain divine quality that has yet to be understood properly.

Finally, the aim for the Moche was not to list all the changes that took place during El Niño events. Instead their objective was to create a symbolic system of everything that was ritually and ideologically significant for the exercise of power.

CHAPTER 6

CHILDREN AND WARRIORS

The three children deposited in Sand 4 shortly after the construction of the ritual complex are perhaps one of the most intriguing contexts of Plaza 3A (figs. 3.3, 3.5, 3.6). Plaza 3A and Platform II were created as a single architectural project for the sole purpose of performing sacrificial rituals in the plaza and burying sacrificers in the platform, so why were the children positioned there exactly underneath the first sacrificial ritual? Were they ritually placed in the clean sand at the base of the structures only as a dedication to the ceremonial architecture in general, regardless of its eventual function? Were they socially or ritually related to the sacrificial victims just above them in the subsequent layers of sand and sediments? The answers to these questions are not readily apparent in the sands and sediments of the plaza.

As explored in chapter 5, the high degree of contiguity between El Niño conditions and the iconography suggests that Moche visual culture remains the best line of inquiry. The individuals involved in the socially important activities, the rituals performed at Moche sites, and the visual culture are all intimately linked. They form part of a socially unified group. The iconography displayed on various media constitutes a single unifying project dedicated to a dominant ideology concerning Moche identity and its social and political institutions. Therefore this chapter and chapter 7 offer the following research hypothesis. Ritual practices and performances such as the offering of children and the sacrifice of captured warriors documented in Plaza 3A and on complex representations on funerary vessels, wooden and metallic objects, and murals cannot be disconnected from one another. This is not just a unilinear approach where the data from one system are used to explain the second one. On the contrary, the method is really to use a dynamic and discursive approach where the physical evidence of ritual performances is used to contextualize the related representations and where the visual imagery permits us tremendously to enhance the quality and the complexity of the interpretations.

The ritual process involving children is studied in detail by first summarizing the archaeological context in the sacrificial site. Although part of this research has been published elsewhere (Bourget 2001a), in this chapter the original analysis is greatly expanded and includes some of the data collected from the latest excavations at the site. I suggest that this ritual activity is closely related to the concept of ritualized warfare and possibly to a certain social class in Moche society.

BURIALS OR OFFERINGS?

As discussed in chapter 3, the three children found buried in Plaza 3A had been carefully prepared, wrapped in textiles, and, in at least one case, kept elsewhere for some time before being buried in Sand 4 (figs. 3.5, 3.6). Therefore the first concern is to determine whether indeed these children were given standard Moche burials in the plaza or whether they were part of another ritual system. A review of child burials from the Moche period indicates that, while the children buried in the plaza share some similarities with full-fledged funerals, they also differ from them in many respects. As in Moche burials, the children were wrapped in textiles, placed on their backs, and in two cases placed in the classic orientation with the upper part of their bodies toward the south and their feet to the north. But they also diverged from standard practices. First, they were not placed in any form of funerary chambers but just laid down in loose sand (fig. 3.3). This is rather unusual; most burials in the Huaca de la Luna are ensconced within the adobe architecture. Second, apart from a degraded mass of seashells and two whistles, the children did not have any of the usual offerings such as ceramic vessels or metallic fragments in their mouth.

The man found more or less at the same level, which preceded the sacrifices as well, was left wrapped in textiles and propped against a boulder (fig. 3.10). He also did not have the usual set of funerary offerings but possessed what was probably a bag filled with quartz crystals, a few beads, and red pigment. It is thus likely that all these individuals were part of another ritual concept involving their deposition in a specific part of a temple for particular reasons. As suggested in chapter 3, the adult male may have been propped against the boulder as an ad hoc gesture in order to reconsecrate the smaller ritual space created by the precinct. The intentionality of the ritual was already well established from the beginning, so the situation of the children must connect to the wider scheme of the project Plaza 3A/Platform II.

Although the iconography sometimes displays scenes involving children that are apparently borrowed from everyday activities, such as individuals holding or breastfeeding a child (figs. 6.1, 6.2), a corpus of subjects with young individuals reveals a very distinct picture. A survey of Moche ceramics shows numerous representations of children being carried by subjects that are not related to motherhood. They can be carried by the three most prevalent types of actors: human beings, anthropomorphized beings, and skeletonized individuals, which indicates the importance of this theme. Perhaps the single most prevalent aspect cutting across these types of subjects is the activity of whistling, so it seems most logical to begin with this aspect in order to unravel this theme.

WHISTLING AND CHILDREN

As shown in chapter 3, the headless child found at the base of the north wall was firmly holding a small whistle in each hand (fig. 3.6). These instruments were almost identical in every respect (fig. 3.7). But what is the relation between these musical instruments and a headless child? This section investigates the representations of children and whistling individuals in the iconography. The first step is to explore whether a link exists among young individuals, the act of whistling, and decapitation.

One of the most frequent types uniting children with whistling is a person standing up holding a child or carrying it under one arm, wearing a shawl covering the head and the shoulders (fig. 6.3).[1] The shawl is usually tightly secured with a sash around the neck. In most examples consulted, the person holding the child is whistling and the bottle itself often is a musical instrument. The bottle shown in figure 6.4 depicts an individual

FIGURE 6.1. Bottle in the shape of a woman breastfeeding a child. By kind permission of the Trustees of the British Museum, London Inv. no. Am1858.0403.22.

whistling, but this time his face is deeply furrowed by wrinkles and Maltese crosses are painted on his cheeks and chin.[2] This is no ordinary human being: these furrows are part of a tradition that began during the Cupisnique Period. Therefore the whistler in figure 6.4 may well be associated

with a concept of ancientness where much older concepts and iconographies are used to validate contemporary ideological and religious tenets. The Moche apparently began using ancient concepts quite extensively in Phase III on their portable art and also on the polychrome murals adorning their

FIGURE 6.2. Bottle in the shape of a woman holding a child on her lap. Museo Banco Central de Reserva del Perú. Inv. no. ACE-486.

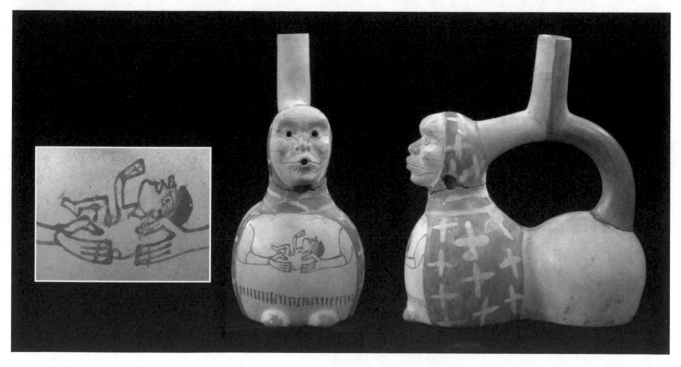

FIGURE 6.3. Whistling individual holding a child. Staatliche Museen zu Berlin, Preußischer Kulturbesitz—Ethnologisches Museum. Inv. no. VA 11437.

FIGURE 6.4. Whistling person with a child. Staatliche Museen zu Berlin, Preußischer Kulturbesitz—Ethnologisches Museum. Inv. no. VA 48201.

FIGURE 6.5. Portrait vessel of an individual whistling and with wrinkles on his face. Staatliche Museen zu Berlin, Preußischer Kulturbesitz—Ethnologisches Museum. Inv. no. VA 4663.

public architecture. A deeply wrinkled whistler has also been depicted on a portrait vessel, further reinforcing the importance of this subject in their symbolic system (fig. 6.5).

Children are also cared for by other entities, such as a skeletonized individual wearing the distinctive shawl (fig. 6.6). As in figure 6.3, this ceramic vessel is a musical instrument, with the air chamber of the whistle situated inside the head of the cadaver. The sound is thus coming through the eyes and the mouth of the dead person. The child is wrapped in a textile or blanket and is being carried on its back, which is somewhat similar to the position of a corpse in a Moche burial.

Children are also transported by anthropomorphized bats. On one vessel the bat being

FIGURE 6.6. Whistling bottle in the form of a skeleton being holding a child. Museo Nacional de Arqueología, Antropología e Historia del Perú. Inv. no. C-01025.

carries a child under one arm and a warrior's mace under the other (fig. 6.7). To my knowledge, this is the only type of a zoomorphic subject holding children. That is a rather important observation, as this subject is consistently linked to ritual bleeding and sacrifice by decapitation (Bourget 1994a; Donnan 1978). The conical helmet and the war mace also establish a positive link with ceremonial combat. When the faces of the children are clearly depicted, their eyes are often closed. This could well be a sign that the child is actually dead.

Thus the young individual in the plaza and the act of carrying a child in the iconography are not only closely associated with real whistles and individuals whistling but also with the feminine gender, death, and sacrificial beings such as bats. But could they also be linked more firmly with ceremonial combat, capture, and El Niño events? In sum, could these children be related to the whole ritual program of the plaza and some of the most fundamental aspects of Moche ideology?

HUNTING, WARFARE, AND SACRIFICE

Three ritual practices depicted in Moche art are fundamentally linked: hunting, warfare, and sacrifice. The same actors—who belong, for lack of a better word, to a warrior class—are consistently observed taking part in these three activities. If the depictions of children and their remains in the

plaza form an integral part of the ideological system, they must also be related to these activities.

Ritual Hunting

An exceptional ceramic (fig. 6.8) bridges the gap between the two distinct ritual systems of the plaza—those with the children and those with the adult males. It is an important artifact because it brings together two sets of information that are usually depicted separately. The first is modeled on top of the bottle and represents a whistling person carrying a child. The second is painted all around the chamber of the bottle. It shows two individuals carrying a large net bundle on their backs. They wield similar bulbous maces in their right hands. A third bundle is also shown as a discrete object between the two individuals, just underneath the sculpture on the summit of the chamber.

These individuals, the net bundles, and the clubs are clearly related to hunting activities. The peculiar clubs that they carry represent a special weapon used in certain scenes of warfare and in the ritual hunts of deer (*Odocoileus virginianus*), sea lions (*Otaria* sp.), and foxes (*Lycalopex sechurae*). Only the first two activities are discussed here. The fox hunts are usually simpler and in many respects very similar to the hunting of deer (fig. 7.32). The fox and the deer as a related pair warrant more concentrated research than can be presented here.

FIGURE 6.7. Bottle in the shape of a bat warrior holding a child. Staatliche Museen zu Berlin, Preußischer Kulturbesitz—Ethnologisches Museum. Inv. no. VA 18083.

FIGURE 6.8. Whistling person holding a child. Museo Nacional de Arqueología, Antropología e Historia del Perú. Inv. no. C-54577.

FIGURE 6.9. Deer hunting with two individuals attending the net. Drawing by Donna McClelland. The Christopher B. Donnan and Donna McClelland Moche Archive, Image Collections and Fieldwork Archives, Dumbarton Oaks, Trustees for Harvard University, Washington, DC.

The first deer hunt takes place just above a net running around the base of the bottle (fig. 6.9). It involves two pairs of humans wearing elaborate headdresses and tunics who are spearing deer to death. Smaller figures, armed with the special clubs, are driving the game toward the hunters. The outfits and the markings on the legs of the four individuals are identical to those of warriors. Donnan (1997: 58–59) has successfully linked these actors to ceremonial combat and the capture of prisoners:

> The many parallels between deer hunting and warfare strongly suggest that these were related activities in the Moche world. The similarities in dress, ornament, body paint, and weapons used in these two activities indicate that the same class of adult males, and perhaps even the same individuals, were participating in both. The purpose of combat was not the conquest of enemy territory, but the capture of opponents for ritual sacrifice. Similarly, the purpose of deer hunting was not to obtain food but to capture deer for ritual sacrifice. By participating in these two activities, high-status adult males could both demonstrate and augment their prestige in Moche society.

Indeed in its anthropomorphized form the deer is often depicted as a warrior holding the very same war mace or as a nude male seated cross-legged with both hands clasped, wearing a rope around its neck (figs. 5.162, 5.163). As shown in chapter 3, many clay statuettes representing nude men in the same position and with a similar tie were recovered from the sacrificial site.

The net bundles transported by the two individuals on the ceramic vessel in figure 6.8 are often represented as carried by other whistlers (fig. 5.185) or placed between individuals involved in the Coca Ceremony (fig. 7.68). In this scene Wrinkle Face raises his clasped hands toward the objects as if to mark their importance and sacredness.[3] This ceremony (discussed in chapter 7) is clearly linked to ceremonial combat and sacrifice. Therefore the net bundles shown in the painting also form part of their paraphernalia. Similar objects are consistently depicted in Phase V attached to the extremities of reed boats (fig. 7.93). Alana Cordy-Collins (1972: 8), who was probably the first person to try to identify these peculiar bundles, suggested that they could have been some type of special bag net used to catch crabs. Although I agree that they may be nets of some sort, I suggest that these bundles consist of the rolled-up nets used in deer hunting.

In the ritual hunt of deer scenes, long nets are systematically depicted on the lower register (figs. 5.65, 5.165). Moreover, the small figures attending the net in figure 6.9 are similar to those painted on the ceramic in figure 6.8. The second attendant,

FIGURE 6.10. Deer hunting. Drawing by Donna McClelland. The Christopher B. Donnan and Donna McClelland Moche Archive, Image Collections and Fieldwork Archives, Dumbarton Oaks, Trustees for Harvard University, Washington, DC.

encased inside the net on the right, has a bulbous mace lying just behind him (fig. 6.9). This would tend to confirm that these big bundles represent long hunting nets rolled up.

The individuals attending the hunting nets or carrying the net bundles are the same actors who perform the second type of hunt, the killing of sea lions (fig. 5.63). These sea lion hunters wear the same tunics, headdresses, and ear ornaments. They also have special bags or sashes tied around their waists like those worn by the net attendants of the deer hunt scene. The sea lion hunt is practiced with the same type of wooden mace. Some sea lion hunters carry war shields, reinforcing the profound connection between hunting and warfare (fig. 5.66). It is also important to note the presence of a woman wearing a shawl toward the right side of the scene in figure 5.63. She is sitting in front of a house and is apparently in the process of preparing offerings. Just behind her, two funerary jars already have been prepared. One of them is decorated with some sort of vine around its neck. Women preparing jars and bottles are also depicted in at least two other similar examples of sea lion killings.

In certain deer hunting scenes (fig. 6.10, far right), these individuals are shown carrying these jars with vines or branches tied around their necks. Thus these sets of recurring actors in both scenes (the hunters or attendants with clubs and the women with jars) seem to confirm that the ritual hunts of deer and sea lions are conceptually

related, although not necessarily absolutely identical. Above all, these elements clearly link both hunting activities to ceremonial combat. But (as discussed further in chapter 7) they may lead to distinct sacrificial systems.

In the deer-hunting scene just discussed, the branches around the jars are very similar to those on the trees surrounding the activity. This might indicate their provenance. Furthermore, these peculiar branches are also depicted on the chests of some of the clay statuettes uncovered in Plaza 3A (fig. 3.106) and also on the shawl of a wrinkle-faced individual carrying a child (fig. 6.11), where the swirling branches terminate in bird heads.

In a previous study (Bourget 1994a), I proposed a sexual dichotomy in the ritual activities and that women were closely associated with the preparation of the cadaver, the funerary offerings, and the victims of sacrifice just before the sacrificial ritual. Men would have been linked with the burial itself, warfare activities, and the actual sacrifices, both as sacrificers and as victims. The carrying of children by individuals wearing shawls—indexes of the feminine gender—would be part of the activities eventually leading to the rituals themselves. Thus the preparation of ceramic vessels, the ritual killing of animals, and the carrying of children would correspond to the intermediary stage of a ritual leading eventually to its conclusion: a burial, a sacrifice, or an offering. I suggest that the women in front of houses in the sea lion hunt-

FIGURE 6.11. Whistling individual holding a child. Courtesy of the Phoebe A. Hearst Museum of Anthropology and the Regents of the University of California. Inv. no. 4-2938.

ing scenes are in the process of preparing funerary offerings: stirrup spout bottles, jars, and gourd containers.

Donnan (1997: 58) has suggested that the jars carried by these individuals in the deer-hunting scene may have contained the blood of sacrificial victims (fig. 6.10):

> Another element linking combat and deer hunting is the fact that females shown in some deer hunting scenes [fig. 6.10] are identical to females who participate in human sacrifice [fig. 6.12]. These women are always shown with long hair, wearing dresses of dark color, and either carry or stand adjacent to large jars. The jars normally have domed lids and branches or rope tied around their necks. They may have contained blood and been conceptualized as the equivalent of prisoners with ropes around their necks.

I would tend to see these vessels as part of the funerary paraphernalia, but these two interpretations are not necessarily mutually exclusive: funerary and sacrificial rituals are probably closely related. After all, these scenes are depicted on funerary offerings. This complex subject requires more research beyond the scope of this study in order to understand the complex relations between gender and funerary and sacrificial rituals.

FIGURE 6.12. Sacrifice Ceremony. Drawing by Donna McClelland. The Christopher B. Donnan and Donna McClelland Moche Archive, Image Collections and Fieldwork Archives, Dumbarton Oaks, Trustees for Harvard University, Washington, DC.

Warfare, Capture, and Sacrifice

Evidence from Plaza 3A and Moche visual culture clearly suggests that deer hunting and the killing of sea lions are closely associated with the war of capture and the sacrifice of warriors. In the iconography, the relation with sea lion hunting is made even clearer in some cases by showing sea lion hunters carrying not only the special maces but warriors' shields. Elizabeth Benson (1995: 258) was probably the first scholar to note the relation between sea lion hunts and a certain form of sacrifice: "Another type of sacrifice—and a possible calendrical one—was the hunting of otaries." This relation was evinced in Plaza 3A by the canine of a very young sea lion purposely deposited on the chest of a victim and by a sea lion painted on the body of a clay statuette (figs. 3.30, 3.113). Moreover, a sea lion vertebra was found in a small recess at the bottom of a posthole on Platform II (fig. 4.4). It is thus very revealing to discover the representation of a victim tied to a sacrificial rack adorned with the heads of sea lions (fig. 6.13). The victim has the same haircut as the statuettes found in the plaza, a further indication of their link with the same sacrificial complex. Although I cannot state that a victim was left in such a rack during the burial of the old man in Tomb 1, other devices used to restrain sacrificial victims are depicted (figs. 7.2, 7.3). In some cases, racks are shown firmly planted in the ground of a plaza in the midst of ceremonial architecture (fig. 6.14).

By a somewhat similar logic, the bulbous head of the mace of a warrior takes the shape of a sea

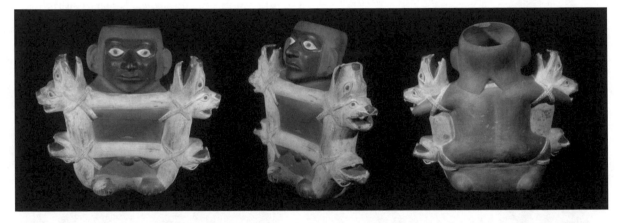

FIGURE 6.13. Victim attached to a rectangular sacrificial rack decorated with sea lion heads. Staatliche Museen zu Berlin, Preußischer Kulturbesitz—Ethnologisches Museum. Inv. no. VA 48078.

FIGURE 6.14. Rectangular rack placed in a plaza in front of a temple. Staatliche Museen zu Berlin, Preußischer Kulturbesitz—Ethnologisches Museum. Inv. no. VA 18282.

FIGURE 6.15. Warrior holding a mace. Museo Nacional de Arqueología, Antropología e Historia del Perú. Inv. no. C-03244.

lion head (fig. 6.15). Therefore both the sacrificial rack and the war club are directly linked with the concept of ritual hunting, reinforcing the idea that these objects are symbolically and metaphorically connected to the killing of these marine mammals. As mentioned in chapter 4, Tomb 1 on Platform II contained a very similar bottle depicting a warrior in the same position holding the same type of mace (fig. 4.7). Thus it seems that the individual resting in this grave, a man in his sixties, might have been closely linked to this ritual.

In addition to the bottle in the shape of a warrior shown in figure 4.8, the tomb of the warrior priest at Huaca de la Cruz contained a bulbous mace (fig. 6.16). This impressive object measuring 143 cm in length ended in an acerated copper point. The scene sculpted around the head of the mace is complex and organized in at least two distinct moments. Near the summit of the mace, three warriors are actively pursuing, fighting, and capturing two other warriors (fig. 6.17). Immediately underneath, in the middle section, two war-

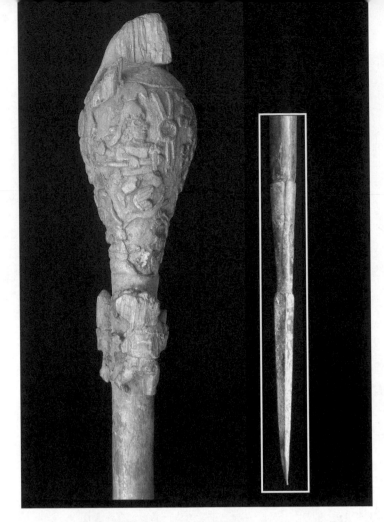

riors are kneeling in front of a seated individual (fig. 6.18); below this scene three prisoners are attached around the shaft of the weapon (fig. 6.16). These finely carved scenes apparently were part of the Warrior Narrative, which includes the battle, the capture, and the presentation of the captives in a ceremonial precinct (Donnan 2010). A series of ceramics in the same tomb is closely related to the themes just discussed: a jar in the form of a sea lion, a deer hunting scene, an individual wearing the headdress of the sea lion hunters, and two almost identical drinking cups in the form of bat heads. Other ceramic vessels also matched those discovered on Platform II, suggesting that the old male in the burial was also a sacrificer.

The use of the same maces in warfare and hunting is certainly not fortuitous and strongly suggests homologous meanings for these activities (Donnan 2010). Ceremonial combat and ritual hunting are so closely related that the war of capture can in fact metaphorically signify the ritual hunting of sacrificial victims, with the deer and sea lions standing for the human victims. This depersonalization process of Moche warriors—transforming them into prey—is further exacerbated by the representations of combatants or sacrificial victims in the guise of anthropomorphized deer (figs. 5.162, 5.163). As suggested by the bottle depicting a child and net bundles (fig.

FIGURE 6.16. Ceremonial mace. Museo Nacional de Arqueología, Antropología e Historia del Perú. Inv. no. MO-10226.

FIGURE 6.17. Ceremonial mace (top part). Museo Nacional de Arqueología, Antropología e Historia del Perú. Inv. no. MO-10226.

FIGURE 6.18. Ceremonial mace (middle part). Museo Nacional de Arqueología, Antropología e Historia del Perú. Inv. no. MO-10226.

FIGURE 6.19. Deer holding a fawn. Museo Nacional de Arqueología, Antropología e Historia del Perú. Inv. no. C-01296.

6.8), the offering of children could be associated with the ritual hunting of deer and by extension with the killing of sea lions. In the logic of Moche iconography, where complex ideas are likely to be delineated in various forms, it is thus not surprising to see deer and sea lions holding their young, as Elizabeth Benson (1972: 54) said, as "a human mother would" (figs. 6.19, 6.20). Chapter 7 discusses the offering of deer in the context of human sacrifice.

Other scenes are related to children, sacrificial victims, and the act of whistling and offering.

Whistling, Offering, and Sacrifice

The act of whistling is associated not only with the offering of children but also with sacrificial victims. One bottle represents the act of whistling on the summit of the chamber (fig. 6.21).[4] Perhaps the same victim, painted on the chamber, is being held by a woman on each side (fig. 6.22). Severed arms, legs, and a head are also represented. Another individual inside a building is looking toward the group and a jar with branches around its neck. It has been suggested (Donnan 1997: 58) that these three individuals are women closely

related to those carrying the jars in the deer hunt scene (fig. 6.10). An eventual sacrificial victim thus also performs the act of whistling. The women holding the victim prior to his sacrifice are associated in other scenes with the preparation of the funerary offerings before the burial ritual itself and in relation with sea lion hunting (fig. 5.63). These two events precede the resolution of their respective ceremonies, the sacrifice and the burial. It is also worth noting that a small whistle in the form of a bird was found among the sacrificed warriors of Plaza 3A (fig. 3.63). The same concept applies to death and its rituals, as indicated by a ceramic that depicts a whistling man transporting funerary offerings (fig. 6.23). The act of whistling is linked with the crucial moment of a ritual just before the offering of a child, the sacrifice of a victim, or the burial itself. It is thus possibly a sound produced to index or symbolically connect with the following phase of these rituals.

An additional aspect linking children and sacrificial victims is the act of offering, which shows considerable overlap between the two types of subjects. A number of vessels display an individual holding a sacrificial victim almost like a child (fig. 6.24). In this example, the skin of the naked male

FIGURE 6.20. Sea lion holding two pups. Museo Nacional de Arqueología, Antropología e Historia del Perú. Inv. no. C-01500.

FIGURE 6.21. Whistling victim standing on top of a sacrificial ritual. Private collection. Photograph Christopher B. Donnan.

is covered with the same designs as those encountered on the clay statuettes of Plaza 3A. His left arm rests on his leg, while he makes the fist gesture with his right hand. This second example blends together the child and the sacrificial victim. The child sitting to the right of a bigger individual is partly covered with a shawl (fig. 6.25). He has a special hairdo, which includes a forelock. This hairstyle is clearly associated with certain types of warriors (fig. 7.19).

SUMMARY

Shortly after the completion of the plaza, dedicatory offerings of children were made. It is not possible to say whether they were sacrificed, decapitated, or simply offered to the huaca after their natural death. Given the nature of the representation of children in the iconography and their numerous links with other subjects such as skeletonized individuals, bats, deer, and sea lions, these young individuals form part of the whole sacrificial and ritual liturgy of the Moche. In a manner which is still difficult to document completely, they are associated with the ritual hunt and killing of deer and sea lions. They are also linked with the sacrificial system, and the removal of their heads may be a strategy to further this connection. Once

FIGURE 6.22. Sacrificial victims and human remains. Drawing by Donna McClelland. The Christopher B. Donnan and Donna McClelland Moche Archive, Image Collections and Fieldwork Archives, Dumbarton Oaks, Trustees for Harvard University, Washington, DC.

FIGURE 6.23. Individual carrying funerary offerings. Private collection. Photograph by Christopher B. Donnan.

FIGURE 6.24. Individual holding a sacrificial victim. Staatliche Museen zu Berlin, Preußischer Kulturbesitz—Ethnologisches Museum. Inv. no. VA 18040.

FIGURE 6.25. Individual under a shawl standing alongside a smaller figure with a forelock. Staatliche Museen zu Berlin, Preußischer Kulturbesitz—Ethnologisches Museum. Inv. no. VA 64330.

more the iconography clearly shows this aspect of the ritual by displaying individuals carrying children whose heads are missing (fig. 6.26).

The sacrificial victims of the plaza are closely linked not only with the El Niño phenomenon but also with the world of the sea and especially the ritual hunting of sea lions. One of the principal reasons for choosing these marine mammals as surrogate victims might be because of the transformation of their predatory activities during El Niño events. During this period, sea lions are deprived of their main sources of proteins, sardines and anchovies. They have to plunge deeper and deeper to get their food and become extremely hungry and aggressive. Even now they frequently destroy the nets of the fishers in order to get their food (Schweigger 1947: 209). During difficult periods of El Niño events, the Moche and the sea lions had to compete for the same resources. The sight of big sea lions attacking their fishing nets must have been just as impressive for the Moche as it is for the present-day fishers. According to Thor Heyerdahl (1995: 209), during a short El Niño–like period at the beginning of the 1990s, the fishers of Lambayeque had "to cease fishing due to the numbers of huge sea lions which destroyed their nets and gathered on the beaches."

But one question remains: what was the relation between the children and the slain warriors? Were their remains randomly selected from deceased children in the local population or were they part of the same social group as the warriors? An adequate answer to this fundamental aspect still eludes me. Perhaps some clues lie in Tomb 3 on Platform II, where a group of three vessels showed a warrior at three stages of his life (fig. 4.46). Donnan (2004: 156) suggested that his status may have been inherited, so the older man in that tomb was depicted at different epochs of his life. The same situation may have occurred with the warriors deposited in the sacrificial site. Children dying at a young age who belonged to this social group may have been deemed proper to be united with their older counterparts.

FIGURE 6.26. Individual holding a child with its head missing. Staatliche Museen zu Berlin, Preußischer Kulturbesitz—Ethnologisches Museum. Inv. no. VA 4701.

CHAPTER 7

HUMAN SACRIFICE
AND RULERSHIP

Moche ritual sacrifices—both in the archaeology and in the iconography—have mostly been discussed in general terms without any real attempt to put these practices into a detailed chronological framework. The actors and the rituals that they performed have often been perceived as timeless and unchanging, forming part of permanent institutions sometimes lasting over four centuries:

> The fact that the Sacrifice Ceremony was so widespread in both time and space strongly implies that it was part of a state religion, with a priesthood in each part of the kingdom composed of nobles who dressed in prescribed ritual attire. When members of the priesthood died, they were buried at the temple where the Sacrifice Ceremony took place, wearing the objects they had used to perform the ritual. Subsequently, other men and women were chosen to replace them, to dress like them, and to perform the same ceremonial role. (Alva and Donnan 1993: 226)

The position taken by these scholars at the time is understandable, as the sacrificial contexts needed to put the practice into a historical perspective were still buried under the sands and the sediments of Plazas 3A and 3C. Yet the burial contexts at Sipán and its related iconographies reveal that these activities, which constituted the most important Moche ceremonies detected to this date, must have been directly associated with the highest ranks of rulership. This linkage between ritual violence and political structures implies that transformations in the organization of the latter would logically affect the former. Multiple representations suggest that these rituals are consistently depicted in relation to the most elaborately attired subjects. The two central tenets of the iconography during Phases III and IV—warfare and human sacrifice—are always overseen by these individuals. Therefore hypothetical changes in

Moche political structures during these two phases must have triggered concomitant changes in these ritual practices and their representations.

This chapter addresses the diverse relationships of Moche visual culture, ritual practices, and political institutions and begins to map the transformations in these structures during this part of Moche history. By uniting the iconography with the archaeology, my aim is to offer some views regarding the nature of the rituals and political configurations created and maintained by the Moche from the late third to the late eighth century. In a sense, the overarching objective is to introduce a dimension of historical depth into these institutions. The information from a single Moche site would not suffice to cover these five centuries. Although most of the data are provided by the Huacas de Moche site, additional information is drawn from Dos Cabezas, Huaca el Pueblo, Sipán, and San José de Moro.

During a period falling approximately between AD 250 and AD 700, two chronological and stylistic phases have been firmly established at the Huacas de Moche site. Phase III and Phase IV have been found in a clear stratigraphic context at the site. As discussed in chapter 1, these phases form part of the five-phase seriation established by Larco Hoyle (1948). In addition to their stratigraphic position, they can be recognized by changes in the form and decoration of certain ceramic vessels, including principally stirrup spout bottles, flaring bowls, and dippers. These ceramic vessels are predominantly found in burial contexts (Chauchat et al. 2008; Tello, Armas, and Chapdelaine 2003). Thus fineware vessels and fragments encountered not only in funerary assemblages but also on the floors of the urban sector and in the fill of the Huaca de la Luna construction phases can be used to date these contexts. Phase III has been dated from 250 to 450 years AD and Phase IV from 400 to 700 years AD (Chapdelaine 2001: 73). These two periods should not be considered definitive. More detailed research will need to be conducted in order firmly to establish the relative time frame of Phase III, which has been defined so far on the basis of only a handful of radiocarbon dates.

Although many of the artifacts presented in this chapter have been looted—orphaned from their original context—the phase to which they pertain is established through similar vessels excavated at the Huacas de Moche and based on a number of physical characteristics, including the form of the vessel, its size, and its decorative techniques. This is rather important. One of the postulates of this analysis is a direct relationship between the political and social transformations in Moche culture and the stylistic and especially iconographical changes taking place in Phase III, Phase IV, and Phase V. In short, I suggest that the iconography is representative of the transformations taking place in the Moche superstructure because it served primarily to disseminate their ideology.

Rafael Larco Hoyle (1948) perhaps first suggested that Moche style changed because of qualitative changes in their society. For him, each of these five stylistic phases was related to some form of progress or evolution of the Moche. The model ascribed to the usual evolutionary scheme begins with a period marked by external influences (Phase I), followed by the development of the arts and industries (Phase II), culminating in a period of technological, religious, and artistic achievements (Phases III–IV), and ending with a period of decadence, leaving the Moche exposed to foreign invasions (Phase V) (Larco Hoyle 1948: 28–50). This scheme was based in part on a rather impressionistic reading of the iconography, on general views of native coastal populations, and on accepted ideas prevalent at the time regarding the development and collapse of ancient civilizations in general. In the 1940s Moche archaeology was at its beginnings. The iconography was thus perceived as a convenient tool for providing insight into Moche culture and social institutions. The approach favored here also considers these phases—at least III, IV, and V—as indexing changes in Moche society. But my approach does not imply some received ideas as to how a society changes or evolves. It principally aims at reuniting the archaeological data with the visual culture for every phase, in order to present a coherent model for each one.

For each stylistic phase and period under consideration, I begin with the iconography, which provides the comparative basis for the archaeological contexts. In the second part of the demonstration, I use the information gathered during more than two decades of excavation at some of the most important Moche ceremonial centers to explore the intricate relationships between rituals—largely funerary and sacrificial—and rulership. I discuss some of the work carried out at the Huacas de Moche by Claude Chapdelaine in the urban sector, by Santiago Uceda Castillo and his colleagues on the Huaca main platform and Plaza 3B, by Moisés Tufinio and John Verano in Plaza 3C, and by myself in Plaza 3A and Platform II (chapters 3 and 4). Admittedly, using only the data from the Huaca de la Luna and the urban sector offers a limited view of the site. Long-term excavations have yet to be fully initiated at Huaca del Sol. Nevertheless, the discussion should provide a substantial view of this symbolic system, as the Huaca de la Luna was probably the place for the most important and elaborate ritual performances.

THE VISUAL CULTURE OF SACRIFICE

Human sacrifices are extensively depicted in Moche iconography. The types of sacrifice are equally varied. Moche warriors are devoured by felines (fig. 7.1). Males and even females are fed to diverse species of vultures (figs. 5.74, 5.75, 7.2) or offered to an Andean condor by black vultures (fig. 5.76). Others are attached to V-shaped trees or strapped to wooden structures, perhaps during certain funerary rituals (figs. 5.127, 7.2, 7.3) (see

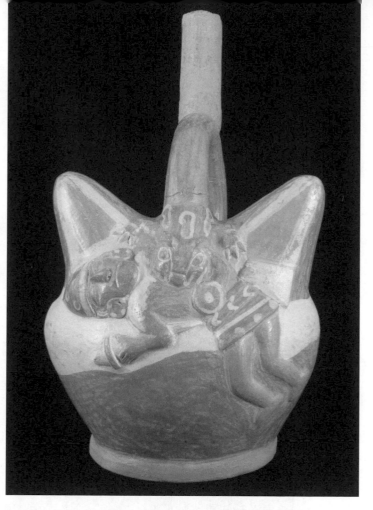

FIGURE 7.1. Moche warrior devoured by a feline. Museo Larco, Lima, Peru, Phase IV. Inv. no. ML001780.

FIGURE 7.2. Sacrificial victim attached to a V-shaped structure. Museo Larco, Lima, Peru, Phase IV. Inv. no. ML001475.

FIGURE 7.3. Sacrificial victim attached to a V-shaped structure. Staatliche Museen zu Berlin, Preußischer Kulturbesitz—Ethnologisches Museum. Inv. no. VA 17575.

FIGURE 7.4. Zoo-anthropomorphic being holding a human head and a sacrificial knife. Museo Larco, Lima, Peru. Inv. no. ML003470.

chapter 6 and Bourget 2006). Sacrifices also may be performed by zoo-anthropomorphic individuals or by beings possessing supernatural attributes (figs. 5.139, 7.4). Among all these varied practices, perhaps the most complex sacrificial rituals in Moche visual culture are those of the Mountain Sacrifice and the Sacrifice Ceremony. These two sacrificial rituals depict distinct activities and different protagonists. They are also related to the most elaborately garbed subjects, indicating the prominence of these rituals and their relationships with the highest Moche elite. First I describe the Mountain Sacrifice, as this ritual tradition is depicted on a ceramic style that chronologically and stratigraphically precedes those vessels illustrating the Sacrifice Ceremony. Indeed, the Mountain Sacrifice occurs prominently on Phase III vessels, while the Sacrifice Ceremony is not visually portrayed before Phase IV.

THE MOUNTAIN SACRIFICE AND THE COCA CEREMONY COMPLEX

The analysis here demonstrates that the Mountain Sacrifice and the Coca Ceremony are related to one another and that they represent the visually most important activities depicted during Phase III. The demonstration begins with the Mountain Sacrifice, which puts into interaction all the main subjects of this symbolic system, including those of the Coca Ceremony.

THE MOUNTAIN SACRIFICE

This section constitutes an extension of chapter 2, where I have suggested (1) that Huaca de la Luna was physically and symbolically linked to the Cerro Blanco and (2) that the Mountain Sacrifice may have been performed in a specific place on the hillside (figs. 2.4, 2.27). The Mountain Sacrifice is first depicted in the Phase III stylistic period. During this phase, it is mostly associated with two specific but related subjects, Wrinkle Face and Iguana. On this single-peak

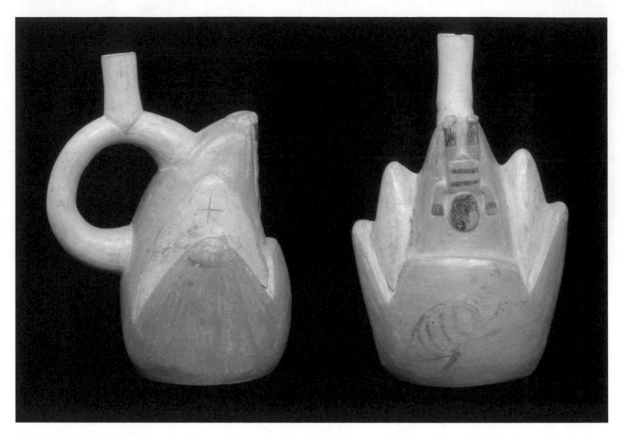

FIGURE 7.5. Mountain Sacrifice showing a victim and a snail. Museo Nacional de Arqueología, Antropología e Historia del Perú. Inv. no. C-03289.

mountain, Wrinkle Face and Iguana flank a victim draped on its summit (fig. 2.23). In most scenes, the long mane of hair of the victim is flowing down from the top of his head, perhaps as a way to highlight its significance for this ritual or to assist in the identification of the subject submitted to the ordeal. In the example shown in figure 2.23, a temple with a double-step design on its roof-comb is located at the foot of the mountain, immediately underneath the central victim. A second victim lies decapitated at the base of the building. There is no indication whether the second victim was intentionally decapitated or whether the fall caused his injury. To the right of the bottle, a leishmaniasis amputee is kneeling alongside the temple, just underneath the left elbow of Wrinkle Face.

A Phase III blackware bottle shows a slightly more elaborate ritual consisting of essentially the same subjects (fig. 5.28). The victim on the central peak is once more flanked by Wrinkle Face and Iguana. A second victim lies decapitated just underneath a large land snail. This relationship

between human victims and land snails scattered at the base of the mountain is not incidental. As suggested in chapter 5, the leishmaniasis amputee, the land snails, and a host of other animal species formed part of a complex ritual ecology centered on El Niño events (fig. 5.112). This third Phase III example of the Mountain Sacrifice (fig. 7.5) shows a victim falling directly on top of an oversized land snail painted at the base of the mountain. Such a direct connection between the sacrificial victim and the land snail is further enhanced by the Phase III bottle briefly discussed in chapter 5, which depicts a mountain sacrifice victim literally being swallowed by a land snail (fig. 5.114). The posterior and the legs of the squatting figure can be seen just underneath the head of the gastropod. In other cases, the relationship between anthropomorphic figures and land snails might even be of a metamorphic nature. A Phase III fineline painting shows a Wrinkle Face being and another subject with land snail shells and the longer pair of tentacles with eyes on their backs (fig. 5.117). With the help of the shell as a wing, they appear to be flying and collecting *ulluchu* fruits, which are connected to sacrifice. This transformation into a land snail being is probably more intricate than the few examples shown here. The individual being swallowed by the land snail in figure 5.114 not only adopts the posture of the victim crouching on the mountaintop; he also possesses snake-like extensions protruding from his back, which are usually assigned to Wrinkle Face beings and subjects with supernatural attributes.

The Mountain Sacrifice ceremony begun in Phase III, including its relationship with land snails, is pursued with greater intensity in Phase IV (Donnan and McClelland 1999: 121). The land snails have literally replaced the sacrificial victims on the mountain peaks of a Phase IV ceramic bottle (fig. 5.113). At the base of the mountain, a fineline painting depicts nine individuals collecting land snails with a bag and a small stick. As noted by Donnan (2004: 72), the facial paintings and the headdresses of these individuals are nearly identical to those depicted in the portrait vessel tradition, which is firmly related to ceremonial combat and sacrifice. The warriors collecting the land snails are also the same type of actors that carry out the ritual hunts of sea lions and deer

(figs. 5.63, 5.65). In the deer hunting scenes and the land snail collections, the individuals frequently wear the same elaborate headdresses and have identical facial paintings (fig. 5.113). Therefore the gathering of land snails could have been symbolically construed as a form of ritual hunting as well. Snail gathering is thus an activity that refers to sacrifice and ceremonial combat, further reinforcing the quasi-interchangeability between a victim on the mountaintop and a land snail.

As noted in chapter 5, land snail proliferation may be associated with humid conditions triggered by El Niño events. Consequently, the Mountain Sacrifice (at least those clearly depicted with land snails) may also have been related to these conditions (figs. 5.112, 5.113). The designs painted on the rectangular base of the bottle in figure 5.114 are similar to those painted on the wings of the stingray shown in figure 5.3 and shown in association with limpets (fig. 5.71). They may refer to an octopus, which proliferates during El Niño events like the land snail.

Wrinkle Face often presides over a complex ritual in Phase IV, including numerous attendants making specific gestures or carrying animals, usually a deer, in their arms (figs. 5.130, 7.6).

FIGURE 7.6. Mountain Sacrifice. Staatliche Museen zu Berlin, Preußischer Kulturbesitz—Ethnologisches Museum. Inv. no. VA 48095.

FIGURE 7.7. Coca ritualist. Museo Larco, Lima, Peru. Inv. no. ML001064.

The gestures made by the attendants are very precise and have been faithfully reproduced in other scenes of the same type (figs. 2.25, 5.112). In other cases, a human or even an anthropomorphized fox may oversee the rituals in lieu of Wrinkle Face. In its human form, the attendant regularly wears a semicircular headdress (fig. 2.25). This is one of the most prominent warrior helmets in Phase III (see figs. 7.12, 7.14 discussed below).

Although the Mountain Sacrifice extends from Phase III to Phase IV, some related rituals such as the Coca Ceremony appear to pertain largely to the earlier Phase III ceremonial sequence. The Coca Ceremony is clearly associated with the Mountain Sacrifice. Therefore I return to this sacrificial ritual in relation with the Coca Ceremony in the following section.

THE COCA CEREMONY

The Coca Ceremony is a ritual activity that forms part of the Mountain Sacrifice. Ceramic vessels with modeled sculptures or elaborate fineline paintings apparently depict individuals chewing coca leaves and using special containers and a short stick to apply lime into the quid kept in their cheek (Donnan 1978: 117). A Phase III example, one of a pair from the Larco Museum, shows a coca taker decorated with the most significant attributes of his function (fig. 7.7). His facial painting consists of a Maltese cross with a mustache. His long black hair passes behind the earlobes with no sideburns. He wears disk ear ornaments, a checkerboard tunic, and a circular headdress decorated with raised hands or paws. The lime that would have been contained in such a bottle is depicted with a touch of white slip applied to the tip of the stick.

In fineline paintings, the Coca Ceremony usually includes a group of individuals (fig. 7.8). Before proceeding with analysis of the ritual activity depicted in this figure, it is important to establish the stylistic and chronological placement of what is perhaps the most important depiction of this ceremony. Although Donnan and McClelland (1999: 84) have stated that the fineline painting shown in figure 7.8 pertains to Phase IV, I suggest that this may not be the case. The bottle measures only 23 cm tall, which is almost 6 cm smaller than the average height for Phase IV bottles collected at the Huacas de Moche (fig. 7.9). The size of the bottle matters, as the chambers

FIGURE 7.8. Coca Ceremony. Drawing by Donna McClelland. The Christopher B. Donnan and Donna McClelland Moche Archive, Image Collections and Fieldwork Archives, Dumbarton Oaks, Trustees for Harvard University, Washington, DC.

of Phase III stirrup spout bottles are consistently smaller than those of Phase IV bottles. Phase IV stirrup spouts are generally more elongated, with the base of the arch or the branches of the stirrup itself drawn much closer together. Though Donnan and McClelland (1999: 84) maintain that the three-color technique used in this fineline painting is largely a Phase IV innovation, they also state that it has been noted on a Late Phase III bottle. I would thus suggest that the Coca Ceremony depicted on this bottle also dates to Late Phase III. It is important to place this vessel in its proper stylistic phase, as these phases are related to qualitative and quantitative changes in Moche political structures. Indeed, if we compare the Phase III vessel depicted in figure 7.7 with two of the four subjects depicted in the Coca Ceremony, it is clearly apparent that they are closely related: the first coca taker, seated to the right of the standing individual, wears the headdress with raised hands, whereas the second subject behind him wears the tunic with the checkerboard motif (fig. 7.8). Also, the three coca takers in a seated position have the ubiquitous Maltese cross painted on their faces and all wear large disk ear ornaments. Therefore the two examples belong to the same stylistic period.

The Coca Ceremony and the coca takers appear in direct relation with warfare and sacrificial activities. A coca taker in figure 7.10 is seated just above a mountain scene depicting a feline, four foxes, some cacti, and a weapon bundle composed of a star-shaped club and a square shield (fig. 7.11). The weapon bundle placed just underneath his left knee is nearly identical to those depicted

FIGURE 7.9. Coca Ceremony. Linden-Museum, Stuttgart. Inv. no. L1450-148 (H 23 cm).

FIGURE 7.10. Coca taker. Museo Nacional de Arqueología, Antropología e Historia del Perú. Inv. no. 1-2854.

FIGURE 7.11. Painting of a feline, three foxes, a war bundle, and cacti. Drawing by Donna McClelland. The Christopher B. Donnan and Donna McClelland Moche Archive, Image Collections and Fieldwork Archives, Dumbarton Oaks, Trustees for Harvard University, Washington, DC.

in the elaborate Coca Ceremony in figure 7.8. The weapon bundle is one of the most important symbols of Moche iconography. Its representation is so ubiquitous that Donnan considers it the most prominent symbolic element disseminated throughout the Moche region. In addition to the depiction of the "eared serpent" (snake-fox) and "Spider Decapitator," the presence of the weapon bundle would, in his opinion, index the existence of a state religion with its focus on human sacrifice:

> The primary symbol of the Moche state religion appears to have been the weapon bundle. This choice is understandable, because the bundle alludes to the capture of prisoners through ceremonial combat, and it appears in most stages of the Warrior Narrative. It can be portrayed in various ways, from simple to elaborate and frequently is anthropomorphized. Other symbols of the Moche state religion include the eared serpent and the Spider Decapitator. (Donnan 2010: 59)

As stated in chapter 1, the term "state religion" poses a problem in the context of this study. I consider these ritual practices, and the individuals involved in these activities, largely in political terms and in a historical perspective. Furthermore, Donnan is largely concerned with the Sacrifice Ceremony in this essay. On the basis of certain elements, he believes that it may have remained unchanged from approximately CE 350 until CE 720 (Donnan 2010: 68). The Sacrifice Ceremony in this perspective would have been maintained for a much longer period and would have fully encompassed three stylistic periods (Phase III, Phase IV, and Phase V). Nonetheless, with this caveat in mind, if we were to replace the term "religion" with "ideology," I would agree with Donnan regarding the unifying powers of these symbols and, perhaps more importantly, the unifying powers that such rituals as the Coca Ceremony, the Mountain Sacrifice, and the Sacrifice Ceremony related to these symbols may have represented.

A late Phase III bottle depicts a sculpted warrior with a semicircular headdress seated above a fineline painting of two warriors, one captured victim, and two weapon bundles (figs. 7.12, 7.13). The clothing and the war implements included in the bundle behind the naked captive were likely

FIGURE 7.12. Moche warrior sitting above a representation of Ceremonial Combat. Private collection. Photograph by Christopher B. Donnan.

taken from him as part of the ritual following the battle (Donnan 2010: 58). Equal importance is placed on the captured victim and on the warrior's clothing and weapons. An additional battle scene from the same stylistic phase shows a similar type of individual with the semicircular headdress, presiding over the capture of two warriors (figs. 7.14, 7.15). Thus the capture of warriors and the prominent display of these weapon bundles constitute some of the most dominant aspects of the ritual. The weapon bundles would stand for the captured warriors themselves and, when depicted in the Coca Ceremony, would act as indexes by linking this ceremony with the activity of ritual combat (fig. 7.8).

The two activities are represented side by side on a rather rustically rendered Phase III quadrangular bottle (fig. 7.16). The coca taker, with his back against a weapon bundle with a star mace, is

FIGURE 7.13. Painting of two warriors, a captive, and two war bundles. Drawing by Donna McClelland. The Christopher B. Donnan and Donna McClelland Moche Archive, Image Collections and Fieldwork Archives, Dumbarton Oaks, Trustees for Harvard University, Washington, DC.

FIGURE 7.14. Moche warrior sitting above a representation of Ceremonial Combat. Private collection. Photograph by Christopher B. Donnan.

looking toward the battle waged on the adjoining face. The coca taker and the captured individual possess the same hairstyle and similar disk ear ornaments, indicating that the capture of a prisoner and the coca taking may be part of a wider narrative that includes both activities. The narrative sequence is not entirely clear in this case, as the scene following the capture where the captive is despoiled of his warrior's attributes has been omitted. It would appear, however, that the display of a weapon bundle behind the coca taker also follows the outcome of the battle and the eventual capture of the defeated warrior. Therefore the Coca Ceremony may have been performed after the ceremonial combat activity.

At this stage, it is imperative to reiterate that the individual with the semicircular headdress (figs. 7.12, 7.14) is shown overseeing the sacrifice (fig. 2.25) in some of the Mountain Sacrifice scenes. His presence demonstrates that the victims provided for the Mountain Sacrifice originated from specific activities of ritualized warfare. These victims are therefore also intimately connected to the Coca Ceremony. In one of the best examples of the Mountain Sacrifice known so far (fig. 7.6), the individuals painted at the base of the mountain possess the same long hair. The naked prisoner to the far left of the painting has a mark on the chin reminiscent of a section of the Maltese cross (fig. 7.17). More detailed research will have to be conducted on the complex subject of facial paintings, but it appears that the warriors still engaged in the ritual battles in Phase III wear only the vertical

FIGURE 7.15. Ceremonial combat. Drawing by Donna McClelland. The Christopher B. Donnan and Donna McClelland Moche Archive, Image Collections and Fieldwork Archives, Dumbarton Oaks, Trustees for Harvard University, Washington, DC.

FIGURE 7.16. Low relief of a coca taker and combatants. Staatliche Museen zu Berlin, Preußischer Kulturbesitz—Ethnologisches Museum. Inv. no. VA 18373.

FIGURE 7.17. Painting of four sacrificial victims and a dog. Drawing by Donna McClelland. The Christopher B. Donnan and Donna McClelland Moche Archive, Image Collections and Fieldwork Archives, Dumbarton Oaks, Trustees for Harvard University, Washington, DC.

FIGURE 7.18. Individual with his arms crossed and eyes closed. Museo Nacional de Arqueología, Antropología e Historia del Perú. Inv. no. C-00591.

arm of the Maltese cross with the mustache (figs. 5.4, 7.12, 7.14, 7.48, 7.49). When they become coca takers, they display the full Maltese cross (figs. 7.7, 7.8).

The hairstyle worn by the mountain victims is also quite specific and apparently is related to the same type of subject involved in other activities. As noted with the modeled coca taker of figure 7.7, the hair is very long, resting on the back, with no sideburns. This hairstyle is also present on the other individuals sitting in between the peaks of the mountain. These mountain individuals may

often be depicted as free-standing sculptures (fig. 7.18). The similarities between the captured warriors and the attendants depicted in the Mountain Sacrifice scenes suggest that these are eventual sacrificial victims. Thus the specific gestures and the animals (mostly deer) carried by these attendants are directly associated with the larger concept of human sacrifice.

A second type of hairstyle may be related to the mode of capture during the battles. It consists of bringing the long hair from the top of the head to the front in a sort of comb-over (fig. 7.19).

In battle this lock of hair facilitates and symbolizes the capture of the defeated warrior (fig. 7.15). The individuals are captured by the opposing warrior by grabbing the lock of hair. The forelock is then shaved before the sacrifice, as shown with the naked victim to the left in figure 7.13. Many subjects with similar long hair but with a circle incised on top of their heads or with the top of their heads flattened, perhaps to symbolize the missing hair, appear in Phase III. These individuals often have the characteristic Maltese cross on their face and wear the ubiquitous disk ear ornaments (fig. 7.20). In Late Phase III and Phase IV battles between a warrior armed with a conical war club and another one wielding a star-shaped club, the latter is always defeated (figs. 5.35, 7.13, 7.21).

The ensuing mountain scene provides important linking of the Coca Ceremony, the coca takers, and the sacrificial victims (fig. 7.22). It shows seven individuals located above two buildings and surrounded by two mountain peaks. Although the heads of two figures are missing, it is clear from the attributes that they still possess that one of them is a victim and the other one belongs to the larger group of attendants. Thus four subjects wore the headdresses with raised hands or paws. Two figures are sacrificial victims with a forelock holding a lime container and a spatula. The last one wears a shawl and is standing in between the peaks with his or her hands clasped (figs. 7.22, 7.23). The individuals with the headdresses have in their mouths what appears to be a complete human head or a human face attached to a sort of textile with fringes (fig. 7.23). The subject standing on top of the following Phase III bottle in the shape of a mountain clearly shows that the

FIGURE 7.19. Captive with a mustache, a goatee, and a forelock. Museo Larco, Lima, Peru. Inv. no. ML002043.

FIGURE 7.20. Individual holding a *Strombus* trumpet. Museo Larco, Lima, Peru. Inv. no. ML002217.

FIGURE 7.21. Ceremonial combat. Drawing by Donna McClelland. The Christopher B. Donnan and Donna McClelland Moche Archive, Image Collections and Fieldwork Archives, Dumbarton Oaks, Trustees for Harvard University, Washington, DC.

head and the rectangular textile with fringes are in fact two distinct pieces (fig. 7.24). He clenches the human head in his mouth, whereas the associated textile is dangling from his back. The individual also wears a feline-with-raised-paws headdress and disk ear ornaments and bears the special club. This blackware bottle thus presents a complex subject, bringing together the Mountain Sacrifice and the Coca Ceremony. Two smaller warriors with coni-

cal helmets stand beneath this imposing figure. They may represent a pair of warriors about to engage in one-on-one combat.

The victims-to-be with the forelock (such as the one depicted in fig. 7.19) form part of a very specific group of ritual warriors illustrated especially during Phase III. Nicknamed "Bigote" (Mustache), this subject, whom Donnan (2004) considered to be a specific individual, can be recognized

FIGURE 7.22. Mountain scene with coca takers and a sacrificial victim. Staatliche Museen zu Berlin, Preußischer Kulturbesitz—Ethnologisches Museum. Inv. no. VA 18297.

FIGURE 7.23. Mountain scene with coca takers and a sacrificial victim (close-ups). Staatliche Museen zu Berlin, Preußischer Kulturbesitz—Ethnologisches Museum. Inv. no. VA 18297.

FIGURE 7.24. High-ranking warrior wielding a club and standing on top of a mountain. Private collection. Photograph by Christopher B. Donnan.

by the mustache, goatee, and forelock. As hinted by the Coca Ceremony associated with one-on-one combat in figure 7.16, the captive in figure 7.19 would represent a coca taker dispossessed of most of his attributes. Only the disk ear ornaments and the facial hair have been maintained. Therefore the coca taking is part of the warfare ritual and the coca takers (at least those of an age to participate) are also warriors. This hypothesis is clearly reinforced by the mountain scene discussed earlier, where two warriors with forelocks are holding a lime bottle (fig. 7.23). A similar coca taker wearing an elaborate headdress and disk ear ornaments is depicted in another Phase III example as a warrior holding the star-shaped club and a square shield wearing a short tunic with incisions suggesting metallic plates (fig. 7.25). The face, the mustache, and the goatee are nearly identical to those of the captive shown in figure 7.19,

prompting Donnan (2004: 117–118) to suggest that these portraits may have represented a single individual who lived during Phase III, as all the known depictions of Bigote pertain to this stylistic period:

> It is clear that several of the individuals in our portrait sample were warriors who participated in combat and were ultimately captured. One of these can be easily recognized by his large bushy mustache, round goatee, and forelock. We have named him Bigote, the Spanish term for "mustache." Bigote wears only hanging disc ear ornaments—usually one in each earlobe or one in each earlobe and another in the upper part of each ear. All of the ceramic portraits of him appear to be from Phase III, suggesting that he lived during that phase.

Bigote would have been depicted at different stages of his career from a full-fledged ritual warrior to a captive. Although the suggestion that the sequence of representations depicts a single individual remains a possibility, it is impossible to substantiate archaeologically. I suggest that the goatee is apparently a shorter rendition of a much longer beard frequently depicted on coca takers (fig. 7.26). A fragment of such a subject was tossed among the slain warriors in Plaza 3A (fig. 3.32).

Therefore an alternative possibility is that depictions of Bigote do not represent a distinct individual portrait but a generic type of coca taker at a younger age, when the subject was still involved in the ritual battles. The mustache and the beard would then be shorter in accordance with the younger age of the individual and his status as a still active warrior. In the portrait vessel tradition of Phase III which continues into Phase IV, when the individuals are depicted as captives, they are shown with long hair and no sideburns (fig. 7.27) or with the addition of the tuft of hair on the forehead (fig. 7.19). They may represent two distinct types of sacrificial victims or may

have had their mustache and goatee cut before the sacrifice. During this period, the noncaptive portrait vessels also are dominated by individuals wearing the disk ear ornaments and the characteristic headdresses of the coca takers (fig. 7.28). In this stylistic period, the ritual battles were largely associated with the Mountain Sacrifice. The Sacrifice Ceremony, which began in Phase IV, did not exist yet, so its cohort of distinctive warriors and captives had yet to be created.

Finally, one extraordinary Phase III portrait vessel depicts an individual—probably a being with fangs—with a feline head ring, disk ear ornaments, and the textile with human head on it in its mouth (fig. 7.29). Beings with fangs are intimately related to Moche rulership and to a notion of power expressed through all these elaborate rituals. This bottle clearly demonstrates that the portrait vessel tradition represents types of subjects, and perhaps in some cases apotheosized individuals, linked to the most important aspects of Moche ritual and political life.

FIGURE 7.25. High-ranking warrior holding a club and wearing a square shield. Museo Larco, Lima, Peru. Inv. no. ML001597.

FIGURE 7.26. Coca taker. Museo Nacional de Arqueología, Antropología e Historia del Perú. Inv. no. C-54674.

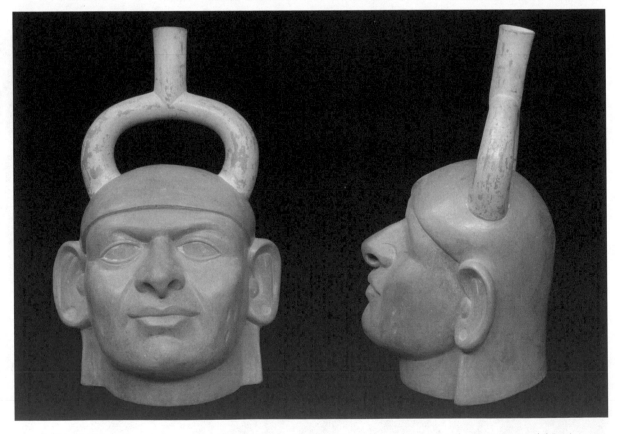

FIGURE 7.27. Portrait vessel of a sacrificial victim. Museo Nacional de Arqueología, Antropología e Historia del Perú. Inv. no. C-54685.

FIGURE 7.28. (*Above*) Portrait vessel of a coca taker. Museo Larco, Lima, Peru. Inv. no. ML013563.

FIGURE 7.29. (*Below*) Portrait vessel of a fanged being with a human effigy in his mouth. Private collection. Photograph by Steve Bourget.

RITUAL HUNTING AND CEREMONIAL COMBAT

As hinted earlier, ritual hunting is an additional activity forming part of the Phase III ritual system described so far. The same actors involved in the Coca Ceremony and the Mountain Sacrifice figure prominently in it. The mountain scene in figure 7.30 is crucial, bringing together warriors engaged in battle and the ritual hunting of a fox. Therefore this example bridges the gap between warfare and hunting. In symbolic terms, hunting a fox may not be too different from clubbing sea lions, collecting land snails, or hunting deer (figs. 5.66, 5.113). To the left of the central part of the mountain in figure 7.30, two warriors wearing conical helmets are fighting with war clubs; two other warriors hold a spear and war clubs as well. The second two warriors wear the type of headdresses and ear ornaments usually assigned to the coca takers (figs. 7.8, 7.10). Just underneath these warriors, a fifth individual is about to spear a fox. The scene in the central portion of the bottle depicts two warriors wearing conical helmets topped with crescent-shaped diadems and armed with conical war clubs confronting two other warriors wearing distinct

outfits and armed with different war clubs. This scene recalls those discussed earlier involving these distinct types of warriors (figs. 7.13, 7.21). It is not clear at this juncture what the pairing of those distinct types of warriors means. Were they meant to represent distinct Moche polities engaging in these activities? Is there a hierarchy between these types of warriors?

As mentioned in chapters 5 and 6, fox and deer hunting are associated not only with the Mountain Sacrifice but also with ceremonial combat. In Phase III iconography, deer and sometimes foxes are consistently pursued by three types of warriors: those with conical helmets and semicircular headdresses (fig. 7.31) and those linked to the Coca Ceremony (fig. 7.32). Anthropomorphized deer and foxes are also depicted as warriors and, in the case of deer, as sacrificial victims (figs. 5.144, 5.162, 5.163). Donnan (1997) has suggested that hunting and warfare are analogous activities and that the hunting of deer and fox may in fact represent metaphors of ceremonial combat and human sacrifice. Therefore the individual carrying a deer in the Mountain Sacrifice can be perceived as being in continuity with the ritual hunting of these animals and their status as sacrificial victims (fig. 7.6).

FIGURE 7.30. Ceremonial combat and fox hunting on a mountain. Museo Nacional de Arqueología, Antropología e Historia del Perú. Inv. no. C-54622.

FIGURE 7.31. Deer hunting. Drawing by Donna McClelland. The Christopher B. Donnan and Donna McClelland Moche Archive, Image Collections and Fieldwork Archives, Dumbarton Oaks, Trustees for Harvard University, Washington, DC.

FIGURE 7.32. Fox hunting. Drawing by Donna McClelland. The Christopher B. Donnan and Donna McClelland Moche Archive, Image Collections and Fieldwork Archives, Dumbarton Oaks, Trustees for Harvard University, Washington, DC.

As discussed in chapter 6, the carrying of a deer is also consistent with the theme of offering children and other animals such as sea lions (figs. 6.19, 6.20). The similarities noted between these different types of activities suggest that they form part of a closely related group. This symbolic system or complex includes the activities of coca taking, ceremonial combat, capture, Mountain Sacrifice, and ritual hunting. In the following section on the archaeological evidence for such a specific complex, I use the term "Coca Ceremony Complex" to encompass these five distinct but interconnected activities. This is done in order to differentiate it from at least three other ceremonial complexes that appeared during the following stylistic periods: the Sacrifice Ceremony in Phase IV and the Burial Theme and the Blood Ceremony in Phase V/Late Moche.

ARCHAEOLOGY OF THE COCA CEREMONY COMPLEX

I now focus on the archaeological contexts at Huaca de la Luna and at some other sites to evaluate whether the iconographical information presented so far fits some of the data collected at these sites. It is critical to establish such a link because I contend that the iconography is directly related to the social, ritual, and political activities carried out by the Moche at these ceremonial sites. The demonstration of a high degree of agreement between the visual culture and the archaeological information is an important step for the framing of Moche social institutions and ritual activities into a historical perspective.

Despite the intense looting of the ceremonial center, elements and individuals associated with the Coca Ceremony have clearly been detected at Huaca de la Luna. Archaeological evidence of this ceremony, of the individuals involved in it, and of the visual culture have been found in the construction layers of Platform I, in the tombs located within the architecture, and in the sacrificial remains left in two adjacent plazas—Plazas 3C and 3A. The contexts associated with the Coca Ceremony are discussed first, then the sacrificial and funerary contexts.

THE COCA CEREMONY ON PLATFORM I

As discussed in chapter 1, Platform I was the heart of the ceremonial complex at Huaca de la Luna. At least five overlapping buildings have been identified and labeled from top to bottom, A, B/C, D, E, and F (the oldest structure known so far). During the excavation of the fill covering Building D—which formed part of the construction of Building B/C and the fourth major renovation of Platform I—a rectangular basket made of reeds was found (Tufinio 2004a). Although this cache was located near a looted burial (Tomb 18), it was perhaps meant as an offering to the temple. The basket had intentionally been put right in front of the striking octopus murals within the solid mudbrick fill (fig. 7.33). In addition to the cache, the fill of Building D contained the remains of two looted tombs, Tomb 17 and Tomb 18. Both burials included among their disturbed contexts a few Phase III ceramic vessels. Therefore these burials and the ceramic fragments collected in the fill indicate that the interment of Building D was carried out toward the end of Phase III. Building B/C (the new building built in the process) could not be associated with the beginning of a specific phase because of lack of conclusive evidence, but Tomb 1 and Tomb 2, discovered in the fill for the construction of Building A, are stylistically related to Phase IV. All the material collected in the following Building A also pertains exclusively to Phase IV. This would support the hypothesis that Building D was buried intentionally to mark the gradual transition from Phase III to Phase IV.

An elaborate feline effigy was deposited in the reed basket (fig. 4.15), along with numerous metallic objects. Most of these objects were probably detached from tunics and headdresses. They included disk ear ornaments, platelets, and small modeled objects. A long textile band sewn to the top of the effigy clearly indicates that the 65-cm-long effigy was meant to be worn. Most of the objects deposited in the box, including the animal effigy, have been recognized by Uceda Castillo (2008) as forming part of the regalia of coca takers. The feline effigy is clearly a more elaborate rendition of the animal effigy dangling from the neck of the individuals in the Coca Ceremony (fig. 7.8). For example, such a finely made effigy is found on the back of the warrior depicted on an Early Moche bottle (fig. 7.34).

Just above the fill where the basket containing the feline effigy was found, Tomb 1 and Tomb 2 were encountered in the fill for the final construction phase of Building B/C. Each funerary context contained the body of a male twenty-eight to thirty-five years old, laid to rest with a number of ritual vessels and a copper bottle for lime with its spatula (fig. 7.35). All the stirrup spout bottles found in these two tombs belong to Phase IV. In addition to the lime container, the deceased individual in Tomb 2 had a dismantled metallic effigy placed on his face (Uceda Castillo 2008: 163, fig. 9.14) and numerous bottles including the duck warrior shown in figure 5.106. The bottles and the feline effigy are nearly identical to those depicted with the attendants of the Coca Ceremony in figure 7.8. The feline effigy, though, is a much less elaborate version of the Phase III example deposited in the reed basket left in the fill of the previous structure (Building D) (fig. 4.15). Perhaps this is indicative of the diminished importance of coca takers during Phase IV. The Moche might have retired the most prominent regalia of the coca takers, who were arguably some of the most important individuals during Phase III, in order to give prominence in Phase IV to the high-ranking individuals associated with the Sacrifice Ceremony.

Additional indices of the Coca Ceremony and the associated regalia have been found in the Chicama Valley and Jequetepeque Valley as well. These additional contexts are discussed further below for comparison with these examples from Huaca de la Luna. Admittedly, because of the rebuilding process of Platform I (the earlier con-

---

FIGURE 7.33. (*Opposite*) Ritual container deposited in the fill of Building D, Huaca de la Luna.

FIGURE 7.34. Warrior in a crouching position wearing a feline effigy on his back. Private collection. Photograph by Christopher B. Donnan.

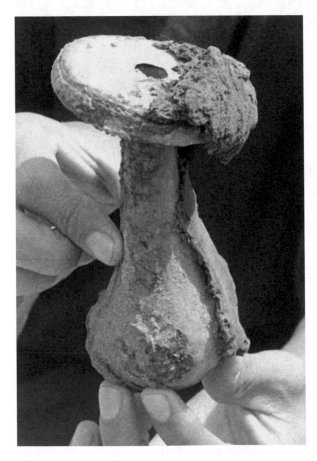

FIGURE 7.35. Lime container for coca taking, Tomb 2, Platform I. Huaca de la Luna. Museo Huacas de Moche, Trujillo.

struction phases being embedded within the new architecture) and the intense looting, the evidence of the Phase III Coca Ceremony is scant. Nonetheless, Plaza 3C (located immediately to the east of Platform I) has provided tantalizing clues about the whole Coca Ceremony Complex.

RITUAL CONTEXTS IN PLAZA 3C

The architectural and archaeological contexts in Plaza 3C are clearly related to human sacrifice and the Coca Ceremony. The iconography illustrated on objects retrieved from one of the tombs found in the plaza closely matches the activities of ceremonial combat and deer hunting as depicted in Phase III. Plaza 3C was organized into two spaces: a quadrangular area containing a small room (Room 1) and a smaller rectangular precinct immediately to the east of it (fig. 2.10). The contexts were recognized as part of two distinct but related events: (1) the fill that eventually formed the base of the plaza and (2) the plaza proper, including Room 1 (fig. 7.36). Both the fill and the floor of the eastern part of the plaza contained remains of sacrificial victims, which are briefly described below.

The walls on each side of the single entry door of Room 1 were decorated with low-relief clay murals depicting a feline overpowering a human victim (fig. 7.37). The victim, a male with the characteristically long hair of the warriors, lies on his back in a defensive posture. He attempts to thwart the attack by raising his left arm between the legs of the feline. The overtaking of a sacrificial victim by a feline is a well-known theme of Moche iconography during Phases III and IV. It is largely associated with the victims possessing forelocks and facial paintings with dots and Maltese crosses (fig. 7.38). Warriors or high-ranking individuals, often with the ubiquitous facial markings and holding small felines, are probably part of the same theme (figs. 7.39, 7.40). Although admittedly it is quite speculative at this stage, I believe that these three types of scenes (a seated high-ranking individual flanked by a feline, a feline in

the arms of a warrior, and a victim overtaken by a feline) may have formed part of the narrative. The feline is making its way from the seat of power (fig. 7.40), both physically and metaphorically, to the eventual overtaking and sacrifice of the victim (fig. 7.38).

The presence of a feline associated with the highest-ranking individual in Phase IV is maintained in the Sacrifice Ceremony. For example, a feline accompanies Individual A, carried in his litter in figure 5.156. The animal is located just in front of him. In the best-known example of the Sacrifice Ceremony, the same type of litter with a feline resting in it is located immediately underneath Individual A, standing just above it on top of the bicephalous arch (fig. 7.50).

In addition to the sacrificial subject portrayed on the walls of the chamber, two deposits containing the remains of a minimum of sixty-one sacrificed male individuals were found just outside the eastern wall of this structure (Sutter and Verano 2007). It is important to stress that the contexts in the fill and those on the floor of the plaza constituted only the final resting places of the remains. These individuals were probably killed, processed,

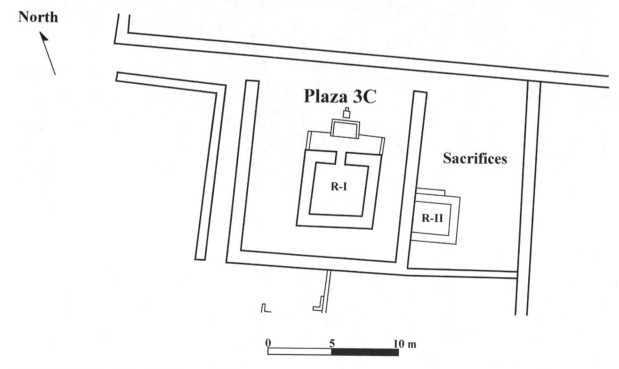

FIGURE 7.36. Plan of Plaza 3C, Huaca de la Luna.

FIGURE 7.37. Low-relief mural on the wall of Room I, Plaza 3C, Huaca de la Luna.

FIGURE 7.38. Feline on the back of a sacrificial victim, Phase IV. Museo Larco, Lima, Peru. Inv. no. ML002804.

FIGURE 7.39. Individual with a forelock holding a feline on his lap, Phase IV. Museo Larco, Lima, Peru. Inv. no. ML001160.

FIGURE 7.40. Individual seated on a throne with a feline on his right side. Museo Larco, Lima, Peru. Inv. no. ML000639.

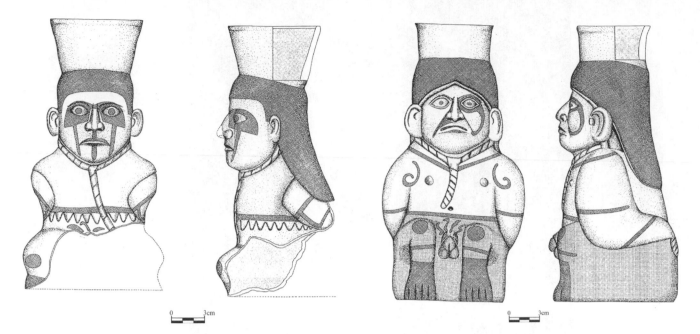

FIGURE 7.41. Reconstructed prisoner effigies from Plaza 3C. Drawings by José Armas Asmad.

and used elsewhere before being discarded in this sector. As such, these contexts would constitute the ritual deposition of human remains that would have served other purposes elsewhere in the huaca.

The earliest group of human remains was encountered deposited in the fill of the plaza. It is not clear whether these remains were deposited in this sector over the years or whether they were placed in a purposely created fill for the construction of Plaza 3C. In such a case, the bones could have been collected from elsewhere and integrated into the construction process. The skeletal remains include a group of at least thirteen individuals and numerous concentrations of bones (Verano, Tufinio, and Lund Valle 2008). Numerous ceramic sherds were retrieved from the fill. Most of the diagnostic examples pertained to Phase III. A number of jar fragments took the form of seated prisoners with long hair, with their hands tied behind their backs and a rope around their necks.

The second group of skeletal remains was left dispersed on the floor of Plaza 3C just above the fill containing the previous group. This context consisted of eight individuals with concentrations of bones. Ceramic fragments mostly dating to late Phase III were recovered with them. Two largely complete jars depict seminaked prisoners with their hands tied behind their backs (fig. 7.41).

Some early Phase IV fineline painting sherds were also found at the site, including fragments depicting Ritual Runners (Tufinio 2001).

John Verano, who excavated the context with Moisés Tufinio and studied the human remains, indicates that all of the Plaza 3C remains were males and had been captured during some form of violent encounters (Sutter and Verano 2007). On the basis of numerous cut marks on the bones, he also suggests that most of these corpses had been carefully defleshed (fig. 7.42) (Verano 2001b: 121). The articulations of the skeletons were still in place, so it would appear that the intention might have been to create some form of skeletonized person:

> Apparently the Moche were not cannibalizing the bodies of their victims, but seem to have been more interested in the skeletons themselves—using them, or parts of them, for display or some other ritual purpose. . . . The extensive and time-consuming defleshing of these bones, while carefully maintaining their articulations, suggests intentional preparation for some purpose rather than simple butchery and consumption. (Verano 2008: 208)

The defleshing of the sacrificial victims is a particularity that was not registered in Plaza 3A. Although the sample is still small (with only two comparative sites), this practice may have been

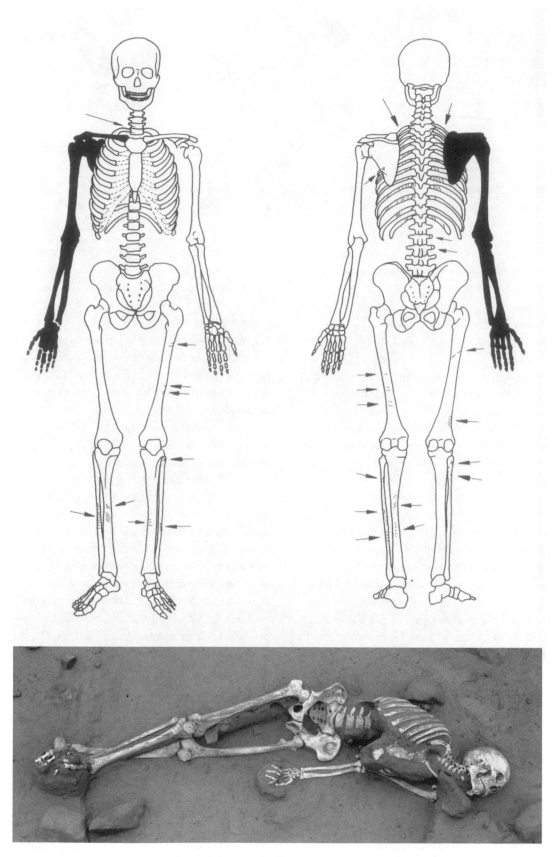

FIGURE 7.42. Location of cut marks and photograph of Skeleton E4. Photograph and drawing by John Verano.

FIGURE 7.43. Sacrificial victims and human remains. Drawing by Donna McClelland. The Christopher B. Donnan and Donna McClelland Moche Archive, Image Collections and Fieldwork Archives, Dumbarton Oaks, Trustees for Harvard University, Washington, DC.

abandoned by Phase IV. We may never know exactly why the skins and the soft tissue were peeled from these victims. Verano, Tufinio, and Lund Valle (2008: 252) suggest that the Moche's intent may have been to use some of these defleshed body parts for ritual display:

> Our hypothesis is supported by the discovery of cord fragments wrapped around the wrists, the legs, the feet, the trunk, and also the neck of skeletons, suggesting that they were initially suspended from some object. Supporting our hypothesis, diverse representations of severed upper limbs with ropes around them are known in Moche art.[1]

It is true that the iconography in certain contexts represents body parts (usually legs, arms, and heads), sometimes associated with naked males. But these body parts are always depicted with their flesh still adhering firmly to the bones (fig. 7.43). These scenes, which mostly date to Phase IV, may in fact depict the types of activities that were carried out in Plaza 3A and not those in Plaza 3C. In the former Phase IV context, many of the craniums, arms, legs, and part of trunks were deliberately dismembered (figs. 3.85–3.88). The imprint of the flesh in the mud of Plaza 3A would indicate that dismemberment took place shortly after death, or at least before the complete dissolution of the soft tissue.

The treatment of the Plaza 3C skeletal remains is drastically different and does not suggest this kind of practice. The flesh was carefully removed, the bones were scraped clean, and most of the skeletons were found still articulated. Therefore the objective was not to dismember the corpses but to fashion authentic anatomical skeletons. As

an alternate hypothesis, the objective may have been to create for some rituals skeletons such as those so prominently depicted in Phase III. During this phase, the iconography frequently shows skeletons dancing, playing music, and performing various activities (fig. 7.44). Skeletons often carry a deer, linking them with ritual hunting and perhaps with the Mountain Sacrifice (fig. 7.45). These skeletons could have been used as props within the Huaca de la Luna temple during some funerary or sacrificial rituals, such as those depicted in the iconography. Sometime after their usefulness had ended, the skeletons would have been deposited in the fill or on the floor of Plaza 3C. Moche ritual life is complex, and these human remains could represent the carefully discarded shells of these activities. Like Verano, Tufinio, and Lund Valle (2008), I suggest that the cord fragments found still wrapped around the bodies may have served to mount the skeletons into some sort of wooden structure so that they could be manipulated.

A number of fragments of effigy jars depicting prisoners were found scattered among the human remains both in the fill and above the floor. The two examples that could be reconstructed are similar to the types of captured warriors depicted in Phase III (figs. 7.13, 7.41). The two nearly complete pieces and all the fragments recovered depict the same type of subject, a naked male with long hair passing behind his ears and resting on his back. The presence of these objects clearly demonstrates a link between the human remains and the theme of ceremonial combat. This is consistent with both Phase III iconography and Plaza 3A, where the theme has clearly been pursued into Phase IV.

FIGURE 7.44. Skeletonized musicians. Staatliche Museen zu Berlin, Preußischer Kulturbesitz—Ethnologisches Museum. Inv. no. VA 62199.

FIGURE 7.45. Skeletonized individual carrying a deer, Phase IV. Museo Larco, Lima, Peru. Inv. no. ML002284.

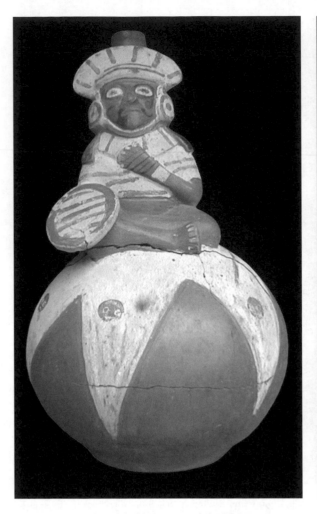

FIGURE 7.46. Warrior holding a round shield. Museo Huacas de Moche, Trujillo. Inv. no. Plz3C-094-T2.

FIGURE 7.47. Sacrificial victim in a seated position. Museo Huacas de Moche, Trujillo. Inv. no. Plz3C-103-T2.

In addition to the defleshed skeletons, Tomb 2 (created just alongside this context) contained the body of an adult male with three children wrapped in a bundle to his right side. The offerings included the fragment of a metallic chisel and fifteen vessels. The subjects depicted on four of these ceramics are directly related to the theme of ceremonial combat and human sacrifice. The first one is a stirrup spout bottle depicting a warrior seated on the summit of the chamber (fig. 7.46). He wears the same semicircular headdress associated with subjects dominating the scenes of ceremonial combat (figs. 7.12, 7.14) or presiding over the Mountain Sacrifice (fig. 2.25). Indeed a mountain setting is probably referenced by the presence of these alternating red and white triangles lightly incised and painted on the chamber of the bottle (fig. 7.46). The same decorative tech-

nique was used with a coca taker discussed earlier (fig. 7.10).

Three additional vessels from the tomb are also directly related to the theme of ceremonial combat, representing a seminude warrior (fig. 7.47), a portrait vessel of a captured warrior (fig. 7.48), and the same type of subject modeled on the handle of a dipper (fig. 7.49). Both subjects have long hair with no sideburns and a mustache and bear the vertical arm of the Maltese cross. This is the same facial painting as the human face in the ray in figure 5.4 and the warrior wearing a semicircular helmet in figures 7.12 and 7.14.

An additional piece of information relating to this symbolic system is the representation of a deer hit by two spears painted within a lozenge on the back of the dipper, just underneath the head of the captive (fig. 7.49). Once more the hunting of deer

(fig. 7.31), the long hair with no sideburns (fig. 7.27), and sometimes the distinctive facial paintings are consistent with the victims and attendants associated with the Mountain Sacrifice (fig. 7.6). It is not necessary to restate the complete argument: like the two adults found on Platform II, the male individual in this tomb may have acted as a sacrificer and these vessels may have formed part of a set linked to his function.

In addition to the proximity of Tomb 2 to the sacrificial deposit and the iconography associated with ceremonial combat, the ritual function of the tomb occupant is reinforced by the presence of the chisel-like knife fragment. Verano (2008: 204) and I thus agree based on our assessments of the Tomb 2 context that the individual was a sacrificer.

Apart from serving as a funerary ground and the repository of skeletal remains, the exact function of Plaza 3C remains unclear. The small chamber with the mural may have been used to contain the captured warriors before their ordeal.

FIGURE 7.48. (*Left*) Portrait vessel of a sacrificial victim. Museo Huacas de Moche, Trujillo. Inv. no. Plz3C-093-T2.

FIGURE 7.49. (*Below*) Dipper with the handle in the shape of a human head. Museo Huacas de Moche, Trujillo. Inv. no. Plz3C-104-T2. Photograph by John Verano.

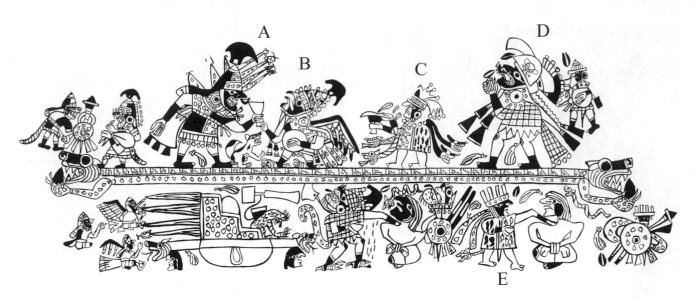

FIGURE 7.50. Sacrifice Ceremony on two registers. Drawing by Donna McClelland. The Christopher B. Donnan and Donna McClelland Moche Archive, Image Collections and Fieldwork Archives, Dumbarton Oaks, Trustees for Harvard University, Washington, DC.

Four radiocarbon dates were processed from the deposits of defleshed skeletons. The first two dates were associated with the remains deposited in the fill and give calibrated dates of AD 50–230 (Beta-158974) and AD 110–330 (Beta-158975). The second pair of dates is associated with the human remains resting on the floor of the plaza. The contexts have provided calibrated dates of AD 460–650 (Beta-146465) and AD 410–600 (Beta-146464). Verano, Tufinio, and Lund Valle (2008: 251) suggest that the four dates demonstrate that these remains were left in this sector in various centuries. An alternative hypothesis could be considered. These deposits would correspond with two distinct periods during Phase III. The first one, in the fill, would date from the beginning of the phase at around AD 230–250, whereas the second one, above the floor, would date to late Phase III and early Phase IV at around AD 420–460. This proposition is also consistent with the type of ceramic vessels and fragments found at the site.

I now turn to the following phase. Once again I begin with Phase IV visual culture and link the data with the archaeological contexts.

THE PHASE IV SACRIFICE CEREMONY

As stated at the beginning of the chapter, the Sacrifice Ceremony did not exist before Phase IV (fig. 7.50). This does not mean that the subjects involved in the activity were created at this moment and for this new ritual only. Individuals wearing conical helmets topped by a crescent-shaped diadem such as those worn by Individuals A and B, or what appears to be an earlier version of the V-shaped diadem of Individual D are already present in Phase III (fig. 2.30). The Phase III variations of the V-shaped diadem are sometimes worn by Wrinkle Face and Iguana as well (fig. 5.130). What is innovative in Phase IV is the grouping of these subjects and the activities being performed (figs. 7.51, 7.52). Slight changes in the form of these diadems and headdresses (or elements surrounding some of these subjects) may be evidence of more profound changes in Moche political organization than heretofore suspected. The essence of politics and ideological efficacy often lies in the minutest details.

The capital letters assigned to the subjects of the Sacrifice Ceremony were ascribed by Donnan in 1975. Although these individuals are usually perceived as clearly distinct, the bird impersonator, Individual B, is sometimes depicted with the V-shaped diadem, indicating a degree of fluidity between subjects B and D that should be explored further (figs. 7.50, 7.52). A goblet in the form of an owl being wearing a V-shaped diadem and adorned with the head of an owl shows this situation beautifully (fig. 7.53). This is clearly consistent

FIGURE 7.51. Sacrifice Ceremony with Individual C presenting a goblet to Individual D. Drawing by Donna McClelland. The Christopher B. Donnan and Donna McClelland Moche Archive, Image Collections and Fieldwork Archives, Dumbarton Oaks, Trustees for Harvard University, Washington, DC.

FIGURE 7.52. Sacrifice Ceremony on the upper register with a battle scene on the lower register. Drawing by Donna McClelland. The Christopher B. Donnan and Donna McClelland Moche Archive, Image Collections and Fieldwork Archives, Dumbarton Oaks, Trustees for Harvard University, Washington, DC.

with the Sacrifice Ceremony, as the owl impersonator is usually the person presenting the goblet of blood (figs. 7.50, 7.52, 7.54). This device of blending both the actor and the action has already been noted in chapter 6 with the example of the head of a club morphing into a sea lion's head (fig. 6.15).

The victims in the Sacrifice Ceremony are the product of ritual combat, which is sometimes depicted just underneath the ceremony (fig. 7.52). It usually entails a sort of duel or one-to-one combat. The warriors usually fight with the typical Moche clubs. One of the most elaborate paintings encompassing both activities (fig. 7.54) follows a sequence named the Warrior Narrative by Donnan (2010). The sacrificial victims in this painting appear to have been recovered from the battlefields (A) and brought to the ceremonial precinct

FIGURE 7.53. Goblet in the form of the head of an owl being. Museo Larco, Lima, Peru. Inv. no. ML003805.

FIGURE 7.54. Complex narrative culminating in the Sacrifice Ceremony. Drawing by Donna McClelland. The Christopher B. Donnan and Donna McClelland Moche Archive, Image Collections and Fieldwork Archives, Dumbarton Oaks, Trustees for Harvard University, Washington, DC.

(B) to be presented (C), prepared (D), and thereafter sacrificed (E). The blood of the victim would then have been exchanged between Individuals A and B (F).

One crucial aspect of the Sacrifice Ceremony that sets this activity apart from the Mountain Sacrifice is the ritual exchange of the blood of these victims. The cups being exchanged in these scenes purportedly contained human blood, as indicated by the bat being bleeding a prisoner to the far left of figure 7.51. Furthermore, the captured warrior in one extraordinary painting (fig. 7.55) bleeds directly into the right hand of Individual A.

vidual A, dispensing the use of a cup. This is perhaps a way of highlighting the ritual gesture of the extended hand, associated with the concept of blood giving by the sacrificial victim (fig. 7.56).

Pedestal goblets such as those prominently depicted in the Sacrifice Ceremony are present in numerous collections and have been found at a number of archaeological sites, such as Sipán, San José de Moro, and Huaca de la Cruz. A ceramic goblet from the Ethnological Museum in Berlin depicts in low relief a group of fourteen individuals around its rim (fig. 7.57). Six pairs of warriors are dueling. They are depicted at different stages

FIGURE 7.55. Sacrifice Ceremony with captive warrior bleeding in the hand of Individual A. Drawing by Donna McClelland. The Christopher B. Donnan and Donna McClelland Moche Archive, Image Collections and Fieldwork Archives, Dumbarton Oaks, Trustees for Harvard University, Washington, DC.

FIGURE 7.56. Ritual bleeding. Drawing by Donna McClelland. The Christopher B. Donnan and Donna McClelland Moche Archive, Image Collections and Fieldwork Archives, Dumbarton Oaks, Trustees for Harvard University, Washington, DC.

FIGURE 7.57. Goblet with a low-relief scene of ceremonial combat. Staatliche Museen zu Berlin, Preußischer Kulturbesitz— Ethnologisches Museum. Inv. no. VA 47985.

of the Warrior Narrative: one is shown receiving a blow to the face, another one is brought down by a warrior and held with a rope around his neck, and a third one is captured by his hair (fig. 7.58). In the midst of this fierce battle stands a man wearing a semicircular headdress and a backflap. He is playing the conch shell trumpet and standing on top of a round object (fig. 7.59). This high-ranking musician is reminiscent of the one playing right above the Sacrifice Ceremony discussed earlier (figs. 5.36, 7.51). The presences of these musicians highlight once more the importance of the conch shell trumpet in the activities of ceremonial combat and blood sacrifice. Therefore the sound of the instrument features as an integral part of these activities.

In order to bridge the gap between the iconography and the reality, Margaret Newman and I (Bourget and Newman 1998) tested this cup, an additional one from the Museo Nacional de Arqueología, Antropología e Historia del Perú (MNAAH), and, as mentioned in chapter 4, the wooden club from Tomb 1 (fig. 4.14) for the presence of human blood. The inside walls of these goblets and the surface of the club were covered with a black residue, which was collected for analysis. These samples were tested against the antisera of eleven distinct animals, including bear, camel (camel, llama), cat (bobcat, lynx, lion, cat), chicken, deer, dog (coyote, wolf, fox, dog), guinea

FIGURE 7.58. Low-relief scene of ceremonial combat (close-ups). Staatliche Museen zu Berlin, Preußischer Kulturbesitz—Ethnologisches Museum. Inv. no. VA 47985.

FIGURE 7.59. Low-relief scene of ceremonial combat. Staatliche Museen zu Berlin, Preußischer Kulturbesitz—Ethnologisches Museum. Inv. no. VA 47985.

pig, rabbit, rat, sheep, and human (human, monkey). Strong positive reactions only to human antiserum were obtained from these samples, confirming the presence of human blood, and human blood only, in the cups and on the club.

It would thus seem that collecting blood from male victims became the most prominent ritual during Phase IV, between the fifth and the eighth centuries AD. The physical appearance of the victims involved in the Sacrifice Ceremony is somewhat different from that seen in the Mountain Sacrifice. The forelock is gone. The hair is still long on the back but is cut short and straight just above the eyebrows. The warriors and the sacrificial victims also wear long sideburns (fig. 4.56). Instead of the usual disk ear ornaments seen during Phase III, the Phase IV warriors usually wear tubular ear ornaments before their capture (figs. 4.47, 4.48). Once they have been captured and deprived of their clothing and ornaments, the telltale signs that these ear ornaments have been removed are the extended ears and the round openings in the earlobes (figs. 5.1, 5.2). As the Mountain Sacrifice continues in Phase IV, slightly transforming the appearance of the warriors and the sacrificial victims in the context of other types of sacrificial rituals such as the Sacrifice Ceremony may have been a device to indicate their eventual destination.

The archaeological evidence and the iconography suggest that the sacrificial victims depicted in these two phases would also have known a different fate. Those with the forelock or with the long hair and no sideburns would have been dispatched in the Mountain Sacrifice or transformed into some kind of anatomic skeleton, as evinced by the remains in Plaza 3C. Those in the Plaza 3A site would have been sacrificed during El Niño events and during the Sacrifice Ceremony as well. The Sacrifice Ceremony and its concomitant subjects are perhaps the single most important change between Phase III and Phase IV. The Moche sites of Sipán, Huaca el Pueblo, and Huaca de la Cruz have provided tombs of a number of high-ranking individuals who may have been involved in the Sacrifice Ceremony. In each case, the individuals were buried with regalia clearly corresponding to that illustrated on the Sacrifice Ceremony individuals. Nevertheless, Plaza 3A remains the main site that provides solid evidence of the ritual activities themselves.

Consistent with his view regarding the Warrior Narrative, Donnan sees the Plaza 3A sacrificial context as the final phase of the ritual sequence: the victims would have been killed during the Sacrifice Ceremony and then taken to Plaza 3A for dismemberment and further treatment (personal communication, 2009). This point of view, largely based on a strict reading of the iconography, is not necessarily in disagreement with my analysis of the archaeological contexts, although I would not make that connection so forcefully. Plaza 3A presents a very complex picture of the practice of human sacrifice during Phase IV, including aspects heretofore unsuspected, such as the association with El Niño conditions, the extensive manipulation and postmortem treatments of human remains, and the offering of domestic sherds indicating repeated visits by the local population. Therefore it is not inconceivable that some of the victims could have been sacrificed elsewhere during the Sacrifice Ceremony and others sacrificed in the plaza in rituals that may have included those performed during rainstorms. After all, the Sacrifice Ceremony is not the only form of sacrifice depicted during Phase IV. The Mountain Sacrifice still plays a prominent role (fig. 7.6), and victims are tied to sacrificial racks (figs. 5.127, 6.13, 7.2, 7.3). One such device is even shown between two buildings in the center of a plaza (fig. 6.14).

RITUAL CONTEXTS IN PLAZA 3A

As described in detail in chapters 3 and 4, the site Plaza 3A/Platform II was built during Phase IV sometime between the sixth and the seventh centuries AD. Two radiocarbon dates were obtained from bone material in Plaza 3A. Due to the small size of the samples, they were analyzed by accelerator mass spectrometry (AMS) at the Oxford Radio Carbon Accelerator Unit. The first sample produced a conventional radiocarbon age of 1500 ± 40 BP (OxA-7661), with a 2 sigma calibrated result of Cal AD 528–643. The second sample gave a conventional radiocarbon age of 1550 ± 55 BP (OxA-7889), with a 2 sigma calibrated result of Cal AD 402–620. These dates clearly confirm the Phase IV placement of the sacrificial contexts.

All the sacrifices and ritual activities in Plaza 3A took place in front of a rocky outcrop, which I suggest constitutes a symbolic extension of the Cerro Blanco. The studies of the physical anthropologists John Verano (2001a, 2001b, 2008), Laurel Hamilton (2005), and Florencia Bracamonte (1998) have revealed that the site contained at least seventy-five male individuals aged between thirteen and forty-five years. Many of them had healed injuries consistent with the practice of violent activities. At least eleven of these had fresh injuries, indicating that they may have been captured after some kind of battle. The ritual activities in the plaza were extensive, including reorganization of some of the corpses, manipulation of the human remains, and destruction of at least fifty-two clay statuettes to accompany the victims. The statuettes represent naked men with a rope around their necks, mostly seated cross-legged with their hands resting on their knees (figs. 3.89–3.108).

These clay statuettes seem to have been taken from the Phase IV ceramic and fineline painting traditions, as they clearly depict the same types of individuals with identical hairdos and body decorations (fig. 7.56). Even the blood drops spurting from the nose of the victim in the fineline painting are depicted as red dots on the upper lip of one of the clay heads (fig. 5.1). These sculptures are thus fully consistent with the victims depicted in this phase (especially with those associated with the Sacrifice Ceremony) and firmly link the visual culture and the ritual actions. Although a direct relationship between the sacrificial rituals performed in Plaza 3A and the Sacrifice Ceremony could not be established, a number of elements suggest that the two ritual systems were closely related and that the victims in the plaza may have provided the blood used in some of these ceremonies:

- The clay statuettes are similar to the depictions of the sacrificial victims used in these ceremonies. Their hairstyle, body markings, and facial paintings are drawn from the same repertoire. These statuettes are more than mere extensions of the iconography: these objects were purposely fashioned to accompany the sacrificial victims and were carried throughout the Huaca de la Luna during the rituals. Fragments of the same type of clay statuettes were found in Plaza 3B wedged in between Platform I and Plaza 3A (fig. 2.10) (Montoya 1997). This indicates that some of these objects and perhaps the victims as well may have transited through this part of the building.

- Cut marks have been detected on the cervical vertebrae of sixty-one individuals (nearly 75 percent of sacrificial victims) (Hamilton 2005). Of these sixty-one individuals, forty-five had their throats slit. Therefore bloodletting and perhaps blood collection is indicated by cut marks left on the cervical vertebrae of a large portion of the sample. Decapitation of the victims is also a major theme in both the iconography and the sacrificial site, with thirty isolated crania.

- As outlined in chapter 5, the iconography relating to the theme of El Niño dominates Moche visual culture. The accouterments and the regalia of high-ranking individuals are replete with subjects related to these conditions (table 5.6). El Niño events were thus physically linked with some of the events that took place in Plaza 3A and symbolically associated with high-ranking individuals by their use of selected animal species displayed on their clothing and regalia. ENSO events permeated some of the most important aspects of Moche political and ritual life. Thus the sacrificial activities that took place during the rainstorms were probably fully embedded within the Sacrifice Ceremony.

Concrete evidence of individuals or architectural features such as murals directly associated with the Sacrifice Ceremony has not yet been found at the Huacas de Moche site. I suggest that the members of the Sacrifice Ceremony must have existed at the Huacas de Moche as well, which might be another avenue of research. But their resting place was not located at the Huaca de la Luna. Rather, it was likely situated in or around the Huaca del Sol. During the impressive extension of Huaca del Sol during Phase IV, this building might have served as a palace for this class of rulers. Future research may tell us whether the looters have left any clues of their presence, despite the intensive looting suffered by the huaca throughout the colonial and republican periods.

Sometime during the rituals conducted in Sand 2 in Plaza 3A, a fragment of a Phase III

FIGURE 7.60. Phase III bottle decorated with an archaic motif. Museo Nacional de Arqueología, Antropología e Historia del Perú. Inv. no. C-03357.

ceramic was placed on the face of one of the victims (figs. 3.31, 3.32). A pair of circular ear ornaments was found in the same layer, tossed among the human remains (fig. 3.128). These fragments of molded ear ornaments were most certainly broken from another Phase III vase, but the rest of the vessel was not recovered. That indicates that this was not a fortuitous event and that these fragments were carefully selected. It is interesting to find a pair of ceramic ear ornaments in the midst of dozens of clay effigies of defeated male warriors made ready for sacrifice. The iconography suggests that the real warriors who had been captured would have been deprived of their warriors' garments and their ear ornaments. Donnan (2004: 114) has also suggested that the removal of the clothing and the ornaments would have been part

of the sacrificial ritual and indicated their change in status.

These ear ornaments and the face fragment belong to two ceramics depicting the bearded individual associated with the Coca Ceremony (fig. 7.26). This may represent a strategy to reconnect this Phase IV ritual with the preceding sacrificial system—ancient practices validating the present. This strategy has also been noted on some of the murals from the north wall of Platform I, where ancient subjects dating as far back as the Cupisnique Period have been the source of inspiration for at least three murals. The ideological manipulation of a distant past seems to become prominent during Phase III, with the appearance of numerous vessels decorated with motifs inspired by the Formative Period (fig. 7.60). The deeply grooved technique for outlining the motif is also reminiscent of the Formative Period.

RITUAL CONTEXTS ON PLATFORM II

As described in chapter 4, four tombs were found on Platform II. Although they had been looted in the past, two of them contained the bodies of old men buried with an adolescent as well as a number of objects and ceramic vessels. A bottle depicting a warrior with a conical helmet and a club covered with human blood were found with the deceased in Tomb 1 (figs. 4.7, 4.13).

Tomb 2/3 housed an old man with an adolescent male and contained a number of vessels associated with the portrait vessel tradition, warriors with conical helmets, three captives, depictions of war objects, and references to blood sacrifice (figs. 4.43–4.46, 4.48, 4.52–4.57, 4.62). These elements from Moche visual culture, the wooden club covered with blood, and the position of the tombs in a purposely built platform right above a sacrificial site suggest that these two old men could have officiated during sacrificial rituals, perhaps even during those conducted in Plaza 3A.

THE SACRIFICERS

The Phase IV tombs from Platform II evolved from an earlier tradition, presenting many similarities with the Phase III tomb from Plaza 3C. Both contained elements associated with warfare, human sacrifice, and the portrait vessel tradition, indicating that these may have been the very resting places of the sacrificers themselves (table 7.1). This is further supported by the tools of sacrifice, such as the chisel-like knife from Tomb 2 in Plaza 3C and the wooden club in Tomb 1, Platform II. In both phases, these three men were buried alongside extensive evidence of human sacrifice, further reinforcing the types of activities associated with them.

The data collected at Moche sites suggest a very close relationship of the archaeological contexts, the stylistic phases, and the visual culture. One of the main tenets of the thesis developed here is that these three elements are linked to social and political changes in Moche society.

Table 7.1. Iconographic Correspondences

Plaza 3C, Phase III	Platform II, Phase IV
Warrior with semi-circular headdress	Warrior with conical helmet
Prisoner	Prisoner
Portrait vessel of victim	Portrait vessel of mutilated individual
Deer hunting	Deer scene

POLITICAL STRUCTURES, IDEOLOGY, AND STYLISTIC CHANGES

My aim in this final section is to suggest a model for the evolution of Moche political structures and the ritual apparatus between AD 250 and AD 800. This exercise is admittedly in its early stages and fraught with difficulties, because the information currently available is still scant, especially for the last period. One of the main tenets of this model is that broad stylistic transformations in the iconography are triggered by changes in Moche society concomitant with important changes in Moche political and ritual institutions. Therefore a general proposition concerning Moche political and ritual organizations can be offered by bringing together the archaeological and iconographic information for a given period.

I suggest that transformations of stylistic periods (such as those of the Southern Region: Phase III, Phase IV, and Phase V) are created by important changes in the political structures of Moche rulership. Therefore the representations in each of these phases would be demonstrative of the Moche political structure at the time.

As noted in chapter 1, the distinction between the Southern and the Northern Moche has largely been based on stylistic differences. The research presently underway strongly suggests that the same larger tradition existed in both regions, regardless of these differences. This is the reason why some of the high-ranking individuals found at Sipán and Huaca el Pueblo and dating to the Middle Moche in the Northern Moche region could be identified very precisely with the iconography dating to Phase IV in the Southern Moche region. I suggest that each of the corresponding stylistic phases could be paired together:

Table 7.2. Moche Stylistic Phases in the Southern and Northern Regions

Southern Region	Northern Region	Stages
Phase V	Late Moche	Stage C
Phase IV (AD 400–700)	Middle Moche	Stage B
Phase III (AD 250–450)	Early Moche	Stage A

Phase III with Early Moche, Phase IV with Middle Moche, and Phase V with Late Moche. For ease of discussion, the contemporary pairs of stylistic phases for the two regions have been united under three consecutive stages: A, B, and C (table 7.2).

The three stages A, B, and C serve to highlight the suggestion that sites on either side of the Pampa de Paiján fully participated in the Moche ideology because their political structures were closely linked. Admittedly, the degree and nature of these links need to be defined and substantiated archaeologically. At these sites on either side of this natural divide, the presence of materials and corresponding iconography such as the individuals with leishmaniasis and the feline pelts and themes such as the Coca Ceremony and the Sacrifice Ceremony indicates that real individuals playing these roles were also present: rulers, coca takers, sacrificers, ritual warriors, and amputees with facial mutilations.

The models developed here for each of these stages do not attempt to cover all the subjects that may have been part of the Moche symbolic apparatus of a given phase, only those that are intimately associated with the sacrificial systems explored in this research. The aim here is to present the model most closely representative of the data, which for Stages A and B have been mostly recovered at Huaca de la Luna. This first undertaking will undoubtedly need to be further developed as new information becomes available.

STAGE A: PHASE III/EARLY MOCHE (AD 250–450)

The nature of Moche rulership during Stage A is not well understood. Admittedly, the archaeological data are still largely missing. Apart from the deposit of sacrificial victims in Plaza 3C, only a few burials of high-ranking individuals have been sci-entifically excavated. In addition to Huaca de la Luna, this section presents contexts from the Chicama Valley (El Brujo) and the Jequetepeque Valley (Dos Cabezas) (fig. 7.61).

Wrinkle Face Tradition

The Wrinkle Face subject (prominently depicted in Stage A in numerous activities, including the Mountain Sacrifice and the Coca Ceremony) originated from a more ancient religious and political structure, perhaps dating as far back as Cupisnique. In Moche culture, it represents more than just a vague subject—a distant memory or artifact of a long-gone symbolic tradition. It includes a series of concepts fundamental to Moche symbolic and ideological domain, such as the feline pouncing on a sacrificial victim (figs. 7.37, 7.62), and the prisoner with a topknot (Jones 2010). The exact mode of transmission of these subjects over the centuries is largely unknown, and formal connections between the Late Formative and Early Intermediate Period have yet to be properly established (Cordy-Collins 2001). Nonetheless, the presence of these subjects in Moche iconography and the resurgence of Cupisnique-like subjects on the walls of Huaca de la Luna bespeak a system that was successfully transmitted and kept at the forefront of Moche ideological preoccupations (fig. 5.77).

The Wrinkle Face tradition culminates during Phase III with the Mountain Sacrifice ritual (figs. 2.23, 5.28). In addition to this subject, among the prominent high-ranking individuals at the time are Iguana, the coca takers, and the warriors. Much research remains to be conducted, but evidence of the Coca Ceremony has been found in the southern and northern Moche regions, indicating the widespread practice of this ritual and the high degree of cohesion achieved in the Moche political structure by the fourth or fifth century AD. In addition to the sacrificial deposit at Huaca de la Luna (Plaza 3C), iconographical evidence of the Coca Ceremony has been found at El Brujo in the Chicama Valley and at Dos Cabezas in the Jequetepeque Valley.

A small bottle in the form of a coca taker was found at El Brujo in the burial of the third attendant accompanying a high-ranking woman named the Lady of Cao (Mujica Barreda et al. 2007: 215).

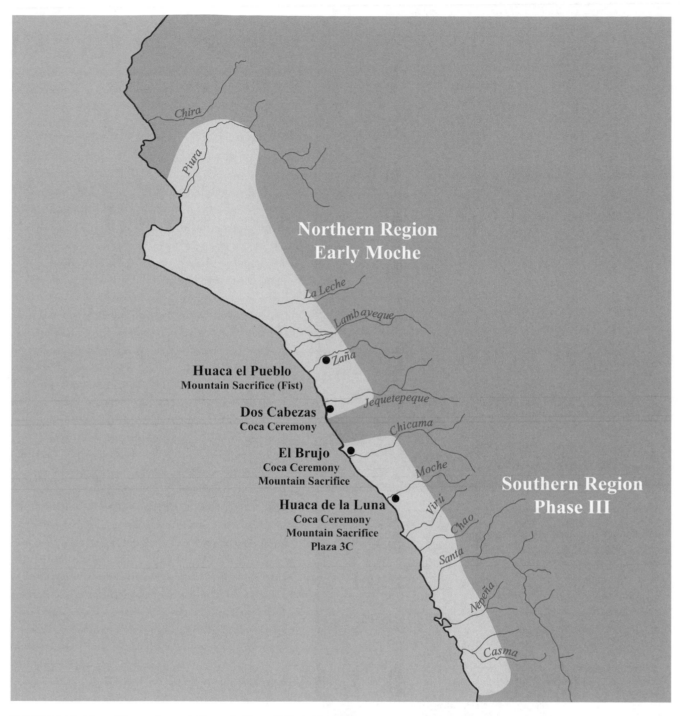

FIGURE 7.61. Map of the north coast, Stage A: Phase III/Early Moche.

Along with other vessels in the funerary chamber, this bottle is in the Early Moche style, similar to the one encountered in the Jequetepeque Valley at sites such as Dos Cabezas and La Mina. In addition to the coca taker, an effigy was found in the bundle of the individual. It consists of a sort of cape made of leather and textile covered with

gilded copper disks and a face mask with hands and feet in the same metal (Mujica Barreda et al. 2007: 216). This striking object fits directly with the Coca Ceremony scenes and Early Moche warriors dressed wearing these objects and could be related to the feline effigy encountered at Huaca de la Luna (fig. 4.15). The feline and the human

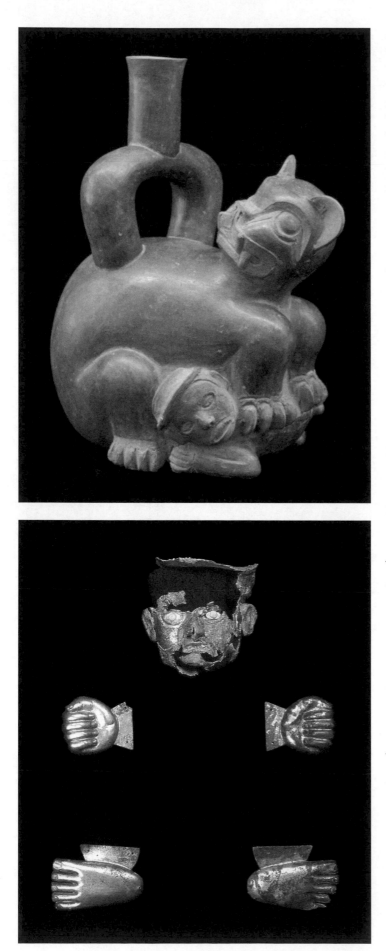

effigies are nearly interchangeable: the feline would stand for the sacrificer, while the human would stand for the victim.

A similar set of gilded copper objects representing a human head, hands, and feet was found in Tomb 2 at Dos Cabezas (fig. 7.63) (Donnan 2007). These objects were positioned on the back of the main male individual. This suggests that he was wearing such an effigy at the time of his placement in the chamber.

In addition to Tomb 2, Donnan (2007) recovered a series of other high-ranking tombs in the southwestern corner of the building during the study of the Huaca Dos Cabezas. About 1 m from Tomb B, which had been looted, Donnan (2007: 30) and his team encountered the remains of an offering consisting of burned textiles and intentionally broken ceramics. Among the ceramic fragments was a matched pair of large jars depicting modeled coca chewers. One of them could be reconstructed (fig. 7.64). The individual portrayed on this beautiful jar wears the hairdo consistently associated with the Mountain Sacrifice subject.[2]

As shown in chapter 5, additional ceramics recovered at Dos Cabezas from these contexts, such as a macaw (fig. 5.55), a seahorse (fig. 5.99), a seated figure wearing a necklace of sea lion heads and an octopus diadem (fig. 5.91), and an individual afflicted with diffuse cutaneous leishmaniasis (fig. 7.65), indicate that the Moche of the Jequetepeque Valley clearly participated in the same ritual structure as the Moche from the south. To highlight the link between the Early Moche and Phase III, the leishmaniasis theme also exists further north. At Huaca el Pueblo in the Zaña Valley, a ceramic illustrating an individual with the facial lesions created by mucotaneous leishmaniasis was located in a partially looted funerary chamber pertaining to the Early Moche (fig. 2.6).

Although scenes of Mountain Sacrifice have not been found to the north of the Pampa de Paiján for Stage A, a stone object excavated at Huaca

FIGURE 7.62. (*Top*) Cupisnique vessel of a feline overtaking a human. Museum zu Allerheiligen, Schaffhausen, Sammlung Ebnöther. Inv. no. Eb15830.01.

FIGURE 7.63. (*Bottom*) Metallic effigy from Tomb 2, Dos Cabezas. Museo de Sitio de Chan Chan. Photograph by Christopher B. Donnan.

FIGURE 7.64. Jar in the form of a coca taker from Tomb B, Dos Cabezas. Museo de Sitio de Chan Chan.

FIGURE 7.65. Individual resting on his right side. Tomb 2, Dos Cabezas. Museo de Sitio de Chan Chan. Inv. no. 13-01-04/IV/A-1/13,437. Photograph by Johnathan Watts, MEG.

el Pueblo may provide the first clue that this ritual concept was also present among the Northern Moche. We have found in the fill of a Middle Moche (Stage B) tomb at that site a natural stone that had been slightly modified by pecking to resemble the back of a human hand and arm (fig. 7.66). With these small changes, the rock took the form of the half-fist gesture, mimicking the mountain depicted in the iconography: "Like the mountain scenes, the half fist emphasizes a central point with symmetrically arranged protrusions to each side" (Donnan 1978: 154). This modeled hand in a half-fist position integrates the concept of both the gesture and the mountain (fig. 7.67). The back of the hand is made in the form of five peaks. Thus the gesture is not just a hand signal that forms part of the corpus of hand signs depicted in the Mountain Sacrifice (fig. 7.6). This hand gesture literally symbolizes the mountain (Donnan 1978).

STAGE B: PHASE IV/MIDDLE MOCHE (AD 450–700)

Stage B presents the richest body of information of all three stages. This period includes among other things the high-ranking burials of Sipán, Huaca el Pueblo, and Huaca de la Cruz, the Plaza 3A sacrificial site, and the full expansion of the Moche culture. It is also marked by the most elaborate visual culture on all types of media.

When Archaeology Meets Iconography

The people and the rituals associated with them during Stage A, including the Coca Ceremony and the Mountain Sacrifice, do not disappear during Stage B. But a new group of individuals and rituals comes into prominence: those of the Sacrifice Ceremony. In some cases (such as the Huaca de la Cruz site in the Virú Valley), the main person found in Tomb 12, who pertained to the Wrinkle Face tradition but became known as the "warrior-priest," may have also accumulated functions associated with this new symbolic system and political organization (Bourget 2006; Strong and Evans 1952). In his tomb are elements (including wooden staffs and ceramic vessels) associated with both Stage A and Stage B, such as scenes of a Mountain Sacrifice, a warrior with the segmented conical helmet (fig. 4.8), a portrait vessel with the

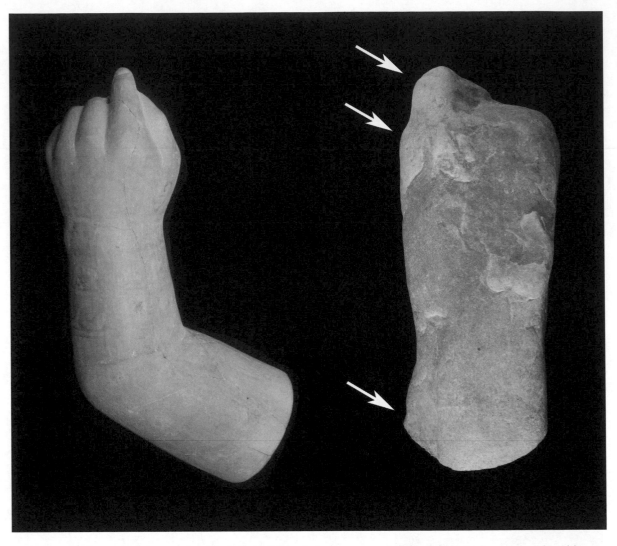

FIGURE 7.66. Comparison between a ceramic in the form of a human arm and a reworked stone from Huaca el Pueblo. Museo Nacional de Arqueología, Antropología e Historia del Perú. Inv. no. C-00275.

Phase III hairdo and Maltese cross facial painting (fig. 5.177), a deer hunting scene, and two portrait vessels clearly pertaining to the Sacrifice Ceremony tradition. Burial 10 located nearby contained the remains of a female eventually identified as one of the representatives of Individual E from the Sacrifice Ceremony (fig. 7.50) (Arsenault 1994).

The mixing of both traditions within Tomb 12 is perhaps not too surprising. The Sacrifice Ceremony is not a replacement of the previous ritual system but an addition to it. It evolved from elements already present during Phase III. As an example, in an unusual depiction of the Sacrifice Ceremony subjects (which I suspect is a late Phase IV painting), Wrinkle Face stands to the

right of Individual A, who is being helped up a ladder by five spider beings wearing V-shaped diadems (fig. 5.194). Thus the Wrinkle Face subject still maintains a prominent role in the Moche ideological system throughout Phase IV. The subject inspired by Wrinkle Face is shown standing up in one of the best renditions of the Coca Ceremony (fig. 7.68), and a number of indices suggest that Individual D of the Sacrifice Ceremony is also inspired by the same subject (figs. 7.50, 7.51). In two cases (figs. 7.68, 7.50), these avatars are holding their hands clasped together, perhaps to index the sacredness of the coca ritual or the blood exchange.

The data collected at Huaca de la Luna, including Tomb 1 and Tomb 2 on Platform I, indicate

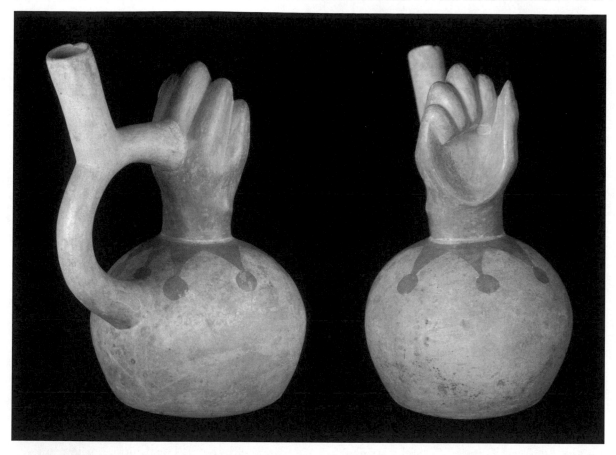

FIGURE 7.67. Human fist in the form of a mountain. By kind permission of the Rautenstrauch-Joest-Museum, Köln. Inv. no. RJM 37839. Photograph by Christopher B. Donnan.

FIGURE 7.68. Coca Ceremony. Museo Larco, Lima, Peru. Inv. no. ML004112. Drawing by Donna McClelland. The Christopher B. Donnan and Donna McClelland Moche Archive, Image Collections and Fieldwork Archives, Dumbarton Oaks, Trustees for Harvard University, Washington, DC.

that the rituals and the concomitant iconography developed in Phase III follow into Phase IV. The Coca Ceremony continues, but it is apparently no longer depicted as an elaborate ceremony such as the one shown in figure 7.8. The cache discussed earlier containing the elaborate feline effigy and the regalia of coca ritualists may indicate the decommissioning of these objects toward the end of Phase III (figs. 4.15, 7.33). The scene of the Coca Ceremony shown earlier, however, likely dates to a transitional period leading into Phase IV (fig. 7.68). It has retained the same tricolor decorative technique shown in figure 7.8, but the painting is created on a bigger and more elongated bottle. At 27 cm tall, it stands 4 cm higher than the example shown in figure 7.9. The upper spout is taller and its sides are parallel. The scene depicts two coca takers accompanied by Wrinkle Face making a supplicating gesture. This gesture is also similar to the one performed by coca takers standing underneath the bicephalous arch in figure 7.8. A fanged being wearing a feline effigy on his back has a bag containing a lime container slung over his left arm. He is facing an assemblage of ritual objects, including a feline headdress, two lime containers, two net bundles, a feline effigy, and a weapon bundle (fig. 7.68).

The Sacrifice Ceremony, a new sacrificial ritual that began in Stage B with its own set of individuals, shows continuity from Stage A as well by using the fanged being tradition as a source of inspiration for Individual D. This symbolic association does not suggest a total break from the previous traditions but the appearance of a new political formation grafted onto the previous one, which already spanned the southern and northern regions from Moche to Zaña. Human beings interred with the attributes of the Sacrifice Ceremony subjects have been found in the northern and southern regions, including Sipán, Huaca el Pueblo, Pacatnamú, and Huaca de la Cruz (Alva and Donnan 1993; Arsenault 1994; Bourget 2008, 2014; Strong and Evans 1952; Ubbelohde-Doering 1983). Indeed objects pertaining to Individual D but without a clear provenance are reputed to have been found at Loma Negra to the far north of the Moche region, whereas a mural inspired by the same ceremonial formation has been found as far south as Pañamarca (figs. 7.69, 2.8) (Bonavia 1985; Donnan 2010). The presence of buried indi-

viduals wearing this regalia and other elements of material culture found throughout the Moche region, from Piura to the north to Nepeña to the south, demonstrates the remarkable political and structural stability and homogeneity achieved by the Moche at this stage of their history.

Table 7.3 lists the individuals that have been linked with their iconographical counterparts so far in order to clarify these correspondences.

Although individuals associated with the Sacrifice Ceremony have been found in both regions, in Stage B the fineline scenes that led to their identification do not exist north of the Pampa de Paiján (Bourget 2008). The reasons why the northern Moche did not adopt the fineline painting style so prevalent in the southern region are unclear. Nonetheless, the objects and the regalia used north of Paiján are consistent with the representation of the same objects in Phase IV iconography. It would seem that the northern rulers did not feel the need to adopt this type of representation and that the Middle Moche style, which developed in synchrony with the Phase IV style, was deemed sufficient to fulfill their propaganda needs.

Even with the fineline painting so eloquently displaying the Warrior Narrative absent from the northern region, an important element that may index the presence of ceremonial combat leading to the Sacrifice Ceremony is the portrait vessel tradition. As noted by Donnan (2004), portrait vessels depict the ritual warriors and their full range of activities/roles, including the stage leading to the sacrifice proper. The presence of portrait vessels in the burials of Plaza 3C and Platform II at Huaca de la Luna and in the Warrior-Priest tomb at Huaca de la Cruz indicates that the old men buried in these tombs are sacrificers. This is consistent with the position stated earlier that the occurrence of ceramics depicting activities of warfare, human sacrifice, or coca taking signals the practice of these rituals at the site. I suggest further that the presence of portrait vessels, which are eminently associated with ceremonial combat, capture, and human sacrifice, also indicates the site's participation in these activities.

Our understanding of the distribution of the portrait vessel tradition at Moche sites is still incomplete. Nevertheless, it has been found at nearly all Moche sites currently under investiga-

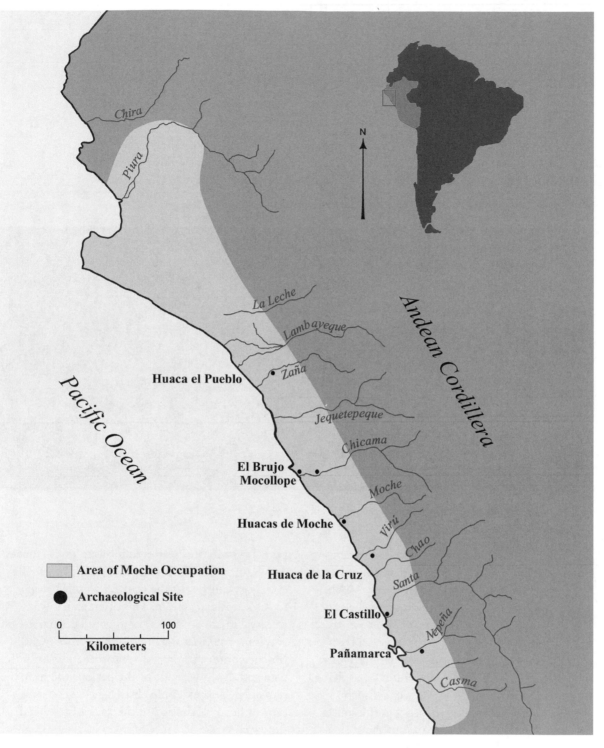

FIGURE 7.69. Map of the north coast, Stage B: Phase IV/Middle Moche.

Table 7.3. Stage B Funerary Contexts

Site	Context	Identity	Period
Huaca de la Luna	Tombs 2 and 3	Coca ritualists	Phase IV
Huaca de la Cruz	Tombs 12–15	Wrinkle Face	Phase IV
Pacatnamú	nos. 74–85	Individual A	Middle Moche
Sipán	Tomb 1	Individual A	Middle Moche
Sipán	Tombs 2, 3, 14	Individual B/D	Middle Moche
Huaca el Pueblo	CH-7	Individual B/D	Middle Moche
Huaca de la Cruz	Tomb 10	Individual E	Phase IV

FIGURE 7.70. Fragment of a portrait vessel, Huaca el Pueblo. Ministry of Culture, Peru.

tion in the southern region and has been mentioned by Larco Hoyle (1938, 1939) at a number of still poorly known sites in the Chicama, Moche, Virú, and Santa Valleys. On the basis of the style and the archaeological evidence, until recently it has been argued that the portrait vessel tradition did not exist in the northern region (Donnan 2004: 19). Such an absence could be explained by stylistic and ideological preferences such as the prevalence of fineline painting in the southern region only before Stage C. But the absence of the portrait head vessel tradition in the northern region severely limits its usefulness to index the important activity of ceremonial combat. This also would not explain why the northern Moche chose to depict the leishmaniasis amputee or the coca taker in minute detail and yet did not use perhaps the single most prominent subject of one of the most important ritual activities. After all, the fifty-two clay statuettes scattered in Plaza 3A at Huaca de la Luna are in essence portrait sculptures. They clearly establish that the portrait vessels belong to the sacrificial system. This discrepancy was resolved in 2008 when a fragmented portrait vessel was found at Huaca el Pueblo in a secure Middle Moche context (fig. 7.70). Unfortunately, only the base and the lower part of the back of the head remained. This example clearly shows the same type of head cloth, tied to the back of the head (fig. 7.71).

At this stage, on the basis of the mounting evidence, the southern and northern division of the Moche can no longer be sustained in terms of ritual and political organizations but only on the basis of stylistic traditions.

FIGURE 7.71. Portrait vessel of a warrior. Museo Larco, Lima, Peru. Inv. no. ML000386.

The Warrior and Sacrifice Ceremony Narratives

Donnan (2010: 55–58) correctly suggests that the numerous scenes that display activities of warfare and sacrifice formed part of a sequence that he refers to as the Warrior Narrative. He identifies ten distinct but interrelated and consecutive actions culminating with the eventual sacrifice and dismemberment of the sacrificial victims (table 7.4):

> Reconstructing the Warrior Narrative demonstrates that the Sacrifice Ceremony was not an isolated ceremony but was the culmination of a much larger ritual complex. The archaeological and iconographic evidence available today indicates that this ritual complex was the central focus of a highly organized religious institution that I will refer to as the Moche state religion. (Donnan 2010: 58)

In general terms, the data and the sequence that Donnan presents are in agreement with the available information, though I suggest that some slightly different views could be offered for some of the scenes, such as those that show blood being spilled. For Donnan, the scene depicted in figure 7.56 represents a ritual that immediately follows removal of the clothing of the captured war-

Table 7.4. Donnan's Warrior Narrative Sequence

1	Figure 7.82	Warriors with elaborate clothing, weapons, and ornaments
2	Figure 7.21	Combat (usually one on one)
3	Figure 7.15	One of the combatants is vanquished
4	Figure 7.13	Clothing, weapons, and ornaments removed and tied in a weapon bundle
5	Figure 7.56	Rope put around the neck and causes bleeding
6	Figure 5.35	The defeated are paraded
7	Figure 7.54	Brought to the summit of a temple
8	Figure 7.51	The Sacrifice Ceremony is enacted
9	Figure 7.52	The blood of the sacrificial victim is consumed
10	Figure 7.43	The bodies are dismembered

riors. The activity consists in making the captives bleed by being hit on the face (Donnan 2010: 56). I suggest rather that this might represent a conflation of two distinct but related themes brought together in a single representation. In the scene, victims are bleeding into the hands of warriors wearing a conical helmet. The blood is in turn offered to the weapon bundles just behind the elaborately dressed warriors, who wear the same accouterments as Individual A of the Sacrifice Ceremony (figs. 5.35, 7.56). An unusual rendition of the Sacrifice Ceremony discussed earlier portrays a warrior bleeding in the outstretched hand of Individual A, demonstrating the validity of my assessment (fig. 7.55).

The representational technique of blending two distinct but related activities is not rare. A similar situation occurs in the Sacrifice Ceremony shown in figure 7.52, where a ritual battle is depicted just underneath the bicephalous arch, while the ceremony itself is crammed into the space just above it. This narrative device of amalgamating two related subjects on a single ceramic was also noted by Donnan and McClelland (1999: 134).

Donnan presents a straightforward and descriptive approach to this complex system, using the iconography and the archaeological data at the same time. I would argue, however, that Moche visual culture allows for a more symbolic reading as well. To address what perhaps may represent the more metaphysical dimensions of the Warrior Sequence, I call upon scenes detailing additional aspects of the Warrior Narrative and Sacrifice Ceremony. As stated by Donnan and McClelland (1999: 113), numerous scenes in Phase IV represent not only human beings engaged in battles and the capture of prisoners but also subjects with supernatural attributes, such as animated objects and zoo-anthropomorphic beings (fig. 7.72). These actors are engaged in activities including sacrifices, funerary rituals, and acts in marine settings. The anthropomorphizing of objects and animals, and the corresponding "zoomorphization" of human beings, is one of the major representational modes of Moche iconography alongside the portrayal of ritualized warfare. Ritual battles and humanized objects and animals are intimately related to one another in the Sacrifice Ceremony and in many other scenes, including the Battle of the Animated Objects (fig. 7.73). This subject represents a key for

understanding some of the basic tenets of Moche ideology and needs to be analyzed further.

The Battle of the Animated Objects

Fineline drawings of anthropomorphized objects capturing human beings were some of the first Moche representations to be analyzed and published. Walter Krickeberg (1928) likened these scenes to a recorded Quiche Maya myth that told of a rebellion of everyday objects and domesticated animals and to a vaguely similar story collected in the seventeenth century in the Peruvian region of Huarochirí. More recently, this proposition has been reinvestigated by Jeffrey Quilter (1990, 1996, 1997) in order to demonstrate that these scenes were part of an ancient myth that spread all over the Americas. The main caveat to this partly structuralist and diffusionist proposition lies in the very nature of the representations themselves. In contrast to the Quiche and Huarochirí texts, Moche iconography does not depict the rebellion of domestic animals or culinary implements against humans. Instead the scenes present animated weapons and ornaments of warriors capturing human beings, who are often denuded. This visual program fits well within the logic of Moche ceremonial combat as reiterated countless times in their visual culture. Weapon bundles and warriors' regalia are prominently shown in ceremonial combat and sacrificial activities. The iconography abounds with scenes representing warriors fighting each other, usually in some form of duel and more rarely in a group. The defeated are then completely or partially denuded, and their outfit and armaments are attached to the war maces of the victorious. The warrior attributes of the losers, fashioned into these weapon bundles, are always prominently represented and seem to be as important as the rest of the depiction (fig. 7.12) (Donnan 2010).

Therefore the anthropomorphization of war implements and attributes is not a radical departure from the Moche mode of representation but forms an integral part of its very structure. Tule boats, vessels, and animals are frequently depicted with human limbs (fig. 5.12). Also, under the guise of warriors, zoo-anthropomorphic and phyto-anthropomorphic subjects abound (fig. 5.164). The anthropomorphization of these objects is directly

FIGURE 7.72. Animated objects capturing warriors. Drawing by Donna McClelland. The Christopher B. Donnan and Donna McClelland Moche Archive, Image Collections and Fieldwork Archives, Dumbarton Oaks, Trustees for Harvard University, Washington, DC.

FIGURE 7.73. Battle of the Animated Objects. Drawing by Donna McClelland. The Christopher B. Donnan and Donna McClelland Moche Archive, Image Collections and Fieldwork Archives, Dumbarton Oaks, Trustees for Harvard University, Washington, DC.

associated with the very core of the Moche ideological system. Human forms, like the individuals of the Sacrifice Ceremony, are often transformed into composite beings with animal components added to their anatomy, such as tails, wings, and heads. Likewise, objects such as vessels, shields, clubs, nose ornaments, and even boats are animated with body parts.

The Munich vase portrays arguably the most complex rendition of the Battle of the Animated Objects. Four actors of the Sacrifice Ceremony (A, B/D, C, and E) appear in the scene (fig. 7.73). I suggest that this scene may represent the precedent event that eventually led to the Sacrifice Ceremony scene. In accord with Quilter (1990), who published the most extensive analysis of this scene, I think that it portrays a narrative involving two distinct groupings of actors. But I would like to propose an alternative sequence to his argu-

ment that it represents a revolt on the lower register brought under control by the rayed deity on the upper register (fig. 7.73 A) (Bourget 2005). I argue that this two-step narrative should be read in the opposite order, starting with the upper section and leading into the lower part of the representation.

On the upper register are Individuals A and C supervising a group of anthropomorphized animals (fig. 7.74). To the left and to the right, a puma, a fox, an ocelot, and a human are literally dragging toward the couple a large belt, a conical hat, and two nose ornaments. In the center of the representation, just below the couple, a duck and two raptorial birds are respectively fighting a warrior's tunic, a shield, and a serpent-fox belt. This represents the first part of the narrative, with A and C sending their zoo-anthropomorphic and human helpers to bring ritual implements to take

FIGURE 7.74. Upper section of the Battle of the Animated Objects. Drawing by Donna McClelland. The Christopher B. Donnan and Donna McClelland Moche Archive, Image Collections and Fieldwork Archives, Dumbarton Oaks, Trustees for Harvard University, Washington, DC.

FIGURE 7.75. Lower section of the Battle of the Animated Objects. Drawing by Donna McClelland. The Christopher B. Donnan and Donna McClelland Moche Archive, Image Collections and Fieldwork Archives, Dumbarton Oaks, Trustees for Harvard University, Washington, DC.

part in the sacred battle taking place just below this part of the painting.

On the lower register (fig. 7.75), humanized implements are defeating and capturing human warriors and an anthropomorphic deer. This battle takes place under the supervision and guidance of an owl impersonator wearing a V-shaped diadem (Individual B/D) and Individual C. In this complex battle scene, human warriors are captured, stripped of their clothing, and taken prisoner under the watchful eyes of the same indi-

viduals: A, B/D, and C of the Sacrifice Ceremony. Furthermore, the characteristic staff with four prongs (identified as E in fig. 7.73) is also involved in the taking of prisoners.

I suggest that the action following the capture of sacrificial victims in the overall story is the ritual running activity. It provides a transition between the ritual battle and the Sacrifice Ceremony. Ritual running is always performed by human warriors or zoomorphic beings in the guise of Ritual Runners or warriors. They consistently wear *tumi*-shaped or disk diadems (fig. 7.76). The following excerpt (fig. 7.77), taken from the complete painting presented in figure 5.35, demonstrates the logic of inserting the Ritual Runner at this juncture within the larger Warrior Narrative. In the center of the painting, a warrior carrying the bag of the Ritual Runners is positioned between a battle to the right and a naked man shedding blood to the left—between the capture and the sacrificial act. The warrior firmly holding this captive is in turn offering his blood to a weapon bundle behind him. This captor wears the conical helmet topped with a crescent-shaped diadem that is also assigned to Individual A of the Sacrifice Ceremony. This does not mean that this is Individual A, but rather that warriors with these attributes are linked to this subject. Therefore the complex painting in figure 5.156 depicts Individual A being carried in a litter by two zoo-anthropomorphic warriors holding the telltale bags of Ritual Runners. They are accompanied by fifteen zoo-anthropomorphic warriors, five snake-foxes, and seven animals. What the bags carried by the runners and those holding the litter may contain is unclear. But the bags also appear in scenes of deer hunting (fig. 5.165, 7.31), and the Ritual Runners are often surrounded by lima beans and *ulluchu* fruits.

Because of the involvement of the Sacrifice Ceremony subjects in the battle and the running shown in figures 7.73 and 5.156, I suggest that this sequence culminates in the eventual sacrifice of the captives during the Sacrifice Ceremony (fig. 7.50). All the categories of actors depicted in the Battle of the Animated Objects and in the journey of Individual A in the litter are also represented in this scene: human beings, zoo-anthropomorphic beings, and animated weapon bundles. The Sacrifice Ceremony would also consist of a two-step narrative. In the first part, situated underneath the bicephalous arch (fig. 7.78), the litter of Individual A rests on the ground. Three zoo-anthropomorphic warriors, two birds and a fox, are sitting behind it. The feline that accompanied Individual A in the litter is still inside it. An anthropomorphized feline and a humanized staff with four prongs on the lower register are collecting the blood from sacrificial victims. Both sacrificers are represented with their corresponding weapon bundles. In the following part of the ritual narrative on the upper register, A and B are partaking of blood brought by woman C in a special container (fig. 7.79).

Other iconographic scenes and sculptures show a considerable amount of overlap between Individual B—the Bird Impersonator—and Indi-

Hummingbird Raptorial Bird Duck Dragonfly Hummingbird Bat Puma Lizard

FIGURE 7.76. Ritual Runners. Drawing by Donna McClelland. The Christopher B. Donnan and Donna McClelland Moche Archive, Image Collections and Fieldwork Archives, Dumbarton Oaks, Trustees for Harvard University, Washington, DC.

FIGURE 7.77. Ritual bleeding and ceremonial combat. Drawing by Donna McClelland. The Christopher B. Donnan and Donna McClelland Moche Archive, Image Collections and Fieldwork Archives, Dumbarton Oaks, Trustees for Harvard University, Washington, DC.

FIGURE 7.78. Lower section of a Sacrifice Ceremony. Drawing by Donna McClelland. The Christopher B. Donnan and Donna McClelland Moche Archive, Image Collections and Fieldwork Archives, Dumbarton Oaks, Trustees for Harvard University, Washington, DC.

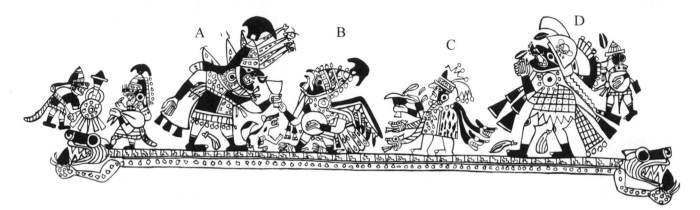

FIGURE 7.79. Upper section of a Sacrifice Ceremony. Drawing by Donna McClelland. The Christopher B. Donnan and Donna McClelland Moche Archive, Image Collections and Fieldwork Archives, Dumbarton Oaks, Trustees for Harvard University, Washington, DC.

vidual D. In the Battle of the Animated Objects (fig. 7.73) and on the striking goblet discussed above (fig. 7.53), Individual B is depicted with the V-shaped diadem usually assigned to Individual D. I suggest that the reason for this overlap is that both belong to the same category or rank.

Animated warrior attributes capturing prisoners could well reinforce the concept of ritualized warfare within the Moche population. For Moche individuals coming from the same social group but fighting each other, these objects could have symbolized the ritual activity itself. In the Battle of the Animated Objects, Individual A as the paramount warlord forces the objects to obey his orders, while Individuals B/D, standing on the summit of a huaca, receive the captives (fig. 7.73). Therefore men vested with the warrior regalia and armed with these weapons become fantastic warriors fighting each other under the guidance of Individuals A, B/D, and C. Those who lost the battle are deprived of these attributes and become captives and eventually sacrificial victims.

The prominence of the warriors outfits and weapons in the iconography is major evidence for the understanding of ritual warfare. In certain scenes, equal statuses are bestowed upon the weapon bundles and the victims (figs. 7.13, 7.56). Seated warriors with their hands clasped together are sometimes depicted presenting their weapon bundle to the *Strombus* monster (fig. 5.118). As we have seen already, *Strombus* shell trumpets figure prominently in the ritual battles and in the Sacrifice Ceremony (figs. 5.35, 5.36, 7.59). Therefore the sound of these trumpets, the vestments worn, and the weapons carried by warriors all contribute to index the commands and the will of the rulers. Hand gestures associated with the battles, the capture, and the eventual sacrifice are also highly codified. I suggest that the closed fist signifies capture (figs. 5.35, 7.3, 7.19), the pointing index finger references the link with sacrifice (fig. 7.54), and the open palm indicates the shedding of blood sacrifice (figs. 5.64, 7.55, 7.56).[3]

An extraordinary bottle from the Museo Larco

is perhaps the most eloquent example of the primary importance of animated weaponry and regalia in Moche symbolic ideology (figs. 7.80, 7.81). The painting is organized into three registers on top of each other, with a thin horizontal line delineating each section. A group of warriors is depicted on the lower section: moving from left to right, Individual A is leading four warriors ambulating toward five others moving in the opposite direction (fig. 7.82). An anthropomorphized hummingbird carrying a large bag accompanies him. In the Sacrifice Ceremony painting shown in figure 7.50, just behind Individual A, is

an anthropomorphized feline shouldering a similar bag. Separating the two groups and linking the action about to happen—the battle—with the middle register is a snake-fox spiral firmly held in the hand of a seated individual (fig. 7.82).

Individual B and a subject with a black tunic dominate the middle register (fig. 7.82). They are facing each other with a pair of *ulluchu* fruits and a fox warrior between them. The person with the black tunic is usually associated with subjects involved with naked prisoners and sacrificial victims (figs. 7.43, 7.54). This individual cannot be directly associated with Individual C due to lack

FIGURE 7.80. Bottle with ceremonial combat and ritual objects, view A. Museo Larco, Lima, Peru. Inv. no. ML010849.

FIGURE 7.81. Bottle with ceremonial combat and ritual objects, view B. Museo Larco, Lima, Peru. Inv. no. ML010849.

of the diagnostic cape and headdress. In the Battle of the Animated Objects, though, Individual C wears her more identifiable attributes, such as her two-pronged headdress and her cape on top of a similar black tunic indicating that we are dealing in these scenes with subjects relating to her (fig. 7.73).

Individual B points toward the *ulluchu* fruits (fig. 7.82), while behind him two seated individuals are guarding a door providing access to four buildings. Both guardians are leishmaniasis amputees. This is a well-known subject: these individuals are once more depicted on this archi-

tectural model with one of them impeding access to the building by holding a stick across the door (fig. 7.83). These scenes may illuminate one of the duties of these mutilated individuals, who are shown in figures 2.5 and 2.6 and were recovered in Tomb 48 in Uhle's platform at Huaca de la Luna (Chauchat et al. 2008).

To the right, the subject with the black tunic and the fox warrior point toward a large group of objects (depicted to the left in the roll-out drawing). The elongated ones with fox heads at their extremities may represent spears, clubs, or sticks (fig. 7.82). The group of four Y-shaped objects,

FIGURE 7.82. (*Above*) Ceremonial combat and ritual objects. Drawing by Donna McClelland. The Christopher B. Donnan and Donna McClelland Moche Archive, Image Collections and Fieldwork Archives, Dumbarton Oaks, Trustees for Harvard University, Washington, DC.

FIGURE 7.83. (*Below*) Individuals with leishmaniasis guarding the door of a building, Phase IV. Museo Larco, Lima, Peru. Inv. no. ML002892.

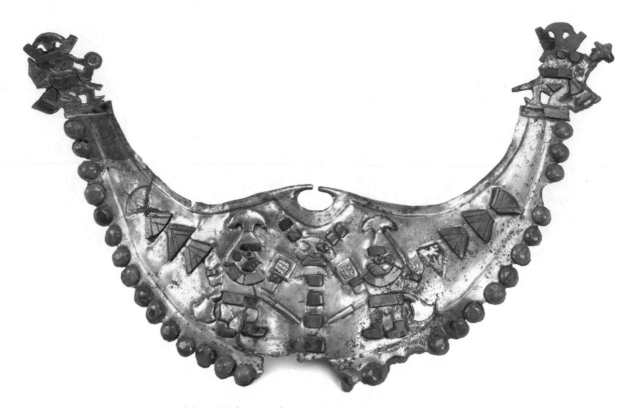

FIGURE 7.84. Nose ornament with low-relief scene of ceremonial combat, Lord of Ucupe burial, Huaca el Pueblo. Ministry of Culture, Peru. Inv. no. CH7-19. Photograph by Johnathan Watts, MEG.

with a human face in their middle, most likely stand for the sacrificial implements that are usually shown with victims attached to them (figs. 5.127, 7.2, 7.3). An almost identical example is depicted on one of the nose ornaments from the Lord of Ucupe burial at Huaca el Pueblo. This beautiful object, in silver with turquoise inlays, depicts the very same Y-shaped object with a human face in its center between two warriors (fig. 7.84).

The upper section of the scene, dedicated to animated regalia and weaponry, includes (from left to right) a crescent-shaped diadem, a cape or pectoral, a belt, two spearthrowers, a tunic, a helmet, a backflap, and a shield (fig. 7.82).

As in the Battle of the Animated Objects narrative, Individual A in the lower register commands the battle and is accompanied by an anthropomorphized hummingbird shouldering a bag (figs. 7.74, 7.82). Hummingbirds are frequently shown with high-ranking individuals (fig. 6.18), carrying Individual A swiftly across the landscape (fig. 5.156), hovering in the midst of battles (fig. 7.85), and migrating toward weapon bundles (fig. 5.108). As suggested by the upper register of the Battle of the Animated Objects (fig. 7.74), the animated

weapons and regalia fall under the purview of Individual A and are directly related to the acts of warfare and capture. Therefore the regalia index the paramount ruler (Individual A) as the greatest warrior, and the weapons signal that the battle is directed by and fought for him.

The central section is overseen by Individual B. It relates largely to the second phase of the ritual—the sacrificial activities. This takes place within the architectural structures of a ceremonial building. It apparently shows the objects used in the sacrificial rituals including the Y-shaped racks, the clubs, and other tools that are yet to be identified properly. Blood is symbolized by the *ulluchu* fruits and by one of the two snake-fox spirals being held by a seated individual. The composite animal extends its bifurcated tongue in the lower register, where a battle is about to begin (fig. 7.82). The forked tongue becomes the very ground upon which the warriors and Individual A tread.

Thus anthropomorphized implements signified the will of the Moche ruling elite. Numerous scenes give equal importance to the warriors, the prisoners, and the war implements. The fre-

FIGURE 7.85. Ceremonial combat. Drawing by Donna McClelland. The Christopher B. Donnan and Donna McClelland Moche Archive, Image Collections and Fieldwork Archives, Dumbarton Oaks, Trustees for Harvard University, Washington, DC.

Table 7.5. Narrative Sequence from the Battle of the Animated Objects to the Sacrifice Ceremony

Battle of the Animated Objects	1	A1: Capture of the ritual objects	Figure 7.74
	2	A2: Sacrificial victims captured by objects	Figure 7.75
Transition to Sacrifice	3	B: The sacred outfit is removed and shown	Figure 7.13
	4	C: The victims are shown naked	Figure 7.13
	5	D: Journey to the Sacrifice Ceremony	Figure 5.156
Sacrifice Ceremony	6	E1: Arrival	Figure 7.78
	7	E2: Collecting of blood	Figure 7.78
	8	E3: Transport of blood by Individual C	Figure 7.79
	9	E4: Individual B offering the blood to Individual A	Figure 7.79

quent representations of weapon bundles and in some cases of people literally worshipping these objects demonstrate their paramount importance. Like the animals in the iconography, these are not simple objects but subjects in their own right, taking an active role in the construction of the ideology transmitted with this system of representation.

Table 7.5 shows the narrative sequence suggested by the analysis. Nine consecutive moments lead from the capture of the ritual objects to the offering of blood to Individual A. This sequence should not be perceived as a proposition replacing the sequence suggested by Donnan and summarized in table 7.4. Donnan's sequence aims at describing the most likely order of ritual actions

that may have been carried out from the ritual battle to the eventual disposal of the human remains. The sequence that I suggest here dovetails with the first one and endeavors to highlight the more symbolically charged aspects of these activities.

In its narrative format, the Battle of the Animated Objects is a late Phase IV subject and marks the transition into Phase V. One bottle, whose spout is in the Phase V style, clearly shows this transition: painted on it is a rendition of this battle (fig. 7.86). The confrontation takes place around a woman with a long tunic standing inside a small building, above a wave populated by sea lions and borracho fish (fig. 7.87). This association with a maritime subject is important, as Stage C ico-

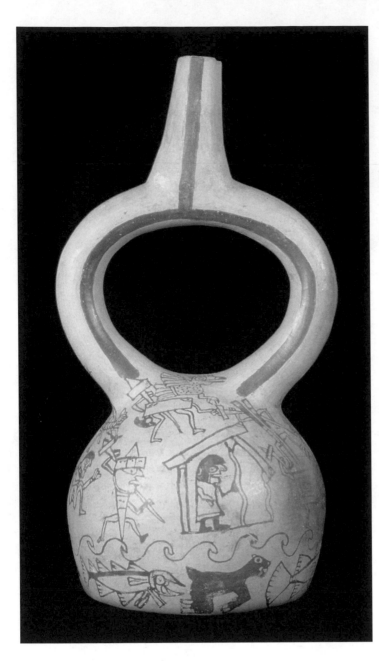

nography becomes dominated by this world. The transitional nature of the Battle of the Animated Objects is also the reason why a mural depicting this theme—probably the first mural found at the Huaca de la Luna by Seler in 1910—is located within Platform III (Bonavia 1985: 73–84). As the following section shows, the symbolic sequence developed in Stage B is pursued with significant changes in the Battle of the Animated Objects, the journey to the place of sacrifice, and the Sacrifice Ceremony.

STAGE C: PHASE V/LATE MOCHE (AD 700–800)

Stage C represents the final stage and the end of Moche culture as we know it. Unfortunately, at present the data to understand such an important moment of Moche history largely come from a single site: San José de Moro, located at the northern margin of the Jequetepeque Valley (fig. 2.1). Although this admittedly limits the scope of the analysis, the visual culture and the archaeological contexts at the site are remarkable and can be used in unison to provide a model that could be tested in the future when other contexts from the same period from other sites become available.

FIGURE 7.86. (*Left*) Animated objects capturing sacrificial victims. Staatliche Museen zu Berlin, Preußischer Kulturbesitz—Ethnologisches Museum. Inv. no. VA 62194.

FIGURE 7.87. (*Below*) Animated objects capturing sacrificial victims. Drawing by Donna McClelland. The Christopher B. Donnan and Donna McClelland Moche Archive, Image Collections and Fieldwork Archives, Dumbarton Oaks, Trustees for Harvard University, Washington, DC.

As shown in this chapter, the past is constantly remodeled throughout the history of Moche iconography within the ideology of the new political structures. The old cultural categories of Wrinkle Face and Iguana, which were present in the two preceding periods, have once more acquired new functional values. For example, a Phase IV painting that depicts Wrinkle Face and Iguana offer-

ing *Strombus* seashells to a high-ranking individual seated in a temple (fig. 7.88) is only a fragment of a more complex theme (the Burial Theme) that will gain prominence during Stage C (fig. 7.89) (McClelland, McClelland, and Donnan 2007). In this complex rendition, the conch shell exchange is located in the lower left side of the painting. The painting constitutes a narrative in which Wrinkle Face and Iguana are involved in all four activities.[4] This Burial Theme is especially impor-

FIGURE 7.88. Being with fangs presenting a *Strombus* seashell to a high-ranking individual. Drawing by Donna McClelland. The Christopher B. Donnan and Donna McClelland Moche Archive, Image Collections and Fieldwork Archives, Dumbarton Oaks, Trustees for Harvard University, Washington, DC.

FIGURE 7.89. Burial Theme. Drawing by Donna McClelland. The Christopher B. Donnan and Donna McClelland Moche Archive, Image Collections and Fieldwork Archives, Dumbarton Oaks, Trustees for Harvard University, Washington, DC.

FIGURE 7.90. Bottle with a painting of the Burial Theme. Private collection. Photograph by Christopher B. Donnan.

have almost completely disappeared from the iconography. As mentioned by Donnan and McClelland (1999: 178), and consistent with the present analysis, the iconography is now mostly dominated by the world of the sea and by only the most salient aspects of the Sacrifice Ceremony. The sea and a new form of the Sacrifice Ceremony are now fused together in what constitutes a new narrative sequence. Distinct individuals have also replaced the Phase IV Sacrifice Ceremony lineup. These transformations in both the structure of the representation and the type of subjects warrant a new designation. Here I coin the term "Blood Ceremony" to designate this type of representation.

On a bottle from San José de Moro, the Blood Ceremony takes place inside a temple underneath a gabled roof decorated with war clubs (figs. 7.91, 7.92). The couple exchanging a goblet, which is presumably filled with human blood, consists of a man with a conical helmet topped by a crescent-shaped diadem and a woman with a tasseled headgear and an elaborate tunic. Both subjects originated from within the Sacrifice Cere-

tant: McClelland, McClelland, and Donnan (2007: 101) suggest that a number of morphological and stylistic characteristics indicate that this bottle originated from the southern region (fig. 7.90). The Burial Theme became one of the most important themes depicted in the San José de Moro fineline painting tradition. Therefore the theme reaffirms the great cultural continuity and political unity between the two regions and provides further justification for considering the two regional fineline traditions within the same stage.

Stage C is also marked by drastic changes throughout the iconography. As I suggest, these changes reflect the transformations that took place in Moche political structures and the need to redefine the ideological discourse. During this period, the Mountain Sacrifice, the coca takers, and the ritual hunting of felines, foxes, and deer

FIGURE 7.91. Bottle with a painting of the Blood Ceremony. Private collection. Photograph by Christopher B. Donnan.

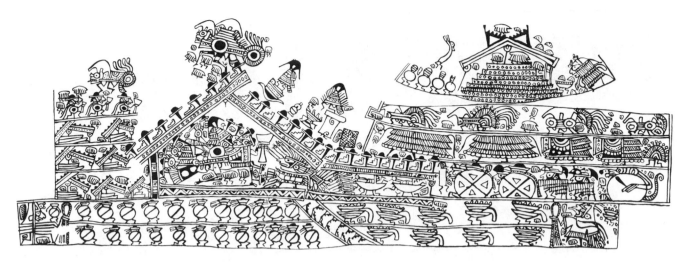

FIGURE 7.92. Blood Ceremony. Drawing by Donna McClelland. The Christopher B. Donnan and Donna McClelland Moche Archive, Image Collections and Fieldwork Archives, Dumbarton Oaks, Trustees for Harvard University, Washington, DC.

mony. The man surrounded by *Strombus* shells and war clubs is an avatar of Individual A, whereas the distant source of inspiration for the woman may have been Individual C (fig. 7.50). In what may be a transitional Phase IV/V bottle, the woman with tassels is depicted in a crescent moon at the apex of a complex scene involving Individuals A, B, and D (figs. 5.193, 5.194). Except for one scene introduced later, the woman with large tassels or plumes in her headdress known as Individual C has disappeared from Stage C iconography. The women who have replaced her in all the activities (including the boat scenes, the Burial Theme, and the Blood Ceremony) consistently wear a net dress and a large plumed headdress. In the Burial Theme example shown in figure 7.89, eight of these women, holding staffs, are standing just above the left side of the coffin. These women are different enough from the Priestess C canon to necessitate a distinct label by McClelland and Donnan: Net Shirt women.

As we have seen in Stage B, animated objects clearly formed part of the Sacrifice Ceremony. These subjects also appear in the Blood Ceremony as this tradition continues. A large array of animated vessels, headdresses, tunics, weapon bundles, *Strombus* seashells, and musical instruments surround the temple where the Blood Ceremony is performed. Animated objects in figure 7.92 are no longer battling but surrounding the couple exchanging the goblet within a temple. The design has also been simplified, and only very simple legs have been added to animate the objects. There-

fore this scene represents a conflation into a single fineline painting of the narrative sequence including ritual battle, capture, and the Blood Ceremony. Another complex painting constitutes perhaps the best rendition of the Blood Ceremony framed into a narrative sequence (fig. 7.93):

> Utilizing the spiral format, the narration proceeds from the bottom to the top of the chamber, apparently relaying successive moments in a story. At the bottom of the spiral, inanimate objects, including a reed boat, come to life and capture humans. Continuing up the spiral are three reed boats, each containing a different individual. They navigate toward a lean-to structure, the site of a ritual presentation of goblets. (Donnan and McClelland 1999: 182–183)

The action sequence suggested by Donnan and McClelland is fundamentally correct. I only wish to expand on it while discussing the sequence in its entirety. Warlike activities are performed in the lower and central section, and warriors are captured by anthropomorphized objects and an animated reed boat (fig. 7.94). A warrior with a conical helmet, a Net Shirt woman, and an individual sitting in a dark recess in the lower lefthand corner of the scene observe or take part in the activities. The seated figure wears the marine headdress, and an *ulluchu* fruit hovers just above his nose.

On the second section above (fig. 7.95), three boats are journeying toward a temple. The individuals in the boats may represent the subjects seen in the taking of prisoners: the first one leading the journey wears a two-pronged headdress,

FIGURE 7.93. Blood Ceremony complex, view A. Drawing by Donna McClelland. The Christopher B. Donnan and Donna McClelland Moche Archive, Image Collections and Fieldwork Archives, Dumbarton Oaks, Trustees for Harvard University, Washington, DC.

FIGURE 7.94. Blood Ceremony complex, view B. Drawing by Donna McClelland. The Christopher B. Donnan and Donna McClelland Moche Archive, Image Collections and Fieldwork Archives, Dumbarton Oaks, Trustees for Harvard University, Washington, DC.

the second one is a Net Shirt woman, and the third wears a headdress with a crescent-shaped diadem. In this case, the boatman is no longer a human being but rather an anthropomorphized feline.

Two similar activities are simultaneously taking place on the section above, to the left (fig. 7.96). The first involves the partaking of sacrificial blood by a person with a crescent-shaped headdress sitting in a temple and a bird-being with a two-pronged headdress. The second, to the left of the temple, includes two Net Shirt women exchanging a goblet. Therefore this narrative may involve three consecutive moments: the capture of warriors/sacrificial-victims-to-be; the journey on reed boats; and the ritual partaking of human blood. Additionally, the bottles seen here and there between the reed boats (fig. 7.95) and during the exchange of goblets in the last section may have served to carry the blood

of the sacrificed warriors. Structurally speaking, the narrative shown in this figure is nearly identical to the one shown in Stage B leading to the Sacrifice Ceremony: the Battle of the Animated Objects (fig. 7.73), the ritual running of the zoo-anthropomorphic warriors (fig. 5.156), and the sacrifice proper (figs. 7.78, 7.79). An important difference exists between the two ritual complexes: who are these Net Shirt women so prominently depicted throughout Stage C iconography? I suggest that the archaeology conducted at San José de Moro provides an answer to this question.

The Archaeology of Stage C

The elaborate tombs of a number of adult women were found at San José de Moro in a large plaza appended to the front of the main ceremonial building, Huaca la Capilla (Castillo Butters 2005).

FIGURE 7.95. Blood Ceremony complex, view C. Drawing by Donna McClelland. The Christopher B. Donnan and Donna McClelland Moche Archive, Image Collections and Fieldwork Archives, Dumbarton Oaks, Trustees for Harvard University, Washington, DC.

FIGURE 7.96. Blood Ceremony complex, view D. Drawing by Donna McClelland. The Christopher B. Donnan and Donna McClelland Moche Archive, Image Collections and Fieldwork Archives, Dumbarton Oaks, Trustees for Harvard University, Washington, DC.

Two of these burials are of a particular interest. Each one consisted of a sizable subterranean chamber made of adobe bricks, set deep within the floor of the plaza. In addition to the women, other human remains were located at their feet and at their sides. Camelid offerings had been deposited, and both chambers were also laden with numerous metallic and ceramic objects, including ceremonial knifes, masks, necklaces, and bracelets. Both females were buried in nearly identical cane coffins wrapped in textiles and decorated with sheet-metal objects representing legs, arms, jars, and a large mask. In addition to these elements sewn to the side and the front of each coffin, two large metallic plumes forming a diadem had been inserted on the top end just above the mask (figs. 7.97, 7.98).

On the basis of the two large sets of copper plumes inserted in the two reed coffins and a bowl containing small cups and a goblet in Tomb M–U41, Donnan and Castillo Butters (1994) suggested that these two women were once the living representatives of Priestess C as depicted in the fineline painting of the Sacrifice Ceremony and on the Pañamarca mural (figs. 7.50, 2.8). The two-tasseled headdress worn by the priestess in the iconography was likened to the metallic plumes decorating the coffins. Donnan (2008: 77–78) suggested further that the addition of these elements to the cane coffins transformed them into anthropomorphic containers bearing strong associations with both priestesses and reed boats as depicted in Late Moche iconography:

Reed boats closely resemble cane coffins. Both have long elements that are bound together intermittently along their length with sedge rope. They are made entirely from plant material and are yellowish brown. Apparently, the Moche made an analogy between reed boats and cane coffins, and they buried the Priestesses in cane coffins as though placing

FIGURE 7.97. View of the tomb of one of the priestesses, San José de Moro. Photograph by Christopher B. Donnan.

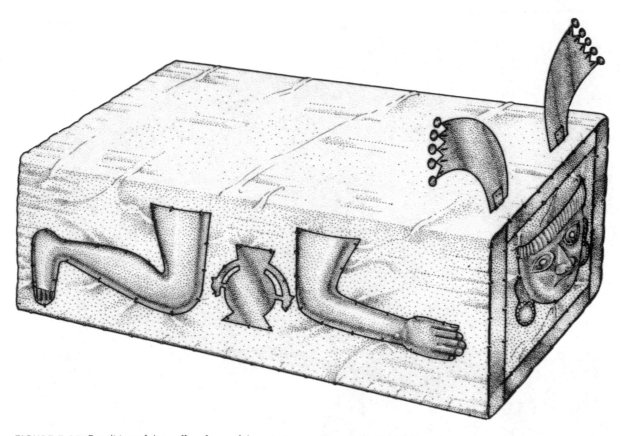

FIGURE 7.98. Rendition of the coffin of one of the priestesses. Drawing by Patrick Finnerty.

them in their reed boats. To underscore this analogy, they anthropomorphized the cane coffins in the same way they anthropomorphized her reed boat in fineline paintings: with arms and legs along the sides, and a face at the end. They even added sheet metal depictions of jars with ropes around their necks, analogous to the jars shown on the reed boats transporting the Priestess [figs. 7.98, 7.99, 7.100]. The two plumes in the top of the coffin would have clearly indicated that it contained a Priestess, for this is a unique characteristic of her ritual attire.

This proposition has two distinct aspects: first, the identity of the main individuals in these burials; second, the symbolic nature of the coffins.

Although I agree that the identity of these two women originated from Individual C of the Sacrifice Ceremony, this precise identity may not have been retained during Stage C. Neither woman had any regalia that could have been directly associated with the identity of Priestess C. The large metallic plumes forming the diadems were not associated with them but with their coffins. These copper plumes were not meant to be worn by these women but to form part of the funer-

ary rituals. Furthermore, the bottles with fineline paintings associated with these persons in their funerary chambers consistently depict Net Shirt individuals. Although these new subjects may have originated from Priestess C, as suggested here, they also represent a clear departure. The tomb excavated in 1991 contained a fineline painting illustrating a Net Shirt woman within a crescent boat. The second tomb, found the following year, contained three bottles with fineline paintings. Two of them also illustrated Net Shirt women in crescent boats. The third example showed the Burial Theme, with Net Shirt women figuring prominently in the assembly on top of the coffin and in the exchange of a *Strombus* seashell to the lower left of the painting (fig. 7.101).

Women wearing an identical two-tasseled headdress do not exist in the San José de Moro sample. The only known examples that resemble this type of headdress are three fineline paintings of a woman with a headdress composed of three plumes vaguely resembling those of priestess C. The most prominent one is the Moche-Huari example mentioned earlier (figs.

FIGURE 7.99. Boat scene. Drawing by Donna McClelland. The Christopher B. Donnan and Donna McClelland Moche Archive, Image Collections and Fieldwork Archives, Dumbarton Oaks, Trustees for Harvard University, Washington, DC.

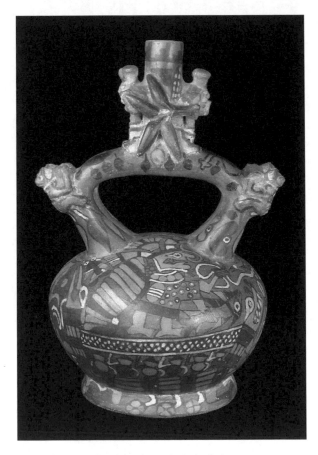

FIGURE 7.100. Bottle with a painting of a boat scene. Museo Amano, Lima. Photograph by Christopher B. Donnan.

7.99, 7.100); the other two belong to the Burial Theme. Perhaps more importantly, Priestess C is not depicted in the Blood Ceremony. Only Net Shirt women are involved in this ritual activity. I would therefore suggest that Priestess C has become a mythological figure, like Wrinkle Face and Iguana—a symbolic vessel in the shape of an anthropomorphized coffin to carry the bodies of Net Shirt women.

Animated boats in Stage C iconography are always decorated at the prow and the stern with animal heads; the addition of a human face wearing a diadem is not depicted. Therefore I suggest that the two anthropomorphic coffins are both animated boats as proposed by Donnan and represent a mythological reference to Priestess C.

In table 7.6 the themes, subjects, and elements discussed in each of the three stages are reunited for ease of comparison.

FINAL REMARKS ON HUMAN SACRIFICE AND POLITICAL AUTHORITY

The scope of any research on an ancient society is always limited by the type and the quality of the data that can be retrieved from archaeological sites. With this caveat in mind, it is clear that the sacrificial and ritual data recovered mostly from Huaca de la Luna are particularly detailed. Very few sites in the Americas have given such a wealth

FIGURE 7.101. Burial Theme. Drawing by Donna McClelland. The Christopher B. Donnan and Donna McClelland Moche Archive, Image Collections and Fieldwork Archives, Dumbarton Oaks, Trustees for Harvard University, Washington, DC.

Table 7.6. Themes and Elements Depicted in Stages A, B, and C

Stage A *Phase III: Early Moche*	Stage B *Phase IV: Middle Moche*	Stage C *Phase V: Late Moche*
Mountain Sacrifice	Sacrifice Ceremony	Blood Ceremony
Wrinkle Face and Iguana	Individuals A, B, C, D, E	Avatars of A and C
Coca Ceremony		Animated objects
Victim with comb-over/*bigote*	Victim with sideburns	Boat journey
Disk ear ornaments	Tubular ear ornaments	
Star-shaped/round club	Club with conical head	
Deer/fox hunting	Sea lion hunting	
Half fist gesture	Fist gesture	

of information. Only the Aztec Templo Mayor (López Luján 1993; Matos Moctezuma 1984, 1987) and the Feathered Serpent Pyramid at Teotihuacan (Sugiyama 2005, 2010) come to mind. Huaca de la Luna provides excellent evidence on sacrificial systems for at least the two major stylistic phases linked, I suggest, to changes in Moche society. Although the chronology still needs refining, these activities, which covered a period of about three hundred to four hundred years, are intimately associated with the history and development of Moche political and ritual structures.

Admittedly, the information on the rise and development of Moche political institutions is still limited. Because of the richness of the artifacts and the close proximity of the funerary chambers and platforms to monumental architecture,

the looting has been quite systematic. Most of the contexts have been destroyed. On the basis of the archaeological and iconographic evidence presented in this chapter, however, I offer the following interpretation regarding the development of Moche rulership.

STAGE A (PHASE III/EARLY MOCHE)

The authority depicted in the iconography in Stage A appears to rest largely in the hands of coca takers. That does not mean that higher-ranking individuals might not have existed, but the coca ritualists are the individuals who would have been most closely linked with the activities of ceremonial combat and sacrifice. The fruits of the sacrifices were apparently not offered to anybody or to any entities in particular. The ritual violence and its related activities are directed toward something that is not readily visible. In the Coca Ceremony, which has firmly been tied to the activities of warfare, capture, and sacrifice, the coca ritualists sometimes raise their clasped hands toward a bicephalous arch spanning across the sky (figs. 7.8, 7.68). A number of Phase III mountain scenes also depict this same arch embedded within the form of the mountain (fig. 2.30). Therefore the Coca Ceremony and the sacrificial rituals including the Mountain Sacrifice are closely related to this arch. The main subjects, including the coca ritualists, the beings with fangs, and Iguana, serve as sacrificers. They are apparently not the recipients of this largesse.

STAGE B (PHASE IV/MIDDLE MOCHE)

Significant changes and additions are made to the ritual system during Stage B, apparently to commemorate a specific group of individuals. The activity still includes ritual battles and sacrifices, but now human blood is collected in a goblet and offered to an individual with specific attributes. The cast involved in the most complex rendition of the Sacrifice Ceremony includes a retinue of at least four main subjects: Individuals A, B, C, and D (figs. 7.50, 7.52). They are no longer standing underneath a bicephalous arch like the coca ritualists but are firmly standing on top of a horizontal arch, which provides a convenient platform. The bicephalous band marks a separation between distinct but related types of activities. Below the band, we usually see the activities leading to the offering of blood: warfare, capture, the arrival of Individual A in a litter, and the blood-taking from the victims. On top of the band, the collected blood is then offered to Individual A in a tall goblet. The blood offering may mark the sacred nature of the Moche ruler himself.

The subjects from the earlier stage have been somewhat demoted. They remain ritualists (they still perform the Coca Ceremony and the Mountain Sacrifice), but they have been superseded in the iconography and in the archaeology by this additional class of individuals. The archaeological evidence recovered at Huaca de la Luna, Sipán, and Huaca el Pueblo supports this hypothesis. The regalia and the objects found with individu-

als identified as A, B, and D strongly suggest that these were the highest-ranking subjects of Moche society at the time at any given Moche ceremonial center.

Data collected in Plaza 3A suggest that the ritual sacrifices and the offering of blood were witnessed by the Moche population. In all likelihood, members of the Moche populace provided the warriors and of course the art used in the sacrifices. They also witnessed the aftermath of the sacrifices and marked their connection with this ritualized violence by tossing worn potsherds into the midst of the victims. These sherds would have represented tokens of their allegiance to Moche ideological values and beliefs and of their identity as Moche, as part of a community ruled by the like of Individuals A, B, C, and D.

The Sacrifice Ceremony presented in figure 7.51 marks a departure from the other scenes, as the goblet is instead offered to Individual D. I have suggested (Bourget 2014) that this scene dates from the transitory period between Phase III and Phase IV (or between Stage A and B) and celebrates the paramount ruler at the time. Subjects dating from this period and associated with this ubiquitous V-shaped diadem have been found archaeologically in Tombs 3 and 14 at Sipán and in Tomb CH-7 at Huaca el Pueblo (Alva and Chero Zurita 2008; Alva and Donnan 1993; Bourget 2008, 2014; Chero Zurita 2008).

STAGE C (PHASE V/LATE MOCHE)

During the last stage, the iconography of power and rulership has been transformed once more to reflect a new political development in Moche society. The assembly of the Sacrifice Ceremony has all but disappeared, and the ritual itself has been recast in the Blood Ceremony, with only two main types of actors. The cast includes a paramount ruler standing for Individual A and a retinue of Net Shirt women originating from Individual C. Within this group of women, one of them seems to stand out: her outfit is always slightly more elaborate. She is regularly depicted inside a crescent design or a reed boat. She may have been the main consort of the ruler (fig. 7.93). I suggest that by this time the Blood Ceremony had been created, not only to mark the divine nature of a paramount ruler but also to acknowledge its lineage via the offering of blood to the Net Shirt women as well.

As suggested, the tombs of the two women discovered in the plaza in front of Huaca la Capilla at San José de Moro would have contained representatives of these Net Shirt women, who are, icono-graphically at least, linked with a paramount ruler. One or more of these rulers might have been buried within the now severely looted huaca. At this stage this suggestion is woefully speculative, I admit, as Huaca la Capilla has not yet been excavated.

CHAPTER 8

VIOLENCE IN THE RISE OF SOCIAL COMPLEXITY

To conclude this investigation is not an easy task. The research on its various aspects is still ongoing, despite the many years that separate this contribution from the unearthing of Plaza 3A sacrificial site in 1995. Numerous issues are still largely unresolved, such as the relationships between the southern and the northern regions, the complex nature and evolution of Moche rulership, and exactly how ideology—through both ritual acts and symbolic statements—contributed by promoting, explaining, and maintaining the development of social inequalities. Here I have largely dealt with only the two most prominent forms of ritual violence and sacrifice depicted in the iconography: the Mountain Sacrifice and the Sacrifice Ceremony. Admittedly, these are the ritual systems most closely related to rulership during two critical phases of its development and offer some contextual data from Huaca de la Luna, Sipán, Huaca el Pueblo, and to a lesser extent at some other sites. In this final chapter I do not intend to rehash all the arguments that have been made throughout the book. I address three main points here: (1) the roles and nature of the violence, (2) the relationships between power and ritual ecology, and (3) the effectiveness of Moche ideology.

ON THE NATURE OF VIOLENCE AND ITS ROLES IN THE RISE OF SOCIAL COMPLEXITY

The prominence of sacrificial rituals in Moche culture has created a certain amount of scholarly discussion. The main bones of contention have been the nature of the battles and the origin of the sacrificial victims found at the Huaca de la Luna site, especially those from Plaza 3A and Plaza 3C.

The ritual aspect of the skeletal remains within the temple has never been a subject of disagreement, but how and from what social contexts these sacrificial victims were obtained remain controversial. It has often been said that two camps have evolved: those who support a more ritualized provenance for the victims based on staged battles (Donnan and I and some others are apparently the main proponents of this view) and those who contend that these individuals were obtained through regular warfare between different groups or competing polities. Although the two categories are not mutually exclusive, I consider them such for the sake of this discussion.

A number of methods have been used to attempt to investigate the problem, including iconographical analysis, ethnohistorical comparisons, ancient mtDNA, biodistance, and isotopic studies (Bourget 2001b; De Bock 2005; Donnan 1997; Shimada et al. 2005, 2008; Sutter and Cortez 2005; Sutter and Verano 2007; Topic and Topic 1997; Toyne et al. 2014). Alas, none of these approaches has resolved the issue once and for all. To my knowledge, no conclusive data can confidently demonstrate whether the sacrificial victims encountered in Plaza 3A and 3C were the product of secular warfare or ceremonial combat. Therefore, regardless of the statistical methods applied to the biometric measurements, the model for a secular nonlocal origin of the captured warriors has often been reinforced with the support of analogical examples drawn from ethnohistorical documents or from the Inca or even Aztec and Maya cultures (Sutter and Verano 2007).

Admittedly, the use of comparative models that largely use unrelated sets of information is misleading and does not enlighten us on the nature of Moche symbolic and ritual systems. It demonstrates only that institutionalized violence and sacrifice were also carried out by other pre-Columbian societies. It is perhaps incidental, for example, that victims were obtained through acts of regular warfare by the Aztecs, as the captives were often ritually processed before their sacrifices on the summit of the temples or involved in some gladiatorial combats in the sacred precincts, usually in front of the same edifices. But the combats that the Moche depicted do not show foreigners against Moche warriors and do not celebrate great victories over other groups or Moche

polities. Nor do they show asymmetrical combats like the Aztecs, where nearly naked captives wielding wooden sticks are fighting fully dressed warriors armed with *macuahuitl* (wooden swords with obsidian blades). Moche combats overwhelmingly show one pair or a few warriors confronting similarly garbed and armed opponents (hence the term "ceremonial combat" originally coined by Donnan 1997 to describe such activities). It is important to note that the garments, headdresses, diadems, and weapons definitely belonged to the topmost echelon of Moche society. Only the highest-ranking burials have provided examples of such objects. Old, well-healed injuries suggest that many of the victims encountered in Plazas 3C and 3A were seasoned warriors. Therefore it is likely that these objects were created for and kept within the ceremonial centers to be lent to the warriors for ceremonial combats.

The approach that I have taken throughout this book is a contextual analysis that endeavors to utilize all the currently available information from Moche archaeology and visual culture. The aim is to gain an in-depth view of the system as ritually performed in Moche ceremonial centers and as abundantly depicted on portable art, regalia, and ceremonial architecture. The iconography on these elements is not vague about the symbolism, ritual processes, paraphernalia, and type of individuals involved. To the contrary, the symbolic system is very precise throughout the history of the Moche, at least from around AD 250–300. Even with the fragmentary nature of the data collected so far, two distinguishable but interrelated sets of visual culture—the ritual ecology (chapter 5) and the ritual actions (chapter 7)—have been found at all the major Moche sites under investigation. They would have led to the establishment of common ideological systems and rulership structures throughout the Moche ceremonial centers of the north coast. Local styles may have differed (for example, certain stylistic traditions such as Phase IV fineline painting may have been restricted to the southern region), but the message was clearly transmitted and successfully exchanged even in its most minute details.

The consistency with which major ceremonial and urban sites other than the Huacas de Moche adopted the symbolism associated with activities that included ritualized violence, capture, and sacrifice suggests that they too participated in these actions. The presence of elements depicting specific rituals (such as a jar modeled as a coca taker with a sacrificial victim hairdo at Dos Cabezas) indicates that the Coca Ceremony and its related activities would have been enacted at the site (fig. 7.64). I do not know at this stage of the investigation what types of relations were entertained between these ceremonial centers, but I suggest that the four thematic sets—the Coca Ceremony, the Mountain Sacrifice (Stages A–B), the Sacrifice Ceremony (Stage B), and the Blood Sacrifice (Stage C)—demonstrate that these rituals were fully known, accepted, and performed at all these sites by similarly dressed individuals. These rituals are shared ideologies and demonstrate that these sites were participating in interwoven social and political systems. The iconographies disseminated by the elites residing at these ceremonial centers are only artifacts of a more complex system of political actions and ideological values. High-ranking individuals associated with an activity like the Sacrifice Ceremony have been found at sites such as Huaca de la Cruz, Pacatnamú, Huaca el Pueblo, and Sipán, which indicates that the concomitant rituals of such offices must also have been performed, because the main contenders of such sacrificial activities exerted their offices at these sites (Donnan 2010: 67). In that regard, related polities with similar elites would undoubtedly have staged ceremonies involving ritual battles and human sacrifices. But would they have raided each other for the procurement of sacrificial victims? That is the question.

As noted, a principal point of debate surrounds the nature or source of the actual warriors that participated in the Warrior Narrative. In the past ten years, scholarship on the subject has turned to biometric and genetic studies to provide a "scientific" basis on which to address this question:

> Based upon the results reported by this study we tentatively suggest that the sacrificial victims from Huaca de la Luna Plaza 3C represent adult male warriors taken in combat with nearby competing polities (Moche or Gallinazo or both), while individuals from Plaza 3A sample likely came from competing polities located in more distant valleys. When the chronological placement of the two sacrificial samples analyzed by this study is taken into account, we suggest that this

explanation is entirely consistent with the model of warriors captured during combat by the southern Moche with nearby competing polities. (Sutter and Verano 2007: 204)

In general terms, I agree with Sutter and Verano (2007: 204) that the victims deposited in Plaza 3C during Stage A (Phase III/Early Moche) may have originated from nearby polities and that the victims sacrificed in Plaza 3A during Stage B (Phase IV/Middle Moche) may have come from more distant valleys. But that possibility does not make them competing polities or enemies. This biometric study does not demonstrate the bellicose rather than the ritual nature of the battles. It primarily reinforces the archaeological model of an expanding Early State society with a very vibrant and powerful ideology that includes rituals involving organized violence and human sacrifice. The suggestion that different polities during Stage A and Stage B may have provided the sacrificial victims found in Plaza 3C and Plaza 3A is not at issue here. To the contrary, on the basis of the information presented in this study, it is most likely that any polity that recognized such high-ranking individuals as their leaders would have engaged in these rigidly prescribed ritual activities. These individuals wore the same attire and regalia that displayed similar ideologies, which is further proof of strong similarities in ritual actions.

One of the notions utilized to signal that the Huaca de la Luna sacrificial victims were not chosen through ritually sanctioned battles was the apparent lack of respect shown to their remains, "which were left to decompose on the surface rather than being given proper burial" (Sutter and Verano 2007: 195). In that regard, the contexts in Plaza 3C and Plaza 3A need to be discussed separately, as they belong to vastly distinct sets of ritual traditions.

As stated earlier, Plaza 3C is not a sacrificial site but a place where human remains were deposited after having been processed and used elsewhere. Once their usefulness was exhausted, or when they were no longer deemed necessary, the remains and the skeletons were carefully buried within the construction layers of the plaza. They were accompanied by offerings, and a tomb located just alongside contained elements suggesting that the male individual in it may have been a sacrificer. My analysis has shown that all the cultural elements associated with both of these contexts in Plaza 3C (the human remains and the tomb) are fully consistent with Phase III symbolic ideology as depicted in the iconography. Victims transformed into anatomical models are amply shown in Moche art as skeletal beings engaged in all sorts of ritual activities. In real life, these defleshed skeletons may have been used as impressive props in the very same type of rituals. During Phase III, Plaza 3C constituted the eastern extension of Platform I (Building D) toward the Cerro Blanco. It is arguably one of the most important parts of the ceremonial center at the time, so the act of depositing these sacrificial remains there certainly indexes their importance and the unlikelihood of a blatant lack of respect. To the contrary, this would unequivocally highlight the degree of consideration bestowed on these human remains.

The Plaza 3A sacrificial site presents an almost textbook case of human sacrifice as depicted in Phase IV iconography. Although it is not necessary to rehash all the information provided throughout the book, the following points should be taken into consideration in reflecting upon the nature of Moche institutionalized violence during this period:

1. The complex of Plaza 3A/Platform II was created expressly to conduct the rituals and was built on one of the most important parcels of real estate of the Huacas de Moche site. Locating the complex between Platform I and the Cerro Blanco was deemed so necessary that part of an extensive Phase III cemetery was removed and relocated elsewhere. Its construction marks a shift between Phase III and Phase IV and, more importantly, in Moche politics as well. A new political structure came into prominence during Phase IV and created this new Sacrifice Ceremony.

2. The contexts recovered from the plaza are fully consistent with the symbolic system of representation. The injuries and the position of the bodies often replicate the depictions of the iconography or vice versa. The clay statuettes deposited with the sacrificial victims constitute a clear prolongation of the visual culture into the sacrificial arena. These sculptures were probably fashioned by artisans living nearby in the urban sector. The domestic sherds thrown

in the sacrificial site throughout the ritual processes also suggest that members of the local population witnessed these events and left behind these tokens of their connection with the rituals. Therefore the statuettes meant to celebrate the victims and the simple offerings left by numerous individuals do not show a lack of respect: the remains of the sacrificial victims were not desecrated but rather consecrated.

3. It is not possible to demonstrate at this stage that the Plaza 3A/Platform II complex was created in anticipation of El Niño events, but such conditions were fully integrated into the sacrificial process. This is rather crucial to consider in the discussion of the nature of the victims. As discussed in chapter 5, the ritual ecology of El Niño was wholly integrated into the Moche symbolic system. It represented perhaps its most important trope. The elites shown in the iconography, and the artifacts recovered from their tombs, are literally covered with subjects and symbols associated with these conditions. Therefore the sacrificial site, including the geoclimatic conditions during which these activities were carried out, fully participated in an ideological project that clearly aimed at reinforcing the rulership structure. To leave behind a visible and accessible memento of the sacrificial activities for the local population to engage with by throwing potsherds in the arena may have been an overt strategy to reinforce this ideology.

4. Platform II, which formed part of the whole sacrificial complex, was a place dedicated at least to the burial of ritual specialists. A wooden club and the iconography found in their tombs suggest that two of these individuals were sacrificers. The visual culture that survived the depredation at the site is consistent with Phase IV iconography and celebrates these individuals as great warriors, clearly connected at some level with the Sacrifice Ceremony. The act of building a platform dedicated to the burial of such high-ranking ritual specialists further highlights how important the sacrificial arena and its arresting display were to the Moche elite at the site.

With the information currently available to us, only two mutually exclusive propositions seem able to account for such a high level of congruity between the archaeological reality and the symbolic system of representation:

1. The Moche would obtain the captives through regular warfare against enemies, other Moche polities, or foreign groups. These acts of war would have been represented and celebrated through an intricate ritual process, as depicted in the iconography (Verano 2001b; Sutter and Verano 2007).

My arguments against this proposal include the following points. Unambiguous indication of warfare between the Huaca de Moche polity and other groups during their expansion is lacking. No evidence of fortifications, burned villages, or mass executions has been found. In contrast, however, all Stage A and Stage B ceremonial centers display similar sets of ritual evidence. Moreover, the iconography does not support the likelihood that these battles were fought against foreign groups, as it systematically depicts elaborately dressed Moche warriors engaging one another. Furthermore, the captives are largely celebrated through an elaborate tradition of portrait vessels depicting them during all the stages from the battles to their ultimate sacrifice. Why would the Moche choose to celebrate the sacrifice of enemies to the state through the portrait vessel tradition?

2. The Moche would have obtained the sacrificial victims through a selection process involving ritualized battles, as abundantly depicted in their art and manifested in the ample portrait vessel tradition. In such a case, the men could have been battle-tested warriors engaging in these battles and wearing richly decorated garments, headdresses, and weapons provided by ceremonial centers such as the Huaca de Luna. The sacrificial complex that includes these battles would have been created in part to reinforce the social and political position of the elite. Hence we would expect to find sacrificial sites of this type during Stage B (Phase IV/Middle Moche) at all the Moche sites housing such an elite. The presence of such sacrificial sites would resolve the issue by clearly demonstrating the participation of all these Moche ceremonial and urban centers in a similar, rigidly prescribed symbolic system. A discovery made at Dos Cabezas in 2011 suggests that this may be confirmed in the near future.

The Dos Cabezas Archaeological Project was initiated in 2010 with the mapping of the site. Some of the main goals of this project are to study the occupational sequence, to study the relationship between the southern and the northern regions, to investigate the development of the Moche in the Jequetepeque, Zaña, and Lambayeque Valleys, and to take further the research that was conducted between 1994 and 2001 by Donnan and Guillermo Cock. During the 2011 field season, attention was mostly directed at the main huaca, Huaca Dos Cabezas (fig. 8.1). It has suffered great damage, perhaps because of the precious metal that may have been discovered in the building during the colonial period. The looting was so intense that a huge crater created in the center almost divided the building in two: hence the name "Dos Cabezas" (Two Heads) for this huaca.

The study of the inner core of Dos Cabezas, along the sides of this crater largely destroyed by colonial looting, has revealed that the building had at least three phases of construction (fig. 8.2). Each of these building phases presents slightly different construction techniques, clearly demonstrating that each building was associated with a distinct moment of the history of the site. Although the research is still in its preliminary stages, the results suggest that Building 1 and Building 2 pertained to the Early Moche, whereas Building 3 marked the transition into the Middle Moche at the site. Most of the upper part of Building 3 is largely destroyed, but its base is in much better condition, especially on the north and west sides (fig. 8.3). It therefore covers the bases of Buildings 1 and 2.

On the basis of this field season and the field reports kindly provided to us by Donnan and Cock, I am confident that most of their excavations in the southwest sector (where the tombs discussed in chapter 7 were found) pertain to the last building phase. Although the ceramics within these funerary contexts are stylistically Early Moche, they would belong chronologically to a transitional moment between Stages A and B. Therefore I suggest that Building 3 was contemporaneous with the transition witnessed in the Lord of Ucupe burial and with the beginning of the Middle Moche at Huaca el Pueblo. It would also coincide with the transition between Phase III and Phase IV at the Huacas de Moche site, which led to the abandonment of Plaza 3C and the construction of Plaza 3A and Platform II.

Along the west side of the huaca, about 10 m to the north of the sector studied by Donnan and

FIGURE 8.1. Huaca Dos Cabezas, Jequetepeque Valley.

FIGURE 8.2. Study of the inner core of Dos Cabezas.

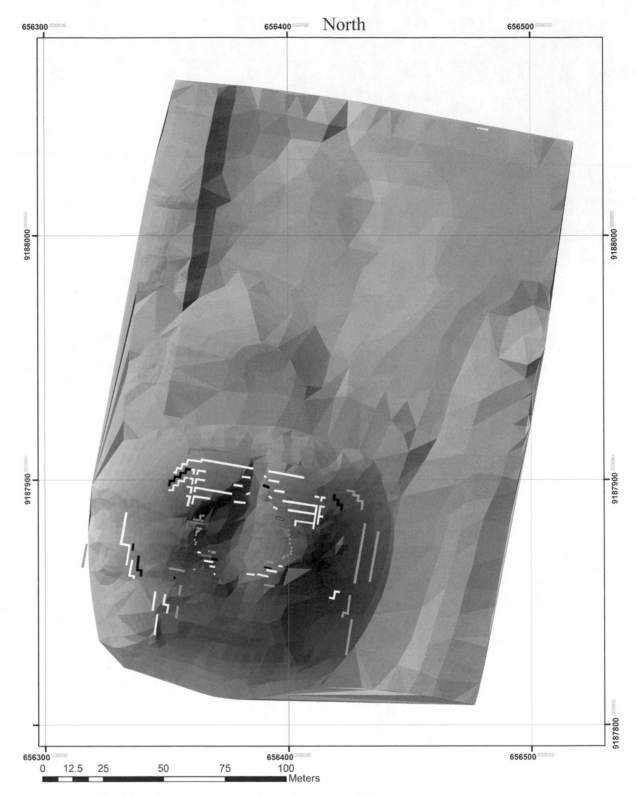

North

656300 °°°°°° 656400 °°°°°° 656500 °°°°°°

9188000 °°°°°°

9187900 °°°°°°

9187800 °°°°°°

656300 °°°°°° 656400 °°°°°° 656500 °°°°°°

0   12.5   25   50   75   100
                                    Meters

FIGURE 8.3. Plan of the walls and isometric rendering of Huaca Dos Cabezas.

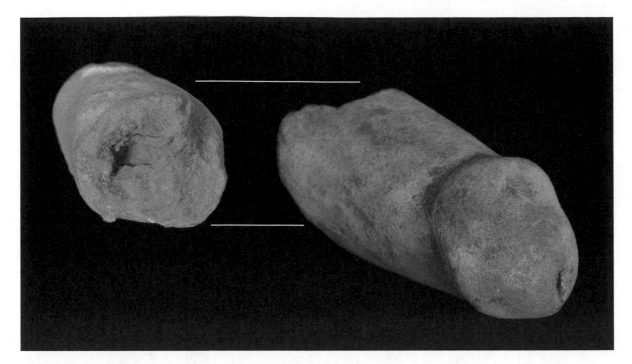

FIGURE 8.4. Penis from a clay statuette. Ministry of Culture, Peru.

Cock (Donnan 2004), in the fill just above a floor of Building 3, a fragment of a clay penis was located (figs. 8.3, 8.4). This fragment must have come from a clay sculpture nearly identical to the fifty-two clay sculptures found in Plaza 3A (figs. 3.94, 3.106). This would confirm not only that Building 3 belonged to Stage B (Middle Moche—Phase IV) but that human sacrifices and perhaps even the Sacrifice Ceremony may have taken place at this site. Admittedly, this is not definitive proof of the existence of a sacrificial site at Dos Cabezas and still represents an isolated example. But it is the first time that such a sculpture has been found outside of Huaca de la Luna and the Moche Valley. It reiterates once more how thoroughly interconnected by a common ideology all the Moche ceremonial centers and their ruling elites were.

ON THE RELATIONSHIPS BETWEEN POWER AND RITUAL ECOLOGY

Perhaps one of the most astonishing aspects of the excavation of Plaza 3A was the realization that many of the sacrificial rituals that took place there were carried out during severe El Niño events. The contexts for these sacrificial activities pre-sented the apparent contradiction of being fully consistent with the ideology developed during Phase IV—amply depicted in the visual culture—and yet being planned to coincide with the mud and rainwater deposition over the clean sand of the plaza. At the time, the prominence of El Niño in Moche symbolism was largely unknown. As a result, on the basis of the available data I concentrated my analysis on its mostly negative aspects (Bourget 2001b) and to a lesser extent on some of the animal species that may have been indicative of certain ecological conditions in the iconography (Bourget 2001a). Thereafter, a more detailed analysis has revealed a much more complex picture. It is true that the impact of El Niño events on the Peruvian north coast could be severe and at times catastrophic, but they involved more than destruction. These events can have both negative and positive aspects. A mega El Niño clearly changes the natural world: it transforms swaths of desert landscape into lakes, providing new conditions for all sorts of wildlife. The rains and the humidity paint the lower part of the Andes a vivid green by waking up dormant vegetation. Countless animal species thrive and multiply, both on the land and in the waters. In sum, the awesome and limitless power of the gods is made visible in the human world. By staging some of the most intricate and complex rituals to coincide with these events, Moche high-ranking individuals sought to manipulate the situation symbolically and to link themselves and their rulership to these conditions—or perhaps more aptly to the gods who created them. The regalia, diadems, and jewelry worn by these individuals are adorned with symbols and subjects linked to these gods and to El Niño animal species. This is an apt metaphor for rulership and for their power to affect and to maintain the balance of the world in their capacity as rulers imbued with a divine nature.

ON THE EFFECTIVENESS OF MOCHE IDEOLOGY

Even if Moche ceremonial centers have lain abandoned for hundreds of years and the hearts of the most important buildings have been thoroughly destroyed, it is most surprising that we still find elements that systematically relate to the Moche symbolic system. Each one of these Moche sites and each of the high-ranking burials faithfully reproduces the same complex set of symbols. Ceramics and objects depicting subjects engaged in specific activities are only a small part of an elaborate ritualized set of actions. At all of these sites, the Moche performed the same rituals, including Coca Ceremonies, ceremonial combat, and human sacrifice, even with similar props such as clay statuettes perhaps imported from other sites. Local stylistic differences are often minor and relate to the overall form of the medium, not the message. But the ceramics left behind, the kingly regalia (crowns, diadems, and jewels), and the murals bespeak a complex set of ideas shared by the elite at all these ceremonial centers. I suggest that only close ties between these centers and the elite can explain such a high level of congruity across Moche visual culture. The people at these sites and its elites (at least those that formed part of Stages A and B, the Coca Ceremony Complex and Sacrifice Ceremony Complex) constituted a political entity that shared common views about the world, similar rituals, and visual cultures aimed at disseminating their values and beliefs.

The use of violence in Moche society was concomitant with the development of social complexity. It separated the rulers from the rest of the society and reinforced the divine nature of their personas and their lineage. Ritualized violence, including battles and human sacrifice, constituted perhaps the most powerful trope of their ideology, uniting the Moche around extremely impressive and charismatic rituals.

Four interrelated notions are consistently depicted in their art, on the walls of their huacas, and perhaps most importantly on sumptuary regalia: ritualized violence, ancientness, the divine, and foreignness. I have already discussed some of these notions elsewhere (Bourget 2008, 2014), but it is worth stating that they form part of the essence of Moche rulership and are constantly reiterated throughout their art and rituals. These notions form the paradigmatic core of their ideology. To study the rise of social complexity in Moche culture, we must address them.

The visual ideology (by blending these four notions together) skillfully and intentionally blurs the lines among these categories in order to present the ruler and rulership as a totality. The rulers as depicted in Stage B iconography and in their final resting places at Sipán and Huaca el Pueblo, adorned with elaborate regalia, are at the same time great warriors, fearful sacrificers, ancient gods, and foreign beings. By amalgamating the categories, Moche ideology erases the ambiguities and the contradictions of encompassing at the same time a human and a divine being, an ancient (local) and a foreign subject, simultaneously the generator of violence through warfare and the receiver of such violence through sacrifice.

Future studies of the nature of warfare and human sacrifice and how and why violence operated in Moche culture and ideology must take into account the ensemble of the data regarding this vast subject, which encompasses the ceremonial architecture, the visual culture, the regalia of the rulers, and the funerary rituals. To pick and choose from the available data, as has often been done in the past, would not do justice to the magnificent symbolic and ritual systems that the Moche created and to the numerous archaeologists and art historians who have contributed to bring this culture to the forefront of ancient Andean studies.

NOTES

CHAPTER 2. THE MOCHE

1. "La regeneración de la arquitectura y del ritual (del cual la arquitectura es el continente) constituye una proposición explicativa de este proceso que adquiere aún mayor significado si se considera que, en los Andes centrales, Moche constituye la más compleja y desarrollada de las formaciones estatales de tipo teocrático, cuyos extraordinarios monumentos arquitectónicos representan la apoteósica culminación de las viejas tradiciones que se iniciaron mucho tiempo atrás con el desarrollo de la arquitectura ceremonial temprana" (Uceda Castillo and Canziani 1998: 157).

2. The very nature of a Gallinazo presence at the Huacas de Moche site and throughout the north coast in general has been a matter of considerable debate in recent years (Uceda Castillo, Gayoso Rullier, and Gamarra Carranza 2009; Millaire and Morlion 2009). It is generally agreed that the domestic ware located in the southeast corner of Plaza 3A (Sector B) is no longer diagnostic of a Gallinazo presence there or at a given site. Nevertheless, the discovery in the Uhle Platform of a diagnostic Gallinazo Negative fineware deposited within a Phase I/II Moche burial strongly indicates that further research is needed at the site to elucidate this question (Chauchat and Gutiérrez 2007: fig. 97).

CHAPTER 3. THE PLAZA 3A SACRIFICIAL SITE

1. Periostitis and osteomyelitis are congenital diseases.

2. These musical instruments are quite rare, and whistles rarely form part of Moche funerary artifacts. Nevertheless, other instruments such as ocarinas have been found in a child burial situated just in front of Huaca del Sol (Millaire 2002).

3. In figure 3.30 the head had already been removed for safekeeping. It was deemed too fragile to be left in situ throughout the excavation of the rest of the body.

4. As mentioned in note 2 in chapter 2, there is no general agreement on a Gallinazo presence at the site before the Moche.

CHAPTER 4. PLATFORM II

1. The sea lion vertebra located in the posthole may indicate a more complex use of this post. This is discussed in chapters 5 and 6.

2. Two additional objects analyzed with the same technique are discussed in chapter 7.

CHAPTER 5. A RITUAL ECOLOGY OF POWER

1. "Sin embargo, los primeros indicios de algunos cambios radicales se presentaron en la región de la Corriente de Humboldt en 1982–83. En diciembre de 1982 los pescadores de la costa central peruana informaron que la mayoría de las especies de peces autóctonas desaparecieron del área de hasta 30 m de profundidad, área explotada por la pesquería artesanal. Entre ellos se pueden mencionar sobre todo los lenguados (*Paralichthys adspersus* y otras especies), la cojinoba (*Seriolella violacea*), la corvina (*Sciaena gilberti*) así como el pejerrey (*Odontesthes regia regia*) que vive cerca de la superficie. Estos fueron reemplazados inicialmente sólo por 'borrachitos,' pequeños peces, que no se venden en los mercados. Con el continuo calentamiento del agua ocurrió una colorida invasión de una variedad de especies tropicales y sub-tropicales, que duró en el sur del Perú hasta abril de 1983 y en el norte hasta el final del EN: barrilete (*Katsuwonus pelamis*) y dorado (*Coryphaena hippurus*), sierra (*Scomberomorus maculatus sierra*) y atún de aleta amarilla (*Thunnus albacares*). . . . Diferentes especies de escualos (sobre todo tiburón martillo, *Sphyrna* spp., y tiburón diamente, *Isurus oxyrhinchus*), grandes rayas águilas (*Myliobatis* spp.) y mantas (*Manta hamiltoni*) rompían las redes, que no fueron diseñadas para los inmigrantes gigantes" (Arntz and Fahrbach 1996: 138).

2. Lavallée identifies the fishes shown in figure 5.78 as anchovies (*Engraulis ringens*), whereas she and some others see in the examples in figure 5.80 representatives of the bonito (*Sarda chiliensis*) (De Bock 1988: 64; Donnan 1978: 38; Lavallée 1970: 50). Anatomical elements, such as the two small appendages below the head and the barbels just above the eyes that do not exist among these species but are present in the borrachos, do not support their suggestions. Furthermore, the constant presence of both types of fish on the same fineline paintings suggests that they belong to the same subject (fig. 5.83).

3. In a personal communication (2009), Donnan suggests that bi-globular ears are often seen on supernatural figures and may simply be a way of indicating that a figure is supernatural. These two views may not be mutually exclusive. Octopus symbolism is one of the most prevalent elements of the iconography. Bi-globular ears on a subject may represent a strategy to add its symbolism to other beings with supernatural attributes.

CHAPTER 6. CHILDREN AND WARRIORS

1. When the genital organs are not visible, recognizing women in Moche iconography is a difficult undertaking. But in this case I propose that the shawl is a marker of this gender.

2. Anne-Marie Hocquenghem (1980, 1987) considers that these are old men offering children at the beginning of a new season or a new reign. She associates the offering of children in Moche iconography with a *rite de passage* between two solstices and especially with the beginning of the humid season. Her interpretations are essentially based on an analogy with the Moche representations and the recorded information on Inca and Quechua rituals.

3. The raised hands gesture is regularly performed to mark the importance of an activity such as the ritual copulation of Wrinkle Face or an encounter with the *Strombus* monster (figs. 5.31, 5.118).

4. Earlier photos of this bottle indicate that the arms were missing. Therefore the arms and the rectangular structure in front of the victim are inaccurate.

CHAPTER 7. HUMAN SACRIFICE AND RULERSHIP

1. "La hipótesis es sustentada por el descubrimiento de los fragmentos de cuerda alrededor de las muñecas, tobillos, pies aislados, troncos, así como también alrededor del cuello de los esqueletos, sugiriendo que fueron originalmente suspendidos de algún objeto. Varias representaciones de miembros superiores amputados con cuerdas atadas alrededor de ellos son conocidas en el arte Moche, apoyando esta hipótesis" (Verano, Tufinio, and Lund Valle 2008: 252).

2. The first field season at Dos Cabezas, conducted in 2011, indicated that the funerary contexts excavated by Donnan (2004) are quite late in the Early Moche sequence of the site. The results are preliminary, but they may relate to the transition from the Early to the Middle Moche.

3. The hand and arms gesture would warrant a separate study. It is a highly codified system. Throughout this book I allude only to the main examples, but a more consistent analysis would certainly provide additional insights into these ritual systems.

4. For a detailed analysis of the Burial Theme, see Bourget 2006.

BIBLIOGRAPHY

ALVA, WALTER

1994 *Sipán.* Ed. José A. de Lavalle. Colección Culturas y Artes del Perú. Cervecería Backus & Johnston S.A., Lima.

2001 The Royal Tombs of Sipán: Art and Power in Moche Society. In *Moche Art and Archaeology in Ancient Peru,* edited by Joanne Pillsbury, pp. 223–245. Studies in the History of Art 63. Center for Advanced Studies in Visual Arts, Symposium Papers XL. National Gallery of Art, Washington, DC.

ALVA, WALTER, AND LUIS CHERO ZURITA

2008 La tumba del Sacerdote Guerrero. In *Sipán: El tesoro de las tumbas reales,* edited by Antonio Aimi, Walter Alva, and Emilia Perassi, pp. 114–137. Giunti Arte Mostre Musei s.r.l., Florence.

ALVA, WALTER, AND CHRISTOPHER B. DONNAN

1993 *Royal Tombs of Sipán.* Fowler Museum of Cultural History, University of California, Los Angeles.

ALVA MENESES, NÉSTOR IGNACIO

2008 Spiders and Spider Decapitator in Moche Iconography: Identification from the Contexts of Sipán, Antecedents and Symbolism. In *The Art and Archaeology of the Moche: An Ancient Andean Society of the Peruvian North Coast,* edited by Steve Bourget and Kimberly L. Jones, pp. 247–262. University of Texas Press, Austin.

ARNTZ, WOLF E., AND EBERHARD FAHRBACH

1996 *El Niño: Experimento climático de la naturaleza.* Fondo de Cultura Económica, Mexico City.

ARNTZ, WOLF E., AND JULIO VALDIVIA

1985 Visión integral del problema "El Niño": Introducción. In *"El Niño": Su impacto en la fauna marina.* Boletín, Volumen Extraordinario. Instituto del Mar del Perú, Callao, Peru.

ARSENAULT, DANIEL

1993 El personaje del pie amputado en la cultura mochica del Perú: Un ensayo sobre la arqueología del poder. *Latin American Antiquity* 4(3):225–245.

1994 Symbolisme, rapports sociaux et pouvoir dans les contextes sacrificiels de la société mochica (Pérou précolombien): Une étude archéologique et iconographique. PhD dissertation, Département d'Anthropologie, Université de Montréal, Montreal.

ASHMORE, WENDY, AND ARTHUR BERNARD KNAPP (EDITORS)

1999   *Archaeologies of Landscape: Contemporary Perspectives.* Wiley-Blackwell Publishers, Malden.

AVENI, ANTHONY F.

1981   The Nazca Lines: Patterns in the Desert. *Archaeology* 39(4):33–39.

1986   Archaeoastronomy: Past, Present, and Future. *Sky and Telescope* 72:456–460.

1990   *The Lines of Nazca* (editor). Memoirs of the American Philosophical Society, Vol. 183. American Philosophical Society, Philadelphia.

2000   *Between the Lines: The Mystery of the Giant Ground Drawings of Ancient Nasca, Peru.* University of Texas Press, Austin.

BAUER, BRIAN S.

1998   *The Sacred Landscape of the Inca: The Cusco Ceque System.* University of Texas Press, Austin.

BAUER, BRIAN S., AND DAVID S. P. DEARBORN

1995   *Astronomy and Empire in the Ancient Andes: The Cultural Origins of Inca Sky Watching.* University of Texas Press, Austin.

BAWDEN, GARTH

1977   Galindo and the Nature of the Middle Horizon in Northern Coastal Peru. PhD dissertation, Harvard University, Cambridge, MA.

1982   Galindo: A Study in Cultural Transition during the Middle Horizon. In *Chan-Chan: Andean Desert City*, edited by Michael E. Moseley and Kent C. Day, pp. 285–320. University of New Mexico Press, Albuquerque.

1996   *The Moche.* Blackwell, Oxford.

2005   Ethnogenesis at Galindo, Peru. In *Us and Them: Archaeology and Ethnicity in the Andes*, edited by Richard M. Reycraft, pp. 12–33. Monograph 53, Cotsen Institute of Archaeology. University of California, Los Angeles.

BENITEZ, LEONARDO

2009   Descendants of the Sun: Calendars, Myths, and the Tiwanaku State. In *Tiwanaku: Papers from the 2005 Mayer Center Symposium at the Denver Art Museum*, edited by Margaret Young-Sánchez, pp. 49–81. Denver Art Museum, Denver.

BENSON, ELIZABETH P.

1972   *The Mochica: A Culture of Peru.* Praeger, London.

1995   Art, Agriculture, Warfare, and the Guano Islands. In *Andean Art: Visual Expression and Its Relation to Andean Beliefs and Values*, edited by Penny Dransart, pp. 245–264. Aldershot, Avebury, UK.

1997   Moche Art: Myth, History and Rite. In *The Spirit of Ancient Peru: Treasures from the Museo Arqueológico Rafael Larco Herrera*, edited by Kathleen Berrin, pp. 41–49. Fine Arts Museums of San Francisco/ Thames and Hudson, New York.

2008   Iconography Meets Archaeology. In *The Art and Archaeology of the Moche: An Ancient Andean Society of the Peruvian North Coast*, edited by Steve Bourget and Kimberly L. Jones, pp. 1–22. University of Texas Press, Austin.

2012   *The Worlds of the Moche on the North Coast of Peru.* The William and Bettye Nowlin Series in Art, History, and Culture of the Western Hemisphere. University of Texas Press, Austin.

BERRIN, KATHLEEN (EDITOR)

1997   *The Spirit of Ancient Peru: Treasures from the Museo Arqueológico Rafael Larco Herrera.* Fine Arts Museums of San Francisco/Thames and Hudson, New York.

BONAVIA, DUCCIO

1985   *Mural Painting in Ancient Peru.* Translated by Patricia J. Lyon. University of Indiana Press, Bloomington.

BOURGET, STEVE

1990a   Caracoles sagrados en la iconografía moche. *Gaceta Arqueológica Andina* 5 (20):45–58.

1990b   Des tubercules pour la mort: Analyses préliminaires des relations entre l'ordre naturel et l'ordre culturel dans l'iconographie mochica. *Bulletin de l'Institut Français d'Études Andines* 19(1):45–85.

1994a   Bestiaire sacré et flore magique: Écologie rituelle de l'iconographie de la culture mochica, côte nord du Pérou. PhD dissertation, Département d'Anthropologie, Université de Montréal, Montreal.

1994b   Los sacerdotes a la sombra del cerro blanco y del arco bicéfalo. *Revista del Museo de Arqueología, Antropología e Historia* 5:81–125. Universidad Nacional de la Libertad, Trujillo, Peru.

1996   Los raptores de almas: Prácticas funerarias en la iconografía mochica. In *Al final del camino*, edited by Luis Millones and Moisés Lemlij, pp. 37–50. Seminario Interdisciplinario de Estudios Andinos, Lima.

1997   Las excavaciones en la Plaza 3a de la Huaca de la Luna. In *Investigaciones en la Huaca de la Luna 1995*, edited by Santiago Uceda Castillo, Elías Mujica, and Ricardo Morales, pp. 51–59. Facultad de Ciencias Sociales, Universidad Nacional de la Libertad, Trujillo, Peru.

2000   Proyecto Huancaco, investigaciones arqueológicas de la capital moche del valle de Virú, costa norte del Perú. Unpublished report submitted to the Instituto Nacional de la Cultura, Lima.

2001a   Children and Ancestors: Ritual Practices at the Moche Site of Huaca de la Luna, North Coast of Peru. In *Ritual Sacrifice in Ancient Peru: New Discoveries and Interpretations*, edited by Elizabeth P. Benson and Anita G. Cook, pp. 93–118. University of Texas Press, Austin.

2001b   Rituals of Sacrifice: Its Practice at Huaca de la Luna and Its Representation in Moche Iconography. In *Moche Art and Archaeology in Ancient Peru*, edited by Joanne Pillsbury, pp. 89–109. Studies in the History of Art 63. Center for Advanced Studies in Visual Arts, Symposium Papers XL. National Gallery of Art, Washington, DC.

2005   Who Were the Priests, the Warriors, and the Prisoners?: A Peculiar Problem of Identity in Moche Culture and Iconography, North Coast of Peru. In

Us and Them: Archaeology and Ethnicity in the Andes, edited by Richard M. Reycraft, pp. 73–85. Monograph 53, Cotsen Institute of Archaeology. University of California, Los Angeles.

2006   Sex, Death and Sacrifice in Moche Religion and Visual Culture. University of Texas Press, Austin.

2008   The Third Man: Identity and Rulership in Moche Archaeology and Visual Culture. In The Art and Archaeology of the Moche: An Ancient Andean Society of the Peruvian North Coast, edited by Steve Bourget and Kimberly L. Jones, pp. 263–288. University of Texas Press, Austin.

2010   Sacrificio humano, poder e ideología en la cultura moche. In El sacrificio humano en la tradición religiosa mesoamericana, edited by Leonardo López Luján and Guilhem Olivier, pp. 577–597. Instituto Nacional de Antropología e Historia: Universidad Nacional Autónoma de México, Mexico City.

2014   Les rois mochica: Divinité et pouvoir dans le Pérou ancien. Somogy Éditions d'Art, Paris; Musée d'Ethnographie de Genève, Geneva.

BOURGET, STEVE, AND KIMBERLY L. JONES (EDITORS)

2008   The Art and Archaeology of the Moche: An Ancient Andean Society of the Peruvian North Coast. University of Texas Press, Austin.

BOURGET, STEVE, AND JEAN-FRANÇOIS MILLAIRE

2000   Excavaciones en la plaza 3a y plataforma II de la Huaca de la Luna. In Investigaciones en la Huaca de la Luna 1997, edited by Santiago Uceda Castillo, Elías Mujica, and Ricardo Morales, pp. 47–60. Facultad de Ciencias Sociales, Universidad Nacional de la Libertad, Trujillo, Peru.

BOURGET, STEVE, AND MARGARET E. NEWMAN

1998   A Toast to the Ancestors: Ritual Warfare and Sacrificial Blood in Moche Culture. Baessler Archiv (Berlin), Neue Folge 46:85–106.

BRACAMONTE, G. FLORENCIA

1998   Los sacrificios humanos en la Plaza 3A afloramiento rocoso Plataforma II Huaca de la Luna: La evidencia de cultos de crisis. Master's thesis, Universidad Nacional de Trujillo, Peru.

BUJARD, MARIANNE

2000   Le sacrifice au ciel dans la Chine ancienne: Théorie et pratique sous les Han occidentaux. Ecole française d'Extrême-Orient, Paris.

BURGER, RICHARD L.

1992   Chavín and the Origins of Andean Civilization. Thames and Hudson, London.

BURKERT, WALTER

1983   Homo Necans: The Anthropology of Ancient Greek Sacrificial Ritual and Myth. University of California Press, Berkeley.

CABANIEL, S. G., T. L. RADA, G. J. J. BLANCO, A. J. RODRÍGUEZ-MORALES, AND A. J. P. ESCALERA

2005   Impacto de los eventos de El Niño Southern Oscillation (IENSO) sobre la leishmaniosis cutánea en Sucre, Venezuela, a través del uso de información satelital, 1994–2003. Revista Peruana de Medicina Experimental y Salud Pública 22:32–38.

CARNEIRO, ROBERT L.

1970   A Theory of the Origin of the State. Science 169(3947):733–738.

CASTILLO BUTTERS, LUIS JAIME

2001   The Last of the Mochicas: A View from the Jequetepeque Valley. In Moche Art and Archaeology in Ancient Peru, edited by Joanne Pillsbury, pp. 307–332. Studies in the History of Art 63. Center for Advanced Studies in Visual Arts, Symposium Papers XL. National Gallery of Art, Washington, DC.

2005   Las Sacerdotisas de San José de Moro, Rituales funerarios de mujeres de élite en la costa norte del Perú. In Divina y humana, la mujer en los antiguos Peru y México, pp. 18–29, Ministerio de Educación, Lima, Perú.

CASTILLO BUTTERS, LUIS JAIME, AND CHRISTOPHER B. DONNAN

1994   La ocupación moche de San José de Moro, Jequetepeque. In Moche: Propuestas y perspectivas, Actas del Primer Coloquio sobre la Cultura Moche, Trujillo, 12 al 16 de abril de 1993, edited by Santiago Uceda Castillo and Elías Mujica, pp. 93–136. Travaux de l'Institut Français d'Études Andines 79. Universidad Nacional de la Libertad, Trujillo, Peru; Instituto Francés de Estudios Andinos, Lima; and Asociación Peruana para el Fomento de las Ciencias Sociales, Lima.

CAVIEDES, CESAR N.

1975   El Niño 1972: Its Climatic, Ecological, Human, and Economic Implications. Geographical Review 65(4):493–509.

1984   El Niño 1982–83. Geographical Review 74(3):267–290.

CHAPDELAINE, CLAUDE

1997   À l'ombre du Cerro Blanco: Nouvelles découvertes sur le site moche, côte nord du Pérou. Les Cahiers d'Anthropologie 1. Département d'Anthropologie, Université de Montréal, Montreal.

1998   Excavaciones en la zona urbana moche durante 1996. In Investigaciones en la Huaca de la Luna 1996, edited by Santiago Uceda Castillo and Elías Mujica, pp. 85–115. Facultad de Ciencias Sociales, Universidad Nacional de la Libertad, Trujillo, Peru.

2001   The Growing Power of a Moche Urban Class. In Moche: Art and Archaeology in Ancient Peru, edited by Joanne Pillsbury, pp. 69–87. Studies in the History of Art 63. Center for Advanced Studies in Visual Arts, Symposium Papers XL. National Gallery of Art, Washington, DC.

2003   La Ciudad Moche: Urbanismo y estado. In Moche: Hacia el final del milenio, Actas del segundo Coloquio sobre la Cultura Moche, Trujillo, 1 al 7 de agosto de 1999, edited by Santiago Uceda Castillo and Elías Mujica, pp. 247–285. Universidad Nacional de

Trujillo, Peru; and Fondo Editorial de la Pontificia Universidad Católica del Perú, Lima.

2010   Moche Political Organization in the Santa Valley. In *New Perspectives on Moche Political Organization*, edited by Jeffrey Quilter and Luis Jaime Castillo Butters, pp. 252–279. Dumbarton Oaks Trustees for Harvard University, Washington, DC.

CHAPDELAINE, CLAUDE, VICTOR PIMENTEL, AND HÉLÈNE BERNIER

2001   A Glimpse at Moche Phase III Occupation at the Huacas de Moche Site, Northern Peru. *Antiquity* 75(288):361–372.

CHATEAUBRIAND, FRANÇOIS-RENÉ

1834   *Oeuvres complètes de M. le Vicomte de Chateaubriand, Tome III*. Chez Furne, Libraire-Éditeur, Paris.

CHAUCHAT, CLAUDE, AND BELKYS GUTIÉRREZ

2007   Excavaciones en la Plataforma Uhle. In *Proyecto Arqueológico Huaca de Luna: Informe Técnico 2007*, edited by Santiago Uceda Castillo and Ricardo Morales, pp. 47–83. Universidad Nacional de Trujillo, Peru.

CHAUCHAT, CLAUDE, BELKYS GUTIÉRREZ, DAPHNÉ DEVERLY, AND NICOLAS GOEPFERT

2008   Recherches sur l'élite de la société mochica: La plateforme Uhle à Moche, sur la côte nord du Pérou. *Les Nouvelles de l'Archéologie* 111–112:116–122.

CHERO ZURITA, LUIS

2008   El reinicio de los trabajos arqueológicos en Sipán: La temporada 2007. In *Sipán: El tesoro de las tumbas reales*, edited by Antonio Aimi, Walter Alva, and Emilia Perassi, pp. 88–113. Giunti Arte Mostre Musei s.r.l., Florence.

CONKLIN, WILLIAM J.

1990   Architecture of the Chimu: Memory, Function and Image. In *The Northern Dynasties Kingship and Statecraft in Chimor*, edited by María Rostworowski de Diez Canseco and Michael E. Moseley, pp. 43–74. Dumbarton Oaks and Research Library and Collection, Washington, DC.

CONKLIN, WILLIAM J., AND EDUARDO VERSTEYLEN

1978   Appendix 1: Textiles from a Pyramid of the Sun Burial. In *Ancient Burial Patterns of the Moche Valley, Peru*, edited by C. B. Donnan and C. J. Mackey, pp. 385–398. University of Texas Press, Austin.

CORDY-COLLINS, ALANA

1972   The Tule Boat Theme in Moche Art: A Problem in Ancient Peruvian Iconography. Master's thesis, Department of Anthropology, University of California, Los Angeles.

1992   Archaism or Tradition?: The Decapitation Theme in Cupisnique and Moche Iconography. *Latin American Antiquity* 3(3):206–220.

2001   Decapitation in Cupisnique and Early Moche Societies. In *Ritual Sacrifice in Ancient Peru: New Discoveries and Interpretation*, edited by Elizabeth P. Benson and Anita G. Cook, pp. 21–33. University of Texas Press, Austin.

DE BOCK, EDWARD K.

1988   *Moche: Gods, Warriors and Priests*. Rijksmuseum voor Volkenkunde, Leiden.

2005   *Human Sacrifices of Cosmic Order and Regeneration: Structure and Meaning in Moche Iconography, Peru, AD 100–800*. BAR International Series 1429. BAR, Oxford.

DE HEUSCH, LUC

1985   *Sacrifice in Africa: A Structuralist Approach*. Indiana University Press, Bloomington.

DOBKIN DE RIOS, MARLENE

1984   *Hallucinogens: Cross-Cultural Perspectives*. University of New Mexico Press, Albuquerque.

DONNAN, CHRISTOPHER B.

1973   *The Moche Occupation of the Santa Valley, Peru*. Publications in Anthropology, Vol. 8. University of California, Berkeley.

1975   The Thematic Approach to Moche Iconography. *Journal of Latin American Lore* 1(2):147–162.

1978   *Moche Art of Peru: Pre-Columbian Symbolic Communication*. University of California, Museum of Cultural History. University of California, Los Angeles.

1982   Dance in Moche Art. *Ñawpa Pacha* 20 (5):97–120.

1986a   The City Walls at Pacatnamu. In *The Pacatnamu Papers, Volume I*, edited by Christopher B. Donnan and Guillermo A. Cock, pp. 47–62. Museum of Cultural History. University of California, Los Angeles.

1986b   The Huaca 1 Complex. In *The Pacatnamu Papers, Volume I*, edited by Christopher B. Donnan and Guillermo A. Cock, pp. 63–84. Museum of Cultural History, University of California, Los Angeles.

1995   Moche Funerary Practice. In *Tombs for the Living: Andean Mortuary Practices*, edited by Tom D. Dillehay, pp. 111–159. A Symposium at Dumbarton Oaks, October 12 and 13, 1991. Dumbarton Oaks Research Library and Collection, Washington, DC.

1997   Deer Hunting and Combat: Parallel Activities in the Moche World. In *The Spirit of Ancient Peru: Treasures from the Museo Arqueológico Rafael Larco Herrera*, edited by Kathleen Berrin, pp. 51–59. Exhibition catalog. Fine Arts Museum of San Francisco/Thames and Hudson, New York.

2004   *Moche Portraits from Ancient Peru*. University of Texas Press, Austin.

2007   *Moche Tombs at Dos Cabezas*. Monograph 59. Cotsen Institute of Archaeology at UCLA, Los Angeles.

2008   Moche Masking Traditions. In *The Art and Archaeology of the Moche: An Ancient Andean Society of the Peruvian North Coast*, edited by Steve Bourget and Kimberly L. Jones, pp. 67–80. University of Texas Press, Austin.

2010   Moche State Religion: A Unifying Force in Moche Political Organization. In *New Perspectives on Moche Political Organization*, edited by Jeffrey

Quilter and Luis Jaime Castillo Butters, pp. 47–69. Dumbarton Oaks Research Library and Collection, Washington, DC.

DONNAN, CHRISTOPHER B., AND LUIS JAIME CASTILLO BUTTERS

1992   Finding the Tomb of a Moche Priestess. *Archaeology* 45(6):38–42. In *Moche: Propuestas y perspectivas, Actas del Primer Coloquio sobre la Cultura Moche, Trujillo, 12 al 16 de abril de 1993*, edited by Santiago Uceda Castillo and Elías Mujica, pp. 415–424. Travaux de l'Institut Français d'Études Andines 79. Universidad Nacional de la Libertad, Trujillo, Peru; Instituto Francés de Estudios Andinos, Lima; and Asociación Peruana para el Fomento de las Ciencias Sociales, Lima.

1994   Excavaciones de tumbas de sacerdotisas Moche en San José de Moro, Jequetepeque. In *Moche: Propuestas y perspectivas, Actas del Primer Coloquio sobre la Cultura Moche, Trujillo, 12 al 16 de abril de 1993*, edited by Santiago Uceda Castillo and Elías Mujica, pp. 415–424. Travaux de l'Institut Français d'Études Andines 79. Universidad Nacional de la Libertad, Trujillo, Peru; Instituto Francés de Estudios Andinos, Lima; and Asociación Peruana para el Fomento de las Ciencias Sociales, Lima.

DONNAN, CHRISTOPHER B., AND CAROL J. MACKEY

1978   *Ancient Burial Patterns of the Moche Valley, Peru*. University of Texas Press, Austin.

DONNAN, CHRISTOPHER B., AND DONNA MCCLELLAND

1979   The Burial Theme in Moche Iconography. Studies in Pre-Columbian Art and Archaeology, 21. Dumbarton Oaks Research Library and Collection, Washington, DC.

1999   *Moche Fineline Painting: Its Evolution and Its Artists*. Fowler Museum of Cultural History, University of California, Los Angeles.

ELING, HERBERT H., JR.

1986   Pre-Hispanic Irrigation Sources and Systems in the Jequetepeque Valley, Northern Peru. In *Andean Archaeology: Papers in Memory of Clifford Evans*, edited by Ramiro Matos M., Solveig A. Turpin, and Herbert H. Eling Jr., pp. 130–149. Monograph 26. Institute of Archaeology, University of California, Los Angeles.

FLANNERY, KENT V.

1972   The Cultural Evolution of Civilizations. *Annual Review of Ecology and Systematics* 3:399–426.

1999   Process and Agency in Early State Formation. *Cambridge Archaeological Journal* 9(1):3–21.

FRANCO, RÉGULO

1998   Arquitectura monumental moche: Correlación y espacios arquitectónicos. *Arkinka* 27:100–110.

FRANCO, RÉGULO, CÉSAR GÁLVEZ, AND SEGUNDO VÁSQUEZ

1994   Arquitectura y decoración mochica en la Huaca Cao Viejo, Complejo El Brujo: Resultados preliminares. In *Moche: Propuestas y perspectivas, Actas*

del Primer Coloquio sobre la Cultura Moche, Trujillo, 12 al 16 de abril de 1993, edited by Santiago Uceda Castillo and Elías Mujica, pp. 147–180. Travaux de l'Institut Français d'Études Andines 79. Universidad Nacional de la Libertad, Trujillo, Peru; Instituto Francés de Estudios Andinos, Lima; and Asociación Peruana para el Fomento de las Ciencias Sociales, Lima.

1998   Desentierro ritual de una tumba moche: Huaca Cao Viejo. *Sian* 3(6):9–18.

2003   Modelos, función y cronología de la Huaca Cao Viejo, Complejo El Brujo. In *Moche: Hacia el final del milenio, Actas del segundo Coloquio sobre la Cultura Moche, Trujillo, 1 al 7 de agosto de 1999*, edited by Santiago Uceda Castillo and Elías Mujica, pp. 125–177. Universidad Nacional de Trujillo, Peru; and Fondo Editorial de la Pontificia Universidad Católica del Perú, Lima.

GAMONAL, ANTONIO

1998   Excavación en el sector suroeste de la Plaza 3b de la Huaca de la Luna durante 1996. In *Investigaciones en la Huaca de la Luna 1996*, edited by Santiago Uceda Castillo and Elías Mujica. Facultad de Ciencias Sociales, Universidad Nacional de la Libertad, Trujillo, Peru.

GHEZZI, IVAN, AND CLIVE RUGGLES

2006   Las trece torres de Chankillo: Arqueoastronomía y organización social en el primer observatorio solar de América. *Boletín de Arqueología PUCP* 10:215–235.

GIERSZ, MILOSZ, KRYSTOF MAKOWSKI, AND PATRYCJA PRZADKA

2005   *El mundo sobrenatural mochica: Imágenes escultóricas de las deidades antropomorfas en el Museo Arqueológico Rafael Larco Herrera*. Universidad de Varsovia, Warsaw, and Fondo Editorial de la Pontificia Universidad Católica del Perú, Lima.

GLYNN, PETER W.

1988   El Niño–Southern Oscillation in 1982–83. Nearshore Population, Community and Ecosystem Responses. *Annual Review of Ecology and Systematics* 19:309–345.

GOLTE, JÜRGEN

1994   *Iconos y narraciones: La reconstrucción de una secuencia de imágenes moche*. Instituto de Estudios Peruanos, Lima.

GUSDORF, GEORGES

1948   *L'expérience humaine du sacrifice*. Presses Universitaires de France, Paris.

HALSTEAD, BRUCE W.

1978   *Poisonous and Venomous Marine Animals of the World*. Darwin Press, Princeton.

HAMILTON, LAUREL A.

2005   Cutmarks as Evidence of Precolumbian Human Sacrifice and Postmortem Bone Modification on the North Coast of Peru. PhD dissertation, Department of Anthropology, Tulane University, New Orleans.

HEYERDAHL, THOR

1995   Túcume and the Continuity of Peruvian Culture. In *Pyramids of Túcume: The Quest for Peru's Forgotten City*, edited by Thor Heyerdahl, Daniel H. Sandweiss, and Alfredo Narváez, pp. 199–229. Thames and Hudson, London.

HOCQUENGHEM, ANNE-MARIE

1980   L'iconographie mochica et les représentations de supplices. *Journal de la Société des Américanistes* 67:249–260.

1987   *Iconografía mochica*. Fondo Editorial de la Pontificia Universidad Católica del Perú, Lima.

JONES, KIMBERLY L.

2010   Cupisnique Culture: The Development of Ideology in the Ancient Andes. PhD dissertation, Department of Art and Art History, University of Texas at Austin, Austin.

KENNER, JULIE, AND PETER WEINA

2005   Leishmaniasis. *eMedicine*, April 14, 2005. WebMD: http://www.emedicine.com/derm/topic219.htm.

KOLATA, ALAN

1993   *The Tiwanaku: Portrait of an Andean Civilization*. Blackwell, Cambridge, MA.

1997   Of Kings and Capitals: Principles of Authority and the Nature of Cities in the Native Andean State. In *The Archaeology of City-States: Cross-Cultural Approaches*, edited by Deborah L. Nichols and Thomas H. Charlton, pp. 245–254. Smithsonian Series in Archaeological Inquiry. Smithsonian Institution Press, Washington, DC.

KRICKEBERG, WALTER

1928   Mexicanische-Peruanische Parallelen: Ein Überblick und eine Ergänzung. *Festschrift/Publication d'Hommage Offerte au P. W. Schmidt*:378–393. Mechitharisten-Congregations-Buchdruckerei, Vienna.

KROEBER, ALFRED L.

1925   The Uhle Pottery Collections from Moche. *University of California Publications in American Archaeology and Ethnology* 21(5):191–234.

1930   Archaeological Explorations in Peru, Part II: The Northern Coast. *Field Museum of Natural History, Anthropology Memoirs* 2(2):45–116.

LANNING, EDWARD P.

1967   *Peru before the Incas*. Prentice-Hall, Englewood Cliffs, NJ.

LARCO HOYLE, RAFAEL

1938   *Los Mochicas (Tomo 1)*. Casa Editorial, Lima.

1939   *Los Mochicas (Tomo 2)*. Empresa Editorial "Rimac" S.A., Lima.

1948   *Cronología arqueológica del norte del Perú*. Sociedad Geográfica Americana, Buenos Aires.

LAVALLÉE, DANIÈLE

1970   *Les représentations animales dans la céramique mochica*. Mémoires de l'Institute d'Ethnologie, 4. Université de Paris, Paris.

LÉVI-STRAUSS, CLAUDE

1966   *The Savage Mind* (1962). University of Chicago Press, Chicago.

LIMA, MAURICIO, JUAN E. KEYMER, AND FABIAN JAKSIC

1999   El Niño–Southern Oscillation-Driven Rainfall Variability and Delayed Density Dependence Cause Rodent Outbreaks in Western South America: Linking Demography and Population Dynamics. *American Naturalist* 153(5):476–491.

LOCKARD, GREGORY D.

2005   Political Power and Economy at the Archaeological Site of Galindo, Moche Valley, Peru. PhD dissertation, Department of Anthropology, University of New Mexico, Albuquerque.

LÓPEZ LUJÁN, LEONARDO

1993   *Las ofrendas del Templo Mayor de Tenochtitlan*. Instituto Nacional de Antropológia e Historia, Mexico City.

LOURIE, S. A., S. J. FOSTER, E. W. T. COOPER, AND A. C. J. VINCENT

2004   *A Guide to the Identification of Seahorses*. Project Seahorse and TRAFFIC North America. University of British Columbia and World Wildlife Fund, Washington, DC.

LUMBRERAS, LUIS G.

1974   *The Peoples and Cultures of Ancient Peru*. Smithsonian Institution Press, Washington, DC.

LUMBRERAS, LUIS G., CHACHO GONZÁLEZ, AND BERNARD LIETAER

1976   *Acerca de la función del sistema hidráulico de Chavín*. Museo Nacional de Antropología y Arqueología, Lima.

LUTZ, BERTHA

1971   Venomous Toads and Frogs. In *Venomous Animals and their Venoms*, edited by Wolfgang Bürcherl and Eleanor E. Buckley, vol. 2: *Venomous Vertebrates*, pp. 423–473. Academic Press, New York.

MATOS MOCTEZUMA, EDUARDO

1984   The Templo Mayor of Tenochtitlan: Economics and Ideology. In *Ritual Human Sacrifice in Mesoamerica*, edited by Elizabeth H. Boone, pp. 133–164. Dumbarton Oaks Research Library and Collection, Washington, DC.

1987   Symbolism of the Templo Mayor. In *The Aztec Templo Mayor*, edited by Elizabeth H. Boone, pp. 185–209. Dumbarton Oaks Research Library and Collection, Washington, DC.

MCCLELLAND, DONNA

2008   *Ulluchu*: An Elusive Fruit. In *The Art and Archaeology of the Moche: An Ancient Andean Society of the Peruvian North Coast*, edited by Steve Bourget and Kimberly L. Jones, pp. 43–65. University of Texas Press, Austin.

MCCLELLAND, DONNA, DONALD MCCLELLAND, AND CHRISTOPHER B. DONNAN

2007   *Moche Fineline Painting from San José de Moro*. Monograph 58, Cotsen Institute of Archaeology. University of California, Los Angeles.

MILLAIRE, JEAN-FRANÇOIS

1997   La technologie de la filature manuelle sur le site moche de la côte nord du Pérou précolombien. M.Sc. Thesis, Université de Montréal, Montreal.

2002   *Moche Burial Patterns: An Investigation into Prehispanic Social Structure*. BAR International Series 1066. BAR, Oxford.

MILLAIRE, JEAN-FRANÇOIS, AND MAGALI MORLION (EDITORS)

2009   *Gallinazo: An Early Cultural Tradition on the Peruvian North Coast*. Cotsen Institute of Archaeology Press, University of California, Los Angeles.

MONTOYA, MARÍA

1997   Excavaciones en la Plaza 3B. In *Investigaciones en la Huaca de la Luna 1995*, edited by Santiago Uceda Castillo, Elías Mujica, and Ricardo Morales, pp. 61–66. Universidad Nacional de Trujillo, Peru.

MOSELEY, MICHAEL E.

1982   Introduction: Human Exploitation and Organization on the North Andean Coast. In *Chan-Chan: Andean Desert City*, edited by Michael E. Moseley and Kent C. Day, pp. 1–24. University of New Mexico Press, Albuquerque.

1983   Central Andean Civilization. In *Ancient South Americans*, edited by Jesse D. Jennings, pp. 179–239. W. H. Freeman, San Francisco.

1992   *The Incas and Their Ancestors: The Archaeology of Peru*. Thames & Hudson, New York.

MOSELEY, MICHAEL E., CHRISTOPHER B. DONNAN, AND DAVID K. KEEFER

2008   Convergent Catastrophe and the Demise of Dos Cabezas: Environmental Change and Regime Change in Ancient Peru. In *The Art and Archaeology of the Moche: An Ancient Andean Society of the Peruvian North Coast*, edited by Steve Bourget and Kimberly L. Jones, pp. 81–92. University of Texas Press, Austin.

MOSELEY, MICHAEL E., AND JAMES B. RICHARDSON III

1992   Doomed by Natural Disaster. *Archaeology* 45(6):44–45.

MUJICA BARREDA, ELÍAS, RÉGULO FRANCO JORDÁN, CÉSAR GÁLVEZ MORA, JEFFREY QUILTER, ANTONIO MURGA CRUZ, CARMEN GAMARRA DE LA CRUZ, VÍCTOR HUGO RÍOS CISNEROS, SEGUNDO LOZADA ALCALDE, JOHN VERANO, AND MARCO AVEGGIO MERELLO

2007   *El Brujo: Huaca Cao, centro ceremonial moche en el valle de Chicama*. Fundación Wiese, Lima.

MURPHY, ROBERT C.

1923   Fisheries Resources in Peru. *Scientific Monthly* 16(6):594–607.

NILES, SUSAN A.

1987   *Callachaca: Style and Status in an Inca Community*. University of Iowa Press, Iowa City.

1999   *The Shape of Inca History: Narrative and Architecture in an Andean Empire*. University of Iowa Press, Iowa City.

ORBEGOSO, CLORINDA

1998   Excavaciones en el sector sureste de la Plaza 3c de la Huaca de la Luna durante 1996. In *Investigaciones en la Huaca de la Luna 1996*, edited by Santiago Uceda Castillo, Elías Mujica, and Ricardo Morales, pp. 67–73. Universidad Nacional de Trujillo, Peru.

PALMA, RICARDO

1913   Huacos antropomorfos mutilados del Perú. *International Congress of Americanists* (Proceedings of the XVIIIth Session, London, 1914) 2:276–279.

PAULSEN, ALISON C.

1974   The Thorny Oyster and the Voice of God: *Spondylus* and *Strombus* in Andean Prehistory. *American Antiquity* 39(4):597–607.

PILLSBURY, JOANNE

1996   The Thorny Oyster and the Origins of Empire: Implications of Recently Uncovered Spondylus Imagery from Chan Chan, Peru. *Latin American Antiquity* 7(4):313–340.

PROULX, DONALD A.

1968   An Archaeological Survey of the Nepeña Valley, Peru. PhD dissertation, Department of Anthropology, University of Massachusetts, Amherst.

QUILTER, JEFFREY

1990   The Moche Revolt of the Objects. *Latin American Antiquity* 1:42–65.

1996   Continuity and Disjunction in Pre-Columbian Art and Culture. *RES: Anthropology and Aesthetics* 29/30:303–317.

1997   The Narrative Approach to Moche Iconography. *Latin American Antiquity* 8:113–133.

REINHARD, JOHAN

1987   Chavín y Tiahuanaco, una nueva perspectiva de dos centros ceremoniales andinos. *Boletín de Lima* 50 (March):29–49.

1988   *The Nazca Lines: Líneas de Nazca, montañas y fertilidad*. Editorial Los Pinos, Lima.

RIDGELY, ROBERT S., AND PAUL J. GREENFIELD

2001   *The Birds of Ecuador: Field Guide*. Cornell University Press, Ithaca.

SAHLEY, CATHERINE T.

1996   Bat and Hummingbird Pollination of an Auto-tetraploid Columnar Cactus, *Weberbauerocereus weberbaueri* (Cactacea). *American Journal of Botany* 83(10):1329–1336.

SAHLINS, MARSHALL

1985   *Islands of History*. University of Chicago Press, Chicago.

1995   *How "Natives" Think: About Captain Cook, for Example*. University of Chicago Press, Chicago.

SAKAI, MASATO

1998   *Reyes, estrellas y cerros en Chimor: El proceso de cambio de la organización espacial y temporal en Chan Chan*. Editorial Horizonte, Lima.

SCHOENER, THOMAS W., AND DAVID A. SPILLER

1992   Stabilimenta Characteristics of the Spider *Argiope argentata* on Small Islands: Support of the

Predator-Defense Hypothesis. *Behavioral Ecology and Sociobiology* 31(5):309–318.

SCHWEIGGER, EDUARD

1947   *El litoral peruano.* Companía Administradora del Guano, Lima.

SELER, EDUARD

1912   Archäologische Reise in Süd- und Mittelamerika. 1910/1911. *Gesammeltze Abhanglungen zur Amerikanischen Sprach- und Altertumskunde* 15:115–151.

SHIMADA, IZUMI

1990   Cultural Continuities and Discontinuities on the Northern North Coast of Peru, Middle–Late Horizon. In *The Northern Dynasties Kingship and Statecraft in Chimor*, edited by María Rostworowski de Diez Canseco and Michael E. Moseley, pp. 297–392. Dumbarton Oaks Research Library and Collection, Washington, DC.

1994   *Pampa Grande and the Mochica Culture.* University of Texas Press, Austin.

SHIMADA, IZUMI, KEN-ICHI SHINODA, WALTER ALVA, STEVE BOURGET, CLAUDE CHAPDELAINE, AND SANTIAGO UCEDA CASTILLO

2008   The Moche People: Genetic Perspective on Their Sociopolitical Composition and Organization. In *The Art and Archaeology of the Moche: An Ancient Andean Society of the Peruvian North Coast*, edited by Steve Bourget and Kimberly L. Jones, pp. 179–193. University of Texas Press, Austin.

SHIMADA, IZUMI, KEN-ICHI SHINODA, STEVE BOURGET, WALTER ALVA, AND SANTIAGO UCEDA CASTILLO

2005   MtDNA Analysis of Mochica and Sicán Populations of Pre-Hispanic Peru. *Biomolecular Archaeology: Genetic Approaches to the Past* 32:61–92.

SILVERMAN, HELAINE

2002   *Ancient Nasca Settlement and Society.* University of Iowa Press, Iowa City.

SILVERMAN, HELAINE, AND DONALD PROULX

2002   *The Nasca.* Blackwell, Malden, MA, Oxford.

SMITH, KENNETH G. V.

1986   *A Manual of Forensic Entomology.* Trustees of the British Museum, Natural History, London; and Cornell University Press, Ithaca.

STANISH, CHARLES, AND BRIAN S. BAUER (EDITORS)

2004   *Archaeological Research on the Islands of the Sun and Moon, Lake Titicaca, Bolivia: Final Results from the Proyecto Tiksi Kjarka.* Cotsen Institute of Archaeology Press, University of California, Los Angeles.

STOLTENOW, CHARLIE, AND GREG LARDY

2012   Cyanide Poisoning. V-1150. North Dakota State University Extension Service, Fargo.

STRONG, WILLIAM D.

1947   Finding the Tomb of a Warrior-God. *National Geographic Magazine* 91:453–482.

STRONG, WILLIAM D., AND CLIFFORD EVANS

1952   *Cultural Stratigraphy in the Virú Valley, Northern Peru: The Formative and Florescent Epochs.* Columbia Studies in Archaeology and Ethnology 4. Columbia University Press, New York.

SUGIYAMA, SABURO

2005   *Human Sacrifice, Militarism, and Rulership: Materialization of State Ideology at the Feathered Serpent Pyramid, Teotihuacan.* New Studies in Archaeology. Cambridge University Press, Cambridge.

2010   Sacrificios humanos dedicados a los monumentos principales de Teotihuacan. In *El sacrificio humano en la tradición religiosa mesoamericana*, edited by Leonardo López Luján and Guilhem Olivier, pp. 79–114. Instituto Nacional de Antropología e Historia, Universidad Nacional Autónoma de México, Mexico City.

SUTTER, RICHARD C., AND ROSA CORTEZ

2005   The Nature of Moche Human Sacrifice: A Bio-Archaeological Perspective. *Current Anthropology* 46(4):521–549.

SUTTER, RICHARD C., AND JOHN W. VERANO

2007   Biodistance Analysis of the Moche Sacrificial Victims from Huaca de la Luna Plaza 3C: Matrix Method Test of Their Origins. *American Journal of Physical Anthropology* 132(2):193–206.

TAMBIAH, STANLEY J.

1985   Animals Are Good to Think and Good to Prohibit. Chapter 5 In *Culture, Thought, and Social Action: An Anthropological Perspective*, pp. 169–211. Harvard University Press, Cambridge, MA.

TELLO, RICARDO, JOSÉ ARMAS, AND CLAUDE CHAPDELAINE

2003   Prácticas funerarias moche en el Complejo Arqueológico Huacas del Sol y de la Luna. In *Moche: Hacia el final del milenio, Actas del segundo Coloquio sobre la Cultura Moche, Trujillo, 1 al 7 de agosto de 1999*, edited by Santiago Uceda Castillo and Elías Mujica, pp. 151–187. Universidad Nacional de Trujillo, Peru; and Fondo Editorial de la Pontificia Universidad Católica del Perú, Lima.

THACHIL, JOSE

1985   *The Vedic and the Christian Concept of Sacrifice.* Pontifical Institute of Theology and Philosophy, Kerala, India.

TOPIC, JOHN R., AND THERESA L. TOPIC

1997   La Guerra Mochica. *Revista Arqueológica SIAN* (Universidad Nacional de Trujillo) 4:10–12.

TOPIC LANGE, THERESA

1977   Excavations at Moche. PhD dissertation, Harvard University, Cambridge, MA.

1982   The Early Intermediate Period and Its Legacy. In *Chan Chan: Andean Desert City*, edited by Michael E. Moseley and Kent C. Day, pp. 255–284. University of New Mexico Press, Albuquerque.

TOVAR, HUMBERTO, AND DEMOSTENES CABRERA

1985   Las aves guaneras y el fenómeno "El Niño." In *"El Nino": Su impacto en la fauna marina*, pp. 181–186. Boletín Volumen Extraordinario. Instituto del Mar del Perú, Callao, Peru.

TOVAR, HUMBERTO, DEMOSTENES CABRERA, AND MIGUEL FARFÁN DEL PINO

1985   Impacto del fenómeno "El Niño" en la población de lobos marinos en Punta San Juan. In *"El Nino":*

Su impacto en la fauna marina, pp. 195–200. Boletín Volumen Extraordinario. Instituto del Mar del Perú, Callao, Peru.

TOYNE, J. M., C. D. WHITE, J. W. VERANO, S. U. CASTILLO, J.-F. MILLAIRE, AND F. J. LONGSTAFFE

2014 Residential Histories of Elites and Sacrificial Victims at Huacas de Moche, Peru, as Reconstructed from Oxygen Isotopes. *Journal of Archaeological Science* 42:15–28.

TUFINIO, MOISÉS

2001 Plaza 3c. In *Proyecto arqueológico Huaca de la Luna: Informe técnico 2000*, edited by Santiago Uceda Castillo and Ricardo Morales, pp. 41–59. Facultad de Ciencias Sociales, Universidad Nacional de Trujillo, Peru.

2002 Plaza 3c. In *Investigaciones en la Huaca de la Luna: Informe técnico 2001*, edited by Santiago Uceda Castillo and Ricardo Morales, pp. 47–58. Facultad de Ciencias Sociales, Universidad Nacional de Trujillo, Peru.

2003 Excavaciones en el frontis norte y plaza 1 de Huaca de la Luna. In *Investigaciones en la Huaca de la Luna: Informe técnico 2002*, edited by Santiago Uceda Castillo and Ricardo Morales, pp. 13–26. Facultad de Ciencias Sociales, Universidad Nacional de Trujillo, Peru.

2004a Excavaciones en la Plaza 3c de la Huaca de la Luna 1998–1999. In *Proyecto Arqueológico Huacas del Sol y de la Luna: Investigaciones en la Huaca de la Luna 1998-1999*, edited by Santiago Uceda Castillo, Elías Mujica, and Ricardo Morales, pp. 99–120. Facultad de Ciencias Sociales, Universidad Nacional de Trujillo, Peru.

2004b Excavaciones en la Unidad 14 de la Plataforma I de Huaca de la Luna. In *Proyecto arqueológico Huaca de la Luna: Informe técnico 2003*, edited by Santiago Uceda Castillo and Ricardo Morales, pp. 13–26. Facultad de Ciencias Sociales, Universidad Nacional de Trujillo, Peru.

2006 Excavaciones en la Plaza 3c y sacrificios humanos en la Huaca de la Luna. In *Proyecto Arqueológico Huacas del Sol y de la Luna: Investigaciones en la Huaca de la Luna 2000*, edited by Santiago Uceda Castillo, Elías Mujica, and Ricardo Morales, pp. 47–63. Facultad de Ciencias Sociales, Universidad Nacional de Trujillo, Peru.

2008 Huaca de la Luna: Arquitectura y sacrificios humanos. In *Actas de la primera conferencia internacional de jóvenes investigadores sobre la cultura Moche, Lima, 2004*, edited by Luis Jaime Castillo Butters, Hélène Bernier, Gregory Lockard, and Julio Rucabado, pp. 451–470. Instituto Francés de Estudios Andinos y Fondo Editorial de la Pontificia Universidad Católica del Perú, Lima.

TURNER, VICTOR

1967 *The Forest of Symbols*. Cornell University Press, Ithaca.

1992 *Blazing the Trail: Way Marks in the Exploration of Symbols*. Edited by Edith Turner. University of Arizona Press, Tucson.

UBBELOHDE-DOERING, HEINRICH

1983 *Vorspanische Gräber von Pacatnamú, Nordperu*. Materialien zur Allgemeinen und Vergleichenden Archäologie 26. C. H. Beck, Munich.

UCEDA CASTILLO, SANTIAGO

2000 El templo mochica: Rituales y ceremonias. In *Los dioses del antiguo Perú*, pp. 90–101. Colección Arte y Tesoro del Perú. Banco de Crédito del Perú, Lima.

2007 Huacas del Sol y de la Luna: Cien años después de los trabajos de Max Uhle. In *Proyecto Arqueológico Huaca de la Luna: Informe técnico 2006*, edited by Santiago Uceda Castillo and Ricardo Morales, pp. 265–290. Facultad de Ciencias Sociales, Universidad Nacional de Trujillo, Peru.

2008 The Priests of the Bicephalous Arc: Tombs and Effigies Found in Huaca de la Luna and Their Relation to Moche Rituals. In *The Art and Archaeology of the Moche: An Ancient Andean Society of the Peruvian North Coast*, edited by Steve Bourget and Kimberly L. Jones, pp. 153–178. University of Texas Press, Austin.

UCEDA CASTILLO, SANTIAGO, AND JOSÉ ARMAS

1998 An Urban Pottery Workshop at the Site of Moche, North Coast of Peru. In *Andean Ceramics: Technology, Organisation, and Approaches*, edited by Izumi Shimada, pp. 91–110. MASCA Research Papers in Science and Archaeology, Supplement to Volume 15. Museum Applied Science Center for Archaeology, University of Pennsylvania Museum of Archaeology and Anthropology, Philadelphia.

UCEDA CASTILLO, SANTIAGO, AND JOSÉ CANZIANI

1993 Evidencias de grandes precipitaciones en diversas etapas constructivas de la Huaca de la Luna, costa norte del Perú. *Bulletin de l'Institut Français d'Études Andines* 22(1):313–343.

1998 Análisis de la secuencia arquitectónica y nuevas perspectivas de investigación en Huaca de la Luna. In *Investigaciones en la Huaca de la Luna 1996*, edited by Santiago Uceda Castillo, Elías Mujica, and Ricardo Morales, pp. 139–158. Universidad Nacional de Trujillo, Trujillo, Peru.

UCEDA CASTILLO, SANTIAGO, HENRY GAYOSO RULLIER, AND NADIA GAMARRA CARRANZA

2009 The Gallinazo at Huacas de Moche: Style or Culture. In *Gallinazo: An Early Cultural Tradition on the Peruvian North Coast*, edited by Jean-François Millaire and Magali Morlion, pp. 105–134. Cotsen Institute of Archaeology Press, University of California, Los Angeles.

UCEDA CASTILLO, SANTIAGO, AND ELÍAS MUJICA (EDITORS)

1994 *Moche: Propuestas y perspectivas, Actas del Primer Coloquio sobre la Cultura Moche, Trujillo, 12 al 16 de abril de 1993*. Travaux de l'Institut Français d'Études Andines 79. Universidad Nacional de la Libertad, Trujillo, Peru; Instituto Francés de Estudios Andinos, Lima; and Asociación Peruana para el Fomento de las Ciencias Sociales, Lima.

1997   *Investigaciones en la Huaca de la Luna 1995.* Facultad de Ciencias Sociales. Universidad National de Trujillo, Peru.

1998   *Investigaciones en la Huaca de la Luna 1996.* Facultad de Ciencias Sociales. Universidad Nacional de la Libertad, Trujillo, Peru.

2000   *Investigaciones en la Huaca de la Luna 1997.* Facultad de Ciencias Sociales. Universidad Nacional de La Libertad, Trujillo, Peru.

2003   *Moche: Hacia el final del milenio, Actas del segundo Coloquio sobre la Cultura Moche, Trujillo, 1 al 7 de agosto de 1999.* 2 vols. Universidad Nacional de Trujillo, Peru; and Fondo Editorial de la Pontificia Universidad Católica del Perú, Lima.

UHLE, MAX

1899   Unpublished letter to Mrs. Stevenson (October 18, 1899). Phoebe A. Hearst Museum of Anthropology, University of California at Berkeley.

1913   Die Ruinen von Moche. *Journal de la Société des Américanistes de Paris* 10:95–117.

VALDIVIA, EDGARD, AND WOLF E. ARNTZ

1985   Cambios en los recursos y su incidencia en la pesquería artesanal durante "El Niño," 1982–1983. In *"El Nino": Su impacto en la fauna marina*, pp. 143–152. Boletín Volumen Extraordinario. Instituto del Mar del Perú, Callao, Peru.

VALERI, VALERIO

1985   *Kinship and Sacrifice: Ritual and Society in Ancient Hawaii.* University of Chicago Press, Chicago.

VÁSQUEZ, VÍCTOR, TERESA ROSALES, ARTURO MORALES, AND EUFRASIA ROSELLÓ

2003   Zooarqueología de la zona urbana Moche, complejo Huacas del Sol y de la Luna. In *Moche: Hacia el final del milenio*, vol. 2, *Actas del Segundo Coloquio sobre la Cultura Moche, Trujillo, 1 al 7 de agosto de 1999*, edited by Santiago Uceda Castillo and Elías Mujica, pp. 247–285. Universidad Nacional de Trujillo and Pontificia Universidad Católica del Perú, Lima.

VÉLEZ LÓPEZ, LIZARDO R.

1913   Las mutilaciones en los vasos antropomorfos del antiguo Perú. International Congress of Americanists. *Proceedings of the XVIII Session* 2 (London, 1914):267–275.

VERANO, JOHN W.

1998   Sacrificios humanos, desmembramientos, y modificaciones culturales en restos osteológicos: Evidencias de las temporadas de investigación 1995–1996 en Huaca de la Luna. In *Investigaciones en la Huaca de la Luna 1996*, edited by Santiago Uceda Castillo, Elías Mujica, and Ricardo Morales, pp. 159–171. Facultad de Ciencias Sociales, Universidad Nacional de Trujillo, Peru.

2001a   The Physical Evidence of Human Sacrifice in Ancient Peru. In *Ritual Sacrifice in Ancient Peru: New Discoveries and Interpretations*, edited by Elizabeth P. Benson and Anita G. Cook, pp. 165–184. University of Texas Press, Austin.

2001b   War and Death in the Moche World: Osteological Evidence and Visual Discourse. In *Moche: Art and Archaeology in Ancient Peru*, edited by Joanne Pillsbury, pp. 111–126. Studies in the History of Art 63. Center for Advanced Studies in Visual Arts, Symposium Papers XL. National Gallery of Art, Washington, DC.

2008   Communality and Diversity in Moche Human Sacrifice. In *The Art and Archaeology of the Moche: An Ancient Andean Society of the Peruvian North Coast*, edited by Steve Bourget and Kimberly L. Jones, pp. 195–213. University of Texas Press, Austin.

VERANO, JOHN W., MOISÉS TUFINIO, AND MELLISA LUND VALLE

2008   Esqueletos humanos de la Plaza 3c de Huaca de la Luna. In *Proyecto arqueológico Huacas del Sol y de la Luna: Investigaciones en la Huaca de la Luna 2001*, edited by Santiago Uceda Castillo, Elías Mujica, and Ricardo Morales, pp. 225–254. Universidad Nacional de Trujillo, Peru.

VIAU, ROLAND

1997   *Enfants du néant et mangeurs d'âmes: Guerre, culture et société en iroquoisie ancienne.* Boréal, Montreal.

WAKE, THOMAS A.

2007   Vertebrate Faunal Remains. In *Moche Tombs at Dos Cabezas*, pp. 211–230. Monograph 59. Cotsen Institute of Archaeology at UCLA, Los Angeles.

WALLACE, MICHAEL P., AND STANLEY A. TEMPLE

1988   Impacts of the 1982–1983 El Niño on Population Dynamics of Andean Condors in Peru. *Biotropica* 20(2):144–150.

WEISS, P.

1961   La asociación de la uta y verruga peruana en los mitos de la papa, figurados en la cerámica moshica y shimu. *Revista del Museo Nacional* (Lima):65–77.

WILLEY, GORDON R.

1971   *An Introduction to American Archaeology: vol. 11, South America.* Prentice-Hall, Englewood Cliffs, NJ.

WILSON, DANIEL

1988   *Prehispanic Settlement Patterns in the Lower Santa Valley Peru: A Regional Perspective on the Origins and Development of Complex North Coast Society.* Smithsonian Institution Press, Washington, DC.

WOLFF, M.

1985   Abundancia masiva y crecimiento de pre-adultos de la concha de abanico peruana (*Argopecten purpuratus*) en la zona de Pisco bajo condiciones de "El Niño" 1983. In *"El Niño": Su impacto en la fauna marina*, edited by W. Arntz, A. Landa, and J. Tarazona, pp. 87–89. Imarpe, Lima.

YACOVLEFF, EUGENIO

1932   Las falconidas en el arte y en las creencias de los antiguos peruanos. *Revista del Museo Nacional* 1(1):33–111.

YACOVLEFF, EUGENIO, AND F. L. HERRERA

1934   El mundo vegetal de los antiguos peruanos. *Revista del Museo Nacional* 3:243–322.

1935   El mundo vegetal de los antiguos peruanos. *Revista del Museo Nacional* 4:31–102.

1938   *El mundo vegetal de los antiguos peruanos.* Impresiones del Museo Nacional, Lima.

YERKES, ROYDEN KEITH

1952   *Sacrifice in Greek and Roman Religions and Early Judaism.* Scribner's, New York.

ZIGHELBOIM, ARI

1995   Mountain Scenes of Human Sacrifice in Moche Ceramic Iconography. *Journal of the Steward Anthropological Society* 23(1–2):153–188.

ZUIDEMA, REINER TOM

1964   *The Ceque System of Cuzco: The Social Organization of the Capital of the Inca.* E. J. Brill, Leiden.

INDEX

burials, 313; and contextual analysis, 407; diet, 6; eco-logical markers of, 3; human sacrifice and political authority in, 402–405; ideology of, 414; power and ritual ecology in, 413–414; and rituals during El Niño, 3, 413; sacred mountains and temples in, 25; state model of, 8; state religion of, 12–13; symbolic system of, 198, 310–311; violence and rising social complexity in, 406–413

Moche political structures, 373–402; Stage A: Phase III/Early Moche, 374–377, 403–404; Stage B: Phase IV/Middle Moche, 377–394, 404; Stage C: Phase V/Late Moche, 394–402, 404–405

Mocollope, 8, 19–20, 25, 30

Morales, Ricardo, 14

Nasca culture, 1

Newman, Margaret, 144–145, 369

north coast of Peru, 2–3, 261–262

Pacatnamú, 2, 12, 380, 408

Pañamarca, 9, 12, 19, 380, 399

Platform II, 19–23; ceramic offerings in Tomb 2 and Tomb 3, 161–178; excavation process of, 139; function of, 139, 409; ritual contexts of, 373; rocky outcrop at, 138–139; sacrificers, 373; Tomb 1 at, 141–145; Tomb 2 at, 145–154; Tomb 3 at, 145, 155–161; Tomb 4 at, 178; tomb markers at, 155–156; wooden club found at, 144–145

Plaza 3A, 19–21, 23, 32–137, 360, 409

—artwork found at: ceramic fragments, 129–133, 404; clay statuettes, 72, 113–129, 193–195, 371–372, 413; reciprocity between human and clay statuettes, 129

—contexts of: Chimú presence, 103; Gallinazo Period occupation, 107; ritual contexts, 370–373; sequence of events, 133–134

—excavation of: precinct, 42–72; rocky outcrop, 134–135; Sand 1, 89–103; Sand 2.3, 2.2 and 2.1, 61–72; Sand 2.3.9 to 2.3.1, 48–61; Sand 3, 42; Sand 4, 34–41; Sector B, 103, 107; Sector C, 107; Sector D, 107; Sector E, 107–108; Sediment 1, 103; Sediment 2.2 and 2.1, 72–88; Sediment 3, 44–48; Sediment 4, 41–42

—human remains found at: child burials, 35–41; exposed to the elements, 110; male burial, 42–44; manipulation of remains, 110; muscoid flies, 110, 123, 126, 128; pairing of remains, 72; pairing of sacrificial rituals, 110–112; physical anthropology of remains, 135–136; *tableau macabre* of, 78, 110

Quilter, Jeffrey, 384

ritual ecology, 196; methodology, 197–198

sacred geography, 2, 25

sacrifice, 30; defleshing of sacrificial victim, 358–360; nature of, 33–34. *See also* iconography: sacrifice

Sahlins, Marshall D., 198

San José de Moro, 9, 394, 396–402; burials at, 398–402; Huaca la Capilla, 405

Sipán, 11–12, 26, 30, 170, 208, 225, 254, 266, 306, 310, 311, 329, 330, 367, 370, 373, 377, 380, 404, 406, 408, 414

symbolic duality. *See* duality

Teotihuacan, 403

Turner, Victor W., 287

Uceda Castillo, Santiago, 14, 18–19, 270, 352

Uhle, Max, 27

Verano, John, 358